DIGITAL TECHNOLOGIES AND LEARNING IN PHYSICAL EDUCATION

There is evidence of considerable growth in the availability and use of digital technologies in physical education (PE). Yet, we have scant knowledge about how technologies are being used by teachers, and whether or how these technologies are optimising student learning. This book makes a novel contribution by focusing on the ways in which teachers and teacher educators are attempting to use digital technologies in PE.

The book has been created using the innovative 'pedagogical cases' framework. Each case centres on a narrative, written by a PE practitioner, explaining how and why technology is used in their practice to advance and accelerate learning. Each practitioner narrative is then analysed by a team of experts from different disciplines. The aim is to offer a multi-dimensional understanding of the possibilities and challenges of supporting young people's learning with digital technologies. Each case concludes with a practitioner reflection to illustrate the links between theory, research and practice.

Digital Technologies and Learning in Physical Education encourages critical reflection on the use of technologies in PE. It is an essential resource for students on physical education, kinesiology or sport science courses, practitioners working in PE or youth sport, and researchers interested in digital technologies and education.

Ashley Casey is a Senior Lecturer in Pedagogy at Loughborough University, UK, and an Adjunct Senior Lecturer at the University of Limerick, Ireland. His research explores pedagogical models, teacher development through social media, and pedagogies of technology. He can be found on Twitter as @DrAshCasey, where he writes about teaching and research in physical education.

Victoria A. Goodyear is a Lecturer in Pedagogy in Sport, Physical Activity and Health at the University of Birmingham, UK. Her research focuses on curriculum innovation, teacher professional learning, and the pedagogical and professional uses of digital technologies and social media. Victoria uses Twitter to tweet about practice and research and she can be found at @VGoodyear.

Kathleen M. Armour is Professor of Education and Sport, former Head of the School of Sport, Exercise and Rehabilitation Sciences at the University of Birmingham, UK, and currently Pro Vice Chancellor (Education) at the same institution. Kathy was a panel member in REF2014; is a Fellow of the Academy of Social Sciences and International Fellow of the National Academy of Kinesiology, USA; and holds an honorary doctorate from the University of Orebro, Sweden. Kathy mainly uses Twitter to retweet great comments made by others, but, just occasionally, she also shares an original thought (@ArmourKathy).

DIGITAL TECHNOLOGIES AND LEARNING IN PHYSICAL EDUCATION

Pedagogical cases

Edited by
Ashley Casey, Victoria A. Goodyear
and Kathleen M. Armour

Routledge
Taylor & Francis Group

LONDON AND NEW YORK

First published 2017
by Routledge
2 Park Square, Milton Park, Abingdon, Oxon OX14 4RN

and by Routledge
711 Third Avenue, New York, NY 10017

Routledge is an imprint of the Taylor & Francis Group,
an informa business

British Library Cataloguing-in-Publication Data
A catalogue record for this book is available from the British Library

Library of Congress Cataloging in Publication Data
Names: Casey, Ashley, editor. | Goodyear, Victoria A., editor. |
Armour, Kathleen M., editor.
Title: Digital technologies and learning in physical education :
pedagogical cases / edited by Ashley Casey, Victoria A. Goodyear and
Kathleen M. Armour.
Description: Abingdon, Oxon ; New York, NY : Routledge, 2016. |
Includes bibliographical references and index.
Identifiers: LCCN 2016023487| ISBN 9781138947283 (hardback) |
ISBN 9781138947290 (pbk.) | ISBN 9781315670164 (ebook)
Subjects: LCSH: Physical education and training—Computer-assisted
instruction—Case studies. | Physical education and training—Study and
teaching—Case studies. | Educational technology—Case studies.
Classification: LCC GV364 .D54 2016 | DDC 613.70285—dc23LC
record available at https://lccn.loc.gov/2016023487

ISBN: 978-1-138-94728-3 (hbk)
ISBN: 978-1-138-94729-0 (pbk)
ISBN: 978-1-315-67016-4 (ebk)

Typeset in Bembo and Stone Sans
by Florence Production Ltd, Stoodleigh, Devon
Printed by Ashford Colour Press Ltd.

Ash: To Nana and Grandpa – Your guidance and support allowed me to get where I am today, even if I didn't fully appreciate that at the time.

Vicky: To Paul, my Mum and Dad, and in loving memory of my Grandmother Anne.

Kathy: To Charlie, Georgina and Jamie. Great 'kids'.

From all of us: And to all the great colleagues who have worked so hard to construct these cases.

CONTENTS

FIGURES

TABLES

CONTRIBUTORS

Jonas Almqvist, Uppsala University, Sweden
Helena Baert, State University New York, USA
Jeanne Barcelona, University of Texas at Austin, USA
Dean Barker, University of Gothenburg, Sweden
Natalie Barker-Ruchti, University of Gothenburg, Sweden
Dylan Blain, University of Wales Trinity Saint David, UK
Gavin Breslin, Ulster University, Northern Ireland
Matt Bridge, University of Birmingham, UK
Rebecca Bryan, State University New York, USA
Lynne J. Bryant, University of Texas at Austin, USA
Sean Bulger, West Virginia University, USA
Shawn M. Bullock, Simon Fraser University, Canada
Antonio Calderón, UCAM Catholic University of Murcia, Spain
Lorraine Cale, Loughborough University, UK
Urban Carlén, University of West, Sweden
Darla M. Castelli, University of Texas at Austin, USA
Fiona C. Chambers, University College Cork, Ireland
Eimear Enright, University of Queensland, Australia
Gareth Evans, Ninestiles Secondary School, UK
Joey Feith, St George's School of Montreal, Canada
Javier Fernández-Río, University of Oviedo, Spain
Tim Fletcher, Brock University, Canada
Béatrice Gibbs, Upper Secondary School, Sweden
Doug Gleddie, University of Alberta, Canada
Elizabeth M. Glowacki, University of Texas at Austin, USA
Mark Griffiths, University of Birmingham, UK
Kathy Hall, University College Cork, Ireland

Stephen Harvey, West Virginia University, USA
Carmel Hinchion, University of Limerick, Ireland
Anna Hogan, University of Queensland, Australia
P. David Howe, Loughborough University, UK
Emily Jones, West Virginia University, USA
Clare Kosnik, University of Toronto, Canada
Håkan Larsson, Swedish School of Sport and Health Sciences, Sweden
Isabel López-Chicheri, UCAM Catholic University of Murcia, Spain
Sam Lucas, University of Birmingham, UK
Catherine MacDonald, State University New York, USA
Matthew Madden, State University New York, USA
Ninitha Maivorsdotter, University of Skövde, Sweden
Matthew S. McGlone, University of Texas at Austin, USA
Jaime Morrison, Coyote Ridge Elementary School, USA
Orla Murphy, University College Cork, Ireland
Déirdre Ní Chróinín, Mary Immaculate College, Ireland
Jacob Nielsen, University of Gothenburg, Sweden
Johnny Nilsson, Stockholm and Dalarna University, Sweden
Wesley O'Brien, University College Cork, Ireland
Melissa Parker, University of Limerick, Ireland
Kevin Patton, California State University, USA
Thomas Quarmby, Leeds Beckett University, UK
Mikael Quennerstedt, Örebro University, Sweden
Jarrod Robinson, Boort District School, Australia
Rick Schupbach, Grundy Center Community Schools, USA
James Sherry, Breifne College, Ireland
Oleg A. Sinelnikov, University of Alabama, USA
Megan Babkes Stellino, University of Northern Colorado, USA
Michalis Stylianou, University of Queensland, Australia
Andy Vasily, Nexus Education
Dana Voelker, West Virginia University, USA
Martin Wahlström, University of Gothenburg, Sweden
Nalda Wainwright, University of Wales Trinity Saint David, UK
Tom Winiecki, Mott Road Elementary School, USA
Helle Winther, University of Copenhagen, Denmark

1

A PEDAGOGICAL CASES APPROACH TO UNDERSTANDING DIGITAL TECHNOLOGIES AND LEARNING IN PHYSICAL EDUCATION

Kathleen M. Armour, Ashley Casey and Victoria A. Goodyear

CHAPTER OVERVIEW

While there is evidence of considerable growth in the availability and use of digital technologies in physical education, we have very little evidence about how these technologies are being used and whether they are optimising student learning. In this chapter, we explain the rationale for this book and explore key terms. We take the 'pedagogical cases' framework and a critical understanding of 'pedagogies of technology' as our starting point. The aim is to stimulate debate within the profession about the value and potential dangers of digital technologies, and to bridge research and practice for the benefit of both.

What did we set out to do?

This book is about learning in physical education. It is important to emphasise *learning* because although the book is also about digital technologies, it is not a technology book. We have resisted the temptation to be dazzled by the tech wizardry and we focus instead on the ways in which digital technologies can be used by practitioners to support and enhance young people's learning. Indeed, the starting point for each chapter is a narrative, written by a physical education practitioner, about the technologies they use in their lessons, why, how, for whom, and to what (if any) benefit. Importantly, whilst accepting the educational potential of digital technologies, we have not made the assumption that they are inherently positive or negative in a physical education pedagogical context.

In many countries, digital technologies seem to have become ubiquitous (either intentionally or unintentionally) in our physical education classrooms, gymnasia, courtyards, fields and other settings (Kretschmann, 2015). The central questions addressed in this book are about the effects of these technologies on practitioners' pedagogies and practices, and on young people's learning. In other words, we wanted to know whether we could expand on Casey's (2015) fledgling ideas about developing theory-grounded and practice-relevant pedagogies of technology to inform the ways in which teachers use these extensive and increasingly accessible technology resources. So, we approached physical education pedagogy experts from around the world and asked them each to bring together a team who could collaborate to write a case study chapter for this book in a common case framework.

Each chapter case team consisted of academics (at least one from pedagogy and three from other sub-disciplines) and a physical education practitioner, all of whom collaborated to co-author their case study chapter. The task for the practitioner was to describe and critically reflect upon an aspect of their practice where digital technologies are used. The sub-discipline academics were asked to use their expert disciplinary lenses to analyse and critically reflect upon the practitioner narrative. The pedagogy academic was tasked with drawing the strands of the case together and was encouraged to 'be brave' in taking our thinking about pedagogies of technology forward in new ways. The aim was to contribute to a wider understanding of pedagogy and technology in physical education. The end result is the thirteen pedagogical cases that make up this book.

Why pedagogical cases?

The pedagogical cases model was created originally by Armour (2014). The first book of twenty pedagogical cases attempted to take a novel approach to bridging research/theory and practice. At the heart of each case was a narrative about an individual young person attempting to learn in physical education. Teams of authors from different academic sub-disciplines, led by a pedagogy academic, undertook a multidisciplinary analysis of the narrative. Importantly, the young person at the heart of the narrative was to be characterised as a complex individual learner rather than a deficit case to be 'fixed'. The ambition was twofold: to pilot a new way of translating knowledge developed in individual sub-disciplines into an accessible, multi- and even interdisciplinary format for students and practitioners; and to create a two-way communication channel between academics and practitioners.

Although it has long been argued that in education new communication channels, and translational mechanisms and resources are needed, rather little has materialized. An extract from the introductory chapter of the first volume of pedagogical cases summarises the rationale for taking this approach:

> In her Presidential Address to the 2012 American Educational Research Association (AERA), Arnetha Ball challenged researchers to 'move away from research designed as mere "demonstrations of knowledge" towards research

that has the power to close the knowing-doing gap in education' (Ball, 2012, p. 283, emphasis in original). Ball argued passionately that although it is important for researchers in education to conduct research that can create new knowledge, 'to know is not enough' because knowing 'is not sufficient to address social problems, mitigate inequalities, or advance innovative methods of instruction' (p. 284). Noting also that 'there is a gap between what we know and what is widely done in the educational arena' (p. 285) Ball made a case for more translational research to close persisting knowledge-practice or research-practice gaps. She argued that what is required is 'persistent, collaborative, and generative work' (p. 285) and 'resources and mechanisms to promote the use of research to improve education' (p. 292). This book introduces the concept of 'Pedagogical Cases' as a translational research mechanism and a professional learning tool for practitioners. The purpose of the cases is to make a contribution to closing the knowledge/ research/practice gap for practising and aspirant teachers and coaches who work with children and young people in physical education/youth sport settings. (Armour, 2014, p. 7)

Reflection on the process of developing that first volume of cases suggests that we were only partially successful in what we set out to do. Indeed, those cases are best described as a pilot and perhaps the key lessons learnt were about the considerable challenges to be faced in synthesising different sub-disciplinary knowledge around an individual learner and moving from multi- to interdisciplinary understandings. In this second volume, the task is both similar and different. The intention remains to take up Ball's (2012) challenge to develop new 'resources and mechanisms' that can help to close knowing/doing or theory/practice gaps to improve both. The aim was to learn from the experience of developing the first pedagogical cases and to improve the model.

In each case/chapter in this book, a case narrative details a practitioner's pedagogical intentions and processes when using digital technologies with specific groups of learners. The narratives are then analysed from three different sub-discipline perspectives to provide a multidisciplinary and critical understanding of the possibilities and challenges of supporting learning with digital technologies. Each case concludes with a pedagogical synthesis and a practitioner reflection to ensure the links between theory/research and practice are robust. The pedagogical cases approach, therefore, offered us the possibility to develop new thinking around pedagogies of technology that are grounded in both theory and practice.

Although the focal point of the case narrative in this book is a practitioner, the ultimate target is improved outcomes for learners in physical education contexts. It is also worth emphasising that as with the first volume of pedagogical cases, the aim is to bridge theory and practice but there is no intention to present the practitioner as a deficit case who needs to be 'improved' by knowledge from research. Instead, the aim is to present a set of collaborative, co-created pedagogical cases that raise issues for debate, discussion and further professional learning. It is worth noting that in this volume, a practitioner is a co-author on each chapter and has both the first (narrative) and last (critical reflection) word to ensure their voices are strong.

What are pedagogies of technology?

New technologies are transforming how we think, work, play and relate to each other.

Technology has dramatically affected virtually every sector in society that you can think of *except* education.

The stark contrast between Robinson's and Fullan's statements is at the heart of this book. It has been suggested that education is often far behind other disciplines (Dumagan, Gill, & Ingram, 2003) and somehow disconnected from the outside world, and this is one argument for aspirations to increase the use of technology in education. Yet, it can also be argued that this is hardly a new or particularly innovative message given that numerous researchers have voiced the expectation that technology will revolutionize education (Beynon, 1992; Papert, 1993; Prensky, 2010; Riel, 1994). Foremost among these has been Papert (1993, p. 37) who has suggested, in different ways and at different times, that digital technology (in this case, the computer) will create an environment where 'new educational ideas can be put into practice today and in the near future'. Indeed, the saturation of technology in the personal lives of many individuals can mean that the step from personal to professional use is barely questioned. Selwyn (2011, p. 1), for example, argues that 'we are faced with a prevailing sense that the use of technology in education is something that does not merit particular critical scrutiny or thought'.

Writing more than two decades ago, Apple (1992) suggested there was a sense of autonomy associated with technology. He felt that technology was afforded a life of its own and was simply expected to grow and progress in its capacity to act as 'something of a savior . . . pedagogically' (Apple, 1992, p. 106). Apple was convinced, however, that we should be willing to find and analyse the potential of technology before simply introducing it wholesale into education. More recently, Selwyn (2014) has voiced a similar distrust of educational technology suggesting that there is a 'gulf that persists between the rhetoric of how digital technologies *could* be used in education and the realities of how digital technologies are *actually* used in education' (Selwyn, 2014, p. vii, original emphasis). To this end both Apple (1992) and Selwyn (2014) have suggested that decisions about technology (i.e. what to purchase and use) are being made too quickly and assumptions are made about the future that are not evidence-based and that rarely come to fruition.

Underpinning all of these concerns is a belief that technology in education has tended to be considered largely uncritically and is viewed as being unquestionably beneficial (Apple, 1992; Oppenheimer, 2003; Selwyn, 2014). The sheer volume, power and pervasiveness of digital technologies means that they are seldom problematised and are, instead, positioned as the solution to a plethora of educational problems (see Fullan, 2013). Yet, as Selwyn suggests:

> Most digital technologies over the past 30 years have been accompanied by promises of widening participation in education, increased motivation and engagement, better levels of 'attainment', enhanced convenience of use and more 'efficient' and 'effective' provision of educational opportunities. Indeed, the field of education and technology is beset by exaggerated expectations over the capacity of the latest 'new' technology to change education for the better, regardless of context and circumstance. (Selwyn, 2014, p. 7)

Clearly there is a large and perhaps irreconcilable gap (at least in the short term) between different positions on the value of technologies in education. Some believe in the natural capacity for educational technology to solve pedagogical ills, while others feel that a tectonic shift needs to occur in the way we debate about digital technologies. The purpose of this book is to open this debate in physical education and consider the potential impact of educational technologies on the pedagogies of our subject. In short, we (with the help of the chapter teams) will argue that the problematisation of technologies has the potential to support the field to reconsider what we want to achieve by asking 'what pedagogical gaps exist that digital technologies can help to bridge?' In other words, how can we be creative in our use of digital technologies so that they enhance, expand and even (optimistically) transform teaching and students' learning?

Conceptualizing pedagogies of technology

As we embarked upon the process of developing this book and the pedagogical cases that comprise it, our starting point was a concern that digital technologies in education may not always be driven by a pedagogical process, but more by *ad hoc* decisions to use specific pieces of hardware and software (Hastie *et al.*, 2010; Palao *et al.*, 2015). Literature suggests that while some teachers are enthusiastic technology adopters, others are more resistant, perhaps feeling they lack the organizational and administrative support or expertise to integrate it (Fullan, 2013; Leh, 2005; Palao *et al.*, 2015). This is perhaps not surprising given that schools and institutions are often not fit for purpose and based on industrialized systems of working (Lawson, 2009; Robinson, 2011). Increasingly, teachers lack autonomy. Indeed, there is a prevailing sense that teachers are being employed not to do what they consider is in the best interests of their students but are instead employed to teach in increasingly scripted ways (Au, 2011; Sloan, 2008). Under such conditions, teachers can be forgiven for failing to think pedagogically about technology and instead simply adopting it uncritically or using it because they have been told they must.

In positioning the idea of pedagogies of technology as a foundational concept for this book, we were also aware of the arguments that suggest we have our concepts 'back to front'. As Fletcher (1996) puts it:

When you go to the hardware store to buy a drill, you don't actually want a drill, you want a hole, they don't sell holes at the hardware store, but they do sell drills, which are the technology used to make holes. We must not lose sight that technology for the most part is a tool and it should be used in applications which address educational concerns. (p. 87)

In considering this analogy as a focal point for the development of pedagogies of technology, it is useful to recall that different schools and different teachers use a variety of technologies to meet their aims (or make holes, so to speak). In short, technology should not be used indiscriminately but should be judged on its ability to facilitate the achievement of our educational aims. Rorty (1999, p. xxiii) argues that 'no matter whether the tool is a hammer, or a gun or a belief or a statement, tool-using is part of the interaction of the organism with its environment'. In the case of education that interaction needs to be pedagogic in nature.

Perhaps the key point to be made is that the development of pedagogies of technology requires pedagogues to have 'an understanding of pedagogical principles that are specific to the use of technology in instructional settings' (Diaz & Bontembal, 2000, p. 2). This means that educators need to understand the interactions that occur between teacher, learner and curriculum, and envision how technology can enhance this process. Fullan (2013) argues that we are 'too busy creating better versions of what was needed for the twentieth century instead of creating and implementing a better, more future-orientated education for all our kids' (p. 25). In the words of Robinson (2011, p. 7) we need to 'disenthral' ourselves from old problems and antiquated pedagogies and find new ways of supporting our students in their education.

In an attempt to disenthrall ourselves from old problems and antiquated pedagogies, therefore, we propose the following tentative – yet also ambitious – definition of pedagogies of technology:

Pedagogies of technology are critically aware and technically competent pedagogies that can be developed in practice to maximise the latent potential of technologies to accelerate learning in meaningful ways that meet the individual needs of diverse learners. The starting point for a pedagogy of technology is a desire to do things differently, rather than to the same things using 'flashy' tools and gizmos.

Importantly, however, while we offer this tentative definition here, it was not provided to our chapter authors prior to them constructing or writing their pedagogical cases. One of our aims of this book was to use multidisciplinary perspectives and practice-based examples to further define effective pedagogies of technology in action. So, we took the decision to provide chapter teams with a summary of terms that have been used widely to describe technology-related pedagogy and learning and we left the space open for them to consider different possibilities and opportunities for pedagogy and learning that are afforded by digital technologies. An extract from our guidance is as follows:

> There are some debates around e-pedagogies and we really want you to be creative in thinking about the issues and adding new insights. For example, drawing on the work of Mehanna (2004) the notion of e-pedagogies emerges from an understanding that, to date, there is little if any definitive evidence that e-learning is more effective than more conventional methods. A basic definition of e-learning might be learning using technologies such as, but not exclusively, the Internet, blogs, wikis and social networking sites. Indeed, e-learning has been held up as the 'dominant technology [although perhaps mechanism would better serve] in supporting new approaches to teaching and learning' (Garrison, 2011, p. 61). That said, education has doggedly adhered to a transmission model (i.e. the face-to-face delivery of knowledge) that has hampered the capabilities of e-learning to create a 'new learning ecology' (Brown, 2000). In contrast e-pedagogy challenges us to 'develop new understanding of effective pedagogies that are specific to these learning contexts' (Mehenna, 2004, p. 280). It is a key purpose of this book to further the debates around the development of the concept of 'e-pedagogies'.

As you read these thirteen pedagogical cases, it will be interesting for you to consider how far we succeeded in generating innovative examples of practice and analysis.

The problem with technology

In addition to a desire to add depth to the concept of pedagogies of technology and offer space for innovation, this book is also underpinned by Fullan's (2013) arguments about technology having the potential to accelerate learning. Undoubtedly, in 2016, we see a generation of young people who identify with selfies, hashtags, and emojis, and where sharing, liking, tweeting, blogging and vlogging are becoming mainstream practices (Selwyn & Stirling, 2016). Digital devices, applications (apps[1]) and social networking sites are readily accessible and are used by many young people on a daily basis (Greenhow & Lewin, 2016). It has been estimated, for example, that 71 per cent of American adolescents use the social networking site Facebook as a platform for communication (Lenhart, 2015). This seemingly unstoppable growth in young people's engagement with digital technologies in their personal lives (Selwyn & Stirling, 2016) means that digital technologies are socially and culturally relevant. This is also a growing opportunity to act as a medium through which to deliver information and/or engage young people in ways that are immediate, attractive and increasingly personalised (Greenhow & Lewin, 2016; Rich & Miah, 2014; Selwyn & Stirling, 2016). Yet while new opportunities exist – and more can be anticipated as we move forward – it is important to be mindful of the challenges and risks presented by digital technologies for young people, physical educators, parents, schools and policy makers more broadly.

Fullan (2013) drew our attention to what he termed the 'dark side' of technology, highlighting key concerns around e-bullying, cyber-spying and the pervasive influence of marketing campaigns on young people's well-being. In education and physical education contexts, however, there are further risks and challenges associated with learning, health and well-being. For example, digital technologies are increasingly creating digitized perceptions of health (Öhman *et al.*, 2014) and digital 'benchmarked' data is becoming a primary determinant of 'good' health (Lupton, 2014). While individuals have been recording their health and lifestyle habits for decades through the use of training and/or food diaries, mobile health apps and digital devices present and frame our understandings of the body in ways that appear to be more 'scientific' thus more valid, reliable and credible (Lupton, 2014). This is particularly prevalent when mobile health apps and exergames hold sensor technologies (e.g. gyroscopes, altimeters and accelerometers) that quantify movement to determine health (Lupton, 2014; Öhman *et al.*, 2014; Williamson, 2015).

Used uncritically, these devices and apps can simply teach young people that they are 'fat' and 'unhealthy', with little recognition of important and relevant differences between individuals (Rich & Miah, 2015). There are also significant risks associated with the contemporary practice of posting 'healthy selfies', where individuals (especially young people) digitally alter and post pictures of their bodies to social media sites as indicators of good health[2]. Indeed, the rise of 'healthism' in adults (an ideological, neo-liberal and public construct of health) and concerns about individual autonomy, self-monitoring and obsession/addiction as a result of digital technologies (Lupton, 2014) are also concerns in youth, and those concerns are growing at an alarming rate (Rich & Miah, 2015). In another example, mobile medical apps have been described as 'a physician in your pocket' (Lupton & Jutel, 2015, p. 128) and health-related digital technologies could be regarded as 'a teacher in your pocket'. This is important contextual information for keen physical education teachers who are seeking to merge digital technologies into their practices in order to be culturally relevant.

Looking across this book, we see a different cautionary note that needs to be highlighted. Although we gave no instructions to the chapter teams about the practitioners they would choose to work with, it is interesting to see that while the academic teams are relatively gender balanced, the practitioners are mainly white males. This may simply be a manifestation of the dominance of white male practitioners who use digital technologies and talk about them extensively on social media. Goodyear *et al.* (2015) identified a group of practitioners known as the 'big names' on Twitter who dominate practitioner-focused social media communities. It would appear that white maleness is perceived by others to confer technology expertise and voice privilege in this space (Goodyear *et al.*, 2015). What this means is that while this book offers a variety of practitioner perspectives and experiences, it is also limited. In the first pedagogical cases volume (Armour, 2014), chapter teams were given similar freedoms in the choice of young person for the case narrative and the result was endless variety and difference. In this second volume, the outcome was homogeneity. In future volumes centring on practitioners, therefore, we may need to take a different commissioning approach.

Using this book to support teachers' professional development

This book has been written to be of interest to students who are learning to become teachers, professional practitioners who want to learn more about the capacity of digital technologies to enhance practice, Continuing Professional Development providers and academics in pedagogy.

The mechanism used in this book to develop the science of learning in our movement fields is 'pedagogical cases' (as described earlier). As in the first volume, these multi-/interdisciplinary cases have been written in an accessible format but at an academically challenging level. It was noted in the proposal for the first volume that Lawrence Stenhouse (1980) had advocated for the wider use of case studies as a resource for practitioners. He argued for cases based on a 'differential response to diagnostic assessment of [learner] needs' (p. 3) and for the development of mixed method case studies, and their 'patient accumulation' (p. 4). Stenhouse felt that this would result in a resource that could be shared and that could support practitioners in educational contexts to: 'make refined judgments about what educational action to take in particular cases lodged in particular contexts' (p. 4). His comments summarise the approach taken in this second volume of pedagogical cases, although the cases themselves have a new format, focus and length (to allow for greater depth in analysis).

The structure of the book and each chapter

In each of the thirteen pedagogical cases, we focus on how a practitioner has attempted to use digital technologies to enhance student learning. Each chapter in this book is a stand-alone pedagogical case. The central focus of each chapter is a case narrative of a professional practitioner (teacher or other educator) who is attempting to use an aspect or aspects of digital technologies to build effective pedagogies and 'technology-accelerated learning'. The format for each case/chapter is as follows:

Section One: A case narrative written from the perspective of a professional practitioner who is using digital technologies in a specified physical education context. The narrative has been written in partnership with a pedagogy academic, who also takes the role of lead chapter author. The narratives detail focal technology/technologies and where, how, why and for which specific learners the digital technologies are used to accelerate learning. The purpose of the narrative is to highlight and illustrate both opportunities and challenges.

Sections Two, Three and Four: These three sections have been written by academics from different disciplines/sub-disciplines usually located in the same national context as the practitioner. Each section contributor has analysed the case narrative from his or her disciplinary perspective. They were tasked with drawing upon classic/cutting edge research in their fields, focusing on the effectiveness of the approach described in the narrative in the context of the stated learning outcomes

Section Five: This section has been written by the lead author – the pedagogy academic – who has taken responsibility for drawing together the previous four sections and locating the key issues raised in an appropriate selection of pedagogy research. The focus is on identifying lessons learned for the development of effective pedagogies of technology to support young people's learning in physical education. We also asked these lead authors to 'be brave' in their analysis so we could move the debates forward.

Section Six: This concluding section is a reflective commentary on the whole pedagogical case from the professional practitioner who was at the heart of the case narrative.

To sum up, we make no claim that these pedagogical cases cover all the ways in which digital technologies can, should or could be used in physical education, nor that they offer recipe-style guidance. The aim, instead, is to present them as analytical examples of practice that can stimulate debate, professional learning and – perhaps – change in the wider physical education profession.

Notes

1 An application program is a computer program designed to perform a group of coordinated functions, tasks, or activities for the benefit of the user.
2 www.healthyselfieapp.com

References

Apple, M. (1992). Is the new technology part of the solution or part of the problem in education? In J. Beynon & H. Mackay (Eds.), *Technological Literacy and the Curriculum*. London: Falmer Press. pp. 105–124.

Armour, K. M. (Ed.). (2014). *Pedagogical Cases in Physical Education and Youth Sport*. Oxon: Routledge.

Au, W. (2011). Teaching under the new Taylorism: High-stakes testing and the standardization of the 21st century curriculum. *Journal of Curriculum Studies, 43*, 25–45.

Ball, A. F. (2012). 2012 Presidential Address. To know is not enough: Knowledge, power and the zone of generativity. *Educational Researcher, 41*(8), 283–293.

Beynon, J. (1992). Introduction: Learning to read technology. In J. Beynon & H. Mackay (Eds.), *Technological Literacy and the Curriculum*. London: Falmer Press. pp. 137–124.

Brown, J. S. (2000). Growing up digital: How the web changes work, education, and the ways people learn. *Change: The Magazine of Higher Learning, 32*(2), 11–20.

Casey, A. (2015). *Developing a theory of technology for physical education pedagogy.* Paper presented at the British Educational Research Association's Annual Conference, Queens University, Belfast, 3–5 September 2015. doi:10.1080/00091380009601719

Diaz, D. P. & Bontenbal, K. F. (2000). Pedagogy-based technology training. In P. Hoffman & D. Lemke (Eds.), *Teaching and learning in a network world.* Amsterdam, Netherlands: 105 Press. pp. 50–54.

Dumagan, J., Gill, G., & Ingram, C. (2003). Industry-level effects of information technology use on overall productivity. In US Department of Commerce (Eds.), *Digital economy 2003.* pp. 45–60. Retrieved from www.esa.doc.gov/sites/default/files/reports/documents/dig_econ_2003.pdf

Fletcher, G. (1996). Former director of the division of educational technology, Texas Education Agency, Executive Vice President of T.H.E. Institute quoted in *T.H.E. Journal, 24*, 87.

Fullan, M. (2013). *Stratosphere: Integrating Technology, Pedagogy, and Change Knowledge.* Toronto, ONT: Pearson.

Garrison, D. R. (2011). *E-learning in the 21st Century a Framework for Research and Practice.* New York: Routledge.

Goodyear, V. A., Casey, A., & Parker, M. (2015). *"Must share without fear of being judged": SNSs capacity to form engaging and impactful professional learning communities.* Paper presented at the European Educational Research Association Conference, Budapest, Hungary, 8–11 September 2015.

Greenhow, C. & Lewin, C. (2016). Social media and education: Reconceptualizing the boundaries of formal and informal learning. *Learning, Media and Technology, 41*(4), 6–30.

Hastie, P. A., Casey, A., & Tarter, A-M. (2010). A case study of wikis and student designed games in physical education. *Technology, Pedagogy and Education, 19*(1), 79–91.

Kretschmann, R. (2015). Physical education teachers' subjective theories about integrating information and communication technology (ICT) into physical education. *Turkish Online Journal of Educational Technology, 14*(1), 68–96.

Lawson, H. A. (2009). Paradigms, exemplars and social change. *Sport, Education and Society, 14*, 97–119.

Leh, A. S. C. (2005). Lessons learned from service learning and reverse mentoring in faculty development: A case study in technology training. *Journal of Technology and Teacher Education, 13*, 25–41.

Lenhart, A. (2015). *Teens, social media and technology.* Pew Research Centre. Retrieved from www.pewinternet.org/files/2015/04/PI_TeensandTech_Update2015_0409151.pdf

Lupton, D. (2014). Apps as artefacts: Towards a critical perspective on mobile health and medical apps. *Societies, 4*(4), 606–622.

Lupton, D. & Jutel, A. (2015). "It's like having a physician in your pocket!" A critical analysis of self-diagnosis smartphone apps. *Social Science and Medicine, 133*, 128–135.

Mehanna, W. N. (2004). e-Pedagogy: The pedagogies of e-learning. *ALT-J, Research in Learning Technology, 12*(3), 279–293.

Öhman, M., Almqvist, J., Meckbach, J., & Quennerstedt, M. (2014). Competing for ideal bodies: A study of exergames used as teaching aids in schools. *Critical Public Health, 24*(2), 196–209.

Oppenheimer, T. (2003). *The Flickering Mind: The False Promise of Technology in the Classroom and How Learning Can Be Saved.* New York: Random House.

Palao, J. M., Hastie, P. A., & Guerrero, P. (2015). The impact of video technology on student performance in physical education. *Technology, Pedagogy and Education, 24*(1), 51–63.

Papert, S. (1993). *Mindstorms: Children, Computers, and Powerful Ideas*. New York: Basic Books.

Prensky, M. (2010). *Teaching Digital Natives: Partnering for Real Learning*. Thousand Oaks, CA: Corwin Press.

Rich, E. & Miah, A. (2014). Understanding digital health as public pedagogy: A critical framework. *Societies, 4*(2), 296–315.

Riel, M. (1994). Educational change in a technology-rich environment. *Journal of Research on Computing in Education, 26*(4), 452–474.

Robinson, K. (2011). *Out of Our Minds: Learning to Be Creative*. Chichester, UK: Capstone.

Rorty, R. (1999). *Philosophy and Social Hope*. London: Penguin Books.

Selwyn, N. (2011). *Education and Technology: Key Issues and debates*. London: Continuum.

Selwyn, N. (2014). *Distrusting Educational Technology: Critical Questions for Changing Times*. London: Routledge.

Selwyn, N. & Stirling, E. (2016). Social media and education . . . now the dust has settled. *Learning, Media and Technology, 41*(1), 1–5.

Sloan, K. (2008). The expanding educational services sector: Neoliberalism and the corporatization of curriculum at the local level in the US. *Journal of Curriculum Studies, 40*, 555–578.

Stenhouse, L. (1980). Curriculum research and the art of the teacher. *Curriculum, 1*, 40–43.

Williamson, B. (2015). Algorithmic skin: Health-tracking technologies, personal analytics and the biopedagogies of digitized health and physical education. *Sport, Education and Society, 20*(1), 133–151. doi:10.1080/13573322.2014.962494

2

DYLAN: THE USE OF MOBILE APPS WITHIN A TACTICAL INQUIRY APPROACH

Victoria M. Goodyear, Dylan Blain,
Thomas Quarmby and Nalda Wainwright

CHAPTER OVERVIEW

This chapter explores how a range of applications (apps) were integrated into a tactical inquiry approach to support students' physical, cognitive, social, and affective learning. Motivational, social justice, and fundamental movement perspectives demonstrate how the diverse and individual needs of young people need to be considered when using apps. From a pedagogical perspective, apps act as a tool to support a student-centred pedagogy. This chapter concludes by suggesting that teachers should engage with an ongoing process of diagnosing, responding and evaluating, where apps can be used to assist and strengthen a teacher's ability to design effective learning experiences.

Practitioner narrative (Dylan Blain)

I have written this case from a personal, yet historical perspective as it explores how, as a teacher, I used iPads and various mobile apps in secondary school physical education. At the time of this case I had been teaching for eight years. I had a traditional games background, having played semi-professional football for fifteen years, but firmly believed in adopting an inclusive pedagogy and promoting learning in physical, cognitive, social, and affective learning domains. I was (and still am) a strong advocate of technology and had been using various devices (laptops, cameras, iPads, iPods) to support learning since I started teaching.

The following narrative presents a retrospective view of my experiences of teaching a basketball unit with a mixed ability class of boys age 13–14. The school was situated in a rural town of Wales, and students were from low- to middle-income socioeconomic groups. The school had recently acquired a set of iPads (tablet computers). This unit, however, signified the first time the iPads were embedded into learning tasks, and it was the first time this class had used them in physical education.

Unit overview

The aims of the ten-lesson basketball unit were to enhance students' physical, cognitive, social, and affective learning. Specifically, the unit goals were:

- Physical: Enhance students' technical skills
- Cognitive: Develop tactical game understanding
- Social: Develop teamwork skills
- Affective: Strengthen students' confidence

A tactical inquiry approach, developed from Bunker and Thorpe's (1982) Teaching Games for Understanding model, was used. Similar to Gurvitch *et al.* (2008), I acknowledged the complexity in planning for, using, and adhering to all key steps and/or benchmarks identified to guide a tactical inquiry approach. Consequently, I identified four of the fourteen benchmarks available (see Metzler, 2011) to use as a focus for my practice:

- Tactical problems as the organising centre for learning tasks
- Beginning lessons with a game form
- Deductive questions to get students to solve tactical problems
- High rates of feedback during situated learning tasks

Students were organised into eight mixed ability teams of four or five members. Each team was required to solve tactical problems (e.g. maintaining possession or defending space) and through their analysis of team strengths and weaknesses, create attacking and defensive strategies. To support learning, each team was provided with one iPad and directed to use varying apps (Table 2.1). I also used an iPad and an Apple TV device connected to a projector in the sports hall. The Apple TV device was used for wireless streaming of content from the iPads to the screen – teaching videos from YouTube or performance analysis from Coach's Eye or Ubersense (see Table 2.1).

Teaching and student learning

The apps created new opportunities to enhance *all* students' learning. The use of more than one app within lessons and over the course of the unit catered for each of the unit learning goals and acted to maintain students' interest in learning and group work. This last point was most significant for those students who appeared less engaged during lessons, for example, those who disliked traditional invasion games. The apps allowed *all* students to understand tasks and their team's

TABLE 2.1 Apps, functions and how they were used

Application	Functions	How the applications were used
Coach's Eye and Ubersense	Performance analysis apps that allow playback of captured video footage in real time, slow motion and frame-by-frame; video clips can be annotated and clips can also be overlaid or placed side by side, alongside allowing for narrated and annotated videos to be created.	• Teams filmed and analysed clips of games. • Students adopted analyst roles to capture footage for analysis. • Teams compared and analysed isolated skills against a 'perfect model'.
Dartfish EasyTag	An app that allows users to identify and select specific movements that are videoed; for example, if a team won possession, this part of the clip could be identified by being 'tagged' as 'win ball'. All of the same clips 'tagged' can then be selected to be viewed together and statistics of key 'tags' are generated; 88% of the clips were 'win ball'.	• Teams captured statistics on performances. • Statistics were used to identify strengths and improvements.
Socrative	Question and answer app for teachers to ask questions and set quizzes	• Dylan sent open-ended and multiple-choice questions and received answers from teams.
Explain Everything	Whiteboard app that creates slides of information that are narrated over, annotated and animated	• Dylan created coaching videos, set plays and created videos of lesson tasks.
Edmodo	Social networking app; teachers create online networks for students and teachers to share resources and discuss learning.	• Content created on Coach's Eye and Explain Everything were shared.

performances, and play an equal role in the team's learning. Previously, and before the use of iPads, this level of engagement was not always achieved without needing to provide specific support, direct instructions, or demonstrations.

Fundamentally, the apps allowed the students to apply their learning in different and more effective ways. The real-time, slow-motion, and frame-by-frame playback features of Ubersense and Coach's Eye developed students' understanding of how they had used tactics within games. The statistical outputs from Dartfish EasyTag added to these understandings by providing numerical indicators of whether students were successful in attack or defence. Without video feedback and numerical data, this level of analysis and subsequent tactical understanding would be difficult to achieve. Instead of understanding and analysis being based on students' reflections on the game, the visuals and statistics provided specific indicators of what happened and aided students in developing new and more effective game strategies.

The apps also changed the way students interacted with one another. Similar to social networking sites (e.g. Facebook and Twitter), Edmodo enabled teams to post resources or videos that they had created and then interact with each other and different teams. An unexpected outcome was that students worked on their resources and videos outside of lessons, including commenting on each other's posts. The desired outcomes of building teamwork and tactical understandings were developed through digital interactions inside and outside the classroom.

During the unit, my interactions with students became more digital, frequent, and specific. Following students' engagement with learning tasks – often from the information sent through Explain Everything – I used Socrative to send questions and prompt students to analyse their team's performances. Through Socrative I prompted students' critical thinking and also supported students to learn at a faster rate. Indeed, I sent either the same questions or personalised questions to each of the teams, and this reduced the time it would take for me to reach each of the groups and ask them face-to-face. I would often then use teams' responses to the questions that were sent to determine if and when I needed to provide teams with further questions or specific face-to-face guidance. When all teams hadn't quite grasped the learning tasks or were struggling to create strategies, the Apple TV then became an additional and useful resource. I used the streaming device to provide visual demonstrations of games and skills from 'expert performers' and individual team's game play to highlight certain tactics or movements. The guidance I could provide through the Apple TV was more detailed and specific than the often inaccurate or poor representations of performance that students – or I – were able to demonstrate. In this way, I feel I was able to be more responsive to my students' learning needs because I could provide higher quality feedback with the support of digital demonstrations.

While the apps were beneficial for learning, I was concerned about the time it took for students to learn how to use the apps and, consequently, the reduced time spent in practical game play. I was disappointed with the reduction in moderate-to-vigorous physical activity (MVPA) and was concerned about whether my students had met the recommended amounts of physical activity for their age as specified in the UK Government's guidance (Department of Health, 2011). In addition, I expressed concerns about my students' self-esteem. While viewing successful performances was certainly rewarding, observing their own mistakes – and repeated mistakes – challenged the confidence levels of some students. For example, where some students made repeated errors I saw that their willingness to try again was reduced, and some team members became frustrated with their peers.

Summary

My narrative provides an example of the integration of technology within a tactical inquiry approach. The range of apps I used supported learning through video analysis (e.g. Coach's Eye), social interactions (e.g. Edmodo), and critical thinking (e.g. Socrative). The iPads and the Apple TV device also acted as tools for me to interact with students and provide fast rates of high quality feedback. Nonetheless, I had (and still have) some concerns about MVPA and the potential for some pupils to develop low self-esteem.

My narrative will now be considered from psychological, social justice and fundamental movement skills perspectives. The pedagogical insights emerging from these will then be discussed to offer insights into the dilemmas I faced in practice.

A psychological perspective (Dylan Blain)

Since the teaching of the unit I have moved into higher education and have begun to examine psychological aspects related to physical education. In this section, I draw on my research around self-determination theory (SDT) to offer an evidence-informed critical analysis of my own narrative.

It is widely agreed that positive engagement and the consistent application of effort are important behaviours required by pupils in physical education if they are to learn effectively (see Haerens *et al.*, 2011). *Motivation* is generally described as a process that underpins these positive behaviours (Roberts, 2012). Many motivational theories highlight the influence social environments have on pupil motivation, and this is particularly evident within SDT.

More than accounting for the quantity of motivation, SDT distinguishes different forms of motivation in terms of quality. According to SDT, individuals are highly motivated when they fully endorse their actions and take part in activities for intrinsic interest and enjoyment (Deci & Ryan, 2000). Such self-determined, or autonomous forms of motivation, are shown consistently to lead to more adaptive responses than controlled, extrinsic forms of motivation (Ntoumanis & Standage, 2009; Standage & Ryan, 2012). A complete lack of motivation or intention to act is known as *amotivation* (Ryan & Deci, 2000b). Although only limited individuals are found to be amotivated in physical education (Ntoumanis, 2002), for those who are, technologies such as the iPad may prompt initial engagement in the subject, as was demonstrated with the "traditionally less engaged" pupils in my lessons. An initial level of engagement can lead to more autonomous forms of motivation (Ntoumanis & Standage, 2009; Standage & Ryan, 2012). This is most likely when an individual's social environment supports their basic psychological need for autonomy, relatedness, and competence (Ryan & Deci, 2000a; Standage *et al.*, 2006).

Autonomy involves having a sense of volition or self-endorsing one's actions (Ryan & Deci, 2000a). Reeve (2009) states that autonomy-supportive teachers are those who adopt the students' perspectives; welcome students' thoughts, feelings and behaviours; and support students' motivational development and capacity for autonomous self-regulation. My use of tactical problems to structure the unit provided many opportunities for pupils to have input and choice about their actions. The technology clearly supported this strategy. For example, using the Socrative app, I gathered information from all groups and used it to respond to individual group needs, thus placing the students at the centre of decision-making processes.

Relatedness is concerned with being connected to others through feelings of belonging and being valued (Ryan & Deci, 2000b). Teachers can support pupils' need for relatedness through creating close, caring, warm, and respectful environments (Standage & Ryan, 2012). The interactive group activities used within my lessons provided opportunities for satisfaction of students' needs for relatedness. For example, through analysing video replays and statistical data, groups were encouraged to work together to develop strategies to improve team performance. In addition, Edmodo extended social interactions beyond lesson time and had the ability to enhance students' feelings of belongingness through online collaboration on tasks developed in lessons.

Competence is expressed as feeling effective in one's environment (Ryan & Deci, 2000a). Competence is often developed through structured activities that provide all pupils with opportunities for success whereby the motivational climate can influence how achievement-based goals are judged (Nicholls, 1984). Simply stated, tasks involving climates or mastery climates support effort and cooperation, emphasise learning, and allow students to be assessed on self-referenced criteria (Ames, 1992). My integration of technology supported a mastery focus within lessons, specifically in relation to developing attacking and defensive strategies. Although the target was to win games, the focus remained on improving game performance. For example, the use of Dartfish EasyTag to collect statistical data on performance indicators within the game enabled pupils to set specific improvement targets for game processes, such as successful passes. The collection of these statistics, in combination with video replays via Coach's Eye, provided detailed information for groups to enable them to plan and trial improvements. This focus on task improvement offered opportunities for all teams to experience success and thus develop competence.

While the technologies could have developed students' autonomy, relatedness, and competence, it is also important to consider my concerns about the impact of video analysis on my students' self-esteem. In particular, unsuccessful experiences, and resulting negative feedback observed from video, could frustrate the need for competence, and possibly relatedness, if individuals feel exposed by their poor performances within group situations. In the SDT literature it is acknowledged that excessive frustration of the basic psychological needs can have negative effects on motivation and well-being (Vansteenkiste & Ryan, 2013). Drawing on Ryan and Deci (1989) it might, therefore, be more appropriate to use video feedback for informational feedback rather than in a judgmental or controlling manner. Ryan and Deci (1989) argue that informational rather than controlling feedback has a positive impact on students' basic psychological needs.

In summary, SDT can be used to interpret how digital technologies may support or hinder students' motivation. This analysis has shown that technology can be used as a tool to strengthen students' sense of volition (autonomy), promote feelings of belonging (relatedness), and ensure students have positive self-perceptions about their capabilities (competence). Despite this, there is a need to be mindful that technology could exemplify negative feelings of self and reduce students' motivation. Technology integration, therefore, requires teachers to pay careful attention to their students' individual needs to ensure motivation can be accelerated through digital technologies and not decelerated.

A social justice perspective (Thomas Quarmby)

Many would argue that physical education has a role to play in addressing issues of social justice (see Fitzpatrick, 2013; Tinning, 2002), particularly for vulnerable and disadvantaged young people. Dylan's class comprised students age 13–14, from predominantly low- to mid-income socioeconomic groups. It is important to recognise, however, that there will be 'hidden' students within the class who are disadvantaged in multiple ways and at risk of social marginalisation. One group that characterises multiple disadvantages is 'looked after children' (Children in Care). While not all such children are disengaged, there is strong evidence to suggest they are more likely to be the subject of particular forms of social vulnerability, play truant from school and engage in disruptive behaviour (McAuley & Davis, 2009; Scott, 2011). It is helpful, therefore, to consider the learning needs of this group of young people in an analysis of Dylan's narrative.

Although social justice is a highly contested notion (Rivzi & Lingard, 2010), most attempts to define it centre on a belief that that we should endeavour to tackle the unfair disadvantages faced by some individuals and groups in society. Hence, social justice is about distributing – or even redistributing – resources and opportunities in an attempt to empower *all* young people to realise their potential (Kirk, 2006; Tinning, 2002) and learn across the physical, cognitive, social and affective domains. Importantly, teachers' practices and pedagogies could make a difference to issues of social justice and inclusion (Hayes *et al.*, 2006). In relation to Dylan's practice, and perhaps somewhat counter-intuitively, the integration of specific digital technologies may provide an initial means of tackling issues of social justice for looked after children.

Dylan believed the integration of iPads encouraged student interest in learning and group work, particularly for those who were often disengaged. As an increasingly prominent part of popular culture, the use of iPads may resonate with young people's experiences beyond school. For example, Ofcom (2014) reported that 71 per cent of 5–15-year-olds had access to a tablet at home. Though no figures exist specifically for looked after children, it could be argued that Dylan's introduction of technology may have made the lessons more 'relevant' for young people which may have helped to capture student interest.

For looked after children, learning across the social and affective domains may be particularly relevant and important since they tend to have narrow social networks, poorer interpersonal skills and suffer from low self-efficacy (Gilligan, 1999). By enhancing teamwork and offering new ways to improve interactions with other students (social domain), coupled with developing student confidence (affective domain), Dylan attempted to address these issues. The use of Edmodo, Explain Everything and Socrative facilitated communication and collaboration between students. Edmodo acted to empower students and allowed for creative expression (Kirk, 2006), while Explain Everything and Socrative encouraged students to take ownership of their learning and work at their own pace when reviewing the information. These actions differentiated the learning experience and created a more inclusive learning environment (Whipp *et al.*, 2014). By diversifying learning experiences, Dylan found novel ways to engage with young people who may otherwise have not achieved their full potential through more traditional approaches.

The use of iPads and various apps is not, however, unproblematic. Despite the potential for digital technology to begin to address issues of social justice, there is a need to consider how the uncritical integration of technology may further marginalise some young people.

While technology is increasingly accessible for young people in general, Fursland (2014) highlights the dangers of assuming that looked after children have access to technology and can engage digitally in the same way as other young people. Moreover, the use of computers, mobile phones and tablets is often seen as a threat to looked after children who are more likely to be victims of cyberbullying (Fursland, 2014). Foster carers and those acting as corporate parents have a duty of care to protect children in both the real and virtual worlds, and, as such, many local authorities and care staff tend to restrict access to digital technologies for looked after children (Rotherham Metropolitan Borough Council, 2015; Leeds City Council, 2015). Looked after children may, therefore, be in danger of digital exclusion through economic, cultural or safety reasons, and getting to grips with new technology and apps may be difficult and time consuming. Thus, if only certain students have access to the technology beyond school, they immediately have an advantage over their peers in school. Additionally, this may impact on looked after children's capacity to work on resources and videos outside of lessons, and their ability to engage in teamwork and enhance their social capital through digital interactions.

Apple (2012) emphasises the need to be critically aware of the influence of digital technologies on children's learning. A prevailing emphasis on standards, measurement and competitive individualism can further marginalise young people (Apple, 2012). As such, there is a danger that the performance analysis apps could have foreground students' differences. Where participants have low perceived ability (which applies disproportionately to disadvantaged young people, such as looked after children [Safvenbom & Samdahl, 1998]) and feel unattached to other individuals in a lesson, low self-esteem may follow, which could lead to an increase in disaffection and truancy (Bailey *et al.*, 2009). This may be particularly problematic when children compare their own performance against a 'perfect model', where looked after children may learn that they lack physical 'ability' or talent and, subsequently, develop feelings of alienation and insecurity (Dowling *et al.*, 2014).

This section has shown that technology provides new opportunities for expression, communication and collaboration that could support learning. Uncritical application of technologies, however, has the potential to foreground differences leading to further marginalisation. Teachers must ensure that any messages conveyed about the use of technology reinforce and reflect, rather than contradict, the messages looked after children receive about safe use/practice at 'home'. Failure to adopt a critical approach could have wider implications for learning in physical education and may unwittingly contribute to social injustice.

A fundamental movement perspective (Nalda Wainwright)

The importance of developing children's fundamental movement skills in order to facilitate longer-term engagement with physical activity is well established (Goodway et al., 2013; Stodden et al., 2008). Stodden et al. (2008), for example, suggest that a lack of proficiency in motor development acts as a barrier to later participation in physical activity. Goodway et al. (2013, p. 122) further this point by claiming that 'children who are more highly skilled and motor competent will self-select higher levels of physical activity'. The pedagogical practices underpinning the development of fundamental movement skills are, therefore, important. This section will consider Dylan's pupils' stages of motor development before discussing how technology can be used by teachers to support the development in pupils' fundamental movement skills.

At ages 13–14, it would be expected that children in Dylan's class are in the specialized movement skill phase. Gallahue et al. (2012, p. 306) describe this phase as being when fundamental movements are 'refined and combined to form sport skills and other specific complex movement skills'. Although age serves as a useful frame of reference for determining motor development stage (Gallahue et al., 2012), being able to perform refined movements and specific complex movement skills is dependent on young people's prior level of motor development. Before moving into the specialised movement skill phase young people need to have achieved proficiency in a range of fundamental movement patterns (Clark & Metcalfe, 2002; Seedfelt, 1980; Stodden et al., 2008).

Movement proficiency typically develops as young children (age 18–120 months) embed elements of their movement vocabulary to movement memory, and integrate movement capacities such as balance and coordination, precision and fluency (Maude, 2010; Whitehead, 2010). Motor proficiency, however, does not develop naturally or through free play (Goodway & Branta, 2003). The environment, developmentally appropriate tasks, structured activities, alongside experience and maturation all influence motor skill development (Logan et al., 2011). Consequently, it cannot be assumed that all pupils within Dylan's class were in the specialised movement skill phase, as this would be assuming they all experienced similar environments, tasks, and activities and were at the same levels of maturation. Hence, teachers like Dylan need to have sufficient understanding of their pupils' stages of motor development to be able to identify appropriate tasks and environmental conditions to support the development of motor competence (Gallahue *et al.*, 2012; Maude, 2010). Dylan's narrative provides some useful insights into how teachers can support the development of fundamental movement skills.

Supporting the development of fundamental movement skills

Teachers need to be able to manipulate tasks by adding or removing constraints to ensure there is an appropriate level of challenge for the child's developmental stage (Newell, 1984). Not only does this require teachers to be aware of the developmental stages of children, but teachers also need to understand that the mastery of motor skills is non-linear and so is not a smooth or hierarchical process (Gallahue *et al.*, 2012). For example, children may respond to one task with a movement that demonstrates mastery, but in another environment they may respond with a less mature action. One explanation for this centres on the demands of the task and how securely the child has mastered the skill (Garcia & Garcia, 2002; Goodway *et al.*, 2003). To support the child's motor development, teachers can reduce the number of tasks or environmental constraints on the task until he or she has mastered the skill (Langdorfer, 1990; Lorson & Goodway, 2007).

Technology, as demonstrated by Dylan, could be an appropriate tool for teachers to use to understand their pupils' motor development and set appropriate challenges. Albeit on a team and class level, Dylan was aware of his students' performances in movement tasks through videos of their performances and their responses sent through Socrative or Edmodo. Dylan then used this digital evidence to modify tasks and/or offer additional whole class demonstrations. The apps acted as useful tools to extend Dylan's understandings of his pupils and be able to respond effectively.

In addition to the type of tasks, a wide literature base suggests that the environment in which the task is situated influences skill development (Caldwell & Clark, 1990; Haywood & Getchell, 2009; Newell, 1984). Maynard *et al.* (2013, p. 214) argue that motor development is not something internal belonging to the child but is an 'interaction between the child and his or her social and cultural context'. This view of development as interaction with the wider environment resonates with physical literacy; that is, the 'existentialist belief that individuals create themselves as they live in and interact with the world' (Whitehead, 2010, p. 23). The implications of environment influencing motor development are that teachers need to alter task constraints in a context and environment, which is relevant, meaningful and socially appropriate (Gilbert, 2002).

To some extent, Dylan created an appropriate environment for his students' motor development through the tactical approach. Drawing on Metzler (2011), tactical games are underpinned by a situated learning perspective, meaning that skills are learnt, developed and refined within the social and cultural context of the game. The technology furthered this meaningful and developmentally appropriate context because it enabled the pupils (and not only the teacher) to identify aspects to develop and improve. Dylan's approach not only gave pupils a reason for needing to improve skills but also enabled them to carry out further in-depth analysis of movements, using Coach's Eye and Ubersense, with their peers. As such, the tactical approach and technology created a legitimate environmental context for pupils to learn in the specialized movement phase.

In summary, developing movement competence is a complex task since young people vary in their levels of proficiency. By understanding pupils' stages of development, designing developmentally appropriate tasks and creating meaningful and relevant learning environments, teachers can begin to respond to students' diverse movement capabilities.

A pedagogical perspective (Victoria Goodyear)

An overarching message emerging from this chapter has been that the tactical inquiry approach, together with digital technologies, supported students' physical, cognitive, social and affective learning. Since these outcomes are regarded as the legitimate learning outcomes of physical education that can fulfil the subject's purpose of promoting the physically active life (Kirk, 2013), this is an important message for physical education regarding technology use. This section aims to draw conclusions from the narrative and the three perspectives to offer pedagogical insights into the uses of digital technologies in physical education.

Pedagogically, it should be noted that the digital technologies used by Dylan and the students did not create a new or radically different teaching and learning environment. The functions of the digital technologies that supported "group work", "questioning", "feedback", "demonstrations", "assessment" and "group discussions" are established practices within classrooms that do not use digital technologies (Hattie, 2012). Instead, and drawing on the work of Selwyn (2013), the digital technologies enabled Dylan and the students to teach and learn in more efficient and effective ways. For example, Dylan's narrative demonstrated how through technology he was able to provide "more specific and detailed guidance" and students were able to "learn at a faster rate". Consequently, and in conceptualizing pedagogies of technology, digital technologies should be regarded as tools for teaching and learning that can be used in the pedagogical context to enhance students' ability to engage and practice established learning tasks. How these digital technologies can be used effectively and for maximum impact on learning is now considered through two themes that seem to be consistent within this chapter: (i) students' diverse and individual needs and (ii) student-centred pedagogy. Following this, the pedagogical implications are considered.

Students' diverse and individual needs

Students have diverse, complex and individual learning needs that impact on their ability to engage and learn (see Armour, 2014). While numerous differences between students exist, we can see from this chapter that students differ in their motivation of and for learning, their levels of social vulnerability and their stages of motor development, all of which can be influenced by their prior or current experiences within a social and cultural environment. Consequently, and as Dylan believed, teachers need to diversify how they support learners and adopt an "inclusive pedagogy" (Oliver & Kirk, 2015). Technology, however, adds a heightened level of complexity to the pedagogical context that can alter, in sometimes unpredictable ways, different types of students' engagement (see Goodyear *et al.*, 2014). The social justice perspective suggested that such engagement can be influenced by the potential for technology to "foreground differences and further marginalization". Both the social justice and psychology perspectives used examples of video analysis to illustrate how technology can make differences more "visible" to the individual student and/or students' "hidden" differences can become more visible to others. As noted in earlier work (Fisette, 2011), making the body and performance more visible to others was linked in this chapter to lower levels of motivation and feelings of self that can hinder engagement with learning. Using technology as tool, therefore, requires teachers to assess whether technology is capable of meeting *all* students' diverse and individual needs. If technology, as the psychological perspective suggested, could "decelerate" learning and engagement, it may not be an effective addition to the classroom.

While caution should be applied when considering how technology may exclude students, we must not lose sight of ways in which technology can also be used by teachers to increase understandings of their students' learning needs (see Enright & O'Sullivan, 2012). Evident in this chapter was Dylan's claim that information sent by students through apps extended his understanding of their learning needs. The fundamental movement skills perspective also stressed that there was significant potential for teachers to use video-playback features to learn of their students' stages of motor development in order to design appropriate learning environments. As such, digital technologies can and should be viewed, not only as a tool to support student learning but also as tools for teachers to learn about their students' diverse and individual learning needs.

Student-centred pedagogy

All three perspectives identified that the development in students' physical, cognitive, social and affective learning was related to Dylan's approach in supporting student autonomy, ownership, choice and decision making. Since these terms are often associated with student-centred approaches (Jones, 2007; Le Ha, 2014), it can be argued that technology extended Dylan's ability to promote a student-centred environment. This claim is aligned to the views of Hattie (2012) and Jones (2007) on student centredness. It suggests that the technology supported students' ability to become their own teachers by providing opportunities for collaboration, promoting student assessment of learning and helping students to evaluate their knowledge claims. All of these practices were suggested to have the potential to strengthen students' motivation, reduce issues of social injustice and promote motor development.

A common misconception with student centredness, however, is that students are left alone by teachers and that their beliefs and plans dictate everything in the learning setting (Hattie, 2012; Jones, 2007). In Dylan's narrative it was evident that technology was used as a tool for him, as a teacher, to provide information to teams, question students, respond to students' questions and assist groups or individuals as and when needed. As Dylan claimed, the digital technologies enabled his interactions to become more "personalized" and "frequent". The high level of teacher-student interaction certainly contrasts with the prominent definitions of teacher facilitation associated with student centredness, where it is suggested that teachers should only interact with learners when students face a barrier to learning (Bähr & Wibowo, 2012). Instead, the teacher behaviours displayed by Dylan and his ability to promote autonomy, ownership, choice and decision making are characteristics identified in Hattie's (2012) meta-analysis of teaching and learning to have the greatest impact on learning outcomes. Consequently, it might be suggested that technology can be used to promote student-centred learning activities, and learning and achievement can be maximized when teachers also use digital technologies to interact with students.

Pedagogical implications

It has been highlighted in this chapter that teachers need to consider how students' social and cultural experiences/backgrounds and feeling of self can shape what students engage with and learn through digital technologies. In addition, a key message is that digital technologies provide teachers with a mechanism to view digital representations of learning that enables them to assess and respond to students needs. Drawing on Hattie (2012, p. 18), it seems reasonable to suggest that digital technologies can have a positive impact on student learning when teachers see "learning through the eyes of their students".

Many of the discussions around how Dylan used and could have used digital technologies to support learning are similar to the pedagogical processes explained in clinical teaching models (Biggs, 2012; Hattie, 2012) and within guidance for effective teacher behaviours (Wibowo, Bähr, & Groben, 2014). Both lines of research indicate that effective practices and pedagogies involve teachers engaging in an ongoing assessment of students' learning needs, where evidence drawn from the local context is used to drive subsequent pedagogical actions. Assessment and the use of appropriate pedagogical actions are considered possible when teachers engage in a process of diagnosis, intervention and evaluation (or checking) (Dinham, 2013; Wibowo *et al.*, 2014). The narrative and the three perspectives help us to see the importance of these three processes for supporting students' individual and diverse learning needs, particularly where technology can be used by teachers to engage with these processes more "efficiently and effectively". The term *response*, however, seems more appropriate than intervention. *Intervention* is rather medical;

it assumes that something is required to be changed, and that this will occur in a short time period. Yet Dylan used digital technologies to engage in an ongoing assessment of students' learning and to respond and develop learning, rather than change the direction of learning. Thus, the pedagogical implications of using digital technologies are that teachers should engage with an ongoing process of diagnosing, responding and evaluating where technology can be used to assist and strengthen teachers' abilities to design effective learning experiences.

- *Diagnosing*: Teachers need to be able to diagnose their students' diverse and individual needs.
- *Responding*: Teachers need to be able to respond to students in needs supportive ways providing frequent and personalized support.
- *Evaluating*: Teachers need to be able to evaluate and assess student learning to be able to respond effectively to students' emerging and ongoing learning experiences.

Practitioner reflection

The literature in this chapter suggests that technology integration can support students' basic psychological needs for autonomy, competence and relatedness. However, this process has reinforced my concerns about technology highlighting some pupils' poor performances observed on the iPad, or their lower levels of digital competence. Further understanding of how these issues can be approached in lessons would be beneficial. I would be interested in investigating the *lived experience* of students engaged in learning using the iPad.

The technology also allowed for more effective and personalised interventions by me as a teacher. Socrative is an example of a technology that helped me to guide feedback and target groups with specific topics and questions based on their responses. It has become clear that I could develop this approach to attend to students' personalised needs further, such as their movement competencies. The use of technology to extend this learning beyond the classroom is an important avenue for physical education to explore. While students engaged with tasks unexpectedly outside of lessons, I could use the pupil-response system to prompt physical activity outside of school.

As this was the first experience of using iPads for this class, I selected the apps to maintain structure to lessons. In future units, it may be interesting to allow pupils to select appropriate apps or technologies to use in response to inquiry or problem based tasks. This could provide more *real-life* learning that may transfer outside of school. For example, pupils could be given a task to develop an exercise programme in school. Exploring a range of apps in school may encourage their use outside of school, thus promoting physical activity. However, as highlighted in the social justice perspective, acknowledging that not all pupils will have access to digital technologies outside of school is important. If the use of digital technologies in physical education does promote learning and, importantly, physical activity outside of school, provision of such tools by the school may be a worthwhile consideration. Indeed, many schools are now adopting one-to-one iPad schemes.

From my experiences of using technology, its integration with an appropriate pedagogical approach is essential. This process has highlighted how we must firstly consider the needs of the pupils prior to selection of a pedagogical approach and the integration of technology. Where the use of technology supports the pedagogical approach in achieving the outcomes sought, its integration should be encouraged. However, in order to make these decisions, a level of knowledge and understanding of how the technology can be integrated with a range of pedagogical approaches, and the outcomes of them, are required. It is my hope that the use of the iPad to support learning with a tactical inquiry-based approach has provided an insight into one technological-pedagogical approach for physical education.

Lessons from the case: How can the use of digital technologies accelerate pupil learning in physical education?

- Digital technologies act as learning tools to enhance students' engagement with established learning tasks.
- Students have diverse and individual learning needs that will impact on their engagement and learning with and from digital technologies.
- Digital technologies can be used to strengthen teachers' ability to promote a student-centred approach to learning.
- Digital technologies can strengthen teacher's ability to provide timely and developmentally appropriate feedback.
- To accelerate learning, teachers should engage with a process of diagnosing, responding and evaluating where technology can be used to assist and strengthen teachers' ability to design effective learning experiences.

References

Ames, C. (1992). Classrooms: Goals, structures, and student motivation. *Journal of Educational Psychology, 84*(3), 261–271.

Apple, M. W. (2012). *Can Education Change Society?* London: Routledge.

Armour, K. (2014). *Pedagogical Cases in Physical Education and Youth Sport.* London: Routledge.

Bähr, I. and Wibowo, J. (2012). Teacher action in the cooperative learning model in the physical education classroom. In B. Dyson and A. Casey, eds., *Cooperative Learning in Physical Education: A Research-Based Approach.* London: Routledge. pp. 27–41.

Bailey, R., Armour, K., Kirk, D., Jess, M., Pickup, I. and Sandford, R. (2009). The educational benefits claimed for physical education and school sport: An academic review. *Research Papers in Education, 24*(1), 1–27.

Biggs, J. (2012). What the student does: Teaching for enhanced learning. *Higher Education Research & Development, 31*(1), 39–55.

Bunker, D. and Thorpe, R. (1982). A model for the teaching of games in the secondary school. *Bulletin of Physical Education, 10*, 9–16.

Caldwell, G. and Clark, J. (1990). The measurement and evaluation of skill within the dynamical systems perspective. In J. E. Clark and J. H. Humphrey, eds., *Advances in Motor Development Research*. Brooklyn, NY: AMS Press. pp. 165–200.

Clark, J. E. and Metcalf, J. S. (2002). The mountain of motor development: A metaphor. In J. E. Clark and J. H. Humphrey, eds., *Motor Development: Research and Review: Vol. 2*. Reston, VA: NASPE. pp. 163–190.

Deci, E. L. and Ryan, R. M. (2000). The "what" and "why" of goal pursuits: Human needs and the self-determination of behavior. *Psychological Inquiry, 11*(4), 227–268.

Department of Health (2011). UK Physical Activity Guidelines, www.gov.uk/government/publications/uk-physical-activityguidelines (accessed 18th March, 2015).

Dinham, S. (2013). The quality teaching movement in Australia encounters difficult terrain: A personal perspective. *Australian Journal of Education, 57*(2), 91–106.

Dowling, F., Fitzgerald, H. and Flintoff, A. (2014). Narratives from the road to social justice in PETE: Teacher educator perspectives. *Sport, Education and Society*, iFirst Article.

Enright, E. and O'Sullivan, M. (2012). 'Producing different knowledge and producing knowledge differently': Rethinking physical education research and practice through participatory visual methods. *Sport, Education and Society, 17*, 35–55.

Fisette, J. L. (2011). Exploring how girls navigate their embodied identities in physical education. *Physical Education and Sport Pedagogy, 16*(2), 179–196.

Fitzpatrick, K. (2013). *Critical Pedagogy, Physical Education and Urban Schooling*. New York: Peter Lang.

Fursland, E. (2014). The IT crowd: How technology is helping children in care. *Children and Young People Now, Special Report: Technology in Care*, 22 July–4 August, 23–25.

Gallahue, D. L., Ozmun, J. C. and Goodway, J. D. (2012). *Understanding Motor Development: Infants, Children, Adolescents and Adults* (7th edition). Boston: McGraw-Hill.

Garcia, C. and Garcia, L. (2002). Examining the developmental changes in throwing. In J. E. Clark and J. H. Humphrey, eds., *Motor Development: Research and Review: Vol. 2*. Reston, VA: NASPE. pp. 62–95.

Gilbert, I. (2002). *Essential Motivation in the Classroom*. London: Routledge.

Gilligan, R. (1999). Enhancing the resilience of children and young people in public care by mentoring their talents and interests. *Child and Family Social Work, 4*(3), 187–196.

Goodway, J. D. and Branta, C. F. (2003). Influence of a motor skill intervention on fundamental motor skill development of disadvantaged preschool children. *Research Quarterly for Exercise and Sport, 74*, 36–46.

Goodway, J. D., Brian, A., Chang, S. H., Famelia, R., Suda, E. and Robinson, L. E. (2013). Promoting physical literacy in the early years through project SKIP. *Journal of Sport Science and Physical Education, 65*, 121–129.

Goodway, J., Crowe, H. and Ward, P. (2003). Effects of motor skill instruction on fundamental motor skill development. *Adapted Physical Activity Quarterly, 20*, 298–314.

Goodyear, V. A., Casey, A. and Kirk, D. (2014). Hiding behind the camera: Social learning within the cooperative learning model to engage girls in physical education. *Sport, Education and Society, 19*, 712–734.

Gurvitch, R., Blankenship, B. T., Metzler, M. W. and Lund, J. L. (2008). Student and teachers' implementation of model-based instruction: Facilitators and inhibitors. *Journal of Teaching in Physical Education, 27*(4), 466–486.

Haerens, L., Kirk, D., Cardon, G. and De Bourdeaudhuij, I. (2011). Toward the development of a pedagogical model for health-based physical education. *Quest, 63*, 321–338.

Hattie, J. (2012). *Visible Learning for Teachers: Maximizing Impact on Learning*. London: Routledge.

Hay, P. and Penney, D. (2013). *Assessment in Physical Education.* New York: Routledge.

Hayes, D., Mills, M., Christie, P. and Lingard, B. (2006). *Teachers and Schooling Making a Difference: Productive Pedagogies, Assessment and Performance.* Sydney, AUS: Allen & Unwin.

Haywood, K. and Getchell, N. (2009). *Life Span Motor Development.* Champaign, IL: Human Kinetics.

Jones, L. (2007). *The Student-Centred Classroom.* Cambridge, UK: Cambridge University Press.

Kirk, D. (2013). Educational value and models-based practice in physical education. *Educational Philosophy and Theory, 45,* 973–986.

Kirk, D. (2006). Sport Education, critical pedagogy, and learning theory: Toward an intrinsic justification for physical education and youth sport. *Quest, 58,* 255–268.

Langdorfer, S. (1990). Motor-task goal as a constraint on developmental status. In J. E. Clark and J. H. Humphrey, eds., *Advances in Motor Development: Vol. 3.* New York: AMS Press. pp. 16–28.

Leeds City Council. (2015). Fostering Service: Statement of Purpose. Retrieved from www.leeds.gov.uk/foster4leeds/Release%20Documents/Statement%20of%20purpose%20 fostering.pdf

Le Ha, P. (2014). The politics of naming: Critiquing "learner-centred" and "teacher as facilitator" in English language and humanities classrooms. *Asia-Pacific Journal of Teacher Education, 42,* 392–405.

Logan, S. W., Robinson, L. E., Wilson, A. E. and Lucas, W. A. (2011). Getting the fundamentals of movement: a meta-analysis of the effectiveness of motor skill interventions in children. *Child: Care, Health and Development, 38*(3), 305–315.

Lorson, K. and Goodway, J. (2007). Influence of critical cues and task constraints on overarm throwing performance in elementary age children. *Perceptual and Motor Skills, 105,* 753–767.

McAuley, C. and Davis, T. (2009). Emotional well-being and mental health of looked after children in England. *Child and Family Social Work, 14*(2), 147–155.

Maude, P. (2010). Physical literacy and the young child. In M. E. Whitehead, ed., *Physical Literacy Throughout the Lifecourse.* London: Routledge. pp. 100–115.

Maynard, T., Waters, J. and Clement, J. (2013). Child-initiated learning, the outdoor environment and the 'underachieving' child. *Early Years: An International Research Journal, 33*(3), 212–225.

Metzler, M. (2011). *Instructional Models for Physical Education* (3rd ed.). Scottsdale, AZ: Holcomb Hathaway.

Newell, K. (1984). Physical constraints to development of motor skills. In J. Thomas, ed., *Motor Development During Childhood and Adolescence.* Minneapolis, MN: Burgess. pp. 106–120.

Nicholls, J. G. (1984). Achievement motivation: Conceptions of ability, subjective experience, task choice, and performance. *Psychological Review, 91*(3), 328–346.

Ntoumanis, N. (2002). Motivational clusters in a sample of British physical education classes. *Psychology of Sport and Exercise, 3,* 177–194.

Ntoumanis, N. and Standage, M. (2009). Motivation in physical education classes: A self-determination theory perspective. *Theory and Research in Education, 7*(2), 194–202.

Ofcom. (2014). Children and Parents: Media Use and Attitudes Report. Retrieved from http://stakeholders.ofcom.org.uk/binaries/research/media-literacy/media-use-attitudes-14/Childrens_2014_Report.pdf

Oliver, K. L. and Kirk, D. (2015). *Girls, Gender and Physical Education: An Activist Approach.* London: Routledge.

Reeve, J. (2009). Why teachers adopt a controlling motivating style toward students and how they can become more autonomy supportive. *Educational Psychologist, 44*(3), 159–175.

Rivzi, F. and Lingard, B. (2010). *Globalizing Education Policy*. London: Routledge.

Roberts, G. C. (2012). Motivation in sport exercise from an achievement goal theory perspective: After 30 years where are we? In G. C. Roberts, and D. C. Treasure, eds., *Advances in Motivation in Sport and Exercise*. Champaign, IL: Human Kinetics. pp. 5–58.

Rotherham Metropolitan Borough Council. (2015). 'Internet Safety Policy for Looked After Children'. Retrieved from http://rotherhamcsyp.proceduresonline.com/chapters/p_internet_safety.html

Ryan, R. M. and Deci, E. L. (1989). Bridging the research traditions of task/ego involvement and intrinsic/extrinsic motivation: Comment on Butler (1987). *Journal of Educational Psychology, 81*(2), 265–268.

Ryan, R. M. and Deci, E. L. (2000a). Intrinsic and extrinsic motivations: Classic definitions and new directions. *Contemporary Educational Psychology, 25*(1), 54–67.

Ryan, R. M. and Deci, E. L. (2000b). Self-determination theory and the facilitation of intrinsic motivation, social development, and well-being. *American Psychologist, 55*(1), 68–78.

Safvenbom, R. and Samdahl, D. (1998). Involvement in and perception of the free-time context for adolescents in youth protection institutions. *Leisure Studies, 17*(3), 207–226.

Scott, J. (2011). The impact of disrupted attachment on the emotional and interpersonal development of looked after children. *Educational and Child Psychology, 28*(3), 31–43.

Seedfelt, V. (1980). The concepts of readiness applied to motor skill acquisition. In R. A. Magill, M. J. Ash and F. L. Smoll, eds., *Children in Sport*. Champaign, IL: Human Kinetics. pp. 31–37.

Selwyn, N. (2013). *Distrusting Educational Technology: Critical Questions for Changing Times*. London: Routledge.

Standage, M., Duda, J. L. and Ntoumanis, N. (2006). Students' motivational processes and their relationship to teacher ratings in school physical education. *Research Quarterly for Exercise and Sport, 77*(1), 100–110.

Standage, M. and Ryan, R. M. (2012). Self-determination theory and exercise motivation: Facilitating self-regulatory processes to support and maintain health and well-being. In G. C. Roberts and D. C. Treasure, eds., *Advances in Motivation in Sport and Exercise*. Champaign, IL: Human Kinetics. pp. 233–270

Stodden, D., Goodway, J., Langendorfer, S., Roberton, M., Rudisill, M., Garcia, C. and Garcia, L. (2008). A developmental perspective on the role of motor skill competence in physical activity: An emergent relationship. *Quest, 60*(2), 290–306.

Tinning, R. (2002). Toward a "modest pedagogy": Reflections on the problematics of critical pedagogy. *Quest, 54*(3), 224–240.

Vansteenkiste, M. and Ryan, R. M. (2013). On psychological growth and vulnerability: Basic psychological need satisfaction and need frustration as a unifying principle. *Journal of Psychotherapy Integration, 23*, 263–280.

Whipp, P., Taggart, A. and Jackson, B. (2014). Differentiation in outcome-focused physical education: Pedagogical rhetoric and reality. *Physical Education and Sport Pedagogy, 19*(4), 370–382.

Whitehead, M. E. (2010). *Physical Literacy: Throughout the Lifecourse*. London: Routledge.

Wibowo, J., Bähr, I. and Groben, B. (2014). Scaffolding as an instructional model for the cooperative learning model in physical education. *Australian Council for Health, Physical Education, and Recreation Magazine, 21*(2–3), 15–18.

3

JAIME: "I COULDN'T TEACH WITHOUT TECHNOLOGY"

A teacher and student learning journey

Melissa Parker, Jaime Morrison, Kevin Patton,
Megan Babkes Stellino, Carmel Hinchion
and Kathy Hall

CHAPTER OVERVIEW

This case examines a primary physical education specialist teacher's use of technology from assessment, child development, literacy, and pedagogical perspectives. The case draws on these various educational and developmental viewpoints to interrogate and distil a set of pedagogical insights, regarding both student and teacher learning. Through the adherence to constructivist learning principles, an active, meaningful, relevant, and social pedagogy of technology was developed. This use of technology, not as an end in itself, but as a means to an end, may serve to challenge prevailing assumptions regarding technology in the classroom.

Practitioner narrative (Jaime Morrison)

I couldn't teach without technology – or if I did, students would lack meaningful assessment, accurate skill development, and I would be overwhelmed with a ton of grading. In this narrative, I share my journey with technology and assessment in physical education. I am an elementary school (ages 6–11) physical education specialist and have been teaching for 12 years in an economically advantaged American neighbourhood. As a top performing school in the area, all stakeholders support physical education and innovation. With that said, I have always struggled with accurate and relevant assessment for the 550 students I teach.

For the first 6 years of my teaching career I used paper-and-pencil exit slips as a cognitive check for understanding and assessed students' psychomotor skills mostly through teacher observation. This process was cumbersome and challenging to provide consistent feedback to students. In addition, students viewed assessment as a separate, not integrated part of the teaching/learning process. As part of a

Master's level project during my seventh year of teaching, I began trying new methods of assessment using video cameras. At the time, the trend was to use video cameras to record students as they completed movement tasks at various stations. This step was then followed by me watching countless hours of video to assess students' skills. It was time consuming and lacked student participation. I wanted to find a more efficient, meaningful, and engaging assessment system.

With $300 in my school physical education budget, I purchased 15 Kidizoom video cameras made by Vtech (see Table 3.1). These personal video cameras were durable and provided an on-camera screen that immediately displayed what was recorded. From the outset, students were interested in seeing themselves on video and talked with excitement about their skill development. After I provided coaching cues to guide the skill practice, students became natural peer coaches, delivering more resourceful and specific feedback to each other than ever before. The technology proved effective for learning fundamental movement skills, but unfortunately the battery life was limited to a week, and after several months the cameras were used sparingly, as the battery replacement process became too time consuming and expensive.

Two years later I was fortunate enough to acquire 30 iPod Touches by Apple (see Table 3.1) that classroom teachers found inadequate. These iPod Touches had built-in video cameras and Wi-Fi connectivity – and they were rechargeable! No more replacing batteries; all I had to do was plug them in and the battery would last all week with every class using them. Just like the Kidizoom video cameras, students used the camera on the iPods to video-record each other's skills and then provide feedback. Shortly after I began using the iPod Touches I discovered an app called iSwing (see Table 3.1). The iSwing app records video in slow motion and is unique as it has a maximum of 7 seconds record time, which prevents students from using too much memory and recording lengthy wasted videos. Tested first with shooting basketballs, students were able to have a peer video-record their skill and then analyse their performance to draw conclusions of why they made or missed a basket. The assessment prompt asked students to investigate and try to identify "what body part specifically caused you to miss?" Students further compared themselves to a teacher demonstration on video to answer the next assessment question that asked, "What does the body part need to do to make the basket?" The result: meaningful and self-directed assessment.

The iPod Touches were also used to help students develop personal- and social-responsibility skills. I learned early to allow time for students to experiment with the iPods without specific step-by-step instructions. Guided discovery instruction works naturally with technology for students to develop curiosity, perseverance, and responsibility. Students would consistently approach me with frustration saying, "It isn't working!" hoping I would fix it for them. Instead I would inquire by saying, "I could help, but your answer is somewhere on the iPod and using perseverance you can fix it on your own, and gain responsibility!" After a couple minutes you can imagine the student's face when they would exclaim "I did it!"

The iPod's internet connectivity also provided the ability to show YouTube clips of athletes' appropriate and inappropriate sportspersonship during game play. Students were then asked to develop a respectful celebration for assessment. Furthermore, students used the voice memos app on the iPod to develop their "press conference" skills after a game. Students asked each other questions about the game they played, and were assessed on whether their answers were focused and respectful. The iPod Touches enhanced the learning outcomes in physical education, but I still struggled for an efficient way to collect and analyse the tasks with which students engaged.

I found a solution to my nightmare of assessing 550 students in the same technology that changed the way the world communicated. I FOUND GMAIL! Gmail offers apps through Google Drive called Google Forms (see Table 3.1), allowing users to create their own online surveys. Initially designed for companies to receive feedback from customers, teachers can use this platform in a similar way to create online worksheets for tests for their students. Best of all, it's free and easy to create. Now I had devices (iPod Touches) that students used to access the assessments (in the form of a survey on Google Forms) that I specifically created to determine what they had learnt. For the next four months I used and experimented with Google Forms to determine the easiest way to assess students. During that time, I was able to overcome some logistical challenges by adjusting my assessments to be more user friendly. For instance, to save time and keep consistent data, instead of students typing their name in, they would select their name from an alphabetical list. I also discovered an app called Scan.me which creates and scans QR codes (see Table 3.1) that can be linked to the Google Form assessments I created. Modifications like these made the assessments time efficient and, on average, students would complete them in two minutes!

The flexibility of online assessments also allowed me to modify my assessments, sometimes even while the class was occurring. In addition, Google Forms generates a compiled summary of the students' responses for assessments. Time may be the most critical component a teacher has with students and what used to take three hours to consolidate now takes me three minutes! Every day I would review the students' answers and then create my lesson plan for the next day based on their performance. Using technology to efficiently input and compile data meant that this was the first time in my career that my instruction was completely guided by assessment.

Recently, I purchased thirty Fit Smart watches by Adidas that provide students' heart rate, distance, activity time, and calories burned instantly while they move throughout the class (see Table 3.1). Students, as young as six, are gaining additional knowledge about their individual fitness and are then able to input their performance into the Google Form assessment for tracking. For example, a fourth-grade class had an average heart rate of 143, covered close to a mile, were moving for thirty-four minutes, and burnt 224 calories in one physical education class.

When I asked my students what they thought about the technology, the most common response was that "it is fast and easy". That is a huge relief, especially as

TABLE 3.1 The different forms of technology used by Jaime

Device/application	Function(s)	How it was used
Kidizoom camera	Handheld video camera	Peer coaching on skill development
Google Forms	Create and deliver online assessments	Conduct online assessments that can be analysed immediately
iPod Touch	• Video-recording function • Wi-Fi internet connection • Device allows for apps to be used and downloaded	Connect to internet to input answers for Google Form assessment
iSwing app	Video-recording in slow motion used on the iPod Touch	Peer and self-assessment of skill development in slow motion
Voice memo app	Record audio files	Sportspersonship press conferences
Scan.me	QR code[a] generator app used on the iPod Touch	Access the Google Form assessment without any typing and by scanning a code using the camera
Fit Smart watch	A wearable device that provides individual student heart rates, calories burned, distance travelled, and activity time	To input fitness data into Google Form assessment

a A QR code is a machine-readable code consisting of an array of black and white squares, typically used for storing URLs or other information for reading by the camera on a smartphone.

I still hear about other physical education teachers who spend laborious hours passing out papers, making copies, grading each student, and summarizing it all into a grade book, all of which could be done effortlessly using today's technology.

In the following sections of this chapter Jamie's narrative is examined through assessment, developmental, and literacy perspectives. Following this, the narrative and all perspectives are considered pedagogically and key implications arising from Jaime's uses of digital technologies are provided.

An assessment perspective (Kevin Patton)

Student assessment plays a critical role within the current accountability and standards-based educational context. In the U.S., federal policies require states to implement standardized assessments as student achievement measures and these policies emphasize the use of assessment data to guide instruction and individualize student programming (U.S. Department of Education, 2010). Similarly, the international agenda continues to convey a growing interest in assessment as a tool to support learning and enhance teaching (Leirhaug & MacPhail, 2015). Teachers, therefore, must be assessment literate (DeLuca & Bellara, 2013; National Council for Accreditation of Teacher Education [NCATE], 2008). *Assessment literacy* is defined as understanding how to construct, administer, and score reliable assessments and communicate student learning (Stiggins *et al.* 2012), and involves integrating assessment practices, theories, and philosophies to support teaching and learning within a standards-based framework of education.

As Jaime's case illustrates, accommodating the promises of reform efforts with regard to assessment is problematic. Physical education teachers' use of formal assessment, in general, is often reported to be lacking due to time constraints, a general disbelief about the necessity of assessment, and a gap between teachers' knowledge of assessment theory and practice (Hay & Penney, 2013; Veal, 1988). As a result, physical education assessment practices are underpinned by little consensus, questionable validity, and a slow ability to change (Annerstedt & Larsson, 2010; Hay & Penney, 2013). Further, Leirhaug and MacPhail (2015) indicate that assessment in physical education has historically been closely linked to the practice of sport and performance culture, not necessarily with the advances in educational theories of learning.

Jaime, however, overcame the barriers to assessment, in part, by using technology as an assessment tool. Tannehill *et al.* (2015, p. 212) define *assessment* as a process, "where students are given opportunities to demonstrate their knowledge, skill, understanding and application of content in a context that allows continued learning and growth". This definition exemplifies an *assessment for learning* approach (AfL) grounded in constructivist perspectives of learning (Shepard, 2000). In contrast to traditional behaviourist theories of learning, AfL has attracted considerable interest in its potential to enhance student learning and develop teaching and assessment practice (Leirhaug & MacPhail, 2015). At a practical level, AfL turns the assessment process into an instructional intervention designed to increase, not merely monitor, student learning (Stiggins, 2002). Graham *et al.* (2013, p. 175) identify five characteristics of AfL that can be used to examine Jaime's assessment practices and support teachers' use of assessment.

First, *assessment and instruction are linked*. Assessment is used, not only to monitor individual students' progress but also to reflect on teaching to maximize effectiveness. Whereas Jaime's students initially viewed assessment as a separate event, the use of technology meant that they no longer perceived it as something disconnected from learning activities.

Second, *assessment is learner centred*. AfL puts students at the centre of the teaching/learning process, effectively activating them as the owners of their own learning (Wiliam & Thompson, 2007). A frequently overlooked aspect of assessment is its potential to influence student motivation (Martin *et al.*, 2002). Meaningful assessments are framed within a mastery perspective, viewing success as individual and rooted in self-improvement. Doing so increases development of self-regulation and the confidence that results in increased motivation (Martin *et al.*, 2002). It was not until Jaime streamlined the assessment process and made it more meaningful by using the iPod Touches and varying applications that students responded positively. By engaging them in the role of coaches using video technology to provide feedback to peers, assessment became something students valued and in which they assumed an active role.

Third, *assessment is an ongoing part of teaching, not an end or an afterthought.* Assessments should not be viewed as a collection of tools or methods, but rather a series of routes in the process of learning something of value (Lambert, 1999). Frequently, teachers become focused on using the tool or the test (e.g., iPad, Fitnessgram [US fitness programme]), forgetting its intended purpose. Assessment must be more than a data-gathering process; it must be seen as a process of making meaning and providing meaningful feedback to the learner. Jaime could easily have been impressed by with the idea of capturing students' interest with the use of technology. Instead, he utilized various technological innovations on a daily basis, enabling him more time to do what he loves best: teaching!

Fourth, *assessment is comprised of meaningful tasks performed in context.* Within AFL, the assessment task itself becomes a learning experience, challenging students' existing knowledge structures and beliefs, and fostering the active construction of meaning (Shepard, 2000). This develops and challenges students' higher-order knowledge and skills that can be transferred to contexts beyond the classroom (Hay, 2006). Jaime's assessment tasks were both contextually relevant and connected. He described the ways in which students explored sportspersonship by examining their own sporting behaviour and comparing their personal actions to those of professional athletes. As such, students were able to critically examine their own behaviours and to transfer the skills and knowledge obtained in class to their own lives.

Finally, *the criteria for assessment are known in advance.* Assessment criteria must be shared with students before they start the process of learning or assessment. Decreased motivation occurs when students fail because they are assessed on material they have not had time to master (Deci & Ryan, 1985). Assessments, therefore, can and should be a positive influence on student behaviour. While not explicitly stated, we might assume that Jaime shares his expectations ahead of time, clarifying his learning intentions and sharing criteria for success.

Current assessment literature suggests that teachers must be prepared to assess student learning, develop their assessment literacy, and successfully address the complex and diverse social origins and consequences of assessment (Hay & Penny, 2013). Current assessment practices, therefore, need to be grounded in new understandings of learning theories, new curricula that are being developed, and new knowledge and skills necessary to satisfy the accountability requirements of systems and governments.

A developmental perspective (Megan Babkes Stellino)

Developmental considerations from motor learning and social psychology are particularly applicable when analysing the benefits of technology integration in physical education. This section explores connections between Jaime's integration of technology and aspects of motor behaviour and social-psychological developmental lenses.

Motor learning

Of particular relevance to Jaime's teaching methods are the motor learning concepts of attentional capacity, demonstration, and augmented feedback. Many external and environmental cues must be processed for learners. This is challenging for students and teachers, as relevant cues for learning must be distinguished from irrelevant stimuli. Student *attentional capacity*, or the limitations on human information processing, increases linearly as a function of age during normal childhood development (Pennings, 1996). As children age and their cognitive development increases, the ability to pay attention to both appropriate (and more) cues improves. Fewer sources of stimuli are recommended for younger children, as they typically don't, and developmentally can't, attend to the most appropriate cues. Older students have expanded attentional capacity, allowing for appropriate focus on more relevant cues that aid their learning and understanding of concepts being taught. Knowledge of the developmental changes in attentional capacity afford Jaime's case, allowing for understanding of how the integration and use of iPod Touches might overwhelm younger children and how use of video with older children might elicit a focus on the wrong aspects of viewing themselves and others.

Demonstrations, or observational learning, also require consideration of student age and maturity. Jaime repeatedly references having students watch their peers in the learning processes. His examples reinforce well-substantiated research on peer modelling/demonstrations, as particularly relevant for problem solving and motor skill learning success (Magill & Anderson, 2014). Findings suggest watching similar peers (e.g. skill/ability level, age, gender, etc.) creates a powerful benefit to learning and skill acquisition (McCullagh & Weiss, 2001). Younger children, and novices, improve their ability to figure out where they are making mistakes and independently create and experiment with solving these problems in their motor skills when opportunity to watch similar peers is available.

Jaime describes how he used video-related technology with his students. While seemingly intuitive to students of this era, video is a form of augmented feedback that has developmental caveats to successful integration in the learning process. For example, a student might feel that they are bending their legs sufficiently (task-intrinsic sensory information) in a skill, however, upon hearing the teacher say "Your legs are only bent a little, that's not enough" (augmented feedback, specifically knowledge of performance), such additional information aids in skill learning and eventually results in a more accurate interpretation of task–intrinsic information. Children do not inherently attend to the most beneficial aspects of the feedback provided through technology (e.g. video), so there are limitations to the extent to which video feedback effectively augments the learning and performance process (Magill & Anderson, 2014). Jaime's efforts to integrate video technology shows how he provided instruction and direction for what students should be paying attention to in their viewing of video, both of themselves and their peers.

Social-psychological aspects

Social-psychological developmental perspectives focus on factors associated with self-perceptions and motivation. These factors are largely impacted by simultaneous cognitive development and are relevant to the integration of technology in physical education. Of particular importance in Jaime's narrative is how technology relates to motivation. The seminal literature on achievement motivation (i.e. Dweck, 1986; Nicholls, 1989) provides important foundations for understanding how physical education students are capable of interpreting technology-based information into their learning and performance. Individual student learning, performance, and specifically, choice, effort, and persistence, are predicated on the primary focus of all individuals being demonstrations of competence. Children's conception of ability (i.e. social comparison versus mastery) changes developmentally in very significant ways (Nicholls, 1989). As noted by Fry (2001), effort and ability are equated as one and the same (e.g. "I caught the ball; I'm good at catching") in early childhood (ages 5–7 years). With age, cognitive development, and *contextual* experience, children are able to increasingly differentiate and distinguish between various contributions to performance outcomes in achievement domains. In later childhood (ages 9 years or over), effort and ability are differentiated and objective task difficulty is considered in self-assessment of ability (e.g. "Kicking a goal is challenging, the less effort I have to put forth to be successful, the better I am") (Fry, 2001).

The motivational climate, or social context, established within physical education, has a profound impact on students' achievement goals and behaviour, as well as their competence beliefs (Ames, 1992, 1984; Duda & Ntoumanis, 2003; Ntoumanis & Biddle, 1999). When the physical education environment is focused on self-referent, task-involving, effort-based criteria for success and failure, it is considered a mastery motivational climate. In contrast, a performance motivational climate emphasizes other-oriented and ego-involving references for determination of success and failure (Ames, 1984). Extant literature in physical education suggests that when a mastery motivational climate is created it enhances positive aspects (e.g. individual task perseverance, well-being, persistence) and reduces negative aspects (e.g. individual learned helplessness, low effort) within the learning environment (Hastie *et al.* 2014; Roberts, 2012; Shen *et al.*, 2007). Jaime incorporated individual task choices, rewarded learning and effort, and avoided a focus on performance outcomes. In addition to this, Jaime grouped children heterogeneously. In this environment, Jaime created a social context that promoted students motivating one another and learning from one another. Jaime's methods were self-referent, task-involving, and focused on effort-based criteria for success; as such they revealed Jaime's ability to create a mastery motivational climate that benefited his physical education students. Furthermore, how he varied these practices according to student age reflected his appreciation and integration of social-psychological developmental factors.

In summary, Jaime's teaching methods highlight sound pedagogy rooted in evidence-based perspectives associated with developmental factors in student motor learning. The factors included an appreciation of student attentional capacity, the ability to interpret and use peer demonstrations, and the use of augmented feedback. The critical social-psychological factor of achievement motivation has tremendous developmental considerations, and this is also noteworthy in Jaime's integration of technology in the elementary physical education environment.

A literacy perspective (Carmel Hinchion and Kathy Hall)

As we live in a world of burgeoning technological advancement, multiculturalism and globalization, new and complex literacies are required in our teaching and learning (O'Rourke, 2005). Looking in on Jaime's classroom and his 6–11-year-old students, we get a vivid picture through print, visual imagery, and a video hyperlink of this complexity and richness in a physical education setting. There are multiple perspectives on what literacy is, how to define it, and how to teach it (Hall, 2003). Before we go deeper into Jaime's narrative, this section will give some orientation to the reader on our understanding of the concept.

Literacy takes on different meanings depending on the lens through which it is viewed. If for example, literacy is viewed through a psychological lens, the focus is on cognition where the individual develops cognitive skills through an internal locus of meaning making (Hall, 2003). A socio-cultural lens shifts the emphasis from an internal process located in an individual per se to the individual in relation to other individuals, and to the social and cultural context in which literacy occurs (Hall *et al.*, 2010; Leander & Sheehy, 2004; Lewis *et al.*, 2007; Pahl & Rowsell, 2010, 2006, 2005). Furthermore, if literacy is viewed through a socio-political lens, the focus is on how structures in society (class, socio-economic, political) shape literacy capital and determine a sense of agency (Lambirth, 2011). As well as these shaping paradigms, there is a lexicon developing around the concept with references to physical literacy (Whitehead, 2010) and emotional literacy (Goleman, 2014); so, it is easy to see how the concept is somewhat contested and diffuse in meaning.

Fundamentally, to be literate requires us to use and develop our potential in reading, writing, speaking, and listening in order to make meaning and to enhance our belonging, self-expression, power, and critique as we go about living our lives. 'New Literacy Studies' research has provided a language in understanding the contemporaneous, social, contextual, and dynamic practice of literacy (Pahl & Rowsell, 2006), and we subscribe to this understanding here:

> Literacy is primarily something people do; it is an activity, located in the space between thought and text. Literacy does not reside in people's heads as a set of skills to be learned, and it does not just reside on paper, captured as texts to be analysed. Like all human activity, literacy is essentially social, and it is located in the interaction between people. (Barton & Hamilton, 1998, p. 3)

In Jaime's classroom we see evidence of this social situation where he and his students are learning over time and where this learning is an interactive production between Jaime and his students. The digital devices drawn on act as types of cultural artefacts which scaffold and mediate learning (Vygotsky, 1978). Jaime outlines his struggle with finding effective assessment methods for peer assessment and teacher feedback, and we see him searching for digital modes to make formative assessment manageable with large numbers of students to make it time efficient and consistent, and, above all, to make it a participatory process for students. Jaime's own literacy skills enable him to find and access ways to use video cameras, iPod Touches, apps, and Gmail as communicative resources in his pedagogical situation. In a Freirean (Freire, 1970) sense, Jaime empowers himself to empower his students.

With Jaime's text here we move between written print, visual imagery, and a hypertext link to video. Text as a communicative product expands its definition and carries many modes of representation – visual, aural, spatial, gestural, performative, and graphic, all evident in Jaime's classroom, and the materiality of texts and their structure is varied and eclectic, too. The notion of reading has also expanded its definition, and, according to Moss (2003), becomes much more multidimensional as the architecture of the linear page has changed.

In the social playground of Jaime's classroom, students are encouraged to discover technology for themselves, and, in this constructivist way, learn motor skills as well as reading comprehension skills. For students, events can be recorded in the moment and there is immediate feedback on a basketball throw or on skills of catching, kicking, or running. It is obvious from what is written and visually represented in the narrative that reading, writing, speaking, and listening are embodied literacy processes with a physicality and materiality grounded in everyday experiences. Students are learning to assess, navigate, design, interpret, and analyse multimodal texts (Serafini, 2012) in a contextual and natural way through their subject matter. They are emotionally and cognitively engaged in developing varied competencies which not only promotes vocabulary development, communicative competence, teamwork skills, skills of questioning and feedback but also promotes character-building dispositions and attitudes. Physical education and the activities that comprise it become tools for life lessons, and literacy becomes a lived experience with both an implicit and explicit pedagogy in Jaime's classroom.

An interesting question for us in relation to Jaime's case is the notion of access to resources in education and how this impacts literacy capital. We understand this in Bourdieu's sense of cultural capital (2008) and how the systemised practices of schooling can frame experiences and opportunities (Youdell, 2011). Here we see Jaime's students growing in confidence, making meaning, and developing dispositions and skills aided by an innovative teacher, supportive school, and some economic support. Literacy development depends on resources – human, economic, and political, for access, equity, and human flourishing. As Pahl and Rowsell (2005) underline, 'Literacy is about meaning':

This seems obvious and yet is sometimes lost in the plethora of spelling tests and standardized testing. Children use literacy to make meaning and to explore the constraints and possibilities of their worlds. (p. 139)

And we cannot forget this, that we are all embedded in practices, often normalized, habitual, and tacit, which influence our meaning making and our potential and freedom in the world. We as teachers, like Jaime, hold great power in engaging students in the possibilities of literacy, but so too do our policy makers and funding bodies.

This section has tilted a literacy lens on Jaime's classroom. It first set out some definitions of this contested word, concept, and practice, and settles on a socio-cultural understanding of literacy. It then focused on Jaime's interaction with his students as they read, write, speak, and listen with varied texts, including multimodal and digital text. This section concluded by drawing attention to the importance of literacy development for human flourishing, but highlighted its dependence on social, cultural, and political capital.

A pedagogical perspective (Melissa Parker)

As distinct from teaching, which can be classified as an act, *pedagogy* reflects the relationships and "interactions between teachers, students and the learning environment and the learning tasks" (Murphy, 2008, p. 35). While many teachers use technology to design instructional materials, far fewer integrate technology into teaching and learning (Liu, 2011). The concept of teaching and learning through the use of technology is highly complex, and the introduction of technology into a learning environment does not, in and of itself, reflect pedagogy or bring about change in pedagogical practice. Rather, its use is inextricably linked with understandings and beliefs regarding the nature of knowledge and the nature of knowing.

Teacher beliefs play a critical role in technology integration. Whether beliefs guide actions or actions inform beliefs, effective teachers, in whatever approach they take, act consistently in accordance with their beliefs. If not, learners receive confusing messages. Thus, how technology is used determines its effect on learning outcomes (Wenglinsky, 2005). While Jaime's learning goals can only be inferred from his narrative, it is obvious he wants students to gain psychomotor skills enabling them to be physically active for a lifetime, develop cognitive understanding of skill and health related fitness, and develop personal and social responsibility. What is striking in his use of technology, undertaken to accomplish the task of assessment (the proverbial "thorn in the side" for many teachers), is that it more effectively allowed him, either knowingly or not, to enact his beliefs about teaching and learning.

When looking through the three lenses used to examine Jaime's technology use (assessment, child development, and literacy), his pedagogies most clearly reveal a constructivist view of learning. Collectively, they expose an overt focus on meaningful learning, the importance of meeting the needs of the whole child, and an overriding attention to the social nature of the learning. Constructivist learning theory suggests a radically different approach to teaching from the "traditional". Constructivism assumes learners are not empty vessels to be filled, but, instead, are actively attempting to create personal meaning (Brooks & Brooks, 1993); this type of learning is messy and complex (Siemens, 2005). While multiple definitions of constructivism exist, learning from this perspective can be understood "as a self-regulated process resolving inner cognitive conflicts that often become apparent through concrete experience, collaborative discourse, and reflection" (Brooks & Brooks, 1993, p. vii). As such, the teacher's task is to provide opportunities and incentives to build up knowledge rather than dispense knowledge (Fosnot, 2005). Three major constructivist tenets (Rovegno & Dolly, 2006) have implications here.

First, learning is an active process where students are viewed as agents in their knowledge construction and understanding through decision making, critical thinking, and problem solving. Both the learner and the environment are important, as it is the interaction between the two that creates knowledge (Ertmer & Newby, 2013). In this manner, knowledge is co-produced through the activity. For example, the assessment perspective indicated Jaime had students assume various learner-centred roles resulting in the development of self-regulation and confidence which resulted in increased motivation. Similarly, the literacy perspective indicated the movement between written print, visual image, and hypertext actively immersed students in multiple literacy forms. Having students first discover how to use the iPod Touches encouraged them to explore their world, discover knowledge, and reflect and think critically. Asking students to video each other's learning attempts and provide feedback to a peer is not only active, but integrates their developing motor skills while understanding, interpreting, and thinking about the cognitive and affective concepts to be learned. Jaime's use of technology supports an environment where learning domains are fully integrated or aligned within tasks.

Second, students construct knowledge in relation to their prior knowledge and experiences (Rovegno & Dolly, 2006). For these students technology is a way of life. Asking them to use press conference skills around sportspersonship addresses their self-evaluation processes, encouraging them to bring their voice to learning through challenging investigation using both peer and internal appraisal in realistic and meaningful ways. From the developmental perspective, the use of peer models for learning and video feedback allowed for more contextual learning.

Third, knowledge is a social product and knowledge creation a shared experience. Group settings provide experiences in which the social process of knowledge construction occurs concurrently and interactively with individual child development (Borko *et al.*, 1997). As described previously by Hinchion and Hall, "the social playground" of Jaime's classroom is foundational to his teaching; learning and assessment tasks are carried out with peers, and the climate created is mastery oriented (Roberts, 2012), enhancing the positive aspects of learning. Ultimately, these pedagogies supporting constructivist learning allowed Jaime's students to be engaged in the self-directed learning they carried out.

In turn, the same pedagogies supporting constructivist learning also challenge the traditional view of technology as behaviourist. From a behaviourist perspective, technology is an information source where the learning process is characterized as reactive to the conditions in the environment as opposed to the learner taking an active role in discovering the environment (Ertmer & Newby, 2013). Thus, the level of cognitive processing is low (Ertmer & Newby, 2013) and learning is viewed as external to the learner (Siemens, 2005). Technology from this viewpoint can be branded as an input/output process where a learner finds information rather than creates it. In this case, however, Jaime's emerging pedagogy of technology attends to the complex world of personal meaning making, thus negating the prevailing view of technology in favour of constructivist learning perspectives.

Jaime's emerging pedagogy of technology demonstrates an expansion of Shulman's (1986) concept of pedagogical content knowledge (PCK). Mishra and Koelher (2006) proposed the notion of technological knowledge (TK), technological content knowledge (TCK), and Technological Pedagogical Content Knowledge (TPACK), the latter residing at the intersection of content knowledge, pedagogical knowledge, TCK, and TK. As such TPCK (or TPACK as it was later termed),

> encompasses understanding and communicating representations of concepts using technologies; pedagogical techniques that apply technologies appropriately to teach content in differentiated ways according to students' learning needs; knowledge of what makes concepts difficult or easy to learn and how technology can help redress conceptual challenges; knowledge of students' prior content-related understanding and epistemological assumptions, along with related technological expertise or lack thereof; and knowledge of how technologies can be used to build on existing understanding to help students develop new epistemologies or strengthen old ones. (Koelher & Mishra, 2009, p. 401)

Jaime's technology use clearly indicates his TPACK. His focus is on the students – their engagement, their learning – and finding a more effective manner to accomplish that. Through his journey, Jaime developed his own TK and TCK, but most importantly focused on the TPACK that allowed him to meet his students' learning needs. It wasn't technology as end that fuelled his drive, but the use of technology as a means to provide holistic student engagement, emphasizing understanding of key concepts, and the ability to apply these concepts to solve authentic real-world problems.

Teachers have a responsibility to meet the needs of the students they teach, and therefore must be lifelong learners (Armour, 2010). In this case, Jaime took the responsibility to solve his own problems. Though initially developed from what could be regarded as a selfish drive to make assessment easier, his emerging pedagogy of technology has extended from what technology to use, to how technology may be used to facilitate learning. It is doubtful that Jaime knows much about Bourdieu or Freire or for that matter constructivist learning. What he does know is a lot about his students and their needs and what he hopes they learn as a result of his teaching. While his beliefs were rarely stated explicitly, Jaime's journey as a learner of technology has allowed him to more fully implement those beliefs into a pedagogy of technology. A major implication, therefore, is how do other teachers move beyond the fascination with new technological gadgets to a pedagogy of technology to enhance student learning? After all, "while digital technologies can make things possible it is people that make things happen" (Butler *et al.*, 2013, p. 11).

While adhering to important developmental perspectives, enhancing literacy in its broadest sense, and supporting learning through assessment, Jaime's technology use provided an active and relevant learning environment enabling his students to make meaning of their own learning. This resulted in a knowledge-deepening approach where technology supported enquiry and enabled students to work on solving complex real-world problems. From a broader perspective, his use of technology as a learning tool may challenge the assumptions of technology in society. In the current world, technology is easily accessible, often relatively inexpensive, self-controlled, and comparative – just click and you can find the answer. The question remains: What type of knowledge is desirable in physical education for twenty-first century learners – knowledge for today or knowledge for tomorrow?

Practitioner reflection

I feel a sense of pride knowing my technological journey, although humbling in comparison, has similarities to that of Thomas Edison. Explaining it all as part of the process in his invention of the light bulb, Edison said he never failed, but discovered thousands of ways the light bulb didn't work. As I reflect on my technology expedition I find ultimately it was a test of perseverance and patience to overcome challenges and mistakes.

The result of my technological forays went so much further than I could have predicted. Assessments became foundational in every lesson, but more importantly, assessment became integral to my instruction. The guesswork of what to teach became an automatic result of constant analysis and progress. Students' grades were not dependent on perceptions of effort, but actual learning. While simultaneously infusing literacy I continued to reinforce students' linguistic skills in a hybrid of communication and technology.

By engaging in the development of this pedagogical case, I discovered much about my own teaching style. I previously didn't really know how to describe my pedagogical methods, often perceiving them as simplistic. From the constructivist perspective, combined with technological pedagogical content knowledge, I see a teacher who focuses on richer experiences, asking what he really wants students to achieve. Students' own perseverance to solve problems with social and cognitive skills becomes a mirror of my own voyage to set up such an environment. In a sense, my voyage became the students' voyage, and it's an amazing experience to able to share your learning with others. Ultimately, and unpredictably, this expedition took me back to my initial philosophies of teaching. Steve Jobs once said, "Technology is nothing. What's important is that you have a faith in people, that they're basically good and smart, and if you give them tools, they'll do wonderful things with them".

Technology can be exciting and novel. Often we gather information just to gather information, thinking it will enhance student learning. As much as I may have thought technology was the reason for my success, I recently realized technology was just a tool. On our gym wall we have a saying posted: "People are more important . . ." to signify that whatever may follow in that sentence will ultimately lose in comparison. No skills, games, rules, or even technology can ever be more valuable, meaningful, and rich than the human experience of learning.

It's easy as educators to have such a desperate grasp on assessment and grip on technology that we don't have a hand left to hold what is important. Technology didn't make my physical education class a success. Technology simply created an opportunity for me to help students reach their potential. Everything we do as educators is still completely dependent on the human possibility. For every teacher and student that's the true journey.

Lessons from the case: How can the use of digital technologies accelerate pupil learning in physical education?

- Viewing technology as a means to an end, rather than an end in itself, led to the development of a pedagogy of technology through listening to students and keeping educational objectives in mind.
- Considering learning from a constructivist perspective allowed learning to be conceived as active, with technology functioning as an integral part of that activity.
- Reflection allows for reflective practice which facilitates change.
- Assessing teaching through multiple lenses provides scope for enhanced learning.
- Technological gadgets have their place in education, but they're no substitute for knowledge. To avoid sending confusing messages to students, teachers must act consistently in accordance with their beliefs.

References

Ames, C. (1992). Classrooms: Goals, structures, and student motivation. *Journal of Educational Psychology*, *84*(3), 261–271.

Ames, C. (1984). Achievement attributions and self-instructions under competitive and individualistic goal structures. *Journal of Educational Psychology*, *76*, 478–487.

Annerstedt, C. and Larsson, S. (2010). 'I have my own picture of what the demands are . . .' Grading in Swedish PEH – problems of validity, comparability and fairness. *European Physical Education Review*, *16*(2), 97–115.

Armour, K. M. (2010). The physical education profession and its professional responsibility . . . or . . . why '12 weeks paid holiday' will never be enough. *Physical Education and Sport Pedagogy, 15,* 1–13.

Barton, D. and Hamilton, M. (1998). *Local Literacies: Reading and Writing in One Community.* London: Routledge.

Borko, H., Mayfield, V., Marion, S., Flexer, M. D. and Hiebert, E. (1997). Teachers' developing ideas and practices about mathematics performance assessment: Successes, stumbling blocks, and implications for professional development. *Teaching and Teacher Education, 13,* 259–278.

Bourdieu, P. (2008). *Practical Reason.* Oxford: Polity.

Brooks, J. G. and Brooks, M. (1993). *In Search of Understanding: The Case for Constructivist Classrooms.* Alexandria, VA: ASCD.

Butler, D., Leahy, M., Shiel, G. and Cosgrove, J. (2013). 'A Consultative Paper: Building Towards a Learning Society: A National Digital Strategy for Schools.' Dublin: St. Patrick's College and Educational Research Centre.

Deci, E. L. and Ryan, R. M. (1985). *Intrinsic Motivation and Self-determination in Human Behaviour.* New York: Plenum.

DeLuca, C. and Bellara, A. (2013). The current state of assessment education: Aligning policy, standards, and teacher education curriculum. *Journal of Teacher Education, 64*(4), 356–372.

Duda, J. L. and Ntoumanis, N. (2003). Motivational patterns in physical education. *International Journal of Educational Research, 39,*415–436.

Dweck, C. S. (1986). Motivational processes affecting learning. *American Psychologist, 41,* 1040–1048.

Ertmer, P. A. and Newby, T. J. (2013). Behaviorism, cognitivism, constructivism: Comparing critical features from an instructional design perspective. *Performance Improvement Quarterly, 26*(2), 43–71.

Fosnot, C. T. (2005). *Constructivism: Theory, Perspectives, and Practice.* New York: Teachers College Press.

Freire, P. (1970). *Pedagogy of the Oppressed.* New York: Bloomsbury.

Fry, M. D. (2001). The development of motivation in children. In G. C. Roberts, ed., *Advances in Motivation in Sport and Exercise.* Champaign, IL: Human Kinetics. pp. 51–78.

Goleman, D. (2014). 'We Should Be Teaching Emotional Literacy in Schools.' Retrieved from www.google.ie/?gws_rd=cr,ssl&ei=daxXVsDrCYfxO-fqgoAD#q=emotional+literacy

Graham, G., Holt/Hale, S. A. and Parker, M. (2013). *Children Moving: A Reflective Approach to Teaching Physical Education* (9th ed.). New York: McGraw Hill.

Hall, K. (2003). *Listening to Stephen Read: Multiple Perspectives on Literacy.* Berkshire, UK: Open University Press.

Hall, K., Goswami, U., Harrison, C., Ellis, S. and Soler, J. (2010). *Interdisciplinary Perspectives on Learning to Read: Culture, Cognition and Pedagogy.* London: Routledge.

Hastie, P., Sinelnikov, O., Wallhead, T. and Layne, T. (2014). Perceived and actual motivational climate of a mastery-involving sport education season. *European Physical Education Review, 20*(2), 215–228.

Hay, P. J. (2006). Assessment for learning in physical education. In D. Kirk, D. Macdonald and M. O'Sullivan, eds., *The Handbook of Physical Education.* London: Sage. pp. 312–325.

Hay, P. and Penney, D. (2013). *Assessment in Physical Education.* New York: Routledge.

Koehler, M. and Mishra, P. (2009). What is technological pedagogical content knowledge? *Contemporary Issues in Technology and Teacher Education, 9*(1), 60–70.

Lambert, L. (1999). *Standards-Based Assessment of Student Learning: A Comprehensive Approach.* Reston, VA: NASPE.

Lambirth, A. (2011). *Literacy on the Left: Reform and Revolution*. London: Bloomsbury.

Leander, K. and Sheehy, M. (2004). *Spatializing Literacy Research and Practice*. New York: Peter Lang.

Leirhaug, P. E. and MacPhail, A. (2015). It's the other assessment that is the key: Three Norwegian physical education teachers' engagement (or not) with assessment for learning. *Sport, Education and Society*, *20*(5), 624–640.

Lewis, C., Enciso, P. and Birr Moje, E. (2007). *Reframing Sociocultural Research on Literacy*. New York: Lawerence Erlbaum Associates.

Liu, S. (2011). Factors related to pedagogical beliefs of teachers and technology integration. *Computers and Education*, *56*, 1012–1022.

McCullagh, P. and Weiss, M. R. (2001). Modeling: Considerations for motor skill performance and psychological responses. In R. N. Singer, H. A. Hasenblas and C. M. Janelle, eds., *Handbook of Sport Psychology* (2nd ed.). New York: Wiley. pp. 205–238.

Magill, R. and Anderson, D. (2014). *Motor Learning and Control: Concepts and Applications* (10th ed.). New York: McGraw Hill.

Martin, J. J., Hodges-Kulinna, P. and Cothran, D. (2002). Motivating students through assessment. *Journal of Physical Education, Recreation & Dance*, *73*(8), 18–19.

Mishra, P. and Koehler, M. J. (2006). Technological pedagogical content knowledge: A new framework for teacher knowledge. *Teachers College Record*, *108*(6), 1017–1054.

Moss, J. (2003). 'Which English?' In J. Davidson and J. Dowson, J. eds., *Learning to Teach English in Secondary School*. London: Routledge Palmer. pp. 1–17.

Murphy, P. (2008). Defining pedagogy. In K. Hall, P. Murphy and J. Soler, eds., *Pedagogy and Practice: Culture and Identities*. London: Sage. pp. 28–39.

National Council for Accreditation of Teacher Education (NCATE). (2008). *It's All About Student Learning: Assessing Teacher Candidates' Ability to Impact P–12 Students*. Washington, DC: Author.

Nicholls, J. G. (1989). *The Competitive Ethos and Democratic Education*. Cambridge, MA: Harvard University Press.

Ntoumanis, N. and Biddle, S. J. (1999). A review of the motivational climate in physical activity. *Journal of Sport Sciences*, *17*(8), 643–565.

O'Rourke, M. (2005). Multiliteracies for 21st century schools. *Snapshot, Australia: The Australian National Schools Network Ltd*, *2*, 1–12.

Pahl, K. and Rowsell, J. (2010). *Artifactual Literacies*. New York: Teachers College Press.

Pahl, K. and Rowsell, J. (2006). *Travel Notes from New Literacy Studies*. Trowbridge, UK: Cromwell Press.

Pahl, K. and Rowsell, J. (2005). *Literacy and Education*. London: Sage.

Pennings, A. H. (1996). The measurement of mental attentional capacity: A neo–Piagetian developmental study. *Intelligence*, *23*(1), 59–78.

Roberts, G. C. (2012). Motivation in sport and exercise from an achievement goal theory: Perspective after 30 years, where are we? In G. C. Roberts and D. C. Treasure, D.C., eds., *Advances in Motivation in Sport and Exercise* (3rd ed.). Champaign, IL: Human Kinetics.

Rovegno, I. and Dolly, P. (2006). Constructivist perspectives on learning. In D. Kirk, D. Macdonald and M. Sullivan, eds., *The Handbook of Physical Education*. London: Sage. pp. 226–241.

Serafini, F. (2012). Multimodal texts in the 21st century. *Journal of Research in the Schools*, *19*(1), 26–32.

Shen, B., Chen, A. and Guan, J. (2007). Using achievement goals and interest to predict learning in physical education. *The Journal of Experimental Education*, *75* (2), 89–108.

Shepard, L. (2000). The role of assessment in a learning culture. *Educational Researcher*, *29*(7), 4–14.

Shulman, L. S. (1986). Those who understand: Knowledge growth in teaching. *Educational Researcher*, *15*(2), 4–14.

Siemens, G. (2005). Connectivism: A learning theory for the digital age. *Instructional Technology and Distance Learning*, *2*(1), 1–8.

Stiggins, R. J. (2002). Assessment crisis: The absence of assessment for learning. *Phi Delta Kappan*, *83*(10), 758–765.

Stiggins, R., Arter, J. A., Chappuis, J. and Chappuis, S. (2012). *Classroom Assessment for Student Learning: Doing It Right—Using It Well*. Upper Saddle River, NJ: Prentice Hall.

Tannehill, D., van der Mars, H. and MacPhail, A. (2015). *Building Effective Physical Education Programs*. Burlington, MA: Jones and Bartlett.

U.S. Department of Education. (2010). 'A Blueprint for Reform: The Reauthorization of the Elementary and Secondary Education Act'. Retrieved from www2.ed.gov/policy/elsec/leg/blueprint/

Veal, M-L. (1988). Pupil assessment practices and perceptions of secondary teachers. *Journal of Teaching in Physical Education*, *7*(4), 327–342.

Vygotsky, L. (1978). *Mind in Society*. Cambridge, MA: Harvard University Press.

Wenglinsky, H. (2005). Technology and achievement: The bottom line. *Educational Leadership*, *63*(4), 29–32.

Whitehead, M. (2010). *Physical Literacy: Through the Lifecourse*. London: Routledge.

Wiliam, D. and Thompson, M. (2007). Integrating assessment with instruction: What will it take to make it work? In C. A. Dwyer, ed., *The Future of Assessment: Shaping Teaching and Learning*. Mahwah, NJ: Lawrence Erlbaum Associates.

Youdell, D. (2011). *School Trouble*. London: Routledge.

4

JAMES: PHYSICAL EDUCATION TEACHER

Fiona C. Chambers, James Sherry, Orla Murphy, Wesley O'Brien and Gavin Breslin

CHAPTER OVERVIEW

This chapter presents a narrative of James, a secondary school physical education teacher in the Republic of Ireland. The narrative is analysed from three theoretical perspectives: digital humanities, physical activity promotion and sport psychology. In the final section, a pedagogical perspective urges us to rethink pedagogy for an age of digital information and communication (Beetham & Sharpe, 2013, p. 4). A learner-centred model of technological, pedagogical and content knowledge (Koehler & Mishra, 2005) is developed using a design-thinking framework (Brown, 2008) in order to facilitate new forms of learning activity.

Practitioner narrative (James Sherry)

Since qualifying as a teacher in 2001, I have worked in secondary schools in England, Australia and Ireland. While teaching, I completed a Master's degree in education. In addition, I have supported the professional development of secondary school physical education teachers and newly qualified teachers through my role as a PE-CPD tutor. This narrative explores my experiences as a secondary school teacher in Ireland.

In Ireland, the school I began working in is a designated DEIS school (Delivering Equality of Opportunity in School)[1]. I was the only physical education teacher and extracurricular activities coordinator, there. While I inherited poor equipment (dangerous trampoline, one burst indoor soccer ball), I also had brilliant facilities, including a four-court sports hall, grass pitch and all-weather pitch. There was a new principal who was willing to invest in resources to raise the profile of sport and physical education. For me, technology held the key to this. I had dabbled in this in London and Australia, but was actually quite a non-techie person. This was an opportunity to be brave and embrace it fully.

Timing was everything. It so happened that the school's Technical Graphic/ Design and Communication Graphics departments were allocated new computers, and so I liberated one of their old computers. I put this inside the main lobby of the school in a very prominent place and used PowerPoint (see Table 4.1) to advertise (i) lunchtime clubs and activities, and (ii) upcoming fixtures. While the students found the club and fixture information useful, students seemed most captivated by the slideshows of photos taken at matches. These photos displayed students enjoying themselves during fixtures and "in action". I also discovered that software programmes (Microsoft Mail Merge; see Table 4.1), could assist me in producing certificates for the school sports awards ceremony. This raised the profile of sport (and physical education) and was done with a few clicks of a button! Seeing the positive impact of technology, school management further invested by buying a large screen for the lobby, which was then also used to promote Healthy Lifestyle Week, Active Schools Week and other school events.

I further raised the quality and standard of physical education by using carefully selected digital devices and applications across all strands of the physical education curriculum. Specifically, I used the iPad, e-portfolios, exergames and heart rate monitors. These will now be discussed in more detail.

iPad

The iPad has had the single biggest impact on my teaching. It allowed for a seamless use of technology to support learning through the varying apps that are available. One example is my use of the app Dartfish (see Table 4.1). Before the iPad, this was cumbersome to use, as it required a laptop computer with tripod and camcorder, which restricted teacher movement. However, with the iPad, I just needed an Apple TV unit to transmit wirelessly from the iPad wherever I was standing in the sports hall. I even modified the tripod to hold the iPad securely. To fully exploit the iPad, I accessed a variety of affordable apps to support my teaching (e.g. Scoreboard, Ubersense and Video Delay [Table 4.1]). By using Ubersense and Video Delay on the iPad, I could integrate movement analysis and skill development into nearly every class.

e-portfolios

During classroom-based physical education lessons, I used technology to support students to create e-portfolios using Google Docs (Table 4.1). An *e-portfolio* is both a product (a digital collection of artifacts, such as photos, videos, certificates and progress reports) and a process of learning (i.e. it incorporates a reflective process on the digital artifacts and what they represent). Student e-portfolios included personal fitness data (e.g. results of 20-metre shuttle run, 12 minute run, Illinois Agility Test) and tracking of ongoing skill development over the course of a unit

TABLE 4.1 Technology used by James

Devices and applications	Description	How it was used
Microsoft Mail Merge	Generates personalised copies of a document	To produce certificates
PowerPoint	A presentation tool used on computers or the iPad	To show match photos and footage
iPad	A new handheld tablet computing device from Apple, Inc. that first launched in January 2010	Apps on the iPad were used to analyse skills
Dartfish	Analysis of movement and performance software (or app) on the iPad	To analyse skills
Ubersense	A video analysis app that includes tools to video-record performances and then replay, analyse and compare performances against others	To analyse skills
Video Delay	Slow-motion video capture app	To analyse skills
Scoreboard	An app that allows scores in games to be recorded	To keep track of scores during games
Xbox	Game console	To play the Just Dance video game
Just Dance	An exergame available on the varying games consoles, Just Dance is a series of rhythm games in which an avatar is displayed on the screen for players to copy the movements of	To teach dance; students copied the dance movements to a particular video
Kinect Sensor	Xbox sensor to track movement	To track whether the student is copying the dance correctly
Apple TV	Digital media player and micro-console sold by Apple. It is a small network appliance and entertainment device	To stream digital data from websites, cameras and the iPad to TV for playing on the TV screen; Android devices are also compatible
Heart rate monitors	Monitors heart rate during activities	To check heart rate before, during and after exercise
Google Docs	Create and edit web-based documents, spreadsheets and presentations	To create an e-portfolio

(e.g. a six-week period). The e-portfolio provided compelling evidence of progression for the students that supported their learning

Exergames

I have always struggled with teaching dance, and so I searched for a technology fix to help me in my practice. The Just Dance game was ideal. Just Dance is an exergame and works on the Xbox, among other systems (Table 4.1). An interesting feature of the Xbox is the Kinect Sensor which, once attached, allows the Xbox to read the movement of a number of people and award points on the basis of how closely they can copy the on-screen movements. I was able use this with a class of thirty students as the Kinect Sensor tracked students in the front row. The rest of the students simply copied the choreography on the projector screen. By recording their scores and rotating the students who were being tracked by the Kinect Sensor, everybody was fully engaged and made good progress.

Heart rate monitors

Using heart rate monitors brought a real understanding of the effects of exercise on the body. It became much easier for students, who had struggled to find their heart rate by using the traditional approach (i.e. find pulse, count number of beats for six seconds and multiply by ten to get beats per minute). By using the heart rate monitors, students could see the impact of the intensity of exercise on heart rate immediately.

Conclusion

Students live in a digital-centric environment. This has implications for teaching and learning in physical education, particularly given the fact that it will soon be an examination subject in Ireland, and movement analysis is a key component of this. Physical education teachers need to keep abreast of all such changes through effective CPD opportunities.

The following sections explore James' narrative from digital humanities, physical activity promotion and sport psychology perspectives. Following this, the pedagogical implications of the three perspectives for physical education teachers across the continuum of teacher education (Teaching Council of Ireland, 2011) are considered.

A digital humanities perspective (Orla Murphy)

What is digital humanities?

Digital humanities (DH) examines what it is to be human in the digital age (i.e. the relationship between humans and computers). It is a discipline which comprises humanities, arts, social sciences and technology (Gold, 2012). Formerly humanities computing, DH has become synonymous with digital pedagogy and research innovation using emerging technologies. From a DH standpoint, research may consider technology as a tool, study object, expressive medium, exploratory laboratory or an activist avenue[2] (Svennson, 2010).

The role of technology in teaching

According to Tomei (2005), classrooms and schools that are most successful use "best practice" strategies for teaching and learning that are technology enhanced:

> Teachers who serve not only as dispensers of knowledge . . . but also as facilitators alongside their students . . . form true learning communities best supported by the technology-based resources that become part and parcel of their curriculum. (Ibid, p. xii)

It can be said that James emulates a technology-enhanced approach to teaching and learning, despite positioning himself as a self-confessed "non-techie" educator. Indeed, James has achieved an organic integration of technology into his practice. Within the very real defined parameters of finance and managerial support, his engagement with technology has grown in parallel with platform and software development. Initially, technology played a basic role in administration by automating tasks, for example, sports awards certificates. Steadily mirroring his own growth as an educator, his use of technology has become more sophisticated and enables reflection, participation and engagement in an active learning process. James's choice of technology is determined by working with students to identify their learning needs. Such a collaborative approach is central to DH (Spiro, 2012).

Using video as digital pedagogy

James's use of video as a feedback tool in the classroom is an example of how he is developing a digital pedagogy. Through videography, slow-motion capture and photography, students used technology as a reflective tool and developed an enhanced self-awareness and a shared understanding of the skills taught and milestones recorded through e-portfolios. This is termed *video action research practice* (VARP), where students and teachers use video to critically evaluate performances, "positioning themselves in relation to others and sharing this in an empirical form" (Lovett, 2008, p. 72). Video is immediately accessible, and in James's narrative, video allows individuals to see themselves from the perspective of others, to see their movement and interaction. It allows the student to better appreciate their body, their movement and arguably, themselves (McNicol *et al.*, 2014), leading to an objective appreciation of their growth and improvement over a module.

Developing digital literacy

James and his students are "digital natives", meaning they are all "native speakers" of the digital language of computers, video games and the Internet (Prensky, 2001, p. 1). Another term used for this cohort is *millennials*, the Millennial Generation or Generation Y, who were born between 1980s to early 2000s. The assumption is that because millennials use digital devices, they understand the impact of these technologies and the personal data gathered now and into the future. The startling fact is that these digital natives or millennials do not understand the use of these ubiquitous technologies or their impact (Organisation for Economic Cooperation and Development [OECD], 2015). A critical understanding of what these devices do must be intrinsic to the engagement with technology (Ibid). This is called *digital literacy*. Being digitally literate means understanding technologies that map and record personal data, such as personal heart monitors, and having an acute awareness of how this data is being used now and in perpetuity. It is a core capability for someone for living, learning and working in a digital society (Hibberson *et al.*, 2015).

James uses technology in the service of a pedagogical goal, which shows some understanding of the capabilities of these devices and a basic level of digital literacy. However, in his classes, he may not realise the amount of data being generated and how that data might be used. The new technologies used by James, whether texts, visual, oral or literate, present a new image (or new inscription) of the student in the digital sphere. This means bodies are videoed, images captured, movements and distances mapped and pulses measured. All of this data are held on an app's servers and may be shared through social media. This self-inscription is often simultaneously personal and public, local and national/international; in other words, the digital image of the student performing the long jump is not only available to the student but also can be accessed by other students and the teacher, and could be used beyond the classroom nationally or internationally. This is a powerful digital footprint. We assume that millennials are aware of this. However, the recent OECD (2015) report on Students, Computers and Learning notes that far from being digital natives, this "wired generation" needs assistance in navigating the cyber sphere and understanding how their data are used. Both James and his students will need to become more digitally literate, learning how to interrogate the use of data generated in the cyber sphere.

Conclusion

In summary, at the centre of DH is the relationship between humans and computers. Integral to DH are the key notions of digital literacy and the use of technology as a student-centred reflective tool. It is clear that James emulates a DH approach. The narrative demonstrated James's willingness to embrace new ideas in the service of his teaching goals. One key moment shows a change in James's thinking – moving from a video camera with a tripod to carefully chosen apps on the iPad. Here, James changes from using the technology as tool to a more integrated understanding of the possibilities of contemporary technology, where students are actively mapping, visualising, analysing and sharing their learning journeys in a peer-to-peer setting. James's next step will be to educate students to be critical consumers of technology and the data they generate. In this way both James and his students will become digitally literate, moving towards a deeper understanding of ways in which technology impacts on "how we think" (Hayles, 2012).

A physical activity promotion perspective (Wesley O'Brian)

What is physical activity?

A standardised definition for *physical activity* has become accepted as any bodily movement produced by the skeletal muscles expending energy beyond resting levels (Caspersen *et al.*, 1985). From the perspective of childhood physical activity promotion, and, specifically, energy expenditure at a moderate-to-vigorous intensity level, James is demonstrating the effectiveness of digital technologies to promote physical activity.

As an experienced practitioner, James introduces the narrative with some of the early technological developments for teaching and learning in physical education (e.g. PowerPoint, Mail Merge and Dartfish). For James, the arrival of iPads heralds a noticeable 'technological transition' within physical education. In terms of promoting childhood physical activity in dance and across the curriculum, James integrates tools, such as active video gaming (Xbox), heart rate monitors and iPads, for feedback on student performance. From this narrative, the recent technological developments within the fields of 'movement' (Kinect Sensor) and 'physical fitness' (e-portfolios) are enlightening for physical activity promotion within a school environment.

Measuring childhood movement and physical activity participation

Whilst James effectively captures the essence of integrating digital technology in physical education, it is important to consider the complex, multifaceted behaviour of childhood physical activity participation (Bouchard *et al.*, 2007; Ward *et al.*, 2007). Recently, many technology-driven sedentary pursuits (e.g. television, mobile phones, video games) have become the preferred mode of passive entertainment, outside of the school environment (Bickham *et al.*, 2013; Biddle *et al.*, 2010; Oliver *et al.*, 2012). This, in turn, had led to rising levels of childhood physical inactivity, weight status and potential chronic illness. With the rise of 'sedentariness' (Rey-López *et al.*, 2008, p. 242), it seems critical for physical education specialists, similar to the approach of James, to integrate digitally robust tools for measuring childhood movement and physical activity participation (Belton *et al.*, 2014; O' Brien *et al.*, 2015, 2013; Harrington *et al.*, 2014). Most recent evidence highlights a wide variety of methods and approaches used to measure childhood movement and physical activity participation (McKenzie & van der Mars, 2015; Scott *et al.*, 2015; Smith *et al.*, 2015; Tremblay *et al.*, 2015), many of which were acknowledged by James in this narrative. In the future, James might consider direct measures of physical activity, such as systematic observation, which provide contextually rich data on the setting in which the activity occurs (McKenzie & van der Mars, 2015). Many physical educators choose not to embrace the culture of digital technology, with indirect measures, such as self-report, the most widely used assessment tool for physical activity participation (Hands *et al.*, 2006; Murphy, 2009).

The low-validity coefficients observed for self-report instruments (Armstrong, 1998; Kohl *et al.*, 2000; Trost, 2007) suggest that objective measurements of physical activity may indeed be the most appropriate (Rowlands & Eston, 2005; Troiano *et al.*, 2008). For example, the Kinect Sensor employed by James was an effective tool for promoting physical activity participation because it provided visual and auditory cues to help students to learn the dance. Aligned with the promotion of digital technology in physical education, James further comments on the integration of objective physical activity measurement tools such as heart rate monitors and compatible movement analysis software for iPads. In terms of critically analysing the narrative from a physical activity measurement perspective, there is sufficient scope for James to move beyond heart rate monitors in the classroom and embrace the technological advances of objectively measured accelerometry to enhance his students' physical activity levels (Belton *et al.*, 2013; De Vries *et al.*, 2011; Slootmaker *et al.*, 2010).

Research evidence supports the idea that accelerometers are the most efficient measurement protocol during childhood, as they derive a range of physical activity data (intensity, frequency, pattern and duration) (Berlin *et al.*, 2006; Trost, 2007). Interestingly, from a digital technological perspective, these activity monitors have been developed in response to (a) the lack of reliability of self-report measures, (b) the intrusiveness of direct observation, (c) the complexity of heart rate monitoring (Puyau *et al.*, 2002) and (d) the lack of quantitative information provided by the pedometers (intensity, duration, etc.).

In terms of childhood movement and energy expenditure measurement, James has utilised the app Ubersense and the exergame Just Dance in conjunction with heart rate monitors. James clearly understands the benefits of heart rate monitoring during physical education classes to help him understand the link between childhood movement and health. While the correct assessment of physical activity remains an ongoing challenge for researchers (Scott *et al.*, 2015), accelerometers are a unique instrumentation that provide quantitative information relating to the vertical accelerations of the trunk and body segments at user-specified times (Dale *et al.*, 2002; Trost *et al.* 2005; Trost, 2007). From a youth physical activity, physical education and sport perspective, it is important to note that sufficient research reports a strong correlation between accelerometer output and energy expenditure and/or exercise intensity (Freedson *et al.*, 2005; Trost, 2007).

Conclusion

From a physical activity perspective, there is now consistent evidence within the literature (Kimm *et al.*, 2000; O'Donovan *et al.*, 2010; Ortega *et al.*, 2013) to suggest that an age-related decline in physical activity participation occurs during adolescence. In this milieu, the importance of robust protocol for childhood physical activity promotion seems critical. James has outlined how digital technology might be employed to enhance the quality and amount of physical activity for young people. It seems prudent that specialist physical education teachers consider the integration of established, validated and reliable accelerometry within physical education classes.

A psychological perspective (Gavin Breslin)

What is sport psychology?

Sport psychology (SP) is a multidisciplinary field spanning psychology, sports science and medicine, and includes the scientific study of how we think and behave, and encompasses topics such as personality, learning, motivation and cognition (American Psychological Association, 2016). By researching human behaviour and cognition, SP can contribute to interventions that can enhance performance in physical activity contexts. Two main themes are central to this analysis: (a) James's psychological characteristics and (b) skill acquisition and movement technology.

Psychological characteristics

Psychological characteristics refer to the likely traits and prominent behaviours of a person (Ibid). James's psychological traits are manifested when faced with lack of quality physical education equipment (broken trampoline). His response to this was to focus on what he did have – brilliant facilities – and to use technology to engage students in physical education. He 'liberated' a computer from another department and worked on 'up-skilling' himself in the new technology, taking a risk with trying something new to augment his teaching. This behaviour is evidence of a growth mind-set (Dweck, 2012, 2006), wherein he perceived his ability not as fixed but flexible, which can be developed through effort. More-over, the growth mind-set is underpinned by intrinsic and extrinsic motivation to achieve the end goal of enhanced student learning experiences in physical education (Ibid). Those people who possess the characteristics of a growth mind-set typically feel that they have more to learn when engaging in activities (Ibid). When faced with challenges, they ignore the negative voice inside them saying 'I don't know if this is possible to achieve', and believe that they can learn and grow from this new situation (see Table 4.2). Someone with a fixed mind-set, on the other hand, is someone who does not approach the challenge because they feel they either

TABLE 4.2 Examples of interpretations of events by those with a fixed and growth mind-set (Dweck, 2006)

Fixed mind-set	Growth mind-set
I am not good at this.	I can learn from this.
I am not smart enough.	I will learn how to do this.
I cannot make this better.	I can always improve.
This is too difficult.	This may take long.
Others tried this before and failed.	I can work harder at this.

cannot achieve anything from engaging with the challenge or that a positive end result/outcome is unlikely (see Table 4.2).

Skill acquisition and movement technology

To understand the psychology of human performance and learning, psychologists assess movement behaviour. This is referred to as *motor skill acquisition*, and is the process through which learners interact with their environment to become proficient performers (Muratori *et al.*, 2013). Skill acquisition in recent years has been supported by new technology. James's use of skill acquisition processes will be analysed from this standpoint.

It was refreshing to read James's use of the Xbox Kinect Sensor and Just Dance, as this provided his students with real-time feedback. Eaves *et al.* (2011) investigated the role of real-time feedback when acquiring a dance move using burdensome technology. While Eaves *et al.* (2011) concluded that providing feedback was beneficial for learning, providing visual feedback on every trial of practice led to a reliance on watching the teacher and a decrease in learning due to students receiving less feedback. It is therefore important for James to offer students an opportunity to be engaged in their own problem-based learning as opposed to receiving all the information required to achieve a task goal from technology. By using problem-based learning, the learner engages cognitively in problem solving that would then in turn enhance long-term memory, as opposed to a reliance on a continuous source of information that when removed can lead to a detriment in recall and hence performance (Hodges & Williams, 2012).

Modelling is amongst the most frequently used instruction techniques to enhance motor skill acquisition (Gould *et al.*, 1989; Weinberg & Jackson, 1990). By understanding how modelling works teachers can manipulate and make salient important information for students to further enhance learning (Breslin *et al.*, 2009; Hodges *et al.*, 2007). For example, by bringing attention to core information sources of a model's movement through cueing or managing the amount of information provided to learners, skill acquisition can be enhanced (Breslin *et al.*, 2009). In dance, James used the Kinect Sensor to lead students to synchronise their movement with an avatar (model) on the large screen. This practice can facilitate cognitive attentional processes and encoding of information in memory for later retrieval, similar to the face-to-face process of modelling (Hodges *et al.*, 2007). The approach facilitated the retrieval of the memory required to be able to perform the representation of the dance movement seen by students on the screen. Recall or retrieval of memory (remembering) refers to the subsequent re-accessing of events or information from the past, which have been previously encoded and stored in the brain (Jonides *et al.*, 2008).

Conclusion

James demonstrates a positive growth mind-set in terms of reviewing what resources he has for facilitating student learning. Although James refers to himself as a 'non-techie person', he has engaged with new technologies, has taken calculated risks in their use and has embedded technology into the school and his physical education classes. By working with technology, he has triggered individual behaviour change that has arguably led to a cultural shift in his school around the provision of physical education and school sport. Furthermore, James has been able to provide students with a movement-based system that only six years ago presented challenges to researchers. This is to be commended and illustrates the shift in how technology is evolving to allow students to have real time video feedback for skill acquisition in their natural settings.

A pedagogical perspective (Fiona Chambers)

Learning is a set of personal and interpersonal activities, deeply rooted in specific social and cultural contexts. When those contexts change, how people learn changes also (Beetham & Sharpe, 2013, p. 6). The advent of digital technology has caused the sociocultural context for learners to change with almost borderless classrooms encouraging greater learner mobility, choice and access to knowledge (Ibid, p. 7). This new milieu disrupts our understanding of pedagogy and invites new forms of learning activity. Existing pedagogical practices are no longer sufficient. And so, what is required now is a mechanism of 'rethinking pedagogy for an age of digital information and communication' (Ibid, p. 4).

In rethinking pedagogy, it is evident that contemporary physical education teachers, like James, need to have more than just pedagogical content knowledge (PCK) (Shulman, 2007). PCK is a type of knowledge that is unique to teachers, and is based on the manner in which teachers relate their pedagogical knowledge (what they know about teaching) to their subject-matter knowledge (what they know about what they teach). For the modern, networked and borderless classroom (Beetham & Sharpe, 2013, p. 7), Koehler and Mishra (2005) reconceptualised Shulman's PCK. In this new iteration, PCK is infused with technology forging the Technological Pedagogical Content Knowledge (TPACK). The TPACK model delineates teachers' knowledge of technology and describes the situated and complex knowledge required by teachers for technology integration in their teaching in a digital age (Koehler & Mishra, 2005; Thompson & Mishra, 2007). Effective TPACK is a powerful tool, as it enables inclusive practice. It can meet the 'pace and level of learning for each student within the styles and forms of current youth culture' and is optimised in the hands of a trained and digitally literate teacher (Laurillard, 2013, p. xi), a point raised by the digital humanities perspective. Koehler and Mishra (2009) describe how TPACK comprises seven elements including TPACK itself: Content Knowledge (CK); Pedagogical Knowledge (PK); Technology Knowledge (TK); Pedagogical Content Knowledge (PCK); Technological Content Knowledge (TCK); Technological Pedagogical Knowledge (TPK) and Technological Pedagogical Content Knowledge (TPACK) (please see Figure 4.1). In this way, TPACK can be considered a pedagogy of technology.

TPACK research shows that those teachers who are most effective possess a sophisticated knowledge base, wherein content, pedagogy, and Technological Knowledge interplay in high degrees (Koehler & Mishra, 2005). The sport

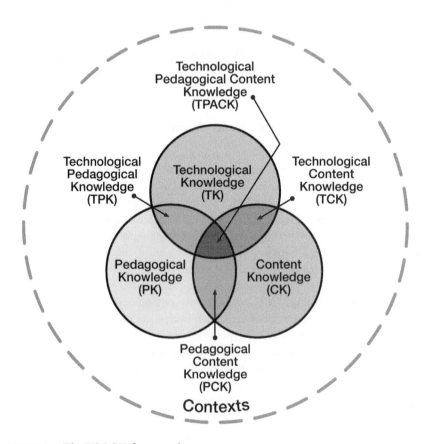

FIGURE 4.1 The TPACK framework.

Reproduced by permission of the publisher, © 2012 by tpack.org psychology and digital humanities perspectives both highlighted how James gained a deep understanding of the pillars of pedagogy, both the educational context and his students' learning needs. This enables him to engage in TPACK – to match technologies to enhance what (he) teaches, how (he) teaches and what students learn (Chen & Jang, 2014), a point raised by the physical activity perspective. All teachers need to be supported to rethink traditional pedagogies/PCK and move toward becoming fluent in TPACK. The design thinking (DT) framework (Brown, 2008) is now used to help rethink traditional pedagogy for a digital age.

Using design thinking to reconstruct pedagogy

Brown (2008) coined the term *design thinking* (DT) to encapsulate the phenomenon when design was not merely construed as a physical process but as a way of thinking. Further, Brown and Martin (2015) assert that Buchanan's 1992 article "Wicked Problems in Design Thinking" made very clear and concrete links to how DT might be used to tackle fluid, assiduous and obstinate challenges. Devitt (2014) describes three types of problems: (a) simple (lack of data), (b) complex (lack of data, unknown algorithm), and (c) wicked (stakeholders' disagreement, interconnected system, unclear goals, poor understanding, no algorithm possible and data uncertainty). *Wicked problems* are

> not stable but are continually evolving and mutating; have many causal levels; have no single solution that applies in all circumstances and where solutions can only be classed as better or worse, rather than right or wrong. (Blackman *et al.*, 2006, p. 70)

DT offers an opportunity to embrace the disruptive nature of digital technology, which by its nature nudges norms, pushing them in new directions; 'challenges assumptions . . . and ushers in completely new forms of learning activity' (Beetham & Sharpe, 2013, p. 4). Digital technology has forced the reconstruction of pedagogy (PCK morphing into TPACK). The reconstruction of pedagogy is a wicked problem, given the fluid nature of the sociocultural context, learner mobility and connectivity.

Rethinking pedagogy demands finding a way to infuse technological content knowledge into pedagogical practice (TPACK) to produce digitally literate students (digital humanities perspective). Moreover, this new form of pedagogy must be delivered by teachers who themselves have a profound digital literacy, noted by the digital humanities perspective. It appears that the quality of TPACK is influenced by a number of mercurial factors, namely: (a) quality of teacher training in TPACK, (b) teacher access to changing technologies (hard and soft), (c) the changing learning needs of students, and (d) the digital literacy of teachers and students (Beetham & Sharpe, 2013).

DT seems to offer a pathway to developing TPACK, as it is 'a human-centric and multidisciplinary approach focused on solving problems through the generation of new ideas by understanding the needs of end-users and final consumers' (Cerejo & Barbosa, 2012, p. 3). Moreover, Hassi and Laakso (2011) concluded that the DT process is itself complex as it is 'based on a three-dimensional framework' where a set of practices interacts with cognitive approaches and a specific (abductive, divergent, open) mindset (Peinado & Klose, p. 102). This encourages abstract solutions to concrete problems (Goligorsky, 2012). The DT framework is a four-stage iterative process: clarify, ideate, develop and implement (Goligorsky, 2012, Puccio *et al.*, 2010). A teacher (e.g. James) may follow these DT steps to develop student-centred TPACK in physical education – a transformational approach to pedagogy in a rapidly changing sociocultural context.

This iterative DT process begins with the 'clarify' stage, which involves using empathy to understand the client (in this case, the students' learning needs).

> Seeing learning from the student's perspective shifts attention to how learners acquire the access, skills, practices and attributes they will need to learn effectively in the digital age. (Sharpe & Beetham, 2010, p. 85)

By understanding the student's preferred learning style and ability, the teacher can move to select the digital technology which allows that student to direct the pace and level of their learning. Then, the teacher (James) applies an iterative process to move across the latter DT stages of ideating (brainstorming solutions), development (creating a model of TPACK which works) and implementation (putting model in place and evaluating efficacy of model) (Borja de Mozota & Peinado, 2013, p. 1). These steps lead to the teacher making sophisticated choices from the suite of digital technologies available. The teacher matches the digital technologies with individual learners and supports them to 'think' and to reflect on their own learning in collaborative learning spaces, for example the use of e-portfolios (reflective praxis), global classroom[3], the flipped classroom[4] or group wikis (cooperative learning). In this way, teachers can be seen as the designers of bespoke learning experiences for each student, a point highlighted in all three perspectives. This is possible because designers (teachers) are trained in observation techniques, experimentation and the continuous testing of their ideas in what are often unstable contexts, as highlighted by the sport psychology and digital humanities perspectives. Designers (teachers) are risk takers who learn how to manage uncertainty via prototyping, based on observation, user awareness and testing (Borja de Mozota & Peinado, 2013, p. 1). All three perspectives acknowledge that James exhibits these qualities coupled with empathy, integrative thinking, optimism, experimentalism and collaboration (Brown, 2008).

Conclusion

The arrival of digital technology has pushed the teaching profession to rethink pedagogy, nudging it to embrace TPACK, which is a sophisticated form of technology-infused PCK. Developing meaningful TPACK can be done using a design thinking approach, which places the student at the centre of the learning experience, encouraging students to think and to reflect through technology-infused learning experiences. In addition, the DT approach allows teachers to develop a wide repertoire of TPACK prototypes, which can be shared through an online repository. This encourages collaborative professional learning.

Practitioner reflection

It has been fascinating to read the three perspectives on my progression, not only in utilising digital technology in physical education but also on my development as a physical education teacher. As physical education teachers, we are taught to be reflective practitioners, and so it is very interesting that Orla observed how the technology and applications we are now utilising also allow the students to reflect on the active learning process. Even though I consider myself a reflective practitioner, I had not connected my own professional journey to developments in technology. This was very evident to Orla, Wesley, Gavin and Fiona. Teachers must keep up with technological developments and not to be afraid to try something if it could have a positive impact on their teaching. Orla and Gavin commented on my ability to advocate for use of technology in a cash-poor school environment. By evidencing the impact of technology on school status and learning, school management were willing to invest in a suite of technologies.

Wesley, Orla and Fiona highlighted how students need considerable teacher guidance to enable them to gain an understanding of all of the data at their disposal, as technology continues to advance and become more affordable. It is important that physical education teachers help students become critical consumers of these types of data to help inform them about how to improve and maintain levels of physical activity in school and beyond school. This in turn allows students to become more physically literate as well as digitally literate.

Each academic expert in his or her field made the point about the importance of digital integration. Wesley and Gavin made a key point when discussing the importance of building an integrated curricular approach and the integration of technology into practise in authentic physical education settings (e.g. Kinect Sensors and the recent Virtual Reality training environments). An integrated approach ensures that technology becomes an activity-led tool used to assist, enthral, engage and inspire our students.

I do believe that high quality CPD will engage physical educators and indeed help them take a few big steps to build up their confidence and proficiency in using technology in physical education settings. Fiona is right in saying that digital technology demands new approaches to teaching and learning (i.e. TPACK). Her idea of an online TPACK repository is a good one, and would allow teachers to share strategies.

When I was asked if I would be interested in participating in this chapter, I didn't feel that my journey using digital technology in physical education would warrant any more than a few hundred words, or that I would fit into any of the established research on this. However, I have been taken aback by the accuracy of the analyses from the academic experts and the amount of theory that highlights how and why these processes occur.

Lessons from the case: How can the use of digital technologies accelerate student learning in physical education?

- DT framework should be used to develop TPACK programme for teacher training across the continuum of teacher education (Teaching Council of Ireland, 2011). DT by its nature guarantees the aforementioned student-centred approach.
- In this digital age, TPACK offers a chance for students to engage in self-directed learning at their own paces and levels.
- Using digital technologies creates an opportunity for students to become more discerning about how their personal data is used and shared. In this way, they become more digitally literate in respect of physical education/physical activity data generated in and outside class.
- Sharing TPACK prototypes through an online repository could build teacher expertise.

Notes

1 The Department of Education and Skills (2015) defines *DEIS schools* as those that house students who show "the impediments to education arising from social or economic disadvantage which prevent students from deriving appropriate benefit from the education in schools" (p. 1).
2 This is where technology is considered in relation to shaping public opinion, for example.
3 Classrooms partner with other international classrooms to conduct joint projects and share their work online both synchronously and asynchronously.
4 The flipped classroom is a pedagogical model in which the typical lecture and homework elements of a course are reversed. Short video lectures are viewed by students at home before the class session, while in-class time is devoted to exercises, projects, or discussions.

References

American Psychological Association. (2016). *Sport Psychology*. Retrieved from www.apa.org/ed/graduate/specialize/sports.aspx

Armstrong, N. (1998). Young people's physical activity patterns as assessed by heart rate monitoring. *Journal of Sports Sciences, 16*, S9–S16.

Beetham, H. and Sharpe, R. (2013). *Rethinking Pedagogy for a Digital Age* (2nd ed.). London: Routledge.

Belton, S., O'Brien, W., Meegan, S., Woods, C. and Issartel, J., (2014). Youth-Physical Activity Towards Health: Evidence and background to the development of the Y-PATH physical activity intervention for adolescents. *BMC Public Health, 14*(122).

Belton, S., O'Brien, W., Wickel, E. E. and Issartel, J. (2013). Patterns of noncompliance in adolescent field-based accelerometer research. *Journal of Physical Activity and Health, 10*, 1181–1185.

Berlin, J. E., Storti, K. L. and Brach, J. S. (2006). Using activity monitors to measure physical activity in free-living conditions. *Physical Therapy*, *86*(8), 1137–1145.

Bickham, D. S., Blood, E. A., Walls, C. E., Shrier, L. A. and Rich, M. (2013). Characteristics of screen media use associated with higher BMI in young adolescents. *Pediatrics*, *13*, 935–941.

Biddle, S. J. H., Pearson, N., Ross, G. M. and Braithwaite, R. (2010). Tracking of sedentary behaviours of young people: A systematic review. *Preventive Medicine*, *51*(5), 345–351.

Blackman, T., Greene, A., Hunter, D. J., McKee, L., Elliott, E., Harrington, B., Marks, L. and Williams, G. (2006). Performance assessment and wicked problems: The case of health inequalities. *Public Policy and Administration*, *21*, 66–80.

Borja de Mozota, B. and Peinado, A. (2013). *New Approaches to Theory and Research in Art & Design Lead Educational Programs – Can "Design Thinking" Sparkle New Answers to Old Problems?* Annual Conference of the College of Art Association (CAA), New York, NY.

Bouchard, C., Blair, S. N. and Haskell, W. L. (2007). *Physical Activity and Health*. Champaign, IL: Human Kinetics.

Breslin, G., Hodges, N. J. and Williams, A. M. (2009). Effect of information load and time on observational learning. *Research Quarterly for Exercise and Sport*, *80*(3), 1–12.

Brown, T. (2008). Design thinking. *Harvard Business Review*, *86*, 84.

Brown, T. and Martin, R. (2015). Design for action: How to use design thinking to make great things actually happen. *Harvard Business Review*, *93*, 56–64.

Buchanan, R. (1992). Wicked problems in design thinking: Design issues. *The MIT Press*, *8*, 5–21.

Caspersen, C. J., Powell, K. E. and Christenson, G. M. (1985). Physical activity, exercise, and physical fitness: Definitions and distinctions for health-related research. *Public Health Reports*, *100*(2), 126–131.

Cerejo, J. and Barbosa, A. (2012). *The Application of Design Thinking Methodology on Research Practices: A Mind-Map of Tools and Method*. Proceedings of the 62nd Annual Conference of the International Council for Education Media on Design Thinking in Education, Media, and Society; 26-29, September 2012, Nicosia, Cyprus.

Chen, Y. H. and Jang, S. J. (2014). Interrelationship between stages of concern and technological, pedagogical, and content knowledge: A study on Taiwanese senior high school in-service teachers. *Computers in Human Behaviour*, *32*, 79–91.

Dale, D., Welk, G. J. and Matthews, C. E. (2002). Methods for assessing physical activity and challenges for research. In G. J. Welk, ed., *Physical Activity Assessments for Health-related Research*. Champaign, IL: Human Kinetics. pp. 19–34.

Devitt, F. (2014). *Design Thinking. Industrial Research and Development Group*. Dublin: Leopardstown.

De Vries, S. I., Engels, M. and Garre, F. G. (2011). Identification of children's activity type with accelerometer-based neural networks. *Medicine and Science in Sports and Exercise*, *43*(10), 1994–1999.

Dweck, C. S. (2012). *Mindset: How You Can Fulfill Your Potential*. London: Constable & Robinson.

Dweck, C. S. (2006). *Mindset: The New Psychology of Success*. New York: Random House.

Eaves, D. L., Breslin. G., Schaik, P. V., Robinson, E. and Spears, I. R. (2011). The short-term effects of real-time virtual reality feedback on motor learning in dance. *Presence*, *20*, 1.

Freedson, P., Pober, D. and Janz, K. F. (2005). Calibration of accelerometer output for children. *Medicine & Science in Sports & Exercise*, *37*, S523–S530.

Gold, M. K. (2012). *Debates in the Digital Humanities*. Minneapolis, MN: University of Minnesota Press.

Goligorsky, D. (2012). *Empathy and Innovation: The IDEO Approach*. Boston: Harvard Business School.

Gould, D., Hodge, K., Peterson, K. and Giannini, J. (1989). An exploratory examination of strategies used by elite coaches to enhance self-efficacy in athletes. *Journal of Sport & Exercise Psychology*, *11*, 128–140.

Hands, B., Parker, H. and Larkin, D. (2006). Physical activity measurement methods for young children: A comparative study. *Measurement in Physical Education and Exercise Science*, *10*(3), 203–214.

Harrington, D. M., Belton S., Coppinger T., Cullen, M., Donnelly, A., Dowd, K., Keating, T., Layte, R., Murphy, M., Murphy, N., Murtagh, E. and Woods, C. (2014). Results from Ireland's 2014 Report Card on Physical Activity in Children and Youth. *Journal of Physical Activity and Health*, *11*(Suppl.1), S63–S68.

Hassi, L. and Laakso, M. (2011). *Conceptions of Design Thinking in the Design and Management Discourses: Open Questions and Possible Directions for Research*. IASDR – 4th World Conference on Design Research. Delft, The Netherlands.

Hayles, N. K. (2012). *How We Think: Digital Media and Contemporary Technogenesis*. Chicago: University of Chicago Press.

Hibberson, S., Barrett, E. and Davies, S. (2015). *Developing Students' Digital Literacy*. JISC. Retrieved from www.jisc.ac.uk/guides/developing-students-digital-literacy

Hodges, N. J. and Williams, A. M. (2012). *Skill Acquisition in Sport: Research Theory and Practice* (2nd ed.). London: Routledge.

Hodges, N. J., Williams, A. M., Hayes, S. and Breslin, G. (2007). What is modelled during observational learning? *Journal of Sports Science*, *25*(5), 531–545.

Jonides, J., Lewis, R. L., Nee, D. E., Lustig, C. A., Berman, M. G. and Sledge Moore, K. (2013). The mind and brain of short-term memory. *Annual Review Psychology*, *59*, 193–224.

Kimm, S. Y., Glynn, N. W., Kriska, A. M., Fitzgerald, S. L., Aaron, D. J., Similo, S. L., *et al.* (2000). Longitudinal changes in physical activity in a biracial cohort during adolescence. *Medicine & Science in Sports & Exercise*, *32*(8), 1445–1454.

Koehler, M. J. and Mishra, P. (2009). What is technological pedagogical content knowledge? *Contemporary Issues in Technology and Teacher Education*, *9*(1), 60–70.

Koehler, M. J. and Mishra, P. (2005). What happens when teachers design educational technology? The development of technological pedagogical content knowledge. *Journal of Educational Computing Research*, *32*(2).

Kohl, H. W., Fulton, J. E. and Caspersen, C. J. (2000). Assessment of physical activity among children and adolescents: A review and synthesis. *Preventive Medicine*, *31*(2), S54–S76.

Laurillard, D. (2013). Foreword to the first edition. In H. Beetham and R. Sharpe, eds., *Rethinking Pedagogy for a Digital Age*. London: Routledge.

Lovett, M. K. (2008). 'Creative Intervention Through Video Action Research and Pedagogy'. University of Illinois Urbana – Champaign. Proquest.

McKenzie, T. L. and van der Mars, H. (2015). Top 10 research questions related to assessing physical activity and its contexts using systematic observation. *Research Quarterly for Exercise and Sport*, *86*(1), 13–29.

McNicol, S., Lewin, C., Keune, A. and Toikkanen, T. (2014). *Facilitating Student Reflection Through Digital Technologies in the iTEC Project: Pedagogically Led Change in the Classroom*. First International Conference, LCT 2014, Held as Part of HCI International 2014, Heraklion, Crete, Greece, June 22-27, 2014, Proceedings, Part II.

Muratori, L. M., Lamberg, E. M., Quinn, L. and Duff, S. V. (2013). Applying principles of motor learning and control to upper extremity rehabilitation. *Journal of Hand Therapy*, *26*(2), 94–103.

Murphy, S. L. (2009). Review of physical activity measurement using accelerometers in older adults: Considerations for research design and conduct. *Preventive Medicine, 48*(2), 108–114.

O'Brien, W., Belton, S. and Issartel, J. (2015). Fundamental movement skill proficiency amongst adolescent youth. *Physical Education and Sport Pedagogy*, iFirst Article.

O'Brien, W., Issartel, J. and Belton, S. (2013). Evidence for the efficacy of the Youth-Physical Activity Towards Health (Y-PATH) intervention. *Advances in Physical Education, 3*(4), 145–153.

O'Donovan, G., Blazevich, A. J., Boreham, C., Cooper, A. R., Crank, H., Ekelund, U., Fox, K.R., Gately, P., Giles-Corti, B., Gill, J.M.R., Hamer, M., McDermot I., Murphy, M., Mutrie, N., Reilly, J.J., Saxton, J.M. and Stamatakis, E. (2010). The ABC of physical activity for health: A consensus statement from the British Association of Sport and Exercise Sciences. *Journal of Sports Sciences, 28*(6), 573–591.

Oliver, M., Duncan, S., Kuch, C., McPhee, J. and Schofield, G. (2012). Prevalence of New Zealand children and adolescents achieving current physical activity and television watching recommendations. *Journal of Physical Activity & Health, 9*(2), 173–187.

Organisation for Economic Cooperation and Development (OECD). (2015). *Students, Computers and Learning: Making the Connection.* Paris: OECD.

Ortega, F. B., Konstabel, K., Pasquali, E., Ruiz, J. R., Hurtig-Wennlöf, A., Mäestu, J., Löf, M., Harro, J., Bellocco, R., Labayen, I., Veidebaum, T. and Sjöström, M. (2013). Objectively measured physical activity and sedentary time during childhood, adolescence and young adulthood: A cohort study. *PLoS One, 8*(4), 1–8.

Peinado, A. D. and Klose, S. (2011). *Design Innovation: Research-Practice-Strategy, Symposium Proceedings: Researching Design Education.* First International Symposium for Design Education Researchers. Cumulus Association/DRS. SIG on Design Pedagogy. Paris, France, May 18–21, 2011, pp. 97–111.

Prensky, M. (2001). Digital natives, digital immigrants: Part 1. *On the Horizon, 9*(5), 1–6.

Puccio, G. J., Mance, M. and Murdoch, M. C. (2010). *Creative Leadership Skills That Drive Change.* Woburn: Sage.

Puyau, M. R., Adolph, A. L., Vohra, F. A. and Butte, N. F. (2002). Validation and calibration of physical activity monitors in children. *Obesity Research, 10*(3), pp.150–157.

Rey-López, J. P., Vicente-Rodríguez, G., Biosca, M. and Moreno, L. A. (2008). Sedentary behaviour and obesity development in children and adolescents. *Nutrition, Metabolism, and Cardiovascular Diseases, 18*(3), 242–251.

Rowlands, A. V. and Eston, R. G. (2005). Comparison of accelerometer and pedometer measures of physical activity in boys and girls, ages 8–10 years. *Research Quarterly for Exercise and Sport, 76*(3), 251–257.

Scott, J. J., Morgan P. J., Plotnikoff, R. C. and Lubans, D. R. (2015). Reliability and validity of a single-item physical activity measure for adolescents. *Journal of Paediatrics and Child Health, 51*, 787–793.

Sharpe, R. and Beetham, H. (2010). Understanding students' uses of technology for learning: Towards creative appropriation. In R. Sharpe, R. H. Beetham and S. De Freitas, eds., *Rethinking Learning for a Digital Age: How Learners Are Shaping Their Own Experiences.* London: Routledge. pp. 85–99.

Shulman, L. S. (2007). Counting and Recounting: Assessment and the Quest for Accountability, *Change: The Magazine of Higher Learning*, 39:1, 20-25, DOI: 10.3200/CHNG.39.1.20-25.

Slootmaker, S. M., Chinapaw, M. J. M., Seidell, J. C., van Mechelen, W. and Schuit, A. J. (2010). Accelerometers and Internet for physical activity promotion in youth? Feasibility and effectiveness of a minimal intervention. *Preventive Medicine, 51*(1), 31–36.

Smith, L., Fisher, A. and Hamer, M. (2015). Prospective association between objective measures of childhood motor coordination and sedentary behaviour in adolescence and adulthood. *International Journal of Behavioural Nutrition and Physical Activity*, *12*(75), 1–6.

Spiro, L. (2012). This is why we fight: Defining the values of the digital humanities. In Gold, M. K., ed., *Debates in the Digital Humanities*. Minneapolis, MN: University of Minnesota Press.

Svennson, P. (2010). The landscape of digital humanities. *Digital Humanities Quarterly*, *4*(1), 1–179.

Teaching Council of Ireland. (2011). *Policy on the Continuum of Teacher Education*. Maynooth: Teaching Council of Ireland.

Thompson, A. and Mishra, P. (2007). Breaking news: TPCK becomes TPACK! *Journal of Computing in Teacher Education*, *24*(2), 38–64.

Tomei, L. A. (2005). *Taxonomy for the Technology Domain*. London: Idea Group, Inc. (IGI).

Tremblay, M. S., Gonzalez, S. A., Katzmarzyk, P. T., Onywera, V. O., Reilly, J. J. and Tomkinson, G. (2015). Physical activity report cards: Active healthy kids global alliance and the Lancet physical activity observatory. *Journal of Physical Activity and Health*, *12*, 297–298.

Troiano, R. P., Berrigan, D., Dodd, K. W., Mâsse, L. C., Tilert, T. and McDowell, M. (2008). Physical activity in the United States measured by accelerometer. *Medicine and Science in Sports and Exercise*, *40*(1), 181–188.

Trost, S. G. (2007). State of the art reviews: Measurement of physical activity in children and adolescents. *American Journal of Lifestyle Medicine*, *1*(4), 299–314.

Trost, S. G., McIver, K. L. and Pate, R. R. (2005). Conducting accelerometer-based activity assessments in field-based research. *Medicine and Science in Sports and Exercise*, *37*(Suppl. 11), S531–S543.

Ward, D. S., Saunders, R. P. and Pate, R. R. (2007). *Physical Activity Interventions in Children and Adolescents*. Champaign, IL: Human Kinetics.

Weinberg, R. and Jackson, A. (1990). Building self-efficacy in tennis players: A coach's perspective. *Journal of Applied Sport Psychology*, *2*, 164–174.

5

BEATRICE: DANCE VIDEO GAMES AS A RESOURCE FOR TEACHING DANCE

Mikael Quennerstedt, Béatrice Gibbs, Jonas Almqvist, Johnny Nilsson and Helle Winther

CHAPTER OVERVIEW

Video games are sometimes used in school physical education in order to fulfil the goals for dance in the Swedish national curriculum. This can be interesting as a way for teachers to teach dance, particularly if the teacher is busy just showing the dance and thus missing the actual teaching. In the chapter, researchers specialising in dance pedagogy, physical education, movement analysis and the use of artefacts in education together discuss this pedagogical case.

Practitioner narrative (Béatrice Gibbs)

I am a physical education teacher and teach students age 15–19 in Sweden. At my school we teach a theme called *dance and movements to music*. However, many of my colleagues often find it difficult to teach dance and worry about whether they will remember all the steps or whether they will just come naturally into the rhythm of the dance. I teach dancing a lot, and wanted to help my colleagues. This resulted in the decision to test dance video games as a technological resource for teaching dance.

Dance video games work in different ways, but, in the ones I use, a digitally animated dancer – called an *avatar* – demonstrates the dance on screen, and the players are expected to follow to the best of their ability (Figure 5.1).

For pedagogical use in physical education, I created a lesson plan of seven lessons using dance video games as a teaching tool. The games include several different songs with different levels of difficulty, and the idea was that the students would work with dance and movements to music, and in that way develop their abilities by creating, expressing and shaping moves to music. The goal was for students to

FIGURE 5.1 Students watching and responding to the dance video game (Gibbs, 2014).

assemble moves, find rhythm, understand how a song was composed and how different aesthetic effects of a dance could be generated. This was a way of preparing them for the final goal to create their own dances in groups and perform them.

In the first four lessons, the twenty-seven students in the class stood in front of the video screen watching the game, and I instructed them to follow the moves of the avatar as closely as they could. They also got different tasks to solve by using the game. I decided not to use any hand controls so that the students would be free to move their entire bodies. I also wanted to avoid the potential limitation of collecting points in the game. In the following two lessons they worked on creating their own dances in groups, and in the last lesson they performed the dances.

How did I proceed? The students were standing in front of the game and tried to imitate the moves of the avatar to the best of their abilities. The activity level was high, they were laughing a lot and they wanted to do more dances. After the very first dance game activity, I demonstrated some of the moves specific to that dance, and they followed me and practised the moves to the count of eight. When they repeated the same dance in front of the screen, it was clear that they could all move accurately to the eight beats we had practised. After another dance display, I told the students to pair up with the person standing next to them and show one particular move from the dance they had just performed. The task was then to assemble the two moves they had chosen to the count of eight and practise them together. In this pair work, the students enthusiastically tried to 'teach' the others 'their' move while discussing how to combine them. While they talked and taught each other, I had the opportunity to circulate and help the pairs that needed it. When they danced the same dance again, I could see that they improved regarding the specific move they have practised in the pairs. The students worked in a similar way in different group constellations with several of the dances in the game. It became clear that by imitating, repeating and practicing the moves, the students gradually learned the moves and sequences of the dance being demonstrated. The idea of having students try out several different dances and encounter different kinds of dance moves was that it would facilitate the creation of their own dances.

Another way of working with the game was to find the rhythm in the songs by clapping our hands to the beat. The students then worked in groups to discover other ways of moving to rhythm and using other parts of the body to feel the beat. This was a way to help them find the beat in different songs. I also showed them how music could be structured and how moves could be adapted to this construction. The students were then divided into two groups. One group danced while the other group watched and took notes. They wrote down when the chorus and verse appeared and which moves the avatar performed in these situations. When the song was played again they switched roles. Afterwards, and in groups of four, they compared notes while I walked around the room and listened to how they had understood the construction of the music. I then explained how the chorus, verses and moves were repeated several times, and that this is important when choreographing and combining moves to music in terms of that moves can be repeated, for example, in each chorus. This was a way of helping them to understand the song they have chosen and facilitate the creation part of the lessons. They also got the opportunity to listen to their own selected song, and I circulated between the groups and helped them out.

An additional way of using the game and preparing them for creating a dance was to show how individuals in a group can organise themselves in relation to each other, so as to create different effects in a dance. I used dances in the games in which two or four avatars were involved. When they danced in pairs there was much laughter, as they were able to dance around and with each other. We talked about what was possible when dancing in pairs compared to dancing alone. The students suggested that they could walk around and hold onto each other. They also danced in groups of four to several different songs. We talked about how individuals in a group could create effects in a dance by working together. The proposals that emerged from the students were to work in canon, two and two, solo and holding on to each other in different ways. This helped the students to realise how they could organise themselves and utilise one another in their own dances.

During the final two lessons, they had the opportunity to use what I had presented to them in the earlier four lessons. The dance games were available, and several groups chose to watch and try out different dances as a way of finding inspiration for their own creation. All groups spread out around the room and used their mobile phones to play their own selected songs. They practised and interacted with one another in order to find the relevant moves and thus solve the final assignment. During these two lessons, the creativity in the groups was obvious, and I could see that they created and combined moves and helped one another in different ways. Some students instructed moves they had created on their own at home to their group members who mimicked the moves. Some others created movement sequences by trying out different moves and putting them together. Some helped each other out by creating stories about every step as a way to remember the steps. Again, I was able to walk around the room and support the groups in different ways by trying to help them move forward in their creative process. In the final lesson, all the groups performed their own dances in front of their classmates.

Finally, what did I discover using dance video games? I realised that, instead of standing in front of the students and teaching a dance at the same time as keeping the beat and remembering the steps, I was able to stand back and observe the students' abilities and how they developed different movements. As a consequence, I could leave the instructor role to the avatar in the game and instead take a more observing and teaching role. While the avatar showed the moves, I could observe my students' movements. Between the dances I could demonstrate different moves that we could practise together, or support students when they practised the moves by themselves. I also realised that the students helped each other out in different ways, both when solving tasks, remembering moves and when creating moves on their own. Among other things, they instructed each other and created stories about each move as a way to remember movement sequences. I could also see that the students learned a lot of movements by imitating, repeating and practising the moves of the avatar. Finally, what became obvious was how involved and active the students were, especially when dancing to the game. What I have shown is that dance video games can be used as tools to demonstrate dances and thereby help teachers to teach dance in physical education.

A dance education perspective (Helle Winther)

For many years I have taught dance and have educated generations of physical education teachers in the art of dancing. I honestly admit that I was somewhat hesitant when I first heard about the use of video games to teach dance. What was the point of playing video games in physical education? What role could they possibly play in education? However, my horizon quickly expanded by Béatrice's pedagogical intervention, which clearly demonstrates that a dance video game can motivate pupils and engage them in the activity.

I would argue that everyone can dance (cf. Sorell, 1986; Laban, 1971; Winther *et al.*, 2015). Children have rhythm in their bodies, and often express themselves musically, even before they can walk. People have danced since the beginning of time, and dance is a form of movement that arguably has both universal and existential qualities (Winther, 2009; Winther *et al.*, 2015). At the same time, dance is closely connected to culture, history and genres of music. Our bodies can be seen as lived bodies, and people express themselves through dance in both conformity with and in dialogue with the tendencies of the surrounding society (Kassing, 2007; Merleau-Ponty 1962/2004; Winther *et al.*, 2015).

In contrast to so many other sporting activities, dance is a phenomenon that is constantly evolving. It involves creativity, expressivity, communication, gender and sensuousness (Kassing, 2007; Winther, 2009; Winther *et al.*, 2015). In relation to this, a dance video game has its own youthful-body cultural expression, which many teachers may find difficult to match. This is also what Béatrice's lesson design sets the stage for. If dance is organised in a way that reflects children's playful energy and matches their level of ability, a whole world of opportunities can unfold. At the same time, all these opportunities in the world of dance can be a challenge for many physical education teachers.

Lundvall and Meckbach's (2008) research shows that it seems as many physical education teachers experience a greater attention to their own bodies and movements while dancing. They feel that they are more focused on doing the dance than on the actual teaching of it. As a consequence, some teachers deliberately limit their teaching in dance (Lundvall & Meckbach, 2008). This insecurity and the feeling of enlargement could be due to the fact that teachers experience the bodily skills required for dance as challenging, even though various teaching methods and approaches could improve the learning and liberate the teacher from having to show all movements (cf. Russell-Bowie, 2013).

Nevertheless, in dance, there is a long tradition of the teacher being a role model. In this form of teaching, the teacher demonstrates how to do the dance and the participants observe and imitate the moves. However, teaching in this way requires the teacher to have mastered the art of dancing. The demonstrations must be precise, every move must be repeated several times and the movements must be chosen in accordance with the participants' abilities (Winther *et al.*, 2015).

This teaching role can be very motivating for pupils, because the teacher has the opportunity to express the joy of dancing and demonstrate bodily competencies with his or her own body, which the pupils can then learn from (Winther *et al.*, 2015). On the other hand, this role can also be challenging. It is therefore important to practise bodily confidence and the movement competencies that are required to demonstrate dance during teacher education. At the same time, a teacher can have other roles and make use of improvisatory teaching methods that appeal to pupils' imagination. These methods have a long history in dance education (H'Doubler, 1925; Green, 2010; Laban, 1971; McCutchen, 2006; Sprague *et al.*, 2006).

Using video games in physical education helps us to develop these methods further and at the same time accommodate the "follow me" model and address the bodily insecurities of the teacher. In a study of the use of video games for teaching dance, Gibbs (2014) states:

> When the dance game is used as an instructor, the learning takes place by the students imitating, repeating, and communicating with their bodies. The students imitate the movements of the avatar and thereafter repeat them every time they are shown. (p. 135)

In the dance games, the *avatar* takes over the task of demonstrating, which leaves the teacher free to take on another role, and, as Gibbs says, "*teach*". When the teacher is able to hand over the instruction to a video game, he or she is free to employ other teaching roles. Thus, Béatrice applies two other teacher roles, which, in the pedagogy of dance, are called the *animator* and the *advisor* or the *coach* (Winther *et al.*, 2015). The *animator* animates and initiates. The role of the animator is often used in improvisation, task-solving exercises and games in which the participants' own movements form the material. The animator organises the lesson in such a way that the scope of the participants' creativity expands as the class progresses. The animator gives the participants physical space and is therefore not in as central a position as for example "the instructor".

The role of the *coach* is employed when the participants work in groups with their own projects. Here, the most important task of the teacher is to encourage, to step back and nourish independence (Sprague *et al.*, 2006). It is important that the coach agrees with and does not stand in the way of the participants' ideas, supporting the participants' initiatives (Winther *et al.*, 2015; Sprague *et al.*, 2006).

The dance video game is an example of task-based, problem-solving teaching using the roles of animator and coach. However, this does not mean that the dance game can or should replace the teacher's professional dance competencies. Rather, teachers need to bring their movement competencies into the pedagogical dialogue with the dance game. The attentive reader will have noticed how Béatrice's pronounced professional movement competencies came to light in the case she presented. This is exactly why she is capable of *teaching*, and, with great authenticity, taking on the role of both animator and coach.

Dance is and will always be connected to the living moment (Engel *et al.*, 2006; Green, 2010). The teacher, with or without a dance game, is responsible for the development that education in movement initiates – a development that could continue well into the future (McCutchen, 2006).

A use of artefacts in education perspective (Jonas Almqvist)

In this section, I will discuss the use of video games to teach dance from the perspective of using artefacts in education. I will also critically touch on an excessive optimism regarding technology in education.

In the description of her teaching practice, Béatrice highlights the possibility of using artefacts to solve a problem in teaching, and, in doing so, describes a dilemma that many teachers face. The Swedish curriculum for physical education states that teachers should teach dance. However, the problem that she addresses in her educational case is that many of her colleagues think that teaching dance is difficult and: "worry about whether they will remember all the steps or whether they will just come naturally into the rhythm of the dance".

In order to solve this problem, Béatrice uses the video game – an artefact – as a teaching assistant. She creates a lesson plan in which the students are expected to learn to dance and to create their own dance routines together in groups. In the described practice, Béatrice not only uses a video game to teach dance moves but also – and this is important to note – creates the lesson plan, instructs the students how to act, gives them different tasks, shows them dance moves, supports them and gives them feedback. She is thus active in her teaching, and only uses the artefact as a teaching aid to solve a certain problem.

Using artefacts to solve a teaching problem is nothing new. The history of education is full of different expectations and optimistic attempts to complement – and sometimes replace – teachers' teaching with artefacts (Cuban, 1986; Ellington *et al.*, 1993; Koschmann, 1996). The use of books, TV, radio, pencils, whiteboards, smartboards and so on are examples of this. There is also a growing body of development projects and research on the use of artefacts in physical education, such as video games or balls (cf. Quennerstedt, Almqvist, & Öhman, 2012; Quennerstedt, Almqvist, Meckbach, & Öhman, 2013).

A central aspect of Béatrice's pedagogical narrative is that she designs the educational setting and uses the artefact as a tool in the setting. She does not expect the artefact to solve the problem on its own. In the planning of her teaching, she then *privileges* a certain content and specific ways of working, and uses the artefact as a means to an end (cf. Almqvist & Östman, 2006; Wertsch, 1998). Béatrice describes how the video games were used as tools and how she was able to stand back and observe the students, how they worked in groups and also how they developed different movements. As a result, Béatrice acted as the teacher and not only as instructor.

Using an artefact as a teaching assistant thus has specific consequences for communication and learning (cf. Säljö, 1999). However, it is also important to note that artefacts can be used in many different ways and that a specific use may have certain desired – or undesired – implications for learning and socialisation (cf. Almqvist, 2005; Quennerstedt *et al.*, 2012). In the case explored in this chapter, the teacher could have been replaced by the artefact, but was not. Rather, Béatrice's ambition is to create a lesson plan and to harness the artefact in order to teach dance. If the video game had been used in a more competitive situation, the users would probably have aimed for high scores rather than learning to dance, although, as Béatrice decided against using hand controls while dancing, she excluded this way of using the game. This contributes to the constitution of the video game as a teaching assistant in the practice described (Almqvist, 2005).

Using artefacts in different ways, for various reasons and with different consequences for teaching and learning constitutes their meaning. This is emphasised in recent research on the design, implementation and use of technology, where the role of the user in the development of artefacts is in focus (Oudshoorn & Pinch, 2005). Here, the use of artefacts is not determined beforehand, as it often is supposed to be. Instead, the different expectations and ways of interpreting and using the artefacts are contingent and constituted in practice (Almqvist, 2005; Bijker & Law, 1994). Privileging between alternatives means that the use of artefacts is far from value free, and that the problems they are supposed to solve are not necessarily those that should be privileged (cf. Feenberg, 1999; Öhman *et al.*, 2014).

In the illustrated case, dance instruction is delegated to the video game in order to facilitate the inclusion of an educational content that is sometimes excluded from physical education. However, all the teaching is not delegated. In contrast to expectations often expressed in history about the use of artefacts as replacements for teachers (Cuban, 1986), Béatrice uses it as a teaching resource while she keeps the role as responsible for teaching.

Another point can be made here concerning the relevance of using artefacts in a specific practice. In the pedagogical case, the specific use of exergames is fully relevant and can facilitate the teaching of dance. It is relevant because dancing in physical education is considered to be relevant, reasonable and valuable. In another practice – for example in science education – this way of using the artefact would perhaps be odd, irrelevant and not a valuable thing to do (cf. Almqvist & Quennerstedt, 2015).

Using artefacts in teaching may be relevant and very worthwhile, although, in order to use them in relevant, reasonable and valuable ways, teachers need to privilege their educational content and ways of working with artefacts (Wertsch, 1998). In fact, privileging may be seen as one of the most central parts of the teaching profession. The lesson plan created by Béatrice is a good example of this.

A movement analysis and physiological perspective (Johnny Nilsson)

From my point of view, I think that at least two general perspectives can be applied to dance in schools: a socio-cultural and an existentialistic perspective. In the first perspective, dance is used to reach certain external goals, such as mediating a specific culture and components of social behaviour. The movements in the different dances are predetermined in pattern and form. Thus, dances should be performed in a certain way, and the students learning should be evaluated using the *know what* and *know how* concepts (Amade-Escot, 2006; Ryle, 1949/2009). Students are examined on how well they can imitate predetermined dance forms. Furthermore, the aim in dance education could be to learn dance moves requiring specific motor skills, such as rotating around the longitudinal body axis combined with learning the biomechanics of spin. Student are then examined to determine how well they perform the movements and whether they can explain why a movement is performed well with regard to biomechanical cause relations (i.e. *know why* from a biomechanical perspective) (see Wilson & Kwon, 2008).

However, in the second perspective, dance in school can also be performed without predetermined movement forms and where the creativity of the students with regard to body, space, rhythm and character is encouraged. The general aim of this form of dance is existentialistic, where dance performance is perceived as rewarding per se and does not need to be evaluated (Winther *et al.*, 2015).

In dances with a predetermined form and movement pattern, the way in which they are performed can be evaluated on the basis of how well the dance moves are done in comparison to an ideal model. In addition, a biomechanical analysis can be performed that evaluates how well the students integrate the biomechanical solutions of the movement requirements in the dance (Wilson & Kwon 2008). This analysis can be a main goal of the physical education teacher in the continuous guiding of the students in the training and development of their dance moves, but it can also be a part of the students' learning outcomes (Mattsson & Lundvall, 2013). It is reasonable to expect that students aiming for higher marks will be able to explain why a certain movement works better with a certain biomechanical solution. By using movement analysis charts, the students can be trained to systematically observe and analyse certain moves in a dance performance (Gibbs, 2014; Laban, 1988; Lees, 2002; Logsdon, 1977). If the dances are recorded with a video camera, the students can then use video analysis software to analyse frame by frame how certain dance moves are performed from a technical and biomechanical point of view. In this way, it is also possible to integrate science into physical education (Hartsell & Yuen, 2006).

Movement analysis in combination with biomechanics is important in order to understand technically demanding dance moves. Let us assume, for example, that during a jump in a dance sequence, a student has to rotate his or her body 360 degrees around the longitudinal body axis and land on the same spot; he or she has to be aware of several biomechanical principles, such as angular momentum, inertia and direction of force. These principles form the basis of the movement analysis (Carr, 1997). It is my belief that movement analysis allows the student to carefully evaluate the technique from a biomechanical point of view.

However, it has been concluded in many investigations that the time devoted to physical education is limited (Nilsson, 2007). Thus, the time allowed in lessons to accomplish the expected learning outcome in the curriculum is short, which emphasises the need to combine the training of several capacities. Thus, in addition to learning the technical aspects of movement technique, other capacities can also be emphasised in dance education, such as strength and aerobic training (Nilsson, 1998; Nilsson & Fredriksson, 2015).

Using an artefact that the students can imitate in order to learn to dance allows the teacher to move freely around the classroom and instruct each student in movement analysis and fitness training. It also allows the teacher to control aspects like muscle strength, aerobic endurance and dance technique (Hodges Kulinna et al., 2003; Gibbs, 2014; Koutedakis et al., 2008).

Further, a dance lesson is often organised in an intermittent way that includes periods of work and rest. During the work periods, short instructions can be given, and during the rest periods, the teacher can provide detailed individual instructions and/or address the class as a whole (see Figure 5.2).

Note that the heart rate increases during the work periods when the student performs the dance interspersed with rest periods that also allow time for specific longer instructions that cannot be transmitted during the dance intervals. The grey zone represents a relative heart rate range between 84–89 per cent of maximum heart rate, which is enough to induce improvement of the maximum oxygen uptake (Branch et al., 2000; Nevill et al., 2003; Nilsson, 1998; Swain & Franklin, 2002).

Aerobic training can then easily be evaluated by recording the heart rate (Figure 5.2). Nowadays, several so-called team systems allow an entire class of students to monitor their heart rates simultaneously, which both during and after the dance

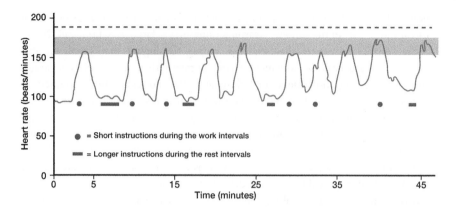

FIGURE 5.2 The recorded heart rate of a typical student during a dance class organised in an intermittent way (adapted from Nilsson, 2008).

class can be summarised by means of computer software giving individual and average reports. This allows the teacher to integrate exercise physiology into the education, which permits students to better understand what kind of training effects can be achieved during dance. The training of muscle strength can also be included in dance by choosing certain moves. For example, extensive lunges will put a heavy load on the knee and hip extensor muscles, and the analysis of the strength component can be integrated into the movement technique analysis chart (Bompa, 1999).

In short, a well-designed dance class can contribute to dance technique training and dance experience, including the training of strength and aerobic endurance. It can also incorporate a theoretical knowledge of biomechanics and physiology. Using artefacts for imitation purposes allows the teacher to focus on individual and collective instructions, instead of being restricted to the object of imitation.

A pedagogical perspective (Mikael Quennerstedt)

The case in this chapter illuminates many things about using pedagogies of technology in a school subject like physical education. To structure the section, I have used what in many European countries is referred to as the *didactic triangle*. In both research and practice, the didactic triangle is a way of understanding and discussing education as the relation between teacher/teaching, student/learning and subject matter (cf. Hudson & Meyer, 2011; Quennerstedt & Larsson, 2015). An important argument in this perspective is that education is always regarded as a relation between all three aspects of the triangle, which are understood in relation to each other. Questions that are often addressed include:

> *what, how* and *why*, in terms of what and how teachers teach, what and how students learn and why this content or teaching is taught or learned. Questions

such as *who* is teaching, *who* is learning, *when*, and *with whom* are also relevant. (Quennerstedt & Larsson, 2015, p. 567)

Further, teaching is never seen to occur in a void, but is always understood in relation to its institutional, cultural and historical context. In this sense, teaching is both a political and moral act imbued with constant choices made in practice.

Putting the *teacher and teaching* in the foreground in the didactic triangle involves considering the different choices of content and form that teachers make. In the illustrated case, and also in the three different perspectives presented in the chapter, it is obvious that the dance game is used by Béatrice as a teaching resource and a way of helping her as a physical education teacher to teach. She uses the game as an instructor, a source of inspiration and a resource for students to use when creating their own dances. The game is thus a teaching resource – not the teacher. She delegates what, from a dance education perspective, can be called the 'follow me' model. This allows her to focus on teaching dance. By adopting the role of 'animator' and 'coach' (Winther *et al.*, 2015), she is free to assume a more pedagogical role of focusing on and observing students' abilities, supporting their creativity, enhancing group work and helping them with their communication. Thus, by using a teaching aid like a dance video game, a teacher can create pedagogical situations that help students to learn and guide them in relation to the subject matter in question.

However, as indicated in the chapter, this requires a competence to teach, for example, by creating lesson plans, choosing the relevant subject matter, instructing the students how to act, giving them tasks, showing them dance moves, analysing the moves from the perspective of dance and biomechanics, giving support and giving feedback. In other words, the teacher needs to be competent in teaching and not simply settling with the game doing all the work.

When *learning and the student* are foregrounded the interest lies in understanding what and how students learn in the practice of physical education. When new technology is introduced in physical education, teachers need to ask themselves what they want the students to learn (Almqvist & Östman, 2006; Quennerstedt *et al.*, 2012). For example, is the aim to learn different movement qualities, a particular dance, rhythm, dance moves, creativity, biomechanical or physiological principles?

To start to unpack these questions in terms of pedagogies of technology, teachers have to be clear about what they want students to learn. In the illustrated pedagogical case, the explicit goal that Béatrice guides the students towards is to

develop their abilities by creating, expressing and shaping moves to music. The goal was for students to assemble moves, find rhythm, understand how a song was composed, and how different aesthetic effects of a dance could be generated.

Here we can see that she is clear about what the students should learn, and that she intends to use the video game in a pedagogical way for this purpose. The next obvious question is, of course, how teachers, or, for that matter, researchers know whether students have learned anything of what was intended.

Looking at the case, Béatrice as a teacher does everything she can to take the direction of student learning into account and support her students' learning in the best possible way (cf. Amade-Escot, 2006). When she delegates the showing and instructing of the dance to the video game, and thereby makes use of the 'follow me' model, she is free to use her teaching skills to create meaningful learning experiences for the students. She can also take a step back, observe the learning that is taking place and continuously assess whether the trajectories of learning are progressing as expected or whether she as teacher should create new tasks, support, redirect, initiate or reorganise the ongoing learning processes (Hay & Penney, 2012; Tolgfors & Öhman, 2015).

In this way, teachers can use their analytical competences both in dance and in movement analysis to create supportive learning environments in physical education (cf. Gibbs, 2014; Lees, 2002). Teachers can also observe and analyse the learning processes that are taking place. It is important to understand not only *what* students learn but also *how* they learn when interacting with the dance game and with each other (Quennerstedt & Larsson, 2015). It is imperative to acknowledge that learning is a complex business and something that teachers should be experts at (Biesta, 2015; Priestly *et al.*, 2015; Quennerstedt *et al.*, 2014). Students learn many things in physical education, including the intended and unintended, and, as the chapter highlights, can potentially learn everything from dance moves to biomechanical concepts. An additional important benefit of the educational processes that are taking place is that students can combine physical training and strength training while learning dance (Nilsson, 2007; 1998).

Looking at the case from the perspective of the *subject matter* in the didactic triangle, it is important to reflect on why this particular content is taught or learned. There are of course significant differences between countries as to whether dance is part of physical education (cf. Hardman & Green, 2011). Other differences are what dance becomes in the context of physical education in the different countries – an activity, a cultural form, a form of exercise or an aesthetic practice and expression (cf. Engel *et al.*, 2006, Mattsson & Lundvall, 2013). According to Mattsson and Lundvall (2013), in Sweden dance has been an important part of the curriculum in terms of its relation to the reconstruction and understanding of cultural traditions, issues of public health and the expression of emotions through movement. The way in which dance video games are used in the case highlighted in this chapter reflects the understanding of dance as an expression of different cultures, of learning different ways of moving to music and of expressing the body in different ways. In this example, a dance video game can fulfil its role in terms of pedagogies of technology (Gibbs, 2014).

It is important to point out that from a didactical point of view, the teaching of subject matter is always inscribed in the cultural, institutional and historical contexts of physical education in school and the particular practice in question. As already mentioned, dance in physical education can be understood from an existential and a socio-cultural perspective. When teaching dance, an awareness of its relation to different movement cultures and different aesthetical cultures can be fruitful, especially in relation to what students are supposed to learn in physical education. In relation to these cultures, teachers have to decide which subject matter and ways of working they are privileging in their teaching (cf. Almqvist & Östman, 2006).

When introducing any teaching resource into education there are both optimistic and critical voices. The same applies when it comes to using video games in physical education (cf. Ennis, 2013; Öhman *et al.*, 2014). In line with these scholars, we would argue that it is important for teachers to decide which educational problems they want to solve when introducing video games in physical education. What is the educational value? All educational problems cannot be solved by technological solutions (Almqvist, 2005; Cuban, 1986; Öhman *et al.*, 2014). Digital technologies are accordingly not *the* solution. They can be aids or tools for teaching dance if, as the case shows, teachers are overly occupied with their own dancing and their own bodies when teaching dance so that they forget to teach. The important question to answer is: What is the problem?

In physical education, 'throwing-in-a-ball' is often criticised as bad teaching. The same can be said for 'throwing-in-a-video-game'. Dance games should be used for a definite purpose and a specific end. As a teacher, there is a great need for competence in teaching, with everything that this involves, in order to use video games fruitfully, however, not necessarily competence in showing a particular dance or dancing yourself in order to fulfil a 'follow me' model of teaching.

Practitioner reflection (Béatrice Gibbs)

As a teacher, I think that having my teaching in dance analysed from different perspectives is very thought provoking. What delights me is that using dance games in teaching not only feels good and works well but also that various researchers can see the benefits of using digital technologies for students' learning, teaching and the subject matter of dance.

From a teacher's perspective, the game enables me to adopt a more planning and advisory role, while the avatar takes an instructional role. As a teacher you do not have to know all the steps of a dance. Instead the main focus should be on teaching. As Johnny writes: "Using an artefact that the students can imitate in order to learn to dance allows the teacher to move freely around the classroom and instruct each student in movement analysis and fitness training". In this way, I can focus on assessing *how* students learn and give them immediate feedback.

From a student perspective, the video game was a way of motivating and engaging them in different ways and allowing them to work according to their own ability. The game and the tasks also encouraged the students' creativity and communication in a variety of ways and helped them to develop and assemble moves. Helle describes it as: "If dance is organised in a way that reflects children's playful energy and matches their level of ability, a whole world of opportunities can unfold". Consequently, it is important that, as a teacher, I reflect on how a dance game can be used so that students learn what they are expected to learn, and not just use them as an activity.

If we look at the content, all four researchers (albeit in different ways) highlight that teachers should consider what purpose the game has in their teaching. A dance game can be used in a variety of ways. In this case, it was used as a tool to help students create movements to music. Based on Johnny's ideas, another way of using the game would be to focus on students' physical health and use it as a tool to work with different heart rate levels.

I would argue that the most important thing to learn from this case is that *what* and *how* students learn when digital technologies such as dance games are used in physical education depends on *how* teachers structure their teaching. Therefore, as Jonas argues, in teaching it is important to take a critical look at pedagogies of technology and not think all teaching problems can be solved by technological solutions. This means that the teacher must be critical of what and how the students learn in the dance games and how this relates to the curriculum. If teachers focus on teaching, such as planning, guiding, supporting and providing feedback, digital technologies can be important resources in the instructional aspects of teaching dance.

Lessons from the case: How can the use of digital technologies accelerate pupil learning in physical education?

In many countries, dance is an important part of physical education in school, at least according to the national curricula. However, research shows that, in general, dance is unfairly treated in the practice of physical education, and that teachers argue that their own abilities in dance limit their teaching. Many teachers testify that they spend a lot of time making sense of their own bodies and movements while dancing, and in this respect demonstrate dance rather than teach it. Other teachers deliberately limit their teaching of dance for similar reasons.

By using different perspectives to look at the case of using dance video games in physical education, we have shown the importance of the teacher in different ways. Some of these are the importance of:

- teachers' competence in teaching as well as competence in dance education;
- teachers' understanding of how learning occurs in physical education practice;
- teachers' understanding of how the particular activity, and in this case artefact, fit into the contexts of the subject matter at hand; and
- an understanding that pedagogies of technology is about *pedagogies* of technology.

In this way the dance game can be used to encourage pupils' creativity and communication and help them to develop new movements together. The game can also act as an "instructor", thus potentially giving the teacher the opportunity to adopt a more pedagogical role.

References

Almqvist, J. (2005). *Learning and Artefacts: On the Use of Information Technology in Educational Settings*. Uppsala: Acta Universitatis Upsaliensis.

Almqvist, J. and Östman, L. (2006). Privileging and artifacts: On the use of information technology in science education. *Interchange, 37*(3), 225–250.

Almqvist, J. and Quennerstedt, M. (2015). Is there (any)body in science education? *Interchange, 46*(4), 439–453.

Amade-Escot, C. (2006). Student learning within the didactique tradition. In D. Kirk, D. Macdonald and M. O'Sullivan (Eds.), *The Handbook of Physical Education*. London: Sage. pp. 347–365.

Biesta, G. (2015). The rediscovery of teaching: On robot vacuum cleaners, non-egological education and the limits of the hermeneutical world view. *Educational Philosophy and Theory*, (ahead-of-print): 1–19.

Bijker, W. and Law, J. (Eds.). (1994). *Shaping Technology/Building Society: Studies in Sociotechnical Change*. Cambridge, MA: The MIT Press.

Bompa, T. O. (1999). *Periodization Training: Theory and Methodology*. Champaign, IL: Human Kinetics.

Branch, J. D., Pate, R. R. and Bourque, S. P. (2000). Moderate intensity exercise interval training improves cardiorespiratory fitness in women. *J Women's Health, 9*, 65–73.

Carr, G. (1997). *Mechanics of Sport*. Champaign, IL: Human Kinetics.

Cuban, L. (1986). *Teachers and Machines: The Classroom Use of Technology Since 1920*. New York: Teachers College Press.

Ellington, H., Percival, F. and Race, P. (1993). *Handbook of Educational Technology*. London: Kogan Page.

Engel, L., Rønholt, H., Svendler Nielsen, C. and Winther, H. (2006). *Bevægelsens Poetik: Om den æstetiske Dimension i Bevægelse*. Copenhagen: Museum Tusculanum.

Ennis, C. (2013). Implication of exergaming for the physical education curriculum in the 21st century. *Journal of Sport and Health Science, 2*, 152–157.

Feenberg, A. (1999). *Questioning Technology*. London: Routledge.

Gibbs, B. (2014). *Wii lär oss dansa? – Om dansspel, rörelsekvaliteter och lärande i idrott och hälsa* (Licentiate thesis). Stockholm: Gymnastik – och idrottshögskolan.

Green, D. F. (2010). *Choreographing From Within: Developing the Habit of Inquiry as an Artist*. Champaign, IL: Human Kinetics.

Hardman, K. and Green, K. (Eds.). (2011). *Contemporary Issues in Physical Education*. Maidenhead, UK: Meyer and Meyer Verlag.

Hartsell, T. and Yuen, S. (2006). Video streaming in online learning. *AACE Journal, 14*(1), 31–43.

Hay, P. and Penney, D. (2012). *Assessment in Physical Education: A Sociocultural Perspective*. London: Routledge.

H'Doubler, M. N. (1925). *The Dance and Its Place in Education*. New York: Harcourt, Brace.

Hodges Kulinna, P., Martin, J. J., Lai, Q., Kliber, A. and Reed, B. (2003). Student physical activity patterns: grade, gender and activity influences. *Journal of Teaching in Physical Education, 22*, 298–310.

Hudson, B. and Meyer, M. A. (Eds.). (2011). *Beyond Fragmentation: Didactics, Learning and Teaching in Europe*. Leverkusen Opladen: Barbara Budrich.

Kassing, G. (2007). *History of Dance: An interactive Arts Approach*. Leeds: Human Kinetics.

Koschmann, T. (1996). *CSCL: Theory and Practice of an Emerging Paradigm*. Mahwah, NJ: Lawrence Erlbaum Associates.

Koutedakis, Y., Owolabi, E. O. and Apostolos, M. (2008). Dance biomechanics – A tool for controlling health, fitness, and training. *Journal of Dance Medicine and Science*, *12*(3), 83–90.

Laban, R. V. (1988). *Modern Educational Dance,* (4th ed.). Plymouth: Northcote House.

Laban, R. (1971). *The Mastery of Movement* (3rd ed.). London: Macdonald and Evans.

Lees, A. (2002). Technique analysis in sports: A critical review. *Journal of Sport Sciences*, *22*(10), 813–828.

Logsdon, B. J. (1977). Physical education: A design for direction. In B. J. Logsdon, K. R. Barrett, M. Ammons, M. R. Broer, L. E., Halverson and R. and McGee (Eds.), *Physical Education for Children: A Focus on the Teaching Process.* Philadelphia: Lea and Febiger. pp. 9–23.

Lundvall, S. and Meckbach, J. (2008). Mind the gap: Physical education and health and the frame factor theory as a tool for analysing educational settings. *Physical Education and Sport Pedagogy*, *13*(4), 345–364.

McCutchen, B. P. (2006) *Teaching as Art in Education.* Champaign, IL: Human Kinetics.

Mattsson, T. and Lundvall, S. (2013) The position of dance in physical education. *Sport, Education and Society*, (ahead-of-print), 1–17.

Merleau-Ponty, M. (1962/2004) *Phenomenology of Perception.* London: Routledge.

Nevill, A. M., Brown, D., Godfrey, R., Johnson, P.J., Romer, L., Stewart, A.D. and Winter, E.M. (2003). Modelling maximum oxygen uptake of elite endurance athletes. *Medicine & Science in Sports & Exercise*, *35*, 488–494.

Nilsson, J. (2008) *Physiological aspects of training illustrated on different activities* (unpublished results).

Nilsson, J. (2007). Att bli sin egen intresserade tränare – träningslära i idrott och hälsa. In J. Meckbach och H. Larsson (Eds.), *Idrottsdidaktiska utmaningar.* Liber: Stockholm. pp. 193–203.

Nilsson, J. (1998). *Puls- och Laktatbaserad Träning.* Stockholm: Sisu Idrottsböcker.

Nilsson, J. and Fredriksson, M. (2015). Peak oxygen uptake and muscle power can be simultaneously improved with hybrid training. *LASE Journal of Sport Science*, *6*(1), 3–15.

Öhman, M., Almqvist, J., Meckbach, J. and Quennerstedt, M. (2014). Competing for ideal bodies: A study of exergames used as teaching aids in schools. *Critical Public Health*, *24*(2), 196–209.

Oudshoorn, N. and Pinch, T. (Eds.) (2005). *How Users Matter: The Co-construction of Users and Technology.* Cambridge, MA: The MIT Press.

Priestley, M., Biesta, G. and Robinson, S. (2015) *Teacher Agency: An Ecological Approach.* London: Bloomsbury.

Quennerstedt, M. and Larsson, H. (2015). Learning movement cultures in physical education practice. *Sport, Education and Society*, *20*(5), 565–572.

Quennerstedt, M., Almqvist, J. and Öhman, M. (2012). Keep your eye on the ball. Investigating artifacts-in-use in physical education. *Interchange*, *42*(3), 287–305.

Quennerstedt, M., Almqvist, J., Meckbach, J. and Öhman, M. (2013). Why do Wii teach physical education in school? *Swedish Journal of Sport Research*, *2*, 55–81.

Quennerstedt, M., Öhman, M. and Armour, K. (2014). Sport and exercise pedagogy and questions about learning. *Sport, Education and Society*, *19*(7), 885–898.

Russell-Bowie, D. E. (2013). What? Me? Teach dance? Background and confidence of primary preservice teachers in dance education across five countries. *Research in Dance Education*, *14*(3), 216–232.

Ryle, G. (1949/2009) *The Concept of Mind.* London: Routledge.

Säljö, R. (1999). Learning as the use of tools: A sociocultural perspective on the human-technology link. In K. Littleton and P. Light (Eds.), *Learning With Computers: Analysing Productive Interaction.* London: Routledge. pp. 144–161.

Sorell, W. (1986). *Mary Wigman. Ein Vermächtnis*. Wilhelmshaven: Florian Noetzel Verlag.

Sprague, M., Scheff, H. and McGreevy-Nichols, S. (2006). *Dance About Anything*. Leeds: Human Kinetics.

Swain, D. P. and Franklin, B. A. (2002). VO_2 reserve and the minimal intensity for improving cardiorespiratory fitness. *Medicine & Science in Sports & Exercise*, *34*, 152–157.

Tolgfors, B. and Öhman, M. (2015). The implications of assessment for learning in physical education and health. *European Physical Education Review*, (ahead-of-print), 1–17.

Wertsch, J. V. (1998). *Mind as Action*. Oxford: Oxford University Press.

Wilson, M. and Kwon, Y-H. (2008). The role of biomechanics in understanding dance movement – A review. *Journal of Dance Medicine and Science*, *12*(3), 109–116.

Winther, H. D. (2009). *Bevægelsespsykologi: Kroppens Sprog og Bevægelsens Psykologi Med Udgangspunkt i Danseterapiformen Dansergia*. Copenhagen: Københavns Universitet.

Winther. H., Engel, L., Nørgaard, M. and Herskind, M. (2015). *Fodfæste og Himmelkys – Undervisningsbog i Bevægelse, Rytmisk Gymnastik og Dans*. Værløse: Billesø & Baltzer.

6

ANTONIO: "I REALLY WANT THEM TO BE ENGAGED AND LEARN"

The use of social media in higher education

Antonio Calderón, Isabel López-Chicheri, Javier Fernández-Río and Oleg A. Sinelnikov

CHAPTER OVERVIEW

Advances in digital technologies, including social media, are changing the ways in which people communicate, collaborate and learn. Scholars have suggested that social media could improve teaching and learning in higher education, while also cautioning about its use. This chapter explores a specific example of social media use with first-year undergraduate-degree students. The aim was to confront and challenge students' core beliefs about coaching youth sport. We illustrate and conclude that the incorporation of social media into educational processes must be based on sound pedagogical principles, and that the construction of a student-centred environment is pivotal to success.

Practitioner narrative (Antonio Calderón)

I am a senior lecturer in physical education and sport pedagogy at a university in Spain. I have taught for twelve years in higher education, most of the time teaching first-year undergraduate students. To develop my practice, I use Twitter as a form of professional learning. Twitter allows me to interact with teacher educators, teachers, and pre-service teachers to share and discuss practice. On Twitter, I tweet (see Table 6.1 for more details) about pedagogy and my uses of digital technologies. I also read and respond to tweets made by others I follow about these topics. For tweets specific to physical education, I follow the hashtag "#physed" and embed this hashtag into my own tweets (see Table 6.1). Due to the benefits I have experienced from using Twitter for professional learning, I decided to begin using social media in undergraduate teacher education classes to develop my students'

Table 6.1 Applications used within the Youth Sport module

Application	Description	Function
Twitter	Twitter is a micro-blogging social media app that allows users to interact with each other via brief online messages.	• **Tweet:** A tweet is a message of 140 or fewer characters that users can send to each other. • **Retweet:** A retweet is a re-posting of someone else's tweet. This isn't an official Twitter command or feature, but signifies that you are quoting another user's tweet. • **Hashtag:** A hashtag, such as #physed, can be embedded into a tweet to signify a specific topic. Users can follow the hashtag to read all tweets made about this topic and they can embed the hashtag into their tweets to contribute to a discussion about a particular topic. • **Follow:** Users can choose to follow other users. This means that all tweets made by those they follow will appear on their Twitter home page.
Google Hangouts	Google Hangouts is an app that functions as an online communications service allowing users to communicate via text, voice or video chats, either one on one or in a group.	Used to debate at the end of every unit about the topic taught, and to activate in the students the need to prepare an online and live debate.
YouTube	YouTube is a video-sharing website that allows users to upload, view, rate, and share videos. Most of the content on YouTube has been uploaded by individuals, but institutions offer some of their material in their channels.	Used to upload the students' reflections after the coaching practice, and to access videos that relate to youth athletes.
Piktochart	Piktochart is a web-based infographic application which allows users to easily create professional-grade infographics using themed templates. Infographics are digital representations of information that are used to present information clearly and quickly.	Used to motivate the students to participate in Google Hangouts and to engage them in the subject.
Google+	Google+ is an interest-based social network to connect with friends and family, and explore all of your interests. Share photos, send messages, and stay in touch with people.	Used to share info related to the online debates and the highlights of every one. To keep students informed about the schedule of the Google Hangouts.

engagement and learning. The following section provides an overview of the ways in which I used social media with my undergraduate students in a first-year module.

The module

The module Youth Sport aimed to confront and challenge students' core beliefs and prior knowledge about coaching youth sport. The module was delivered through three hours of lectures and one practical lesson per week over a four-month period. Students were required to reflect upon, share and debate core topics in order to achieve the targeted learning outcomes:

1. Reflect about the advantages and disadvantages of 'sampling' versus 'specializing' approaches to youth sport;
2. Learn the basic theory and practice of a pedagogical model, such as Teaching Games for Understanding (TGfU); and
3. Enhance students' digital competence and awareness of the benefits of social media and digital technologies for supporting learning.

I embedded various social media sites into the module to extend students' learning. These sites allowed me to share information with my students and initiate debates during and between lectures and practical sessions. Table 6.1 identifies the various sites that were used throughout my module and describes their functions. The discussion below details how these social media sites were used to support students' learning.

Twitter

For this module, I created the hashtag "#fid1415". Every week I tweeted using #fid1415 to share information with my students in the following ways:

1. ***Tweet of the week:*** a relevant and thought-provoking tweet about content related to the module. For example, in week one of the module, I retweeted the following: "Behind the young person in front of you is a child who loves playing your sport. Regardless of their ability you must never extinguish this" (by Dr Martin Toms). The tweet of the week was posted on Mondays at the beginning of a lecture. Before the tweet of the week was shared, I would post another tweet to encourage students to discuss the tweet of the week. For example, "Hi guys, look at this great tweet of the week [link inserted to tweet]. How can we deal with this? Do you agree? (#fid1415)".
2. ***Article of the week:*** a relevant journal article or blog post was tweeted. For example, in the second week, an article was shared that focused on the debate between sampling or specializing in youth sport: "Early specialisation is the best way to have high sporting success [link inserted to article] what do you think? (#fid1415)".

3. ***Twitter chat:*** is a live discussion during class time where students were asked to post tweets using #fid1415 at a specific time point. I displayed this live Twitter feed through the projector. For example, during a lecture, students were asked to watch a video documentary. After the documentary, I posed questions to the class and asked them to tweet about their reflections on this video.

4. ***Daily tweets:*** tweets were posted daily about youth sport trends and issues. For example, in the fourth week pictures were tweeted: "Look at these practice pics! [pictures showing long queues of young athletes waiting to execute an isolated skill] – would you change something? (#fid1415)".

In addition to the varying tweets I sent to initiate and prompt my students to discuss their learning during the module, I also asked my students to post tweets about their wider learning. The students could tweet as individuals from their personal accounts or they could create a team Twitter account to and from which they could post.

Google Hangouts

While Twitter was used on a daily and weekly basis, Google Hangouts was used to support students' learning on a monthly basis. Every four weeks students voluntarily participated in a Google Hangouts session that I moderated to debate and reflect about core content being taught. For every Google Hangout, students were asked to read relevant materials prior to the debates, and I guided them though the debate by posing questions. The debates were announced on social media (Twitter and Google+) with specific infographics that I created using Piktochart (see Table 6.1 for more details) to promote student participation.

YouTube

The Spanish Olympic Committee YouTube channel was used to access videos that related to youth athletes. These videos were shared on Twitter in an effort to extend students' learning, and I encouraged the students to use Twitter to discuss the content of the videos. For example, I shared the following tweet: "Do you know the world youth triple jump Spanish champion? Are you brave enough to live like her? (#fid1415)". Each team was also asked to record a guided team video reflection of their personal coaching practice and upload it (public or private) to YouTube.

#fid1415

Throughout the module students were encouraged to achieve their best, and all teams were considered for "The #fid1415 awards". The winning teams were awarded certificates, gained recognition through the university's social media channels (Twitter and Google+), and could earn bonus points for their grades. These awards were team based and focused on the degree course's learning outcomes:

1. The best-practice lesson (to assess students' pedagogical content knowledge);
2. The best YouTube video team reflection about practice (digital competence and creativity); and
3. The best social media team (active and quality engagements and comments on Twitter, quality resources shared).

This narrative has shown how I used various social media sites in my teaching practice in higher education. It is important to note, however, that I was not completely satisfied with the level of engagement of all students; indeed, some seemed very reluctant to engage fully even though they enjoyed the approach. It seems that the most engaged students were the most technically competent students. The following sections of the chapter show three different perspectives on this narrative: (1) a social media perspective, (2) a teacher educator perspective, and (3) a pedagogical models perspective.

A social media perspective (Isabel López-Chicheri)

The use of social media sites becomes more commonplace every day, and social media is not only changing the way people communicate and collaborate but also the way people learn (Evans, 2014). Consequently, the literature in the field is increasingly focused on analysis of the potential virtues of social media for academic purposes (Graham, 2014).

There are many social media sites and apps that have been tested as learning 'enhancers' including YouTube, MySpace, Facebook or Google (see Tess, 2013, for a review). Although there is limited evidence, Twitter seems to be the most suitable platform for this purpose as it enables public dialogue and idea sharing (Forgie, Duff, & Ross, 2013). Despite controversy regarding the value of the educational role of social media, recent empirical studies suggest that digital technologies could improve teaching and learning experiences (Balakrishnan, 2014). Moreover, the sense of community built among students (and lecturers) through social media improves peer-to-peer communication, increases solidarity in class teams and leads to a better learning and teaching environment (Hamid, Waycott, Kurnia, & Chang, 2015).

Nevertheless, students' perceptions about the integration and usefulness of social media in an academic context vary widely. On one hand, many acknowledge the ability to access academic information quickly, the convenience of direct communication, the improvement of critical thinking skills and a perception that their academic achievement has been enhanced (Gikas & Grant, 2013; Hamid *et al.*, 2015). Conversely, some perceive social media as distracting, time consuming and made for leisure and socializing activities rather than academic purposes (Mao, 2014).

These last perceptions could be significant for students in their first year at university who may encounter their first academic experience using social media as a learning tool. Therefore, before using social media for learning, practitioners need to be aware of previous social network usage by students, and provide them with time and support to become familiar with social media as a learning environment (Graham, 2014).

Research has explored the influence of using social media sites on a variety of academic-related variables: collaborative learning, critical thinking, peer-to-peer and teacher-student communication, perceived efficacy, motivation, writing and language fluency, and student grades (Arquero & Romero-Frías, 2013; Hamid et al., 2015). It is argued, however, that the most comprehensive variable is student engagement, because it encompasses behavioral, emotional and cognitive aspects (Kahu, 2013). Thus, engagement is not a simple construct, but is multidimensional, incorporating the time and effort students devote to activities and impacts on positive academic outcomes, the duration and intensity of thinking, and behavior and feelings of self during the learning process (Chapman, 2003; Kuh, 2009).

Although engagement parameters are not clear in the literature, there is agree-ment that engagement is related to motivation, enhanced achievement and a sense of accomplishment (Steinmann, Beauchamp, Kuntz, & Parsons, 2013). Engaged students are more active in their learning process, take responsibility for their learning and use a variety of cognitive and metacognitive strategies to support their learning (Ibid). Furthermore, engagement is related to trust and a sense of belonging, and these socio-emotional factors affect students' participation and are essential for collaborative learning (Lu & Churchill, 2014). This is particularly noteworthy in case of shy or introverted students, for whom face-to-face interactions could be anxiogenic. Social media, on the other hand, enables them to interact and contribute ideas in a safe context (Forgie et al., 2013; Hamid et al., 2015).

Teacher involvement also impacts students' perceptions about the usefulness of social media for their learning (Irwin, Ball, Desbrow, & Leveritt, 2012). Teachers' awareness, attitudes and perceived ability regarding technologies strongly influence the utilization of social media in class (Ajjan & Hartshorne, 2008). In this case, Antonio's involvement, attitudes and social media proficiency were clear, and yet some students did not engage as much as expected. Other variables relate to engagement and achievement. For example, it has been shown that practitioners who just post teacher-generated content, instead of involving students in critical activities, tend to achieve only superficial engagement (Rambe, 2012). It might, therefore, be concluded that while Antonio's activities have meaningful connections with the curriculum, most of the interactions were superficial. While he designed tasks to prompt dialogic interactions and active reflection, the sheer volume of tasks was excessive. This is especially true when taking into account the other mandatory tasks students were required to complete.

Junco, Elavsky and Heiberger (2013) focus on fostering student engagement and academic achievement using social media, and they propose different types of educationally relevant social media activities. In contrast to Antonio's strategies, most of the posts in this study were related to campus events, class reminders and other practical information. This could be one effective way to integrate selected social media sites into the academic context, gradually changing students' perceptions of the different uses of social media.

Importantly, Antonio's social media tasks were evaluated and graded as an extra reward that could increase students' final marks. Although Antonio's rewards seemed to be a clear motivator for some to become engaged participants, it may not have been enough for 'lurkers' (i.e. those members of an online community who observe, but do not actively participate) (Dennen, 2008). Antonio could consider incorporating the reward of students' efforts into the final grades, rather than an added extra, to deliver more positive outcomes (Lu & Churchill, 2014), even for lurkers.

A teacher educator's perspective (Javier Fernandez-Rio)

Teacher educators are influenced not only by their pedagogical and content knowledge but also by their fears and weaknesses. Technology can be challenging, and the fear it might provoke may influence pedagogical practices. Antonio's initiative to incorporate Twitter and other social media sites into higher education leads me to consider three main ideas relevant in teacher education contexts: communities of practice, student-centred learning, and teacher and students as co-learners.

Communities of practice are groups of individuals who share common interests and have a desire to gain further knowledge in that specific area (Wenger, 2006). Social media sites can help to create open source communities with an established path through which newcomers can participate and quickly develop into trusted members of the community "through a process of legitimate peripheral participation" (Brown & Adler, 2008, p. 19). This means that any member participates from the first time that he or she logs in, increasing relevance in the group through personal inputs.

Social media tools can be positioned to help students feel that they belong to a community, allowing them the opportunity to express themselves, use their knowledge, even author some content, and share it with others. This could be a powerful tool for teacher education, since student interactions with faculty and peers are critical to learning (Rabe-Hemp, Woollen, & Humiston, 2009). For example, teacher educators could use social media to create communities of learners where the face-to-face teaching-learning processes could be augmented. Such communities could offer opportunities for students to integrate content, practices, or technologies and to develop new competences and skills. However, while the role of educators is fundamental for supporting students (Okada, Coelho, Ferreira, & Pinto, 2015), some teachers are afraid of becoming "24-hour teachers" who are almost always "on call" (Grosseck & Holotescu, 2008). Antonio appears able to manage this potential problem, and his perspective serves as a good example of how social media can help to create communities of practice in university settings.

Student-centred learning is viewed as increasingly important in contemporary teacher education settings due to its perceived ability to facilitate "democratic participation, equality, and empowerment to learners" (Le Ha, 2014, p. 1). In seeking to centre learning around the learner – asking them to be active participants in their own learning (growth) – teachers should actively seek opportunities for students to analyse, participate, integrate, and develop knowledge. To achieve this, students should play a dynamic role in their own learning process. Goodyear and Dudley (2015, p. 275) suggested that "student-centred approaches entail developing students' ability to become their own teachers". That said, active teachers (activators) – those who take responsibility and play a dynamic role in helping students learn how to learn (Hattie, 2012) – are also needed.

Social media sites have been found to enhance deep learning by taking the focus away from the teacher and shifting it to the student (Gonzalez, Ingram, LaForge, & Leigh, 2004). Such sites can, therefore, serve as potential platforms for active teachers and self-teaching students. In Antonio's narrative, the ambition is to establish a student-centred-learning context through a combination of all the different mechanisms described: Google Hangouts, live class Twitter chat, and Tweet of the Week. If teacher educators are committed to social media as an educational tool, they have to show their students the educational advantages of its use. "Learning to be a full participant in the field" (Brown & Adler, 2008, p. 19) should be our goal as teacher educators for our students.

The idea of *teacher educators and students as co-learners* is grounded in the work of scholars, such as Freire (1986) and Smith (1996), who argued that teachers and students should cooperate to grow personally and professionally. In physical-education contexts, Casey (2012, p. 83) proposed actors in the teaching–learning process should become co-participants in this "wonderful voyage". Casey wrote of his own experience as a teacher engaged in such a joint venture: "I [teacher] made changes on a lesson-by-lesson basis and changed myself as much as I changed them [students]" (Ibid, p. 83).

This perspective on learning connects with ideas previously explored: student-centred-learning contexts, active teachers, and lifelong learning. It is, however, a step further inasmuch as it is about truly empowering students and acknowledging their capability to engage in "teaching teachers". It is likely that every teacher would say that he or she has learned from their students and that this learning has prompted changes in his or her practice. The circle is completed when the teacher educator returns this newly acquired knowledge to other students and they also learn from it.

It has been argued that the dynamic pace of change in education demands that educators and students "collaborate together in order to co-learn and develop skills for co-creating knowledge anywhere and anytime" (Okada *et al.*, 2015, p. 83). Social media sites can reinforce the notion of viewing teachers and students as co-learners, since their use encourages different forms of interaction. Antonio noted that he "learns a lot from his personal learning environment", which seems to indicate that he considers himself and his students to be co-learners. This is important, because teacher educators can only grow as professionals through a process of continuous learning with and from others, including his or her students. The challenge here is to show teacher-education students that they can learn from a wider social network community, but that this requires a well-planned and coherent instructional design.

In summary, the use of social media in education can support and enhance three recognized mechanisms to enhance student learning in contemporary teacher education: communities of practice, student-centred learning, and teacher and students as co-learners. At the same time, it is important to recognize that there may be something of a generation gap in the ways in which students and teachers understand and accept the role of social media. The challenges faced by tutors must be acknowledged – especially in addressing negative perceptions about teachers' personal–professional balance and workload, students' active role, and traditional views on the teacher–student hierarchy.

A pedagogical model perspective (Oleg Sinelnikov)

This perspective is based on the understanding of a *pedagogical model* offered by Haerens, Kirk, Cardon, and De Bourdeaudhuij (2011) and Kirk (2013). Specifically, a pedagogical model "identifies distinctive learning outcomes and shows how these might be best achieved through their tight alignment with teaching strategies and curriculum or subject matter" (Kirk, 2013, p. 979). To achieve this, a pedagogical model uses a set of non-negotiable features within a certain design specification to allow the interplay of learning, teaching, subject matter and context in the development of a program (Rovegno, 2006). This definition builds on the work of Jewett, Bain, and Ennis (1995), who provided definitions for a *curriculum model*, and Metzler (2011), who proposed the term *instructional model*. Haerens *et al.* (2011), while supportive of this work, argued for the use of "pedagogical models" and positioned it as a neutral term that does not privilege the subject matter (i.e. *curricular*) or the teacher (i.e. *instructional*).

Pedagogical models have become important in the practice of physical education (Casey, 2014a; Kirk, 2013). Conceived initially as an alternative to ineffective teacher-directed traditional practices, they were developed to provide better sporting experiences for children in their physical education experiences (Jewett *et al.*, 1995; Siedentop, 2002). Many scholars have recognized the benefits of implementing pedagogical models in teaching, and have advocated for the use of different models in achieving the breadth and depth of learning in multiplicity of contexts (Lund & Tannehill, 2010; Metzler, 2011).

A number of different pedagogical models have been identified, with the main ones being Sport Education, Teaching Games for Understanding (and their hybrids), Cooperative Learning, Teaching Personal and Social Responsibility, Personalised System of Instruction, Peer Teaching Model, Inquiry Teaching, Health-Based Physical Education, and Physical Literacy. A description and summary of selected models can be found in Metzler's work (2011).

The Sport Education (SE) model (Siedentop, Hastie, & van der Mars, 2011) is one of the more widely researched and well-developed pedagogical models (Kirk, 2013). Nevertheless, research on pedagogical models has predominantly been based in schools and has rarely been conducted in higher education settings. (See Zach & Cohen's [2012] report on Cooperative Learning and Meeteer, Housner, Bulger, Hawkins, & Wiegand [2012] on SE for fuller discussions on the use of pedagogical models in higher education.)

The use of technology has been documented to aid learners in the process of achieving at least some of SE's learning outcomes and contributing to the model's "non-negotiable" features. To date, a number of empirical studies have provided examples of how and when technology and social media can be adopted in SE (Hastie & Sinelnikov, 2007; Sinelnikov, 2012). Specifically, Hastie, Casey, and Tarter (2010) provided an example of using technology within a pedagogical model by incorporating wikis within school physical education in a games-making SE unit. In this study, pupils from two physical education classes in the UK were divided into teams and were given a task to design an invasion game "from scratch" using wikis as the basis for game development (Hastie et al., 2010, p. 81). The findings revealed that the expansion of learning outside of classroom space and time, coupled with the extended community of practice, resulted in a higher quality learning experiences in physical education for the participants.

In another study, college students developed and published web pages representing their volleyball season and showcasing their learning outcomes (Hastie & Sinelnikov, 2007). Each group created a team website comprising pages published by individual team members. The content of each web page varied according to the individual's role on the team. For instance, a student developed and uploaded team training plans, volleyball techniques and tactics to help other team members acquire competency in the game of volleyball. The web pages also served as means for authentic assessment from the instructor's standpoint (Hastie & Sinelnikov, 2007).

The use of technology in the aforementioned studies allowed for the meaningful connection of, and interaction among, learning outcomes, teaching strategy and content. In contrast, the teaching strategies and learning tasks in Antonio's class were more direct and teacher centered. Lund, Gurvitch, and Metzler (2008) and Meeteer et al. (2011) provided precedents of programs in higher education that used SE as a structural discourse for physical education teacher preparation. Importantly, and as cautioned by Kirk (2013), while the non-negotiable features of SE should be retained where possible, they must also allow practitioners to be creative (Lund et al., 2008, p. 581).

Disconcertingly, it has been reported that one of the key structures of SE, learners working in small and persisting groups, has also contributed to some of the unintended and unwelcome outcomes (Hastie et al., 2010). As in many group-work situations, the expectation that all participants do their part equally was not realized, and, as a result, some of the team members became frustrated. The unintended outcomes of unequal or unfair work distribution must also be considered carefully in the use of social media since, in Antonio's narrative, it is apparent that students worked in groups for a considerable amount of time.

In conclusion, scholars have argued that the use of technology in higher education should be driven by three interrelated concepts:

1. The apparently changing nature of students who come to university highly connected, collective, and creative;
2. The changing relationship that current university students have with knowledge consumption, knowledge construction, and formal education; and
3. The de-emphasis of institutionally provided learning and emergence of "user-driven" education (Selwyn, 2010).

All three concepts can work very well with models-based practice, especially if they are linked to the broad conceptualization of pedagogy that recognizes the interdependent elements of curriculum, learning and teaching (Armour, 2011).

A pedagogical perspective (Antonio Calderón, Javier Fernández-Río and Oleg Sinelnikov)

The purpose of this section is to consider the case narrative about the use of social media to support student learning in teacher education as well as the three analytical perspectives. The aim is to identify wider lessons learnt for the development of effective pedagogies of technology. First, it is important to highlight the importance of taking an inclusive approach to technology in order to enhance learning and teaching (Casey, 2014b). Inclusion was certainly the aspiration, but, as is noted in the narrative, there were challenges. There is much literature on the potential benefits of interaction using social media and digital technologies (e.g. Twitter) – engaging with content, peer learning, promoting critical thinking, self-directed learning, self-monitoring of learning progress, interacting with lectures, and enjoying the interactive learning environment (Hamid *et al.*, 2015; Megele, 2015). Yet, although the case narrative reports Antonio's desire to be student centred in order to enhance student learning, as Brady, Holcomb, and Smith (2010) recommended, his approach could be challenged as being too teacher centred.

The social media intervention included activities that may have restricted dialogic interaction such that it was more of a one-directional process of information sharing. For example, in the "tweet of the week", the "article of the week", and the "daily tweets", the practitioner mainly shared content (through tweets) and only a minority of students appeared to be engaged meaningfully. It is also worth noting that these were the most technically competent students. On reflection, it seems clear that the other students were more accurately described as "lurkers". It may be the case that in their personal use of social media, this is the perfectly valid way in which they engage (Dennen, 2008; Sponcil & Gitimu, 2013), so this approach simply transferred to the learning context. Alternatively, it could be argued that Antonio's tweets were too closed and teacher centred, so they simply didn't prompt students to get involved. Rambe (2012) reported the same "superficial engagement" when a teacher posted teacher-generated content instead of involving students in critical activities. The intention was good – the structure of the social media–based intervention attempted to recognize that many of the first-year undergraduates had little previous experience of using social media for learning, however the reality did not match up to Antonio's aspirations.

That said, and as Rafaeli, Ravid, and Soroka (2004) point out, lurking may have allowed novice users to learn the conventions of an online community before they actively participated, thereby improving their socialization when they eventually de-lurk. Mao (2014) notes that in order to be successful in this type of intervention, it is essential to understand students' prior knowledge of social media, as well as their attitudes and beliefs about these digital technologies and related obstacles. For example, in a study of high school students, it was found that they depend on social media in their daily lives for leisure and social connections (Mao, 2014). If the students in Antonio's class were similar, it may explain why some were initially reluctant to use social media for a different purpose.

Looking across the literature and the perspectives presented in this chapter, we might conclude that what really matters is not the technology or the tool but the user's prior experience and uses of technology. Given the relatively low engagement levels, it would appear that some students in Antonio's class faced challenges in separating personal and academic purposes, and struggled to find their digital identity as a learner. Moreover, attempting to force greater collaboration between first-year undergraduates through Twitter – or any other intervention – does not seem to be the most effective solution (Forgie et al., 2013). Instead, and with hindsight, it may be more important to set up a learning environment than attracts students to technology gradually, and in ways that acknowledge their prior beliefs and experiences as users.

Another key issue that arose in both the case narrative and the perspectives was the *process* of developing users' social learning identities and the collaborations between them. To achieve the most effective results in social media–based interventions, it seems clear that practitioners should have a theoretically driven pedagogical basis for their approach and also engage actively with students on the selected platform (Junco, Heiberger, & Loken, 2011). In line with Antonio's beliefs as a pedagogue, the pedagogy underpinning his intervention was built and based on a theoretical framework described by Megele (2015) as "dialectical constructivism and social learning". This framework rejects the idea that knowledge is something that can be delivered from a "knowledgeable source" to someone lacking that "knowledge". Instead, it is an approach that focuses on the processes of student participation and interaction to provide and sustain the context for quality learning experiences.

Despite the best of intentions, however, the case narrative suggests that Antonio's theory was not fully realized in practice. As Casey (2014b) notes, the use of technology needs a clear purpose and an effective combination of technology and pedagogy, and it is this that seems to be the differentiating factor in attracting and keeping students engaged (Megele, 2015). We should not lose sight of the fact that, for the most part, technology is a tool to address educational concerns (Fullan, 2013). It could be argued that Antonio's use of technology was somewhat "mechanical", leading the user to focus on the short-term, day-to-day use of social media with insufficient time for reflection (Hall, 2010).

Perhaps, on reflection, the focus was too much on the excitement of using social media and too little on the learning outcomes and students' individual needs. In order to establish a more authentic student-centred approach, it might have been more effective to have involved the students in solving social or digital technology-based tasks or challenges. This ambition might have been achieved by the use of a pedagogical model such as SE. For example, Antonio could have asked students to design an infographic on the advantages and disadvantages of sampling versus specializing in youth sport. Then, after students had searched and curated the content, they could have shared the outcomes through Twitter in an attempt to connect with other undergraduate students or practitioners in order to open a dialogue and share opinions. Finally, by awarding "fair play points" to those who became engaged rather than simply to those who made the best contribution, Antonio might have "encouraged" greater engagement.

This pedagogical case also raises another issue to be considered critically: that of the non-active participation of some students. This may be linked to the organization of teams that remained the same throughout the programme. As noted in the third perspective, the unintended problems of unequal or unfair work distribution (what Tousignant and Siedentop, 1983, described as "competent bystanding") to complete most tasks need to be carefully considered. In this case, every team had a student who took on the responsibility for leading social media. Team members chose this student and frequently based this decision on the student's previous experience with social media and digital technologies. This could be another reason why not all the students had active engagement and involvement in social media, because, in effect, they had off-loaded the responsibility onto a more experienced teammate. Indeed, in most cases, this same student was the one who also participated in the Google Hangouts sessions and in the rest of the online activities.

In summary, reflection on the case narrative and the three perspectives suggests that an effective pedagogy of technology needs to be grounded in authentic student-centred-learning contexts. It should also promote activities that encourage genuine dialogic interaction between all the actors involved (teachers and students). If most of the content is teacher generated in the first instance, this might help students to bridge the gap between their previous use of social media for mainly leisure purposes and the new educational ambitions, but this teacher-led approach should not dominate. Alternative student-centred approaches (such as models-based practices) could sit alongside such technology use. In this way, these different innovations are positioned to support each other in order to support the students to learn.

Practitioner reflection

I joined Twitter in February 2013, and I started including it in my teaching in October of the same year. Most of my initial tweeting activity included retweets (to repost or forward another user's message – or tweet – on social media sites), marking favorites (letting the author know you like it) and tweeting about places I went to and activities that I thought might be of interest to others (i.e. conferences). Aligned with this personal use of Twitter, my teaching use (i.e. using the hashtag #fid1314) was mainly based around tweeting resources about the subject content in the form of journal articles and audio-visuals which, on reflection, was not very engaging for some first-year undergraduates. One year later, my Twitter connections (followers and people I followed) started to grow. During that time, I tweeted more frequently to let my personal learning network know about my teaching practice. My teaching use (using the hashtag #fid1415) was still based on tweeting resources about the subject content, trying to engage students in their learning and increase their motivation to learn about the use of social media sites. This might explain why students' engagement did increase over time but was still not as fast as I might have wished.

At the point where I was considering the intervention for the next group of students (#fid1516) I decided to change the message of the hashtag for another one that was more creative and engaging. I chose, after a deep searching process, the hashtag #FIDmola (FID is the acronym of the course name and "mola" is the Spanish word that means "cool"). This change of hashtag is not arbitrary but instead represents a major shift. First of all, I do feel a level of security and comfort in using Twitter for professional learning and global connections. My personal learning network is now more or less defined (although remains open), and I feel I learn from it every day. I also started blogging[1] this year. This change of conception has consequences in my teaching use of social media. Having concluded that the first two years of #fid1314 and #fid1415 needed to be improved, I decided to change the focus of the module. My students now have an option, for example, of avoiding formal subject exams if they choose an alternative path. This alternative path consists of a series of mini-challenges to be solved by the students through the use of social technology–based activities. For example, in the second unit, two key concepts in coaching youth sport (traditional/technique or innovative/tactical coaching) are introduced. To engage in this mini-challenge, my students have to: (1) search information from the Internet (I recommend different blogs, journal articles, through attractive challenge-info presentation); (2) curate and sort the information; (3) design an infographic (using specific software) which shows the advantages and disadvantages of both approaches; (4) share through social media sites (Twitter) the outcome, mentioning and trying to interact with at least one of the authors they have chosen to follow to create the infographic; and, lastly, (5) reflect about the whole process on their blogs and tweet about this too, always using the relevant hashtag.

In summary, and as noted earlier, the process of constructing this case and using the expertise from different perspectives to help my critical reflection has led me to some clear conclusions. It is imperative, for example, that in a process of learning and adaptation to the use of social media sites for educational purposes (by students and practitioners) the quality of personal uses of social media is an important component. A pedagogy of technology is, therefore, also a personalized pedagogy. Undoubtedly, as I learn more and the social media landscape continues its dynamic evolution, this principle will become even more important.

Lessons from the case: How can the use of digital technologies accelerate student engagement in higher education?

After my experience with #fid1415, and taking into account the more recent experience of #FIDmola, I can share the following tips:

1. Start reflecting about a theoretically driven pedagogical basis for incorporating social media in your teaching, and set a general educational goal and not a goal of just using social media and technology.
2. Plan the instructional setting and structure of the student-centred intervention using educationally relevant criteria (aligned with standards, technology affordances, personal students' beliefs, needs, previous social media usage, and learning outcomes).
3. Provide the students with enough time and support to become familiar with the social media environment for learning. Sharing teacher-generated content in the first instance might help students to bridge the gap between their previous use of social media for mainly leisure purposes and the new educational ambitions (this teacher-led approach should not, however, dominate).
4. In order to establish an authentic student-centred approach, involve the students in solving social or digital technology–based tasks or challenges. A pedagogy of technology needs to be grounded in authentic student-centred-learning contexts and promote activities that encourage dialogic interaction between all the actors involved (teachers and students).
5. Use different web or mobile applications to encourage students to create their own subject content as a part of every technology-based task or challenge. The process of learning should develop in the students the competences of searching, curating, creating, sharing and reflecting in every challenge, in order to enhance their learning autonomy and engagement.

Note

1   This is the link to the course blog: http://fidmola.blogspot.com.es/

References

Ajjan, H. and Hartshorne, R. (2008). Investigating faculty decisions to adopt web 2.0 technologies: Theory and empirical tests. *The Internet and Higher Education, 11*(2), 71–80.

Armour, K. M. (Ed.). (2011). *Sport Pedagogy: An Introduction for Coaching and Teaching Sport.* Harlow, UK: Prentice Hall.

Arquero, J. L. and Romero-Frías, E. (2013). Using social network sites in higher education: An experience in business studies. *Innovations in Education and Teaching International, 50*(3), 238–249.

Balakrishnan, V. (2014). Using social networks to enhance teaching and learning experiences in higher learning institutions. *Innovations in Education and Teaching International, 51*(6), 595–606.

Brady, K. P., Holcomb, L. B. and Smith, B. V. (2010). The use of alternative social networking sites in higher educational settings: A case study of the e-learning benefits of Ning in education. *Journal of Interactive Online Learning, 9*(2), 151–170.

Brown, J. S. and Adler, R. P. (2008). Minds of fire: Open education, the long tail, and learning 2.0. *Educause Review*, January-February, 18–32. Retrieved from www.johnseelybrown. com/mindsonfire.pdf

Casey, A. (2014a). Models-based practice: Great white hope or white elephant? *Physical Education and Sport Pedagogy, 19*(1), 18–34.

Casey, A. (2014b). Should we have a pedagogy of technology for physical education? Retrieved from http://es.slideshare.net/DrAshCasey/should-we-have-a-pedagogy-of-technology

Casey, A. (2012). A self-study using action research: Changing site expectations and practice stereotypes. *Educational Action Research, 20*(2), 219–232.

Chapman, E. (2003). Assessing student engagement rates. *ERIC Digest.* ERIC Clearing house on Assessment and Evaluation. Retrieved from www.ericdigests.org/2005-2/engagement.html

Dennen, V. M. (2008). Pedagogical lurking: Student engagement in non-posting discussion behavior. *Computers in Human Behavior, 24*(4), 1624–1633.

Evans, C. (2014). Twitter for teaching: Can social media be used to enhance the process of learning? *British Journal of Educational Technology, 45*(5), 902–915.

Forgie, S. E., Duff, J. P. and Ross, S. (2013). Twelve tips for using Twitter as a learning tool in medical education. *Medical Teacher, 35*, 8–14.

Freire, P. (1986). *Pedagogy of the Oppressed.* New York: Continuum.

Fullan, M. (2013). *Stratosphere: Integrating Technology, Pedagogy, and Change Knowledge.* Toronto, Ontario: Pearson.

Gikas, J. and Grant, M. M. (2013). Mobile computing devices in higher education: Student perspectives on learning with cell phones, smartphones and social media. *The Internet and Higher Education, 19*, 18–26.

Gonzalez, G. R., Ingram, T. N., LaForge, R. W. and Leigh, T. W. (2004). Social capital: Building an effective learning environment in marketing classes. *Marketing Education Review, 14*(2), 1–8.

Goodyear, V. and Dudley, D. (2015). "I'm a facilitator of learning!" Understanding what teachers and students do within student-centered physical education models. *Quest, 67*, 274–289.

Graham, M. (2014). Social media as a tool for increased student participation and engagement outside the classroom in higher education. *Journal of Perspectives in Applied Academic Practice, 2*(3), 16–24.

Grosseck, G. and Holotescu, C. (2008). *Can we use Twitter for educational activities?* In 4th International Scientific Conference, eLearning and Software for Education, Bucharest, Romania.

Haerens, L., Kirk, D., Cardon, G. and De Bourdeaudhuij, I. (2011). Toward the development of a pedagogical model for health-based physical education. *Quest*, 63, 321–338.

Hall, G. E. (2010). Technology's Achilles heel: Achieving high-quality implementation. *Journal of Research on Technology in Education*, *42*(3), 231–253.

Hamid, S., Waycott, J., Kurnia, S. and Chang, S. (2015). Understanding students' perceptions of the benefits of online social networking use for teaching and learning. *Internet and Higher Education*, *26*, 1–9.

Hastie, P. A., Casey, A. and Tarter, A. M. (2010). A case study of wikis and student-designed games in physical education. *Technology, Pedagogy and Education*, *19*(1), 79–91.

Hastie, P. A. and Sinelnikov, O. A. (2007). The use of web-based portfolios in college physical education activity courses. *Physical Educator*, *64*(1), 21–28.

Hattie, J. (2012). *Visible Learning for Teachers: Maximizing Impact on Learning*. London, UK: Routledge.

Irwin, C., Ball, L., Desbrow, B. and Leveritt, M. (2012). Students' perceptions of using Facebook as an interactive learning resource at university. *Australasian Journal of Educational Technology*, *28*(7), 1221–1232.

Jewett, A. E., Bain, L. L. and Ennis, C. D. (1995). *The curriculum process in physical education* (2nd ed.). Boston, MA: WCB/McCraw-Hill.

Junco, R., Elavsky, C. M. and Heiberger, G. (2013). Putting Twitter to the test: Assessing outcomes for student collaboration, engagement and success. *British Journal of Educational Technology*, *44*(2), 273–287.

Junco, R., Heiberger, G. and Loken, E. (2011). The effect of Twitter on college student engagement and grades. *Journal of Computer Assisted Learning*, *27*, 119–132.

Kahu, E. R. (2013). Framing student engagement in higher education. *Studies in Higher Education*, *38*(5), 758–773.

Kirk, D. (2013). Educational value and models-based practice in physical education. *Educational Philosophy & Theory*, *45*(9), 973–986.

Kuh, G. D. (2009). What student affairs professionals need to know about student engagement. *Journal of College Student Development*, *50*(6), 683–706.

Le Ha, P. (2014). The politics of naming: critiquing "learner-centred" and "teacher as facilitator" in English language and humanities classrooms. *Asia-Pacific Journal of Teacher Education*, *42*(4), 392–405.

Lu, J. and Churchill, D. (2014). The effect of social interaction on learning engagement in a social networking environment. *Interactive Learning Environments*, *22*(4), 401–417.

Lund, J. L., Gurvitch, R. and Metzler, M. W. (2008). Chapter 7: Influences on cooperating teachers' adoption of model-based instruction. *Journal of Teaching in Physical Education*, *27*(4), 549–570.

Lund, J. and Tannehill, D. (2010). *Standards-Based Physical Education Curriculum Development* (2nd ed.). Sudbury, MA: Jones and Bartlett.

Mao, J. (2014). Social media for learning: A mixed methods study on high school students' technology affordances and perspectives. *Computer in Human Behavior*, *33*, 213–223.

Megele, C. (2015) eABLE: Embedding social media in academic curriculum as a learning and assessment strategy to enhance students learning and e-professionalism. *Innovations in Education and Teaching International*, *52*(4), 414–425.

Meeteer, W., Housner, L., Bulger, S. M., Hawkins, A. and Weigand, R. (2012). Applying sport education in university basic instruction courses. In P. A. Hastie (Ed.), *Sport Education: International Perspectives*. London, UK: Routledge. pp. 58–72.

Metzler, M. W. (2011). *Instructional models for physical education* (3rd ed.). Scottsdale, AZ: Holcomb Hathaway.

Okada, A., Coelho, A. R., Ferreira, S. and Pinto, S. M. (2015). Key skills for co-learning and co-inquiry in two open platforms: A massive portal (EDUCARED) and a personal environment (weSPOT). *Open Praxis, 7*(1), 83–102.

Rabe-Hemp, C., Woollen, S. and Humiston, G. S. (2009). A comparative analysis of student engagement, learning, and the satisfaction in lecture hall and online learning settings. *The Quarterly Review of Distance Education, 10*(2), 207–218.

Rafaeli S., Ravid G. and Soroka, V. (2004). *De-lurking in virtual communities: A social communication network approach to measuring the effects of social and cultural capital.* Proceedings of the 37th Hawaii International Conference on System Sciences.

Rambe, P. (2012). Critical discourse analysis of collaborative engagement in Facebook postings. *Australasian Journal of Educational Technology, 28*(2), 295–314.

Rovegno, I. (2006). Situated perspectives on learning. In D. Kirk, D. Macdonald and M. O'Sullivan (Eds.), *The Handbook of Physical Education*. London, UK: Sage. pp. 262–274.

Selwyn, N. (2010). Looking beyond learning: Notes towards the critical study of educational technology. *Journal of Computer Assisted Learning, 26*, 65–73.

Siedentop, D. (2002). Sport education: A retrospective. *Journal of Teaching in Physical Education, 21*, 409–418.

Siedentop, D., Hastie, P. and van der Mars, H. (2011). *Complete guide to sport education* (2nd ed.). Champaign, IL: Human Kinetics.

Smith, F. (1996). *Joining the Literacy Club: Further Essays into Education*. Portsmouth NH: Heinemann.

Sinelnikov, O. A. (2012). Using the iPad in a Sport Education season. *Journal of Physical Education, Recreation and Dance, 83*(1), 39–45.

Sponcil, M. and Gitimu, P. (2013). Use of social media by college students: Relationship to communication and self-concept. *Journal of Technology Research, 4*, 1–13.

Steinmann, J., Beauchamp, L., Kuntz, J. and Parsons, J. (2013). Alberta initiative for school improvement (AISI). Student engagement research review. Retrieved from www.education.alberta.ca/aisi

Tess, P. A. (2013). The role of social media in higher education classes (real and virtual) – A literature review. *Computers in Human Behavior, 29*(5), 60–68.

Tousignant, M. and Siedentop, D. (1983). A qualitative analysis of task structures in required secondary physical education classes. *Journal of Teaching in Physical Education, 3*(1), 47–57.

Wenger, E. (2006). Communities of practice: A brief introduction. Retrieved from http://wenger-trayner.com/theory/

Zach, S. and Cohen, R. (2012). Using cooperative learning model in teacher education In B. Dyson and A. Casey (Eds.), *Cooperative Learning in Physical Education. A research-based approach*. London, UK: Routledge. pp. 88–89.

7

ANDY: BLOGGING WITH STUDENTS

Educational visions and digital realities

*Tim Fletcher, Andy Vasily, Shawn M. Bullock,
Clare Kosnik and Déirdre Ní Chróinín*

CHAPTER OVERVIEW

We consider the visions and realities underpinning Andy's decision to use blogs with primary physical education students. Academics provide insights into Andy's case from digital technology, literacy, and assessment perspectives. Andy's case demonstrates that e-pedagogies are not limited to the ways practitioners adopt and use new forms of technology. Despite the promises of using blogs, we suggest that the complex situations practitioners face mean decisions about when and why *not* to use certain technologies are crucial in enacting strong e-pedagogies.

Practitioner narrative (Andy Vasily)

I have been a physical education teacher for 16 years, working at International Baccalaureate (IB) schools in Japan, Azerbaijan, Cambodia and China (where I currently work). I see myself as a teacher willing to try out new ideas and who is open minded to change within my own practice; however, I don't jump blindly into the deep end with new teaching approaches. This cautious nature is a result of me wanting the best for my students. I believe the choices we make and the methods of delivery we use in our teaching should have sound pedagogical justification.

In the early part of my teaching career, I attended professional development workshops, read journals, and generally tried to improve my practice. I left no stone unturned in my pursuit of mastery in teaching, and came up against several roadblocks and obstacles along the way. One of these was that I was the only physical education teacher in my school and had nobody in my subject area with whom to collaborate or have professional dialogue with.

About 5 years ago I was applying for a new job and felt I had a pretty good shot at getting it. I soon found out I wasn't even shortlisted! Feeling frustrated and a bit angry, I was forced to evaluate why I didn't get the job. I soon realised that although I was good at teaching and had excellent references from administrators, I had nothing else that genuinely showed the quality of work I was doing. As I weighed my options, I knew that I had to do something different, so I decided to create my own blog. This is when everything really started to change for me.

I set out to blog not only about how I teach and assess my students in physical education, but to also share my reflections about my own learning. Blogging became the spark that helped fuel an even stronger passion for teaching. It had the effect of helping me overcome feelings of professional isolation and played a powerful role in shaping my teaching identity by challenging me to think deeply about my own actions as a teacher and how these influence students' learning. It is one thing to write detailed lessons or summative evaluations of students' learning, but it is an entirely different thing to write about the processes of teaching and the important lessons learned through reflection. I found that writing about my practice had an immediate impact on my effectiveness because it forced me to justify (pedagogically) why I do what I do. Constantly explaining 'why' has been one of the greatest tools for improving my own learning about teaching.

The educational vision for blogging with students

When approached to contribute to this chapter, I was going to write about a form of technology I have implemented successfully. When I thought hard about it, however, I realised it could be more powerful to write about a new idea I was going to test out in the 2014–15 school year. I felt it was important to write about the processes of implementing a new idea regardless of its success, and to share reflections about what did and did not work as part of the process of developing my pedagogies of technology (see Table 7.1).

My new idea builds on something I started about 10 years ago when I created the *Sportfolio* in my primary physical education programme. Each student has their own *Sportfolio*, which is a hard-copy journal geared specifically to students' physical

TABLE 7.1 Technologies used

App/technology	Function	How app/technology was used
Blogs (or Weblog); Blogs referred to in the chapter: *Easy Blog Jr.*, *Edublogs*, *NetNewsWireApp*, *WeChat*, *Weibo*	A blog is an internet site where users can reflect, compile, and/or share their ideas and opinions in the form of an online journal (Wiktionary, n.d.)	It was intended that a blog would provide the technology to digitally store and host students' *Sportfolios* (hard copy physical education portfolios used by Andy with his students)

education and sport experiences and to store assessments, reflections, certificates, and photos. Because I teach a diverse group of learners from different language backgrounds, I have always wanted to digitise the *Sportfolio* but struggled to work out how to achieve this. I evaluated several options and was zeroing in on using a notes programme (such as Evernote™) to create digital *Sportfolios* that would be hosted online.

A notes programme was appealing technologically. However, as I reflected more on my students' needs, I was drawn back to the idea of getting students to blog about their learning journeys in physical education. Because I have had so much experience and success in blogging about my own teaching and learning journeys, I understood many of the technical issues of blogging and could envision what students might gain from this experience. I realised that blogging would offer students numerous options in terms of demonstrating their understanding and interpretation of what they learned and experienced in my classes. Not only would blogging provide them with choice about what to write and how to share their learning experiences, digitising their learning would allow parents and friends to access their work and see their progress. As I began to see the potential positives adding up, I became more excited about the idea of setting up student blogs, shaped by the *Sportfolio*.

The reality of blogging with students

Once I had made the decision to digitise the *Sportfolio* through blogs in July 2014, I contacted our school's IT coach, Tom Johnson. I discussed my plans with Tom, going through the many technical and technological requirements that would be needed. I knew this was going to be a challenging task but even though I had considerable experience of using blogs and had strong beliefs about their value for enhancing students' learning, it soon became clear we couldn't go ahead as planned. Tom explains:

> Testing [the programme] would be good, but we wanted something that would prove useful for the whole school. Our first consideration was to ensure we had one platform that worked on all devices and could be administered by our IT department to allow us to build, help with, and remove content should it infringe upon the school's 'responsible use agreement'. Our next consideration was that we wanted students to add pictures and videos, and be able to comment on one another's posts with ease. Because we would like to cater for students in grade 1 (age 6 years) and above, we wanted a very simple interface. We examined a lot of options, like Weibo, WeChat, and Edublogs, but decided to try Easy Blog Jr., which has worked well in other parts of the world. In China, however, this option was not viable because our Internet is too slow and because sites like this are often blocked. We felt if we were able to host the platform ourselves it should work, but this would take time. Rather than getting set up in a few days or weeks, we

would need a much longer timeline in order to get a host-server running and managed. Setting up blogging at the school would also mean ensuring policies [and rules] were in place, providing a lot of teacher professional development and support, and presenting numerous parent information sessions to ensure they understood the process, ramifications and potential benefits.

We wanted students to be able to take control of their learning but in order to do this, novices needed to be shown how. We realised it would require introducing blogging through scaffolded phases. For example, first, students might blog as a class on one account, allowing the teacher to facilitate appropriate practice for all to see. Second, students would blog through the authorship of a teacher's account, where posts could be vetted before they were published. Ultimately though, we wanted students to have their own sites. We knew they would be excited about this because they could make their sites look the way they wanted and even add widgets, which are fun. The teachers and administrators could view and manage their posts through aggregate programmes like NetNewsWireApp. So, what appeared at first to be a simple process proved to have many elements that needed to be considered, especially given our unique situation here in this part of Asia.

Despite my belief that blogging would offer students a powerful learning experience, working with Tom helped me understand the significant amount of work behind the scenes that would be required. This would necessitate the involvement of numerous stakeholders (students, parents, teachers, and administrators) in a multi-phase approach. Ultimately, we decided to postpone the digitisation of the *Sportfolio* through blogs to give us time to develop and provide the necessary support for students, teachers, and parents. Only by taking this approach could we ensure that the full pedagogical potential of the idea would be realised.

A digital technology perspective (Shawn M. Bullock)

Like Andy, I have been cautiously optimistic about the potential of technology to enhance educational experiences. I made use of real-time sensing software as a physics teacher, and I was quite proud of the class websites I set up in 2000, during my first year of teaching. As both my comfort with using technology for pedagogical purposes and the capability of technologies grew, I incorporated tools such as blogs into my early experiences as a doctoral student and a new teacher educator. An important shift was from thinking of technology as a tool to enhance teaching to considering how technology might engage students in thinking about their learning.

It is tempting to think of blogs as potentially private spaces that have the added bonus of being able to make posts (or the entire blog) instantly and publicly accessible. To complicate this line of thinking, it is useful to consider danah boyd's concept of *networked publics*. boyd (2014) argued that the advent of digital technologies brought a corresponding reconceptualisation of the nature of public space and that technologies such as blogs are *networked publics* in that they are persistent, spreadable, searchable, and visible. Of course, both a physical piece of paper and a blog are persistent in that there is a permanent record that others can view if they have access to the paper or the blog. While a sheet of paper is easily destroyed, the idea of deleting a blog is somewhat spurious. It is possible to click the delete button, but the blog author has no idea about the extent to which others may have kept archived copies of entries or the length of time the blog might remain in either Google's cache of web pages or in backup servers of the blog-hosting companies.

Copying a blog nowadays is much faster than copying sheets of paper; indeed, many blogging services rely on the ease with which content can be spread quickly across the Internet. Perhaps most importantly, the nature and number of visible audiences for anything that gets posted online is ultimately unclear. A blogger will never know how a blog post might be indexed by search engines, how it might be shared via email links or any number of social media services, who might re-post or re-mix a section of a blog (perhaps out of context), or whether the work will be attributed accurately. Privacy issues become even more complicated when taking into account the information embedded in multimedia posts. Pictures have embedded file data (called *EXIF data*) that can be used to determine not only what sort of camera took the picture but also the GPS coordinates of where the picture was taken. All of a sudden, a seemingly innocuous photo of an outdoor learning experience can reveal the precise date, time, and location of a group of people engaged in an activity.

There are at least two sets of concerns regarding the invisible audiences that might review and collect data posted online. The first comes from individuals or groups who can build up reasonably informative profiles of people they have never met based on material posted online. The web is awash with stories of interviewees who have lost jobs because of what potential employers found on their blogs, Twitter feeds, or Facebook pages (Johnston, 2015). The second concern centres on companies themselves. While blogging platforms and social networking sites might be "free" in terms of financial cost for a user, there can be little doubt that companies make the money they need to offer the services provided through advertising and the use of meta-data. In a high profile case, Edward Snowden's revelations about widespread government surveillance of digital technologies revealed the degree to which information can be used in unintended ways (BBC News, 2014). A recent study by Rainie and Madden (2015) revealed that 25 per cent of adults who are aware of government surveillance programs have changed the way they use one or more technologies "somewhat" or "a great deal".

Blogs can be a wonderful tool for educators at all levels. In my own work, for example, I have found blogs particularly useful for accessing how teacher candidates are thinking about their practicum experiences and continuing conversations that began during coursework (Bullock, 2013a). Blogs can facilitate collaborative conversations between teachers, students, and parents, and provide ample opportunities for students to represent their learning in a number of ways using a mixture of text, pictures, video, and sound. But blogs also raise serious concerns about privacy, including the potential of blog posts to be used in ways that were not originally intended by the poster (i.e. teacher). These concerns are magnified when students are involved. Melvin Kranzberg (1986), an historian of technology, suggested that technology was neither good, nor bad, nor value-neutral, and there is no suggestion here that privacy risks should prevent the use of blogs, nor that students should complete all assignments using paper and pencil to ensure that none of their work ends up online. There are many good reasons for using blogs with students of all levels, but the implications for students' immediate and long-term privacy should always be considered. Andy wrote about the importance of choice in shaping digital *Sportfolios*. While I agree that choice can be a powerful motivator, I would also say that discussions about privacy and the use of technology for learning can provide powerful moments of choice for students. Part of the ways in which students might engage with a digital assignment should reflect choices about privacy. These arguments extend to teachers as well. While it is indeed laudable for teachers to engage publicly in the digital realm with ideas about teaching, it is equally important for them to consider the long-term implications of networked publics on their professional and personal lives.

A literacy perspective (Clare Kosnik)

In this section I want to focus on the *potential* value of blogging with students. While Andy chose not to implement blogs for valid reasons now, once he and his school have the appropriate mechanisms in place, digitising the *Sportfolio* offers several powerful and positive implications for his students. Changes in how we communicate, what we communicate, and with whom we communicate are changing the lives of teachers and students. As Booth (2013) suggests:

> Students have the amazing potential to take advantage of vast global networks, huge databases, e-mail archives, rich art collections, and in turn, interactions with millions of users. Our task as educators is to help young people become capable navigators of what is often a complex and disparate landscape (p. 105).

The increasing forms of communication are causing us to 'rethink' literacy, moving away from a view of literacy as a simple process of acquiring basic cognitive skills, to using these skills in ways that contribute to socio-economic development, and to developing the capacity for social awareness and critical reflection as a basis for personal and social change (UNESCO, 2014). Given the many forms of communication available we must move from conceptualising literacy as a defined set of skills taught (transmitted) in a language arts/English classroom to a far more interactive process where social media and multimodal representations are part of regular literacy practices. This broad view of literacy is consistent with Andy's vision because he aims to provide his students with opportunities beyond traditional forms of learning and communication. His intention of letting students blog about their experiences moves literacy from the domain of the language arts/English program to being integrated into physical education where students can improve how they make meaning from their experiences and most likely improve their literacy skills. In this section I only briefly address two topics: multiliteracies and content area literacy.

Multiliteracies

The widely respected New London Group (1996) coined the term *multiliteracies*, a concept that has relevance for physical education. They argue that traditional conceptualisations of 'literacy' (p. 61) are inadequate because *all* teachers should consider themselves as literacy teachers. The New London Group (1996) identified many types of literacy practices including print, sound, gesture, and graphic images, stressing that these modes of communication (and many others) should be acknowledged and supported in the school classroom. This understanding of literacy is becoming increasingly relevant for physical education teachers, not least because *physical literacy* is now part of some school curriculum documents (for example, in Ontario, Canada). In addition, physical education teachers often encourage students to use many forms of communication – such as interpretive dance and drama – and, in this way, movement might be considered a literacy practice.

Given our increasingly diverse society and multiple forms of communication available, schools can no longer focus on a narrow range of literacy practices – some of which 'are never or rarely used in life outside of school' (Gee & Hayes, 2011, p. 65). Students' out-of-school literacy practices (for example, creating sophisticated videos) often contrast sharply with the rudimentary work they do in schools (Alvermann, 2011). Andy's work and ideas provide a fine example of multiliteracies theory actualised. A quick scan of Andy's teaching blog shows many forms of literacy inherent in the site: reading text, watching a video, understanding a picture, recognising an icon (for example, Facebook); interpreting a graph; analysing a picture of children; and listening to a podcast. Similarly, Andy's description of the *Sportfolio* suggests it provides students with many ways to communicate – pictures, graphs, texts, and symbols. Further, Andy and his students can share their out-of-school experiences (for example, participation in a sport or other form of physical activity). By bridging in- and out-of-school experiences he is making education more relevant to his students.

As students are bombarded with information, especially about body images and sports heroes, teachers need space for students to analyse these images and the accompanying rhetoric. Schools need to combine 'information literacy, critical media literacy, and information and communication technology literacy' (Levin & Schrum, 2012, p. 8). Through blogging Andy would provide his students with a place to discuss these issues.

Content area literacy

Understanding multiliteracies opens the way for us to think about content area literacy. Alvermann and Phelps (1994) describe the traditional approach to literacy in the disciplines:

> Most content area teachers assume it is their responsibility to cover their subject matter in a timely, accurate, and effective manner. They also assume . . . that textbooks are necessary (pp. 4–5).

Current research on content area literacy, however, reveals that each discipline has unique forms of communication and that 'content area teachers are asked to help students read like scientists in science classes [and] historians in social studies classes' (Faggella-Luby *et al.*, 2009, p. 459). Fisher and Frey (2012) argue that there is a range of resources *beyond* the textbook. Andy's blogs and the students' *Sportfolios* (whether in hard copy or digital format) help students acquire the conventions and language for physical education and use resources beyond the textbook.

Blogging is a different genre of writing. For example, a blog of 200 words with a graphic and a hyperlink requires a different skill set than writing a 2,000-word essay. Despite being considered as an alternative or new mode of literacy, as blogs become more commonplace there is a growing number of resources about the conventions of blogging, such as how to write an effective blog post or to develop an effective blog site. The website *How To Make My Blog* (http://howtomakemyblog.com/10-elements-of-style-of-blog-post-writing/) lists 10 characteristics of effective blogs, which include: omit needless words; use definite, specific concrete language; be clear; use orthodox spelling; avoid fancy words; and do not take shortcuts at the cost of clarity. What we quickly learn is that blogging requires particular literacy skills.

One of the key features of blogging is that it encourages writers to think carefully about their audience: What do they want to express and why is it important? This level of introspection requires reflection and careful writing. The digital nature of blogs means that the potential audience is massive (as Shawn Bullock suggests in his section). Since readers may be from anywhere in the world our writing could reach far beyond the classroom teacher or fellow students. A key feature of effective teaching is that it motivates students; knowing that others read your work can be incredibly motivating. This makes blogging far more authentic and powerful than the traditional essay that is probably read only by the teacher. The ideas that underpin Andy's work would see students acquiring the skills for blogging while learning the advantages and perils of making connections beyond the classroom. These are life skills that have relevance well beyond the classroom door.

An assessment perspective (Déirdre Ní Chróinín)

Andy's plan to digitise the *Sportfolio* reflects current trends where blogs are being used increasingly in educational contexts (Ray, 2006) and are seen as having the potential to represent an alternative form of assessment in physical education (López-Pastor *et al.*, 2013). Though there is limited research on the use of blogs in physical education, Yuen and Cheung (2013) suggest blogs may serve as an appropriate and enjoyable assessment tool for use in primary schools. In the following section, I focus on the potential added value of blogs in assessment *for* learning (AfL) and summative assessment *of* that learning (AoL).

AfL is focused on informing and supporting student learning (Black *et al.*, 2003). Blogs can support AfL in a number of ways. First, teachers who use assessment *for* learning in physical education share learning intentions and criteria for success with students (Black & Wiliam, 2009). Blog entries can be used by students to set learning goals and demonstrate understanding of assessment criteria. Second, in their blogs, students can devise and record strategies to support identified goals. They can then update their blog regularly to describe their learning experiences and progress related to effort and achievement, thus helping make their learning progress in physical education more explicit (Ní Chróinín & Cosgrave, 2013). Third, feedback can be provided on learning activities; for example, prompts from the teacher can focus student attention on specific aspects of learning, such as effective goals (Cutforth & Parker, 1996). Fourth, interactions with classmates about one another's blogs can activate students as instructional and assessment resources for each other. For example, making decisions related to selection and organisation of blog content gives students ownership of their leaning as well as providing a self-assessment frame to track the learning process. Fifth, students' representations of their learning through work samples can showcase their learning and support AoL by the teacher. The major benefits of blogging as an assessment tool are considered below in relation to: (a) representations of learning and (b) feedback on learning.

Representations of learning

Andy saw that blogs would allow students to capture and represent their learning in a variety of ways, thus providing them with greater ownership of their physical education experience (López-Pastor *et al.*, 2013). For example, written descriptions and evaluations of personal learning experiences can help students develop reflection skills and reinforce important learning outcomes (Cutforth & Parker, 1994). By taking time to model and share examples of his reflection processes, Andy was also teaching students *how* they could reflect on and represent their learning through the *Sportfolio*.

Although blogs carry the potential to develop traditional literacy skills through written text, students can also use blogs to show developments in skill performance using video analysis tools such as *Hudl Technique* and *Dartfish*. The *Hudl Technique* application (www.hudl.com) allows students to record and share skill performance on a mobile digital device. They can review different performances side by side for comparison and track their performances across time. It might also be incorporated into a student's personal blog, or, in Andy's case, *Sportfolio*. Drawings (MacPhail & Kinchin, 2004) and photos (Pope, 2010) are other non-written forms of text that can be incorporated into blogs, both of which can help children demonstrate their learning *and* how they feel about their learning. Scaffolding the selection of non-written items for inclusion in a blog entry by learners can include strategies such as visualisation, labelling items and using reflective prompts such as 'I am choosing this item because' or 'This item shows how I . . .' to help students make sense of their learning (Melograno, 2000). Reviewing a range of learning-related products such as worksheets, drawings, and videos both individually and with peers can promote further active engagement that results in a deeper understanding of specific content.

Feedback on learning

Feedback is central to AfL processes. Feedback on blog entries can create higher expectations for success and motivation to learn, resulting in improved engagement and achievement (Bingham *et al.*, 2010; Ní Chróinín & Cosgrave, 2013). Blogs also provide opportunities for feedback from multiple sources including self, the teacher, peers, parents, or an external expert. Blogging is particularly suited to supporting self-assessment, where self-referenced improvement can be tracked across several blog entries (Bingham *et al.*, 2010). Furthermore, teachers gain valuable insights from blogs into individual learners' attitudes, understandings, and dispositions, and this can help them to individualise feedback.

Structured peer assessment is congruent with social-constructivist learning theories that value interaction, discussion, and collaboration within an interactive learning community. Peers can insert comments into the blog of a classmate that reflect the agreed assessment criteria and feedback protocols. Through response and reaction to new information and ideas, such peer feedback can help students to re-evaluate their own perspectives, resulting in a change in their thinking (Chien *et al.*, 2010).

Blogs also allow parents to access a digital record of learning, offering them the opportunity to understand and acknowledge their child's progress and achievement (Cruz & Petersen, 2002). The online nature of blogs also creates the possibility of connecting with and gaining feedback from others outside the immediate classroom group (Richardson, 2010), for example, sharing a private blog between classes in different schools. Feedback and learning from the perspectives of others through interaction within an online community of learners can promote feelings of value, acceptance, and relatedness (Deci & Ryan, 2011).

Blogging by students in physical education holds the potential to scaffold and enhance every aspect of the assessment process from goal setting through to recording and reporting learning; yet, there is little research on teachers' and students' experiences of using blogs in physical education. Hay and Penney's (2009) socio-cultural perspective on assessment provides a useful framework to examine how blogs might promote learning and privilege particular forms of knowledge in physical education. The impact of individual students sharing their learning processes and products merits particular attention given the public nature of blogging. In any implementation of blogs for assessment purposes teachers should aim to satisfy Hay and Penney's (2009) emphases of authenticity, integration, validity, and socially just approaches. These are recognised as desirable conditions to develop and promote assessment efficacy in physical education. The added value of blogging for the learner provides a compelling case to initiate blogs in physical education. Such innovation is to be welcomed in providing a potential tool that can enhance learning in physical education in ways that personalise and connect this learning to the activities and people central to the learner's experiences.

A pedagogical perspective (Tim Fletcher)

Readers might wonder what this chapter can contribute to a book about technology and e-pedagogies in physical education, given that Andy did not put into practice his ideas for using blogs. It could even be argued that Andy's case showcases an *absence* of technology. Yet if Andy's case is thought of not so much as learning about new technologies but as a foundation from which to *learn about teaching using technology* (Bullock, 2013b), there is much to be gained from his story and the perspectives of the interdisciplinary contributors. In particular, it is clear that a strong and thoughtful pedagogy of technology involves practitioners making critical and intelligent decisions about why, how and when to use (and *not* to use) specific technologies.

Despite the potentially positive outcomes that digitising the *Sportfolio* through blogs could have offered his students, Andy's decision not to use blogs was based on strong pedagogical reasoning involving consultations with many colleagues. Most importantly, students' interests and well-being were always at the forefront of his decision-making process. In the following sections, the themes of using, misusing, and not using technology offer ways to think about and learn from Andy's case in order to inform future decisions related to developing pedagogies of technology in physical education.

Using technology

Andy's extended use of blogging for his personal and professional development meant he had developed the technical proficiency to use blogs. In addition he understood how blogging had helped him learn. This allowed him to understand the pedagogical strengths and limitations of blogging and develop his own digital competencies. That Andy had been developing his digital competency is important for his students' learning, because teachers' digital competencies (combining technical and pedagogical skills and knowledge about integrating digital technology in classrooms) influence students' technological self-efficacy and digital literacy (Aesaert *et al.*, 2015; Hughes, 2005; Papastergiou *et al.*, 2011).

It makes sense that teachers should have some competency using the pedagogical tools they select for teaching. However, the rapid advance of digital technologies can make developing the necessary competencies challenging and time consuming.

For example, in order to appear current to students, parents, and colleagues or to take advantage of the learning features of certain new technologies, teachers may hastily adopt a new digital platform without a strong understanding of the features and drawbacks. Selwyn (2011) intimates that such approaches are common and informed by overly optimistic views of 'harness[ing] the power of technology' (p. 713), but often lack the necessary consideration of the complexities of teaching and learning.

The complexities of teaching are highlighted in Andy's case, particularly when children's involvement in networked publics is considered (see Shawn Bullock's section). Such are the concerns for children's digital privacy, at the time of writing it was announced that a global network of privacy organisations (such as governmental privacy commissioners) would perform a 'sweep' of apps and websites to look at the types of personal information being collected from children (Krashinsky, 2015). Technology companies that track children's personal data or do not insist that children have parents' agreement to their terms and conditions, ran the risk of facing stiff penalties from federal agencies in many countries (including Canada, the United States, most members of the European Union, China, Singapore, New Zealand, and Australia).

Despite some potential perils of online engagement through blogging, there are several positive learning outcomes students may achieve through blogging in physical education. For instance, writing is not often an explicit part of physical education programmes yet, as Clare Kosnik and Déirdre Ní Chróinín suggested, written reflection through blogs or other media contains powerful ways for students to better understand and make sense of their physical educational experiences (O'Connell & Dyment, 2011; Papastergiou et al., 2011).

Taken together, there are two key points to consider about using technology from Andy's case. First, decisions to use digital technologies should be based on their potential to help students achieve educational outcomes (Casey & Jones, 2011). In talking with Andy throughout the writing of this chapter it was apparent he had identified and targeted several key outcomes (literacy outcomes, connecting with peers, reflecting on experiences) well before considering the means through which to achieve them. Only once the outcomes had been identified did he pinpoint blogs as a potential tool to help student achievement. Second, practitioners should consider using technologies with which they are familiar and can demonstrate competence. When a practitioner is not familiar with the many features of the technologies they use, there is a risk that the technology can be misused.

Misusing technology

There are two main ways we might think about the misuse of technology in educational contexts. The first and most glaring is when technology is used in ways that are inappropriate and that put students at risk in some way. For example, requiring students to subscribe and contribute to a publicly accessible class social media account (by posting photos or status updates, for example) could lead to cyberbullying or exposure to online predators (Byron, 2008). The second is when technology is used for purposes that do not advance students' learning. When we previously conducted a collaborative self-study of our online teaching practices, Shawn Bullock introduced me to the technology concept of 'mindtools' (Jonassen, 1996). *Mindtools* are technologies that serve as intellectual partners with the learner to facilitate critical thinking (Moos & Azevedo, 2009). Mindtools often stand in contrast to 'productivity tools', which primarily serve to improve efficiency or simply make things easier, or 'entertainment tools', which offer little more than fancy add-ons or gadgets. This is not to suggest that productivity or entertainment tools have no place in education, however, if student learning is kept at the forefront of teachers' decision making, thinking about the extent to which a technology can serve as a mindtool may help mitigate the misuse of educational technologies.

Andy had experienced ways in which blogging provided opportunities for collaboration and reflection through journal writing, community building, and linking to external readers – all of which characterise blogging as a mindtool. Andersson and Räisänen (2014) identify these as the more powerful features of blogs; however, their research found that Swedish teachers tended to use blogs in a very narrow sense, for example for posting instructions or as supplemental classroom materials (as productivity tools). What this suggests is that adopting a certain technology does not by itself lead to effective student learning; it is the ways in which the technology is used or misused that is of prime importance (Selwyn, 2011). Decisions about the extent to which technology can be used as a mindtool may lead to teachers to decide not to adopt that technology.

Non-use of technology

It is important to make clear that *not* using technology does not mean that its use has been ignored or avoided. In Andy's case, the non-use of technology was based on a rigorous process where student learning was the main principle upon which any decision was made. While the non-use of digital technologies can signal issues of poor access and forms of inequality, it can also be the outcome of a decision-making process reflecting consumers' agency (Selwyn, 2006). For example, Andy was already a competent user of blogs yet chose not to use that technology with his students. Andy's case would be of interest to Selwyn (2006), who encourages us to think of technology users and non-users in a hierarchy (or continuum) rather than in dichotomous terms. Selwyn's (2006) argument serves to remind us that non-use of digital technologies in classrooms is not necessarily indicative of a technophobe or 'Luddite'. Instead, it can be evidence of a reflective teacher who has used her or his agency to make decisions based on what is in the best educational interests of students.

While Andy's decision to not use blogs may limit students' 'hands-on' engagement with digital technology, it does offer important opportunities to discuss technological topics with students. For example, students could have learned about the long-term consequences of posting and sharing online, which could impact their lives well beyond school. Quennerstedt, Almqvist, Mekbach, and Öhman (2013) showed physical education teachers seldom used digital technologies (in the form of exergames) as a springboard to open critical discussions in the physical education classroom. Helping students learn how to be informed consumers and decision makers (for technology or many other aspects of their lives) is arguably an important part of most, if not all, physical education programmes.

In summary, Andy's case demonstrates the importance of practitioners adopting a critical mindset in developing appropriate pedagogies of technology. As Selwyn (2006) suggests, too often technology users and non-users are thought of in extremes – one either does or does not use technology. However, developing pedagogies of technology might be more appropriately considered on a continuum that includes a thorough analysis of the practitioner's adaptability based on the reasons underpinning decisions to use or not use. How a practitioner positions herself or himself on the continuum would shift depending on the different technologies used (or not) and the students with whom the practitioner intends to use the technology. Although Andy is an enthusiastic and proficient user of blogs, in order to avoid misusing blogs with his Grade One students – which might have had negative impacts on student learning – he made an informed decision not to use them. To further develop a pedagogy of technology, discussing decisions about the use or non-use of technology with students opens opportunities for further learning about the role of technology in their lives.

Practitioner reflection

There is no question I was anxious about rolling out digital *Sportfolios*. Although I had good intentions, I began to appreciate the extraordinary amount of work that goes into making important decisions such as this become a reality. It is not just about making this vision a reality for my students and me; it is also about ensuring all stakeholders involved are informed, trained, and fully prepared. I must admit to feeling a sense of doom when I realised my plan was not going to work out, but as I looked at the entire process more objectively, I concluded that waiting a year and setting up digital portfolios properly was in the best interests of my students.

I would like to address some of the meaningful feedback I received from Shawn, Clare, Déirdre, and Tim. I felt I had thought through the entire process of setting up the digital *Sportfolios* for my students. I knew there would be several advantages from different perspectives related to student learning; however, the feedback added new dimensions to my understanding and, hopefully, to theirs too.

Shawn made me aware of the need to revisit privacy issues and understanding the potential risks involved in going digital with student work. Clare's feedback helped me understand the concept of multiliteracies and how digital *Sportfolios* would help expand my students' range of literacy practices for life in the twenty-first century. Déirdre's perspective gave me valuable insight into just how powerful student voice and choice can be in regards to assessment. In particular, I took note of her reference to self-determination theorists Deci and Ryan (2011), who offer further insights and will extend my thinking about some of my decisions in taking *Sportfolios* digital. For example, feedback and learning through interaction within an online community of learners can promote feelings of value, acceptance, and relatedness through affirmation of feelings and ideas (Deci & Ryan, 2011).

As I had worked with Tim throughout the process of writing this chapter, his feedback helped me understand and accept that not moving forward with digital portfolios this year should not be looked at as a failure but as a strong example of sound pedagogical decision making. The other perspectives from Shawn, Clare, and Déirdre also played a role in helping open my eyes to the fact that creating such a huge change in the way I deliver my programme must be looked at from multiple angles in order to have the desired impact I wish for students. In moving forward with digital *Sportfolios* in the future, I know the entire process will not only have been well thought out and planned for; it will have stronger theoretical and pedagogical support.

Lessons from the case: How can the use of digital technologies accelerate pupil learning in physical education?

- Digital technologies should be thought of as tools to potentially assist effective learning, not necessarily as tools that are effective because of their presence. Practitioners should engage in extensive use of digital technologies themselves to understand benefits and risks (inside and outside the classroom) before making any decisions about use or non-use.
- Digital technologies carry the potential to enhance students' learning across the curriculum. Andy's case offered the potential for students to develop literacy and self-/peer-assessment skills in physical education through blogging.
- Practitioners who discuss their decisions about using or not using digital technologies with their students can provide opportunities to enhance student learning about being a technologically literate citizen. For example, Andy's decision not to use blogs was not a matter of 'I don't know how to use it'. He asked questions of himself and knowledgeable colleagues, considered advantages and disadvantages, and thought of privacy concerns before making a decision. Discussing these processes with students may offer an important opportunity to help them think more critically and learn about their own and others' engagement with digital technology.

References

Aesaert, K., van Braak, J., van Nijlen, D., and Vanderlinde, R. (2015). Primary school pupils' ICT competences: Extensive model and scale development. *Computers & Education, 81,* 326–344.

Alvermann, D. E. (2011). Moving on, keeping pace: Youths' literate identities and multimodal digital texts. *National Society for the Study of Education Yearbook, 110*(1), 109–128.

Alvermann, D. and Phelps, S. (1994). *Content reading and literacy.* Boston, MA: Allyn and Bacon.

Andersson, A. and Räisänen, K. (2014). Using class blogs in 1:1 schools – searching for unexplored opportunities. *Computers in the Schools, 31,* 173–196.

BBC News. (2014, January 17). Edward Snowden: Leaks that exposed US spy programme. Retrieved from www.bbc.com/news/world-us-canada-23123964

Bingham, G., Holbrook, T., and Meyers, L. E. (2010). Using self-assessments in elementary classrooms. *The Phi Delta Kappan, 91,* 59–61.

Black, P. and Wiliam, D. (2009). Developing the theory of formative assessment. *Educational Assessment, Evaluation and Accountability* (formerly: *Journal of Personnel Evaluation in Education), 21*(1), 5–31.

Black, P., Harrison, C., Lee, C., Marshall, B., and Wiliam, D. (2003). *Assessment for Learning: Putting it into Practice.* Berkshire, UK: Open University Press.

Booth, D. (2013). *I've got something to say: How student voices inform our teaching.* Markham, ON: Pembroke.

boyd, d. (2014). *It's complicated: the social lives of networked teens.* New Haven, CT: Yale University Press.

Bullock, S. M. (2013a). Learning to teach and the false apprenticeship: Emotion and identity development during the field experience placement. In M. Newberry, A. Gallant, and P. Riley (Eds.), *Emotion and school: Understanding how the hidden curriculum influences relationships, leadership, teaching, and learning* . Bingley, UK: Emerald. pp. 119–140.

Bullock, S. M. (2013b). Using digital technologies to support self-directed learning for preservice teacher education. *The Curriculum Journal, 24,* 103–120.

Byron, T. (2008). *Safer children in a digital world: The report of the Byron review.* DCSF/DCMS. Retrieved from: https://media.education.gov.uk/assets/files/pdf/s/safer%20children%20in%20a%20digital%20world%20the%202008%20byron%20review.pdf

Casey, A. and Jones, B. (2011). Using digital technology to enhance student engagement in physical education. *Asia-Pacific Journal of Sport, Health and Physical Education, 2,* 51–66.

Chien, T.-C., Chen, Z.-H., and Chan, T.-W. (2010). A blog-based peer assessment model to support pupils' composition activity. *18th International Conference on Computers,* pp. 206–210.

Cruz, L. M. and Petersen, S. C. (2002). Reporting assessment results to parents. *Journal of Physical Education, Recreation, and Dance, 73,* 20–24.

Cutforth, N. and Parker, M. (1996). Promoting affective development in physical education: The value of journal writing. *Journal of Physical Education, Recreation, and Dance, 67,* 19–23.

Deci, E. L. and Ryan, R. M. (2011). Self-determination theory. *Handbook of Theories of Social Psychology, 1,* 416–433.

Faggella-Luby, M., Ware, S., and Capozzoli, A. (2009). Adolescent literacy – reviewing adolescent literacy reports: Key components and critical questions. *Journal of Literacy Research, 41,* 453–475.

Fisher, D. and Frey, N. (2012). *Improving adolescent literacy: Content area strategies at work* (3rd ed.). Toronto, ON: Pearson.

Gee, J. P. and Hayes, E. R. (2011). *Language and learning in the digital age.* New York, NY: Routledge.

Hay, P. and Penney, D. (2009). Proposing conditions for assessment efficacy in physical education. *European Physical Education Review, 15*(3), 389–405.

Hughes, J. (2005). The role of teacher knowledge and learning experiences in forming technology-integrated pedagogy. *Journal of Technology and Teacher Education, 13,* 277–302.

Johnston, J. (2015). 'Loose tweets sink fleets' and other sage advice: Social media governance, policies and guidelines. *Journal of Public Affairs, 15*(2), 175–187.

Jonassen, D. H. (1996). *Computers in the classroom: Mindtools for critical thinking.* Upper Saddle River, NJ: Prentice-Hall.

Kranzberg, M. (1986). Technology and history: "Kranzberg's Laws". *Technology and Culture*, *27*(3), 544–560.

Krashinsky, S. (2015). Canada joins global sweep of kids' online privacy. *The Globe and Mail*, May 11 2015. Retrieved from www.theglobeandmail.com/report-on-business/industry-news/marketing/global-sweep-to-focus-on-kids-online-privacy/article24378940/

Levin, B. and Schrum, L. (2012). *Leading technology-rich schools: Award-winning models for success.* New York, NY: Teachers College Press.

López-Pastor, V. M., Kirk, D., Lorente-Catalán, E., MacPhail, A., and Macdonald, D. (2013). Alternative assessment in physical education: A review of international literature. *Sport, Education and Society*, *18*, 57–76.

MacPhail, A. and Kinchin, G. (2004). The use of drawings as an evaluative tool: students' experiences of sport education. *Physical Education and Sport Pedagogy*, *9*(1), 87–108.

Melograno, V. J. (2000). Designing a portfolio system for K–12 physical education: A step-by-step process. *Measurement in Physical Education and Exercise Science*, *4*, 97.

Moos, D. C. and Azevedo, R. (2009). Learning with computer-based learning environments: A literature review of computer self-efficacy. *Review of Educational Research*, *79*, 576–600.

New London Group. (1996). A pedagogy of multiliteracies: Designing social futures. *Harvard Educational Review*, *66*, 60–92.

Ní Chróinín, D. and Cosgrave, C. (2013). Implementing formative assessment in primary physical education: Teacher perspectives and experiences. *Physical Education and Sport Pedagogy*, *18*, 219–233.

O'Connell, T. and Dyment, J. (2011). Health and physical education pre-service teachers' perceptions of journals as a reflective tool in experience-based learning. *European Physical Education Review*, *17*, 135–151.

Papastergiou, M., Gerodimos, V., and Antoniou, P. (2011). Multimedia blogging in physical education: Effects on student knowledge and ICT self-efficacy. *Computers and Education*, *57*, 1998–2010.

Pope, C. (2010). Got the picture? Exploring student sport experiences using photography as voice. In M. O'Sullivan and A. MacPhail (Eds.), *Young people's voices in physical education and youth sport.* Oxon: Routledge. pp. 186–209.

Quennerstedt, M., Almqvist, J., Meckbach, J., and Öhman, M. (2013). Why do Wii teach physical education in school? *Swedish Journal of Sports Research*, *1*, 55–81.

Rainie, L. and Madden, M. (2015, March 16). Americans' Privacy Strategies Post-Snowden. Retrieved from www.pewinternet.org/2015/03/16/americans-privacy-strategies-post-snowden/

Ray, J. (2006). Welcome to the blogosphere: The educational use of blogs (aka edublogs). *Kappa Delta Pi Record*, *42*, 175–177.

Richardson, W. (2010). *Blogs, wikis, podcasts, and other powerful web tools for classrooms.* Thousand Oaks, CA: Corwin Press.

Selwyn, N. (2006). Digital division or digital decision? A study of non-users and low-users of computers. *Poetics*, *34*, 273–292.

Selwyn, N. (2011). Editorial: In praise of pessimism – the need for negativity in educational technology. *British Journal of Educational Technology*, *42*, 713–718.

UNESCO (2014). *Literacy initiative for empowerment.* Retrieved from www.unesco.org/new/en/education/themes/education-building-blocks/literacy/un-literacy-decade/literacy-initiative-life/

Wiktionary (n.d.). blog. Retrieved from https://en.wiktionary.org/wiki/blog

Yuen, G. O. M. and Cheung, W. S. (2013). What students like and dislike about blogs: A two-case study. *New Horizons in Education*, *61*.

8

JOEY: SOCIAL MEDIA AS A TOOL FOR PROFESSIONAL DEVELOPMENT

Doug Gleddie, Joey Feith, P. David Howe,
Håkan Larsson, Lorraine Cale and Ashley Casey

CHAPTER OVERVIEW

Joey is a teacher who uses social media to enhance his professional development and ultimately, his students' learning. Joey's narrative is analysed from three very different perspectives: elementary physical education teacher education, Foucauldian theory and anthropology. It is argued that to develop effective pedagogies of technology, there is a need for authentic professional learning networks (PLN) for pre-service teachers, recognition of power dynamics in social media and an awareness of the "other" to ensure cultural relevance and the establishment of broad networks. The importance of viewing online PLNs analytically and critically is emphasised.

Practitioner narrative (Joey Feith)

One of my goals is to be the best teacher I can be for the students I am privileged to teach. I want to be able to provide them with a world-class, effective and inclusive physical education program. To help me reach this goal, I have been using social media as a tool for engaging in purposeful professional development. The following is an account of how social media platforms have helped change the way I think and go about my teaching.

Of the many social media tools I use, Twitter is the one I engage with the most (see Table 8.1). One of the ways in which I do this is through the bi-monthly Twitter chat '#pechat' that I conceived. This chat explores topics related to physical education. As one of the global #pechat moderators, I am responsible for facilitating the conversation for an hour. In preparation, I usually spend some time on Sunday mornings researching the upcoming topic on Google Scholar (see Table 8.1) and also tapping into my Twitter-based professional learning network (PLN) of over

TABLE 8.1 Technology/apps, functions and how they were used

Technology/app	Function	How they were used by the practitioner
Twitter	Twitter is a popular social media platform that involves users sharing information, links, and other media in short, 140-character messages called "tweets".	Twitter was used as a tool to help Joey connect with like-minded professionals from around the world. It helped him build the foundation of his online professional learning network (PLN).
Google Scholar	Google Scholar is an online search engine that helps users search for academic journals and materials.	Google Scholar was used as a tool to accelerate Joey's research on specific topics prior to professional online chats.
YouTube	YouTube is a video-sharing website and social media platform.	Joey used YouTube to find videos relating to physical education.
Skype	Skype is a popular online video chat software and app that allows people to make free video calls to other Skype users around the world.	Joey used Skype to have online face-to-face conversations with teachers he had connected with via other social media platforms.
Google Forms	Google Forms is a digital form-building tool that is part of the Google Drive productivity suite. The app allows users to create online forms that facilitate data collection.	Joey used Google Forms to create digital reflection sheets for his students in order to better understand the progress they were making in their learning.
QR codes	QR codes, or Quick Response codes, are device-readable codes that allow users to quickly access information that is stored online (e.g. a website or video) by scanning the code using a digital device, such as a phone or tablet PC.	Joey used QR codes to help his students quickly access Google Forms that he had created for his lessons.

20,000 followers that includes teachers, administrators, authors and academics from our field. Having a network of this size accelerated my research efforts and made it simpler to find quality articles that could, in turn, help me moderate. When I 'tweet' questions and requests for literature to this PLN, it does not take very long for fellow Twitter users to respond with helpful tips, links and resources (see Table 8.1 for explanations of the terms used in this narrative).

The #pechat on this particular Monday, on the pedagogical method of scaffolding, progressed as usual. I asked different questions and responded to the wildfire of answers and counter-questions. With each response, I attempted to push fellow teachers to go deeper and to problematize their reasoning and practice. Doing so not only made for a more active chat but it also allowed me to learn as much as possible. For example, the chat forced me to reflect on my own teaching and helped me realize that even though I feel I do a good job of gradually adding levels of support for my students (e.g. modifications to the constraints of the activity, differentiated equipment, etc.), I do not always remove those supports when they are no longer needed.

The next day, with these reflections in mind, I started planning for a striking/fielding unit for my Grade 6 students (age 11–12). I began the process by determining which grade-level outcomes I wanted to help my students reach. From there, I determined the evidence of student learning I would look for throughout the unit. I selected appropriate assessment tools to collect that evidence, designed learning activities that would allow my students to put new concepts/skills/knowledge into practice and then set out to determine the learning sequence of those activities.

This process of 'backwards design' was something I learned last spring when I stumbled across a YouTube video by Terri Drain (a California-based teacher). Terri's video was very logical and comprehensive, and instantly impacted on how I thought about backwards design (especially in terms of determining the desired evidence of student learning prior to the design of learning activities).

The impact of Terri's video was such that I chose to reach out to her via Twitter to initiate a discussion and explore her method of backward design (what Terri called standards-based instructional design [SBID]). As we talked, we realized that we were both attending SHAPE America's upcoming national physical education convention and set a time to meet. Meeting face to face allowed me to better understand her framing of SBID and also gain personal feedback on my own implementation. Specifically, she highlighted the importance of selecting assessment tools designed to collect specific types of student learning evidence (i.e. if a student needs to be able to list critical elements of a skill, the tool must be designed in such a way that allows a list to be created).

Thanks to social media, Terri was not the only person who had a positive impact on the development of my striking/fielding unit. As I determined what evidence of student learning I required, I recalled a Skype conversation I had with Dean Dudley from Australia. Dean and I had connected via Twitter some time ago, and, after talking one day over the social media platform, decided to chat face to face via Skype. Our conversation focused on the importance of being able to show evidence of student learning through the purposeful collection of data. Dean explained that if the grades 'we' (as teachers) assign students came to be argued in court, then the evidence we collect on student learning should be clear and objective enough to convince any jury that our grades were correct.

That conversation stuck with me for a long time. I continued to reflect on this notion, especially in terms of being able to communicate and justify grades clearly and effectively to both my students and other stakeholders (e.g. administrators, parents). Therefore, as I devised my striking/fielding unit, I made sure that my student portfolios and my grade book were all set up. In this way, I could start collecting and communicating evidence from the onset, a process that I believe would have been absent from my planning without my Twitter connections.

Once I'd determined the evidence and assessment tools I needed throughout the unit, it was time to design the learning activities. I like to feel that the process of game design is one of the strengths of my pedagogy. That said, if it were not for the members of my PLN that would not be the case. Of all of the people I have 'tweeted' with over the years, no one has been more influential and had a greater impact on my pedagogical game design than Kelly Ann Parry. Kelly discovered my website, ThePhysicalEducator.com, a couple of years ago and found my Teaching Games for Understanding (TGfU) database amongst the resources. Kelly, who was about to embark on a scholar tour of Canada to learn more about TGfU, began a conversation with me on Twitter and asked if we could meet when she came to Montreal.

We met and discussed the idea of layering games (i.e. modifying games by changing constraints to adjust the tactical complexity) and ensuring that the individual needs of each student are met. Kelly taught me about the difference between primary rules (i.e. rules that define the nature of a game) and secondary rules (i.e. rules that can be modified without changing the nature of the game). She also explained that having different students play with different sets of secondary rules allows each student to work at a developmentally appropriate level without taking them out of the authentic game situation. These conversations completely shifted the way I thought about game design. I used to believe, for example, that students who were not ready for the next tactical progression of a game should instead be given a drill-like activity until they showed progress on the tactics/skills on which they were working. Not any more!

The final piece of my unit planning involved selecting/creating the technological tools to use for assessment. Meaningful use of technology is something I have been interested in for a long time, and I've been very lucky to have great minds from my Twitter PLN help me along the way. Nathan Horne, a physical education teacher in Singapore, was one of the first teachers to show me the 'power' of using Google Forms (see Table 8.1) as a tool to quickly and efficiently collect data on student learning. Jarrod Robinson, an Australian physical education teacher, has also introduced me to the efficiency of using QR codes in education to help students quickly access online materials.

My striking/fielding unit was a success. Not only were my students able to meet the curriculum objectives I outlined, but I am confident that I understand 'where they are at' in their learning and where each student needs to progress. Without the help of my PLN, this unit would not have been as successful. By being purposeful and self-directed in the way I use social media, I have been able to accelerate my own professional development and be a better teacher for my students.

This narrative is just one example of how I have grown as a teacher thanks to the online physical education community. My plan is to keep tweeting, keep reflecting and keep growing as a teacher for as long as I can. The energy, excitement and accessibility of the people I have connected with online keeps my passion for teaching physical education fresh and alive. I only hope more teachers will discover and benefit from the power of social media!

In the following sections, my narrative is considered from elementary physical education teacher education, Foucouldian and anthropological perspectives. The pedagogical insights emerging from them are then discussed to offer insights into the dilemmas I faced in practice.

An elementary physical education teacher education perspective (Doug Gleddie)

Joey epitomizes (albeit superlatively) the growing number of physical education teachers on social media – particularly Twitter. Traditionally, physical education teachers have been rather isolated in their schools and have been provided little opportunity for professional collaboration with those beyond their school or even outside their own classes (Andrew *et al.*, 2014; Templin, 1988). In Joey's narrative, social media serves as a mechanism to circumvent this isolation and connect individual physical education teachers within a PLN. As an elementary physical education teacher educator (EPETE) who works with pre-service teachers in Alberta, Canada, I also use social media with my classes and in my professional networking. However, I am acutely aware of certain limitations and issues surrounding the promotion and use of social media in EPETE. In this section I discuss Joey's case from the perspective of EPETE.

The pre-service teachers at my university are training to become elementary (grades K–6) generalist teachers. Pre-service teachers take curriculum and pedagogy courses in seven subject specific areas, one of which is physical education. I have thirty-six hours with each cohort in which to share all the complexities and nuances of teaching elementary physical education. Time is at a premium, and I must carefully consider what, why and how I teach each class. In some ways, Joey is very much like the majority of my students. They all share the ambition of wanting to "be the best teachers they can be", but there are important differences.

Firstly, the students in my class come from a variety of backgrounds and are *not* physical education majors. This means that while they want to be teachers they do not specifically want to be physical education teachers. Secondly, while Joey's aspiration is to offer his students "a world-class, effective and inclusive physical education program", this is not the case with my students. For many, the pedagogical goals that Joey aspires to, in physical education at least, are not there – certainly not at first. Consequently, before beginning to develop physical education pedagogy, building a professional learning network on Twitter or using Google Forms for assessment with my students, I need to address issues of value and identity, and unpack years of personal prior experience in physical education – much of which has often been poor (Morgan & Bourke, 2008).

As defined by the Oxford Canadian dictionary, *values* are "one's judgement of what is important in life". If my students do not value physical education as part of the education and development of the whole child, they will never build a professional physical education network. If they do not come to value physical literacy as highly as numeracy and literacy (Corlett & Mandigo, 2013), they will never design a TGfU unit. As a starting point in my EPETE class, I take a Deweyan approach and focus on students' past experiences of physical education and activity: both educative and mis-educative (Dewey, 1938). Students engage in autobiographical narrative inquiry (Gleddie & Schaefer, 2014) to examine their past, present and future experiences of physical education, and through this process, the knowledge and experience that pre-service teachers bring to class is affirmed and valued. At the same time, students are encouraged to be critical of their own constructions of physical education and how they impact upon pedagogy (Huber *et al.*, 2013; Morgan & Bourke, 2008; Schaefer, 2013). Narrative inquiry (Clandinin & Connelly, 2000) is strongly influenced by Dewey's pragmatic ontology of experience (1958), and views his framework of continuity and interaction as a fundamental part of the inquiry process. From this point, we begin to move into identity – students beginning to see themselves as "teachers of physical education" (Fletcher, 2012). The passion and drive Joey so clearly demonstrates is built on a foundation of valuing physical education and identifying himself with being a teacher of physical education. Eventually, I do want my students to be like Joey, but I recognize the enormity and complexity of achieving this aspiration in my context.

One of the limitations for EPETE is time. Since students cannot possibly "get" all of the information (and build value/identity) they require at the university, it is important to educate them about how to acquire and develop the knowledge and understanding they need on their own. This is where a community of practice (MacPhail *et al.*, 2014; Parker *et al.*, 2012) or PLN can be very effective. Physical education specialist teachers often feel isolated since they may be the only one in their school (Tannehill *et al.*, 2013). Tannehill *et al.* (2013) cite a physical education teacher's explanation: "There has been no physical education–focused support system for me and there has been no-one that I could turn to during the year with physical education questions" (p. 160). Online opportunities may enable isolated individuals to access the PLNs they desire.

Elementary generalist teachers who value physical education and see themselves as teachers of physical education are also likely to feel this sense of isolation and lack of support. Joey's description of his own PLN, developed through Twitter and supported by #pechat, has great potential to help those who feel they are on their own. Other Twitter chats, such as #espechat (elementary school physical education chat) and #pegeeks (technology integration in physical education), have also found their niches. However, as Joey alluded to, these connections need to move past the surface nature and limitations of 140 characters to become deeper and embedded in practice. I found it interesting that for Joey to truly impact his own pedagogy and the experience of his students, he needed to connect in deeper ways. For example, a Twitter connection with Terri led to watching a YouTube video and eventually a face-to-face meeting, the chat with Dean involved Skype, and whilst the connection with Kelly Ann began on Twitter, it took a physical meeting to really move the connection and process forward.

For my students, I certainly encourage, teach and demonstrate the potential of social media and the use of technology to connect with others outside of one's own school, community or even country. Twitter can be a powerful tool; however, as Joey has narrated, it must be followed up with deeper connections to cause effective change for students in physical education. I agree with Tannehill *et al.* (2013, p. 165) when they say, "Not only must we help pre-service teachers choose to collaborate with one another, we must provide them the space and tools with which to conduct this collaboration". Social media is one such tool and one such space.

A Foucouldian perspective (Håkan Larsson)

Joey's ambition to "be the best teacher he can be for the students he is privileged to teach" is certainly an admirable one. He articulates a desire to develop his teaching utilizing the promises of technology and social media, something that very much signals the approach of a "modern teacher". However, inevitably Joey – or any person for that matter – who wants to improve him- or herself in order to better carry out his or her duties, will also have to face challenges related to power and domination. In order to improve himself, Joey is necessarily both enabled and constrained by forces that transverse the universe where he is acting, forces that are sometimes hard to grasp and act purposefully upon (Foucault, 1982a).

In this section I discuss the balance between power and freedom that is often linked to improving oneself. My writing is based on ideas the French philosopher Michael Foucault developed in the 1980s. Foucault was known as a philosopher of power, but in 1982 he maintained that his purpose was to "create a history of the different modes by which, in our culture, human beings are made subjects" (p. 326). In other words, Foucault was interested in social processes that make people become "somebody", for example, "a criminal" or "a righteous person", "a homosexual" or "a heterosexual". Further, he was interested in what it means to understand oneself as "somebody". In short, Foucault's perspective is about self-understanding and the relationship between how we understand our-selves as human beings and our conduct – in other words, how we behave in the social world.

Foucault identified three modes by which human beings have been turned into subjects: subjects of experience, desire and will – including the will to improve. The first and the second modes are about science and dividing practices (i.e. the way human beings tend to divide each other into categories, like gender, age, professions, sane and mad, teachers and pupils). The third mode, which is interesting for the discussion here, is about how human beings turn themselves into subjects. According to Foucault (1988), humans do this through technologies of the self. These are systematic practices that enable individuals to work on themselves – improve themselves – by regulating their bodies (e.g. through diet or exercise), their thoughts (e.g. through psychoanalysis) and their conduct (e.g. through certain programs facilitating behavioural change). Such technologies afford people the chance to transform themselves in order to attain a certain state of happiness, purity, wisdom, perfection or immortality (Foucault, 1988, p. 18).

Modern societies seem to have re-invented a practice that owes its origins to Greek and Roman Antiquity – namely, the practice of self-formation. Rather than to ask "For what sins do I have to do penance?", modern people tend to ask, as did the Greeks and the Romans, "How can I improve myself?" This might be considered quite unproblematic if technologies of the self were not interwoven with technologies of power (Foucault, 1982a). Technologies of power are "imbued with aspirations for the shaping of conduct in the hope of producing certain desired effects and averting certain undesired ones" (Rose, 1999, p. 52). The interweaving of the technologies of self with the technologies of power does not mean that freedom is impossible (well, perhaps unconditional freedom). Instead, every attempt by a subject to transform him- or herself also calls for a critical awareness of the power relations into which he or she is drawn.

To Foucault, power is relational and it transverses society, rather than flowing through pathways of top-down or bottom-up (Foucault, 1982a). In effect, this means that any attempt by Joey to "push fellow teachers to go deeper and problematize their reasoning and practice" is simultaneously representative of his personal desire to develop the profession as well as a cultural imperative to improve – in the name of the students, the school or society. The same goes for the ambitions to involve technologies in this process of self-improvement. By this, I do not want to imply that using technologies is necessarily a bad thing, but that it may be dangerous (Foucault, 1982b), in particular if we do not consider the sometimes unintended and possibly undesired side effects that are related to the use of technology generally and social media specifically.

What unintended and possibly undesired side effects might Joey encounter? These are related to both intended and unintended online violations and to social media becoming a vehicle for acts such as aggressive marketing. Such marketing may be exercised by companies that target different groups, such as teachers and young people, trying to impose on them commercial or ideological messages. In this sense, while Joey experiences agency in his use of Twitter, Twitter itself – or those who exploit Twitter for their own interests – may exert power over Joey (and his students) and his PLN in unforeseen ways. This example indicates the interconnectedness of technologies of self (i.e. Joey) and power (i.e. Twitter). Furthermore, Joey's use of social media requires an investment in the technology itself, which means that both he and his students are exposed to a world of symbolic meaning.

All cultural practice or use of artefacts (such as technology) also necessarily means involvement with symbolic meaning. No practice is merely "technical"; no technology is culturally neutral (Sewell, 2005). The use of technology includes negotiating a specific set of norms and values that are related to context and what technology is used. Thus, involvement with any practice or any kind of technology will include aspects that the subject did not "intend" to include in the first place, and which he or she will have a hard time grasping. The use of technology might give rise to questions such as: Am I content with simple equipment or will I need to invest in the latest, or a particular brand of, computer or cell-phone? What will my peers think or have to say about this? To some extent these issues may, despite Joey's intentions, affect him and his students in undesirable ways. This is particularly so since struggling against the use of technology might be regarded as retrograde. After all, "a good citizen" in contemporary society is arguably expected to favour the use of technological innovations and the promises of social media (see Jones, 2006).

These examples highlight the continuous need for critical interrogation into the potentially unintended and undesired side effects of using technology in physical education, in particular since personal development often comes out of opportunities that, in Joey's words, we "stumble across". The randomness of this process of engagement with technology might make it even more difficult for individuals to assess the unintended consequences. As Foucault (1982a, p. 327) points out, however, the need for "constant checking" is arguably the most important task for critical thought in this era of self-formation and the will to improve.

Ironically, there is also the danger that instead of achieving the desired self-improvement – with all the risks described above – teachers, and consequently their students' learning, could regress. The interweaving of the technologies of the self with the technologies of power might simply reinforce existing constructions of self and technology. Due to the randomness of information found on social media and the drive for improvement, it is possible that "we" might find better and better solutions in our search for a well-ordered and happy population rather than really challenging, improving and moving our practice on.

An anthropological perspective (David Howe)

In this perspective I focus on the discipline's *raison d'être* – trying to understand the culture surrounding a specific context where a nuanced understanding of the culture, the beliefs, behaviours and objects common to the members of a particular group or society (Harris, 2001) is key. Schools are cultural institutions, which have the ability to transmit dominant cultural values (Bourdieu & Passeron, 1990). In this case, it is the culture surrounding elementary physical education unit planning and, specifically, a unit on striking and fielding games. From the outset, I was struck by the certainty of Joey's position, particularly with his belief that he wants to provide a 'world-class, effective and inclusive physical education program'. This is an important and laudable goal, but one which I question as to whether it can be achieved through the outlined case.

First and foremost, the narrative is ethnocentric. In other words, it shows a distinct tendency to judge or interpret other cultures according to the criteria of one's own culture. Joey draws upon his vast PLN, established in part through a strong Twitter following. In the process of developing a striking/fielding unit, Joey seeks advice and yet the contacts he illuminates in the case are all Western pedagogues. It is important to realise that non-Western pedagogues may also have knowledge upon which we can draw to enhance our teaching and learning environments. As such, we need to be aware of the cultural context in which physical educators are working. Without grounding pedagogical cases in the specificity of the cultural milieu, transferring knowledge from the world's illuminated in academic textbooks to the improvement of day-to-day practice is considerably more difficult.

A simple search indicates that the school Joey works at is in a high socio-economic area. Research suggests that such a school serves a predominantly privileged population and benefits from smaller class sizes and high quality facilities (Owens, 2010; Parman, 2011). Such a working environment is likely to provide time for teachers, like Joey, to draw upon their networks to enhance their teaching practice. This context, however, is likely to be different to an inner city school in Birmingham (UK or USA), where resources are probably tight and class sizes are larger (Richards, 2012).

We need to be mindful of the cultural context in which teachers are actively engaged. Without an understanding of this, pedagogical cases are far less transferrable to other distinctive cultural environments. Bourdieu and Passeron (1990) tell us that the culture of the education system we are part of goes some way to shaping who we shall be as adults, and therefore the opportunities or restrictions placed on us in our childhood can have an influence upon us in the future. Because Twitter is to a greater or lesser extent a global media outlet, it is important that all pedagogues are explicit about the socio-cultural context in which they are working.

As articulated in both Kolb's cycle of experiential learning (Kolb, 1984) and Joey's narrative, the need to collect evidence of student learning is fundamental for pedagogues. However, some teachers are hard pressed to do much more than simply keep control of their class (Richards, 2012). Joey's exuberance, confidence and dedication is clear to see, but it reminds me that we all need to be more mindful of the privileged positions we occupy. For example, due to their privileged background, the children under Joey's charge would arguably have already experienced and acquired basic hand-eye coordination, which one assumes is at the heart of a striking/fielding unit (Wolfenden & Holt, 2005).

Yet assessing their performance through 'grade-level outcomes' seems to fly in the face of the desire to create an inclusive physical education environment. Children all mature at different rates. Inclusion requires that we value everyone as an individual for the movement that they can achieve while also trying to enhance their physical literacy (DePauw & Doll-Tepper, 2000). The adoption of 'grade-level outcomes' can therefore be problematized in pedagogical cases where there is a cultural shift toward inclusive practices.

In considering Joey's narrative, it is important to remember that the cultural mosaic that is celebrated in Canadian heritage means that while the parents of Joey's charges embrace bilingual (English/French) education, many may, in fact, speak a third language at home and could come from a wide range of cultural backgrounds. This may also complicate Joey's lesson plans as the 'collision' of cultures can often produce unforeseen circumstances (Lewis, 1999), such as a conflict with how the parents' culture addresses issues regarding physicality and exposure (or not) of the body in the context of physical education classes.

As well as considering the cultural and physical environment of the school, it might be helpful if Joey reflects upon his access to technology. While there is a wide following of social media platforms such as Twitter, not all great pedagogues embrace such platforms, even in the West. Not all teachers have the time or energy to engage in its use and there are parts of the increasing networked world that it cannot reach. While Joey highlights how social media has made him a better pedagogue, the key question (given the need to investment in this interface and continual stream of huge volumes of information) becomes, how does the teaching community separate high and low quality pedagogical advice? Long before the Internet, McLuhan (1964, p. 57) suggested, 'We see ourselves being translated more and more into forms of information, moving toward technological extensions of consciousness'. Using McLuhan's work shows that, while Joey celebrates the role of social media, it is important to recognise and reflect upon the cultural specificity of the context in which he is working. Furthermore, I would suggest pedagogues in similar positions gather more non-Western input, from a wide variety of sources including social media, if their teaching is going to be truly 'world leading'.

A pedagogical perspective (Doug Gleddie, Lorraine Cale and Ashley Casey)

In this section we apply a pedagogical lens to the three perspectives above. In doing so, we explore issues of power, Westernised culture, self-presentation and account-ability, and suggest that all have the potential to impact on the "type" of teacher technology helps to develop. We conclude by suggesting that while all teachers have (to some degree) the potential to use technology (in whatever form it takes) to enhance their pedagogy, it is a matter of choice and not necessity. Joey is not defined by technology but by the ways in which he uses it to positively impact on his students' learning.

The concept of power can be found throughout the chapter. Joey discusses how he "push(es) teachers to go deeper and problematize their reasoning and practice". Perhaps he is able to do so because of the broad and stable platform that he maintains (20,000+ Twitter followers, a popular physical education website and a hashtag chat that he invented). In the words of Goodyear *et al.* (2015, p. 10), he is one of the "big name[s]" on Twitter, and, as such, is positioned as having "something worthwhile to say" (p. 11).

Alternatively, we see that Joey "pushes" from a culture of technology firmly rooted in ethnocentric Western pedagogy. Although there is nothing "wrong" with this, as both the anthropological and Foucauldian perspectives acknowledge, there needs to be a "constant checking" (Foucault, 1982a, p. 327) process of these power dynamics and an acknowledgment of the potential limiting and exclusionary nature of such cultures.

Interestingly, this "constant checking" (or at least the need for it) has begun to occur naturally within the #physed community. Recent discussions around social media have featured some of the unintended side effects of technology, such as the tendency to only share successes and not failures (see Erwin, 2016 for a fuller discussion). First, due to the very public and very brief nature of Twitter, there may be an inclination towards a lack of authenticity. It has been argued that individuals may post about how amazing things are and expect to get support in return (Carpenter & Krutka, 2014). Second, and as Erwin (2016) summarised, social media is often a quick, free and effective way of sharing resources. Such sharing, however, does not come without the cost/expectation of quality. It is not enough to simply share resources. Instead, "we [must] we hold ourselves accountable for posting and communicating quality information" while simultaneously challenging "others in a professional way when the information that is shared may not be accurate or appropriate" (Erwin, 2016, p. 4).

Casey *et al.* (2015) suggested that a physical education PLN on Twitter starts out as a place where teachers feel they need to show only their "best side" (i.e. the fact that they are up-to-date and effective supporters of learning). It is not until later, when a teacher's social media identity as an innovator or big name is more secure, that they can open up and talk about their perceived failures as well as their successes (Casey *et al.*, 2015; Goodyear *et al.*, 2015). This suggests a different power dynamic than the one suggested by the Foucauldian perspective, inasmuch as these teachers did not voice a need to improve or indeed "do penance". Instead, they positioned others in this way (Casey *et al.*, 2015) and argued for ways in which "we" – as a field – might help "them" – as deficit teachers – improve.

Many teachers do not progress beyond the "amazing" stage of social media use, and for them it simply becomes a forum for seeking external reassurance, recognition and endorsement rather than necessarily about practice (Carpenter & Krutka, 2014). However, it could be said that "amazingness" is often defined in very Westernised ways. Exploring this idea from an anthropological perspective allows us to see that these notions of innovation and currency are Westernised and, as such, lack the worldwide view that we perhaps associate with the World Wide Web. It also begs the question what might we learn and could we further improve upon, from a wider World Wide Web?

For pre-service teachers, the brevity, positionality and Westernisation of pedagogy could also lead to a misperception of what the "real" work of teaching physical education is like. In their book on workplace learning Rossi *et al.* (2015) argued that schools are not neutral places. They are representative of different ways of acting, dressing, talking and being. They are physical spaces that come to be perceived in certain ways (i.e. supportive, conflicted, macho, sexist, etc.). They are spaces that have come to represent certain conceptions of physical education and sport, and they are spaces that are lived. Are the virtual spaces of the World Wide Web significantly different?

Rossi *et al.* (2015) argued that, in some cases, schools can be seen as spaces that evoke certain subjectivities, practices and relationships – indeed the occupants (i.e. other teachers) plan for and expect them. In other cases, schools are spaces of possibility that support and encourage new ideas and which quickly draw emerging teachers towards the centre of practice. However, these are not single spaces. These are "spaces" that have to be understood through their multiplicity and not through any assumed singularity. Each space has certain possibilities. This understanding raises questions as to how safe, secure and non-threatening a learning platform/ forum social media is for pre-service teachers in particular, especially given the challenges that already exist in their professional contexts.

Furthermore, does the promotion of a culture of technology in #physed lead to a power dynamic where teachers who are "tech-savvy" hold sway and influence over those who aren't? If so, what influence does this dynamic have on the shape and direction of physical education pedagogy and the experiences of students? Is being a #pegeek "better" than "just" working in #physed? Ultimately how does the culture and power of technology and its use influence the pedagogies that we employ?

Joey's pedagogy of technology is based on access: to technology (both individually and as a teacher); to social media; and to individuals outside of his local context. However, it is also based on his efforts and his desire to "be the best teacher I can be". Joey is not the only teacher to have access to technology who has that aspiration. His pedagogy of technology is therefore moulded by his choices and his actions. Although his access to technology might outstrip many others, his power in certain communities may be highly significant, and his thinking may be Westernised – his approach *is* replicable across contexts. Technology supports but does not define his pedagogy. Over his career, Joey has developed, supplemented and enhanced his pedagogy. Any motivated practitioner could do something similar. Their approach may be bespoke, with different degrees of access and intent and with different degrees of power resulting in different methods of teaching and learning. Joey's anthropological origins were not his to choose, however, the desire to put pedagogy before technology was. Both Joey's use of technology and his PLN support his practice and help us to see what a pedagogy of technology could, in one guise, look like.

In summary, while Joey has used his PLN to his advantages he has not been driven by technology. It has been used to serve his purposes and those of his students. The learning of others outside of his immediate contexts is of secondary importance to the development of a world-leading education experience for his students. His choices may not be as free as he might have hoped, and while they might be Western in orientation, they are built on his hard work, his honesty and his willingness to share ideas with, and learn from, others.

Practitioner reflection

Reading these responses to my narrative made me reflect on why I started sharing my work online in the first place. Yes, I did it to gain recognition and build my reputation online. It's fun at first to see how your follower count grows or how many website visits you get each day. However, I do remember a distinct moment when I realized that I was starting to have influence over other teachers' work. Teachers began using the ideas and resources I was sharing online with their own classes and I started to receive invited speaker requests for different conferences. It was all very flattering, and, yes, it went to my head (as it still does every now and then).

There are other reasons, however, why I started sharing and connecting with teachers online. I did it because I wanted to learn more about effective physical education pedagogy and improve as a physical educator. I did it because I actually love my job. I feel like I was born to teach physical education, so I might as well be good at it. I did it because I was tired of people mocking my career choice, tired of seeing physical education time being reduced in schools, and tired of seeing great teachers go unrecognized for their work (and slightly afraid that would eventually be me).

Yes, I want to be the best teacher I can be. However, am I doing all I can and setting myself up to be able to achieve that? Are the ideas and methods I learn about online and subsequently adopt actually moving my practice in the right direction? To ensure this, I need to set up systems of "constant checking" to make sure I'm not adopting ineffective or undesirable teaching practices. Systems could involve setting aside time each week to reflect on the ideas and methods I have come across and am excited about, and then following up with some research to establish what evidence supports – or challenges – these. Also, given the amount of expertise available to me via my PLN, I could reach out to experts in the field to seek their opinions on my teaching (similar to how we have done in this chapter). Setting up these "constant checking" systems should help me to avoid the potential pitfall of adopting particular teaching practices simply because I find them exciting. Doing so will allow me to keep exploring best practice and to continue growing as a teacher.

Reading the responses to my narrative also reminded me that, when I share online, I often share the "best" or in other words the refined or rehearsed version of what actually happened in my class. I receive digital pats on the back for my success, but I do not necessarily grow as a teaching professional as a result. To do that, I need to share the things that did not go as well in lessons and discuss what might have been missed opportunities in my teaching. I need to move from a place where I am just "telling", to a place where I am "sharing and asking". I need to put my setbacks out there and ask for help. I believe that the status I have earned within physical education social media circles will not only help me to improve but it might also help other physical educators to see that it is okay to share your struggles with the rest of the community.

I want to thank all of my co-authors in this chapter for helping me to see how I might further improve and for being an additional part of my professional learning journey.

Lessons from the case: How can the use of digital technologies accelerate pupil learning in physical education?

- It is important to consider power dynamics in every aspect of professional development through social media.
- An analysis of culture and an awareness of 'the other' can help us to broaden our networks and make them more authentic.
- Early career teachers in particular need nurturing, support and an authentic view of the profession and professional practice. They should be encouraged to be critical and discerning in their use of social media.
- Creation of online PLNs can be very useful tools but also have to be appropriately managed with 'constant checking', reflection and awareness of impact.

References

Andrew, K., Richards, R., Lux Gaudreault, K., & Templin, T. J. (2014). Understanding the realities of teaching: A seminar series focused on induction. *Journal of Physical Education, Recreation & Dance, 85*(9), 28–35. doi:10.1080/07303084.2014.958251

Bourdieu, P. & Passeron, J. C. (1990). *Reproduction in Education, Society and Culture.* London: Sage.

Carpenter, J. P. & D.G. Krutka. (2014). How and why educators use twitter: A survey of the field. *Journal of Research on Technology in Education, 46,* 414–434.

Casey, A., Goodyear, V., & Parker, M. (2015). *"I think this has been a problem with #PhysEd for a long time": Using social networking sites as a platform for professional discussion.* Paper presented at the Association Internationale des Ecoles Superieures d'Education Physique (International Association for Physical Education in Higher Education) conference, Universidad Europea, Spain, July.

Clandinin, D. J. & Connelly, F. M. (2000). *Narrative Inquiry: Experience and Story in Qualitative Research.* San Francisco, CA: Jossey-Bass.

Corlett, J. & Mandigo, J. (2013). A day in the life: Teaching physical literacy. *PHE Journal, 78*(4), 18–24.

DePauw, K. P. & Doll-Tepper, G. (2000). Toward progressive inclusion and acceptance: Myth or reality? The inclusion debate and band wagon discourse. *Adapted Physical Activity Quarterly, 17,* 135–143.

Dewey, J. (1958). *Experience and Nature:* North Chelmsford: Courier.

Dewey, J. (1938). *Experience and Education.* New York: Collier Books.

Erwin, H. (2016). The use of social media by physical educators: How do we ensure quality control? *Journal of Physical Education, Recreation & Dance, 87*(2), 3–4.

Fletcher, T. (2012). Experiences and identities: Pre-service elementary classroom teachers being and becoming teachers of physical education. *European Physical Education Review, 18*(3), 380–395.

Foucault, M. (1988) Technologies of the self. In L. H. Martin, H. Guttman, & P. H. Hutton (Eds.), *Technologies of the Self: A Seminar with Michel Foucault.* London: Tavistock. pp. 16–49.

Foucault, M. (1982a). The subject and power (Afterword). In H. L. Dreyfus, & P. Rabinow (Eds.), *Michel Foucault: Beyond Structuralism and Hermeneutics* (2nd ed.). Chicago: University of Massachusetts Press. pp. 326–348.

Foucault, M. (1982b). On the genealogy of ethics: An overview of work in progress (Afterword). In H. L. Dreyfus & P. Rabinow (Eds.), *Michel Foucault: Beyond Structuralism and Hermeneutics*. Chicago: University of Massachusetts Press. pp. 208–226.

Gleddie, D. L. & Schaefer, L. (2014). Autobiographical narrative inquiry into movement and physical education: The beginning of a journey. *PHEnex Journal, 6*(3), 1–14.

Goodyear, V. A., Casey, A., & Parker, M. (2015, September). "Must share without fear of being judged": Social Networking Sites (SNSs) capacity to form engaging and impactful professional learning communities. Paper presented at the European Educational Research Association conference, Budapest, Hungary.

Harris, M. (2001) *The Rise of Anthropological Theory: A History of Theories of Culture*. Oxford: Alta Mira Press.

Huber, J., Caine, V., Huber, M., & Steeves, P. (2013). Narrative inquiry as pedagogy in education: The extraordinary potential of living, telling, retelling, and reliving stories of experience. *Review of Research in Education, 37*(1), 212–242.

Jones, J. P. (2006). A cultural approach to the study of mediated citizenship. *Social Semiotics, 16*(2), 365–383.

Kolb, D. A. (1984). *Experiential Learning: Experience as the Source of Learning and Development*. Englewood Cliffs, NJ: Prentice Hall.

Lewis, R. D. (1999). *When Cultures Collide*. London: Nicolas Brealey.

MacPhail, A., Patton, K., Parker, M., & Tannehill, D. (2014). Leading by example: Teacher educators' professional learning through communities of practice. *Quest, 66*(1), 39–56.

McLuhan, M. (1964) *Understanding Media: The Extension of Man*. New York: Gingko Press.

Morgan, P. & Bourke, S. (2008). Non-specialist teachers' confidence to teach PE: The nature and influence of personal school experience in PE. *Pedagogy, 13*(1), 1–29.

Owens, A. (2010). Neighborhoods and schools as competing and reinforcing contexts for educational attainment. *Sociology of Education, 83*(4), 287–311.

Parker, M., Patton, K., & Tannehill, D. (2012). Mapping the landscape of communities of practice as professional development in Irish physical education. *Irish Educational Studies, 31*(3), 311–327.

Parman, J. (2011). American mobility and the expansion of public education. *Journal of Economic History, 71*(1), 105–132.

Richards, J. (2012). Teacher stress and coping strategies: A National snapshot. *The Educational Forum, 76*(3), 299–316.

Rose, N. (1999). *Powers of Freedom. Re-framing Political Thought*. Cambridge: Cambridge University Press.

Rossi, T., lisahunter, Christensen, E. & Macdonald, D. (2015). *Workplace Learning in Physical Education: Emerging Teachers' Stories From the Staffroom and Beyond*. London: Routledge.

Schaefer, L. (2013). Narrative inquiry for physical education pedagogy. *International Journal of Pedagogies and Learning, 8*(1), 18–26.

Sewell, W. H. (2005). The concept(s) of culture. In G. M. Spiegel (Ed.), *Practicing History: New Directions in Historical Writings After the Linguistic Turn*. New York: Routledge. pp. 35–61.

Tannehill, D., MacPhail, A., Halbert, G., & Murphy, F. (2013). *Research and Practice in Physical Education*. London: Routledge.

Templin, T. J. (1988). Teacher isolation: A concern for the collegial development of physical educators. *Journal of Teaching in Physical Education, 7*, 197–205.

Wolfenden, L. E. & Holt, N. L. (2005). Talent development in elite junior tennis: Perceptions of players, parents, and coaches. *Journal of Applied Sport Psychology, 17*(2),108–126.

9

LYNNE: PERSUADING TEENS TO REDUCE HEALTH RISK THROUGH HEALTHY MESSAGING

*Darla M. Castelli, Lynne J. Bryant,
Elizabeth M. Glowacki, Matthew S. McGlone
and Jeanne Barcelona*

CHAPTER OVERVIEW

Lynne wanted to help physical education (PE) students increase their rate of healthy decision making through the creation of student public service announcements (PSAs). Guided by student interest and iPad use, two assignments focused on motor skill assessment, and the PSAs were developed and viewed by a broad audience. Students creating the PSAs experienced the greatest impact and reported making more healthy choices, while PE students suggested that the experience increased awareness. This chapter details Lynne's experiences as a physical educator, provides suggestions for improving the program from psychological and health communication perspectives, and offers recommendations for implementation.

Lynne is an innovative physical educator, because she is among the first to integrate emergent pedagogical strategies across her 30-year career. While serving as a cooperating teacher who provided an effective teaching and learning environment for university pre-service student teachers, she enrolled in the doctoral program with a desire to become a teacher educator. Throughout her doctoral studies, Lynne continued to teach and coach at a local high school. Lynne has a reputation for purposefully selecting meaningful and relevant content for her lessons so her students can connect their in-school learning with their lives outside of school. In her eyes, there are two distinct advantages to this approach: (a) engaging student interest and (b) applying PE content through student interactions. Lynne would be the first to admit that she did not recognize the idea of health promotion and technology integration as her responsibility until the later stages of her career.

Practitioner narrative (Lynne Bryant)

During my first few years of teaching I lived in the state of Illinois, a place where daily PE was mandated for K–12 grades. The curriculum focused on motor skill development and game play tactics. In contrast, my current place of employment, in Texas, mandates only one academic year of PE for students in grades 9–12 (age 14–18). With less instructional time, I had to prioritize what I was going to teach and how I was going to maximize my potential impact on student learning. I decided to focus on relationship building, health-related fitness, and connecting class content with community events. First, I created an open and positive class climate in which individuality is acknowledged and accepted. Once the climate was established, I made difficult choices about the content. I resigned myself to the idea that the reduction of practice time might not be sufficient to improve the motor performance among my students. Ultimately, I elected to provide opportunities for physical activity participation beyond class time and to teach the students how to gain access to what they might need when they were not in my presence (i.e. making healthy choices on the weekend).

I began to think of myself as a health promoter. I still used the same teaching cues, but found myself providing the students with an extended explanation of why we were spending time on specific content. During my doctoral studies, I heard of schools using Public Service Announcements (PSAs) that were created by students. When I think back, it was likely my return to being a student that increased my confidence to integrate iPads into my teaching, as I began to see PE through the students' perspective. I viewed PSAs as a chance to reach all my students, especially those who were not enrolled in PE, as well as a way to advocate for healthy lifestyles in a format that was relevant to them. It was my reflection and feedback from my doctoral peers and university faculty, however, that convinced me to dive in and try.

When we were given iPads, I was excited but nervous because we had not been provided with any professional development, examples of integration, or parameters for use. Because the technology was rolled out to both teachers and students at the same time, I focused on the skills with which we were already familiar (see Table 9.1).

Examples of iPad use during PE

Assessing motor skills using iPads

Students welcomed the integration of iPads into PE classes and naturally began to assume roles similar to those in a Sport Education model (Siedentop, Hastie, & van de Mars, 2011). Teams of 4–5 students were formed and within each group individuals acted as players, videographers, coaches conducting analyses, and producers. My goals during the initial phase of iPad integration were to help students

TABLE 9.1 Technology type and utilization

Application	Function	Class utilization
iMovie	Movie making, editing	Integrate pictures, videos, edits
GarageBand	Music creation, interviews	Add music, overlay audio
Keynote	Presentations	Organize information
YouTube	A online forum for sharing videos	Watch the videos
Dropbox	A secure, online storage space	Sharing videos and other artefacts

identify the critical elements of movement and to apply relevant concepts to improve the quality of their own movement.

Analysis of the problem

When I moved to Texas, I was most concerned about the reduction of instructional time. Instead of having 4 years of daily PE, students now had 1 year. I didn't want to just throw in the towel and teach less; instead, I wrestled with the notion of how to teach more, with less. One particular research finding stuck me as valuable: *the more students discuss or interact with the content outside of the classroom setting, the higher the level of comprehension.* Now known as the pedagogical strategy of *flipping the classroom*, that idea became my driving force. I operated under the assumption that if my students were viewing, editing, and sharing video of motor skills outside of class time, then I may be increasing the likelihood that learning would transpire.

Solution to the problem

I asked groups of students to select one skill from our volleyball unit and to develop a scoring rubric to assess performance of that skill. Using the iPads, they captured video images of at least two people performing the skill in game-like situations. Generating both a rubric and a visual demonstration of each skill, clearly defined my expectations and as a result, the students progressed in their skills more rapidly. Surprisingly, this worked better than I thought it would.

The Keynote and GarageBand apps provided an avenue to produce an example that displayed all of the critical elements of the given skill (i.e. setting, passing, attacking, blocking). Students shared their final videos with their classmates by uploading them to YouTube. I encountered several technological and potentially ethical barriers during the assignment because the sharing of student images emerged as a concern among the parents and other teachers. Today, I use a password-protected portion of the school website and the students provide parental consent to use the videos for educational purposes. Looking back, I think the pedagogy was the easy part, while navigating the school policy proved the most difficult aspect of the initial assignment.

Building public service announcements (PSAs) to promote healthy choices

Analysis of the problem

Students had voiced a need for continued support to make healthy choices. One student told me, "I think [you] need to remind kids like us . . . to be healthy". "Positive behaviors need to be reinforced, because not all of us get that from home", commented a second student. I began to realize that PE was possibly the only place for some of my students to be exposed to the importance of making healthy choices. Further, I was tired of being asked by colleagues to integrate other content such as educational initiatives like anti-bullying campaigns and literacy across the curriculum into PE instruction. I wanted the students in language arts class to be writing about how they struggled to make healthy decisions!

Solution to the problem

To address the problem, I surveyed the students and then asked them to identify a personally relevant health issue (i.e. physical inactivity, stress, etc.) and research that concern in small groups. Videos ranged from students flashing informative cue cards to showing naturally occurring situations in their homes (e.g. parental stress and expectations, academic stress, availability of alcohol and the variety of alternative choices available, and capturing their parents' and personal responses to those situations). Using cooperative learning between film, health, and PE class members, the students were immediately recognized as experts within their domain (e.g. film students were experts at movie making, health students researched the prevalence of the topic, PE students endorsed physical activity as a healthy alternative). The students were given 6 weeks to develop a PSA and then upload it to Dropbox for review by the film teacher, health teacher, and myself. Students of different ages and grade levels were asked to work together. In total, 182 students were part of the production process, while 2,000 students viewed the PSAs.

Lessons learned from the integration of iPads into PE

Using iPads and creating the PSAs were not only feasible but also allowed students to interact with peers and adults through non-traditional experiences. Specifically, the content of the PSAs commonly included peer models immersed in stressful scenarios (e.g. being tempted by a friend to use tobacco, looking at a beer in the refrigerator, wavering between pizza and the salad bar). The content illustrated the depth of some of the perceived pressures experienced by adolescents and how frequently unhealthy outlets were accessed to relieve that stress.

In fact, many students came to me to ask how they could get involved in this project. Consequently, this project became a school-wide conversation about the health issues and pressures that the students face daily. I don't think I can state with absolute confidence that our PE project created sustainable change in the health culture of our school, but I do know that this assignment is now an annual event in which the students look forward to participating. My hope is that the students, particularly those not enrolled in PE, are reminded of the benefits of healthy eating and physical activity, and thereby choose to participate regularly.

A psychological and persuasion perspective (Matthew McGlone)

Lynne's efforts to foster a community of students who create and share health messages shed light on the issues that are pertinent to student health and well-being. Adolescents are frequently targeted by fast food, alcohol, and tobacco companies and yet are often underrepresented in studies evaluating practices for combating the effects of these messages (Shen, Monahan, Rhodes, & Roskos-Ewoldsen, 2009). Despite the significant sums the U.S. and other governments spend on these campaigns, analyses indicate that most exert modest or negligible impact on people's behavior (Dunlop, Wakefield, & Kashima, 2010). Even worse, some ill-conceived campaigns "boomerang", inadvertently encouraging the bad choices (e.g. alcohol abuse) they were created to discourage (Agrawal & Duhacheck, 2010). One common problem is campaign messaging that is not informed by relevant persuasion research and theory (O'Keefe, 2016). Professional PSA designers often rely on intuition about how to persuade people rather than evidence-based principles.

Lynne's PSA class project was an excellent opportunity to promote pro-social learning among students. Future offerings of this project could increase educational impact by treating it as an occasion to learn about the key role of persuasion in promoting healthy behavior.

Peers as actors

The impact of a persuasive message has almost as much to do with who is saying it as what is said (Heesacker, Petty, & Cacioppo, 1983). Traditionally, health-oriented PSAs have employed medical experts as sources in an effort to maximize perceptions of message accuracy. Message validation via source expertise is an effective strategy when audience members are unfamiliar with the course of action recommended by a PSA. However, when the benefits of recommended actions are already accepted by the target audience (e.g. smoking is bad for your health), expert testimonials do little to boost message impact (Atkin, 2000).

In these situations, savvy persuaders pivot from emphasizing the accuracy of a message to enhancing its likeability (Reinhard & Messner, 2009). All other things being equal, audiences like messages from sources they perceive to be like themselves – that is, their peers (Lieberman, Gauvin, Bukowski, & White, 2001). The vast majority of the students' PSAs used students as sources and found settings that their audience (peers) could be expected to recognize (parents nagging them about mobile phone bills, peers pressuring them to use drugs). The students' PSAs enjoy the persuasive advantage of having genuine audience-peers as their stars, not faux ones. Given that actor appeal is crucial for PSA effectiveness (Shead, Walsh, Taylor, Derevensky, & Gupta, 2011) and that adolescents tend to be more influenced by messages about health from their peers (Nash, McQueen, & Bray, 2005), it was wise of Lynne to have the students serve as the "actors" in their PSAs.

Social norms

For PSAs to be successful, their designers must recognize the distinct power of the different norms and focus the target audience on only the social behavior that is consistent with their goal. However, there are numerous examples of PSAs where designers didn't appreciate this distinction and undermined their campaign impact as a result (Payne, 2001). For example, to underscore the need for government action against cigarette smoking among children, the Federal Drug Administration routinely produced PSAs in the 1990s reporting the high number of youth in the U.S. who regularly smoke (Cialdini *et al.*, 2006). As Cialdini and colleagues (2006) point out, these efforts to prevent adolescent smoking were unsuccessful because they relied primarily on descriptive norm messaging (i.e. "25 per cent of adolescents smoke") rather than injunctive norm messaging ("adolescents shouldn't smoke"). Although this claim may be true and well intentioned, its inclusion in PSAs undermines warnings about smoking by drawing attention to the large number of people who do that very thing. This, of course, has the unintended effect of making the undesirable behavior more acceptable (Nolan, Schultz, Cialdini, Goldstein, & Griskevicius, 2008).

Two student-created PSAs committed a similar error. In one, an otherwise congenial set of recommendations for healthy eating was pre-empted by an alarming quotation in bold font announcing, *"Nearly the entire U.S. fails to eat a diet following dietary guidelines"* (emphasis added). A second PSA intended to encourage drug abstinence shows the teenage protagonist surrounded by peers offering him marijuana while the claim "Everybody's doing it" is repeated several times in the soundtrack. In both cases, the prominent display of descriptive norms about the prevalence of an undesirable behavior works against the persuasive goal of preventing or curbing it in the target audience. Eliminating references to the descriptive norms and instead focusing on relevant injunctive norms (e.g. you should eat healthy foods and avoid drugs) would better serve this goal.

Agency

Subtle aspects of the language used to compose a health message can exert a sizable impact on its persuasiveness. One such aspect is *agency*, a term alluding to the source of action designated by a message. In general, we tend to think of message agents as more powerful or potent than other persons or things mentioned in the message

(McGlone, Bell, Zaitchik, & McGlynn, 2013). Strategically assigning linguistic agency can reinforce audience members' self-efficacy in preserving their health, and consequently helps messages be successful in persuading audiences to follow behavior recommendations (Glowacki, McGlone, & Bell, 2016). Two student PSAs used linguistic agency assignments that worked against their persuasive goals. One intending to highlight the health benefits of physical activity abdicated the exerciser's role in this process through an initial series of statements assigning agency exclusively to the process (*Exercise boosts brain power; movement melts away stress; physical activity prevents disease*). A second closes an otherwise clever video sequence in which students drive a car through a cloud of unhealthy "temptations" (fast food, alcoholic beverages, illegal drugs) with the ego-depleting claim that *Life throws you lots of choices . . . so choose wisely*. Both PSAs would benefit from strategic agency assignments that linguistically reinforce audience members' personal involvement in choosing healthy behaviors (e.g. *You make lots of choices in life, so choose wisely*) and reaping their benefits (e.g. *When you move, you melt away stress*).

A health communication and messaging perspective (Elizabeth Glowacki)

To be effective, health messages need to be engaging, informative, and persuasive: engaging so that receivers pay attention, informative so that a desired behavior or practice can be learned, and persuasive so that recipients of the intended message are motivated to take action. Involved and active educators are crucial for the promotion of healthy messages within schools, but those messages will fail to produce the intended effects if they lack specific communication features.

Health messaging that uses bold words that empower the individual to build self-efficacy and autonomy are particularly important during adolescence (Bong, 2001). Statements such as *Fasten your seat belt* or *Eat more fruit* both describe the problem and address it. Messages about health are effective when they garner audience interest and offer a means for taking action. One example of fostering self-efficacy is a video in which the protagonist is sitting alone at home and starts to think about all the people in her life who are upset with her. She initially reacts to her stress by walking to the refrigerator and pulling out a beer, but starts to consider the reactions of those close to her and rethinks the role that she wants alcohol to play in her life. She puts the beer back and goes outside for a run. This presents the audience with a means for coping with stress other than alcohol (exercise) and depicts a clear case of enhanced self-efficacy. The protagonist in the video knew she had the support of family members and friends, but had to take matters into her own hands before engaging in a healthy practice.

Assessing motor skills using iPads

There is no doubt that peer-to-peer education is an effective model for informing audiences (Sloane & Zimmer, 1993), which is why future iterations of this project should incorporate more opportunity for peer feedback and questioning at the front end and throughout the creation of the skill-based videos. If students have the opportunity to hear about other groups' ideas or ask questions of one another early on, they may raise critical points about why some key elements of the movement (e.g. grip, follow through, weight transfer) are given priority over others and why some topics are more salient to some students than others. Additionally, the students may find the process more rewarding if they are encouraged to ask about what each groups' goals are behind the videos and are given the opportunity to pre-screen their videos before they go live for their final submission. Providing this chance for peer feedback without teacher interference may create a "safe space" in which students feel comfortable sharing their thoughts on critical elements of movement without having to worry about disclosing their concerns in front of their educators.

Building public service announcements (PSAs) to promote healthy choices

Of particular interest to me were the health messages developed by the students. Health messages are most effective when they encourage audiences to engage in pro-social behaviors (Cappella & Hornik, 2010). Lynne did a commendable job of getting students to identify health topics salient to their school community and design messages encouraging positive practices related to these issues. However, health messages need to do more than distinguish between good and bad behaviors; they also need to provide audiences with suggestions for overcoming a threat (Beck & Lund, 1981). The extended parallel process model (EPPM; Witte, 1994) posits that audiences conduct two parallel appraisals when evaluating a message: an appraisal of the described threat and an appraisal of their own self-efficacy, or ability to take action against the threat. Fear can be a mechanism for encouraging individuals to take action against a health threat or problem, but only to the extent that those individuals perceive that they are equipped with the proper tools for doing so (Witte & Allen, 2000). In other words, people need to feel that they have a "way out" or means for coping with a perceived threat. This is an especially important component for Lynne's students given that they are at an age when autonomous and informed decision-making practices are needed for confronting peer pressure.

With regard to the student PSAs in Lynne's project, a couple of the videos alluded to health concerns like poor eating habits and peer pressure to take drugs, but offered no alternative recourse. For instance, in one of the videos, the protagonist is faced with multiple offers for engaging in substance use and at the end of the video, simply says "no". The video concludes with, "Don't let peer pressure weigh you down". While the metaphor of physical weight is an apt one for portraying peer pressure, the "just say no" approach has been shown to be ineffective for instances in which children and teenagers are faced with having to make choices about drug use (Hornik, Jacobsohn, Orwin, Piesse, & Kalton, 2008). This video could be improved if it featured an alternative to substance use or gave the protagonist another way out which would thus enhance his sense of self-efficacy or ability to cope with the difficult decisions.

Conclusions

While Lynne put useful protocols in place for obtaining feedback upon completion of the PSAs, future attempts to recreate this process would benefit from conducting a needs assessment at baseline at the outset through the use of focus groups or classroom interviews. This would allow for comparisons to be made between student expectations about the project and actual experiences. Lynne's implementation of a PSA production and sharing processes served as a useful guide for empowering students to engage in discussions about health, but could be refined to allow for more peer feedback and review at the beginning and middle of the production timeline, rather than at just the end. Encouraging students to build up one another's self-efficacy and to talk about alternative solutions to problems can help educators initiate these dialogues in their classroom communities.

A learning perspective (Jeanne Barcelona)

Learning should be student centered, reflective, and address the needs of the whole child, while meeting the mandated standard of learner performance. Student-centered learning (SCL) means different things to different people. Generally, SCL shifts power away from the teacher and to the student (Barr & Tagg, 1995). Instructional strategies that can be used to facilitate SCL might include group discussion, computer-assisted learning, and student choice. Lynne is a teacher who uses a SCL in an era where teaching toward achievement of the educational standard is the norm.

Student reflection

Student reflection fosters ownership of learning. Creating reflective PE students means more than simply a rote debriefing after an outdoor education lesson. *Reflection* is a component of the educational experience that both students and teachers alike should engage in. For this to emerge, the teacher must value reflection on their own pedagogical practices and provide students with the opportunity to reflect on their learning process. Lynne did a fine job of igniting this process with her students by engaging work groups in debriefing interviews. However, reflection should be an ongoing process and not a single, summative event. Continual engagement in student reflection can be facilitated through frequent discussions, interviews, questioning, sentence stems, and logs or journals (Feuerstein, Rand, Hoffman, & Miller, 1980). Further, students must interact with reflective role models who exemplify self-reflection in their own learning (Crosby, 2000). The art of self-reflection is not instinctual; it must be taught and guided (Costa & Kallick, 2008). Teachers who already institute reflective teaching practices at the beginning of lessons are primed and ready to extend students' engagement in self-reflective activities and should provide more occasions throughout the entire learning process. Such efforts to engage students in ongoing reflection at the beginning, midpoint, and end of lessons will help them to take ownership over their learning, making them more aware of objectives they have mastered. Most importantly, continual reflection provides students with the opportunity to set personal goals leading to mastery of health-related learning objectives.

Whole-child approach

The education sector has called for the adoption of a whole-child approach to teaching since healthier children are more ready to learn. It is believed that a whole-child approach will not only lead to an increased achievement of learning proficiencies in reading, writing, science, and mathematics but also advance a child's social and emotional development (ASCD, 2007). When successfully implemented, the whole-child approach fosters a healthy, safe, and supportive environment where students can actively engage in and challenge their own learning capacity. This idea is not new. In 1987, Allensworth and Kolbe called for schools to adopt the coordinated school health model that incorporates the constructs of health and wellness across the mainstream curriculum. The implementation of models such as coordinated school health (which is a mandated policy in Texas) as a whole-child approach has the potential to maximize student learning and health-enhancing behaviors (Lewallen *et al.*, 2015).

Assessing motor skills using iPads

Lynne's use of iPads to assess motor skills is student centered, has value because the lesson recognizes the technological interests of the students, and utilizes technology as a vehicle through which each student can be helped to refine their own motor skills. Additionally, by requiring that all students both engage in the practice of a motor skill and record their participation, Lynne is introducing students to the concept of self-reflective learning. All students have the opportunity to revisit and assess their own level of mastery of the motor skill. Lynne's pedagogical strategies for her iPad and motor skills lesson do indeed foster a student-centered and self-reflective learning environment. However, future lessons should also consider a self-reflective culminating experience where students first pinpoint their degree of mastery over the lesson and then create personal goals that will continue to help them advance their progress with the motor skill objective.

Building public service announcements (PSAs) to promote healthy choices

The integration of PSAs into PE is an example of the whole-child approach. The lesson challenges students by requiring them to both identify relevant health issues as well as providing them with a safe environment where they are encouraged to reflect on and initiate ways of overcoming the issue. Further, this lesson also encapsulates the philosophy of the coordinated school health model by placing students in the role of health promoters and allowing them to educate the larger student body. As these observations suggest, Lynne's lesson creatively unites the whole child and coordinated school health models despite the assertions made by Lewallen and colleagues (2015) that such efforts have not yet been successfully implemented. However, as Lynne stated in her narrative, "I don't think I can state with absolute confidence that our PE project created sustainable change in the health culture of our school, but I do know that this assignment is now an annual event in which the students look forward to participating. At least once a year, PE is the talk of the school". This statement is paramount, as the compilation of the whole-child approach and the coordinated school health model may have the capacity to create a sustainable healthy culture within a school. However, to do so, teachers and administrators must look to the organizational change literature for guidance. Barcelona and colleagues (2015) found that the theory of organizational change provided a useful framework for teachers looking to create a healthy school culture. According to the theory of organization change, Lynne's PSA lesson unfroze the stagnant culture, allowing the school community to embrace health (Schein, 1996). Therefore, the next step for teachers such as Lynne should be to develop additional lessons that support a healthy culture. Through deliberate actions, such as continued use of PSAs and similar health-based lessons that involve the wider school community, Lynne will gain collective buy-in from administration, teachers, and students leading to a sustainable healthy school culture.

A pedagogical perspective (Darla Castelli)

Lynne is to be applauded for her effectual indirect teaching, promotion of healthful living through authentic problem solving and interdisciplinary learning. This case demonstrated that it is feasible to use iPads in interdisciplinary, health-related homework assignments in PE. If effective PE programming is providing *meaningful content, opportunities to learn, assessment and moderate to vigorous physical activity* (SHAPE America & Human Kinetics, 2014), the integration of iPads into PE was a success even if the rate of student healthy decision making is still relatively unknown. Because lifestyle behaviors and personal attributes are affiliated with health and school performance, health-related fitness education has been strongly supported in the Unites States (Welk, Eisenmann, & Dollman, 2006). Further, the integration of the iPads and focus of the corresponding assessments is an example of how the youth physical activity promotion model can be applied in PE (Welk, 1999). Focusing instruction on the predisposing, enabling and reinforcing factors related to physical activity engagement builds self-concept, efficacy and interest of the students. Addressing authentic problems and relevant, developmentally appropriate solutions is both valuable and timely, given the current existing public health issues (Ogden, Carroll, Kit, & Flegal, 2014).

Extending PE content into the health education and film classes was an exemplar of how to provide interdisciplinary learning opportunities, because PE teachers have frequently been expected to take such an approach and integrate other subject matter into their lessons (Rink & Mitchell, 2003). This is particularly true because there are some encouraging secondary by-products of the project. For example, school-wide awareness of health issues and advocacy for the subject matters of physical and health education were surprising but highly positive outcomes. Yet, despite the success of the technology integration, a critical question about the learning approach taken could be posed: Would a more formal embedding of the tenets of problem-based learning (PBL) have had even greater impact on the behaviors of these adolescents?

Fidelity of the tenets of PBL

Formalized in medical education, problem-based learning (PBL) is a teaching method by which students gain knowledge and skills from working for an extended period of time to investigate and respond to a multifaceted question, problem or challenge (Wood, 1994). PBL requires a student to call on integrated, multidisciplinary knowledge to solve a problem. There are eight key elements to include in the PBL approach: (a) defining and applying key knowledge and skills, (b) posing challenging problems, (c) sustained inquiry, (d) authenticity, (e) student voice and choice, (f) reflection, (g) critique and revision, and (h) public product. Yet, sometimes the pedagogical underpinnings are lost in the implementation of this approach (Savery, 2015). In this case, it is clear that knowledge, choice, challenging problems, public product and authenticity were evident, but sustained inquiry, critique and revision and reflection were only emerging, thus the impact on students may have been reduced.

PBL has been applied to teacher education (Oberlander & Talbert-Johnson 2004), specifically to help develop teachers who can identify a problem, make decisions, and solve problems. In this case, Lynne applied these pedagogical constructs to bring out these characteristics in her own students. The simple practice of providing timely and congruent feedback by the teacher to the student can facilitate this process, particularly when integrating technology (Castelli & Fiorentino, 2008). Within PBL, students should give, receive and use feedback to improve the process and product through a cycle of *critique and revision*. From this perspective, it could have been helpful to include more purposeful and distinct points of teacher and peer feedback aligned with the desired outcome of the learning experience. For peer feedback to be effective, the teacher needs to provide examples of what should be said and how it should be stated.

Since some PSAs would benefit from strategic agency assignments that linguistically reinforce audience members' personal involvement in choosing healthy behaviors, perhaps a fourth teacher – one with expertise in language arts – could be added to the project. Using a listing of key elements of a persuasive argument, the extra teacher could help the students attempt to identify the elements on storyboards or in unedited video clips. Additionally, as a prerequisite to this assignment, the students could have used an iPad to capture video of students making healthy choices (e.g. choosing the salad bar, going for a run, etc.) or the students could have conducted a review of existing health PSAs and evaluated the contents as critical consumers. As suggested by the importance of persuasion, the healthy options must be the prominent choice within the messaging. Students would then have an opportunity to revise their messaging and ultimately enhance the potential impact.

Development of teachers' knowledge

One way teachers' knowledge is expanded is through student constructivist learning experiences such as those provided in this present case (Rovegno, 1998, 1993). Of particular interest in the use of iPads to assess motor skills were Lynne's conceptions of skill development and readiness for game play, as the students were tasked with identifying the critical elements of passing, attacking and blocking in volleyball games. Some teachers have been limited by an inability to design developmentally appropriate skill progressions and sometimes lack the pedagogical content knowledge necessary for implementation of such progressions (Rovegno, 1993). Lack of instructional time, over a lack pedagogical content knowledge, was evident in this case. In her narrative, Lynne commented that she had "resigned [herself] to the idea that the reduction of practice time might not be sufficient to improve the motor performance among my students". Drawing on her extensive volleyball coaching experience, she knew exactly what to look for in the student rubrics and videos. By beginning with content well within her expertise, she was able to focus on the integration of technology and policy troubleshooting that was required by this initial assessment of students' knowledge and abilities.

In the case of having students create PSAs, feedback from the content experts and the teacher educator contributed to Lynne's professional reflections. From a constructivist perspective, she learned what to say to the students and when to say it, which was supported by similar research findings whereby Rovegno asked in-service teachers what they had learned from feedback after enacting a movement education lesson (Rovegno, 1993). Because Lynne is an experienced teacher, she thought that by offering more time (6 weeks to complete the project) and less direction, the students would present creative solutions, of their choice. This largely was the case, but the healthy messaging was somewhat underdeveloped. To enhance the PSAs all of the teachers involved in the project could electronically respond to and monitor student progress, thus contributing to the reciprocal feedback cycle. The creation of an interactive forum could also be used for groups to conduct reviews of peer storyboards or early iterations of PSAs. This format could fully embrace the strengths of the diverse groups and teacher expertise. As previously stated, Lynne was more attentive to the students' interests and less attentive to the tenets of problem-based learning. Lynne made this assertion in her own reflection.

Practitioner reflection

This project clearly exemplified how fluid the learning process is for both students and teachers. Collaborating and reflecting are lifelong assets that are keys to success in any field of study. I feel very lucky to be surrounded by professionals with diversified experiences from which I can draw and improve my teaching.

I anticipated that the integration of technology through motor skill assessment and PSA development in PE would increase students' knowledge and make connections for situating that knowledge in their lives, in addition to identifying areas of personal growth that were well within their control and attainment. Yet, I agree with Darla Castelli that frontloading PBL tenets in both the skill assessment and the PSA project while maintaining the PBL format throughout the projects would have stimulated more introspection and possibly more positive action towards healthy behaviors by my students. In addition, Matt McGlone's references to how effective persuasion research can be really made me think and revise my lesson structure. I think my students were mimicking the negative, fear-based messages that frequent the media. Acknowledging this aspect of the media and how to move forward in a pro-social manner is a life lesson in itself.

In my experience, student centered learning increases adolescent human capital by layering knowledge with authentic social interactions fostering resilience to challenges and revealing the interconnectedness of the global community. The positive effects of peer relevance and the development of self-efficacy were confirmed by Elizabeth Glowacki.

Increasing my students' support system concerning healthy behavior choices through the interactions these projects initiated improved the school climate for everyone. I am eager to employ these tactics in my next lesson.

Lessons from the case: How can the use of digital technologies accelerate pupil learning in physical education?

Broadly, there are four lessons learned from this project:

- In the future, a problem-based learning approach using iMovies and Garage Band applications should be integrated from the onset. Using such a process of inquiry may have formalized the steps in the development of the videos.
- Ongoing peer review of the PSA production with and without the presence of teachers may have been beneficial, given the variations in group member ages and experiences. Roles effectively emerged, but more frequent peer feedback from the reciprocal teaching needed to be fostered.
- The third lesson learned was the need to help students understand the importance of messaging and persuasion. Many messages undermined the given intent. Words can empower or undermine adolescent decision making.

- The last lesson learned is one of reflection. The use of blogs and/or e-discussion boards may have aided the students in understanding what facilitators and barriers were confronted and overcome by other groups.

References

Agrawal, N. & Duhachek, A. (2010). Emotional compatibility and the effectiveness of anti-drinking messages: A defensive processing perspective on shame and guilt. *Journal of Marketing Research, 43,* 263–273.

Allensworth, D. D. & Kolbe, L. J. (1987). The comprehensive school health program: Exploring an expanded concept. *Journal of School Health, 57*(19), 409–412.

Association for Supervision and Curriculum Development (ASCD). (2007). *The Learning Compact Redefined: A Call to Action.* Alexandria, VA: Author.

Atkin, C. K. (2000). Theory and principle of media health campaigns. In R. E. Rice & C.K. Atkin (Eds.), *Public communication campaigns* (3rd ed.). Thousand Oaks, CA: Sage. pp. 49–68.

Barcelona, J., Castelli, D. M., Pitt Barnes, S., Wargo, J., & Cance, J. D. (under review). Presidential Youth Fitness Program Implementation: An antecedent to organizational change. *Journal of Physical Activity and Health.*

Barr, R. B. & Tagg, J. (1995). From teaching to learning – A new paradigm for undergraduate education. *Change,* 13–25.

Beck, K. H. & Lund, A. K. (1981). The effects of health threat seriousness and personal efficacy upon intentions and behavior. *Journal of Applied Social Psychology, 11,* 401–415.

Bong, M. (2001). Role of self-efficacy and task-value in predicting college students' course performance and future enrollment intentions. *Contemporary Educational Psychology, 26,* 553–570.

Cappella, J. N. & Hornik, R. C. (2010). The importance of communication science in addressing core problems in public health. In D. Carbaugh & P. M. Buzzanell (Eds.), *Distinctive Qualities in Communication Research.* New York, NY: Routledge. pp. 73–86.

Castelli, D. M. & Fiorentino, L. H. (2008). *Physical Education Technology Playbook.* Champaign, IL: Human Kinetics.

Cialdini, R. B., Demaine, L. J., Sagarin, B. J., Barrett, D. W., Rhoads, K., & Winter, P. L. (2006). Managing social norms for persuasive impact. *Social Influence, 1,* 3–15.

Costa, A. L. & Kallick, B. (2008). *Learning and Leading with Habits of Mind: 16 Essential Characteristics for Success.* Alexandria, VA: ASCD.

Crosby, R. H. J. (2000). AMEE Guide No. 20: The good teacher is more than a lecturer-the twelve roles of the teacher. *Medical Teacher, 22*(4), 334–347.

Dunlop, S. M., Wakefield, M., & Kashima, Y. (2010). Pathways to persuasion: Cognitive and experiential responses to health-promoting mass media messages. *Communication Research, 37,* 133–164.

Feuerstein, R., Rand, Y., Hoffman, M., & Miller, R. (1980). *Instrumental Enrichment: An Intervention Program for Cognitive Modifiability.* Baltimore, MD: University Park Press.

Glowacki, E. M., McGlone, M. S., & Bell, R. A. (2016). Targeting Type 2: Linguistic agency assignment in diabetes prevention policy messaging. *Journal of Health Communication,* e-pub (ahead of print).

Heesacker, M., Petty, R. E., & Cacioppo, J. T. (1983). Field dependence and attitude change: Source credibility can alter persuasion by affecting message-relevant thinking. *Journal of Personality, 51,* 653–666.

Hornik, R., Jacobsohn, L., Orwin, R., Piesse, A., & Kalton, G. (2008). Effects of the national youth anti-drug media campaign on youths. *American Journal of Public Health*, *98*, 2229–2236.

Lewallen, T. C., Hunt, H., Potts-Datema, W., Zaza, S., & Giles, W. (2015). The whole school, whole community, whole child model: A new approach for improving educational attainment and healthy development for students. *Journal of School Health*, *85*(11), 729–739.

Lieberman, M., Gauvin, L., Bukowski, W. M., & White, D. R. (2001). Interpersonal influence and disordered eating behaviors in adolescent girls: The role of peer modeling, social reinforcement, and body-related teasing. *Eating Behaviors*, *2*, 215–236.

McGlone, M. S., Bell, R. A., Zaitchik, S., & McGlynn, J. (2013). Don't let the flu catch you: Agency assignment in printed educational materials about the H1N1 influenza virus. *Journal of Health Communication*, *18*, 240–256.

Nash, S. G., McQueen, A., & Bray, J. H. (2005). Pathways to adolescent alcohol use: Family environment, peer influence, and parental expectations. *Journal of Adolescent Health*, *37*, 19–28.

Nolan, J. M., Schultz, P. W., Cialdini, R. B., Goldstein, N. J., & Griskevicius, V. (2008). Normative social influence is underdetected. *Personality and Social Psychology Bulletin*, *34*, 913–923.

Oberlander, J. & Talbert-Johnson, C. (2004). Using technology to support problem-based learning. *Action in Teacher Education*, *25*, 48–57.

Ogden, C. L., Carroll, M. D., Kit, B. K., & Flegal, K. M. (2014). Prevalence of childhood and adult obesity in the United States, 2011–2012. *Journal of the American Medical Association*, *311*(8), 806–814.

O'Keefe, D. J. (2016). *Persuasion: Theory and Research*. Thousand Oaks, CA: Sage.

Payne, R. A. (2001). Persuasion, frames and norm construction. *European Journal of International Relations*, *7*, 37–61.

Reinhard, M. A. & Messner, M. (2009). The effects of source likeability and need for cognition on advertising effectiveness under explicit persuasion. *Journal of Consumer Behaviour*, *8*, 179–191.

Rink, J. & Mitchell, M. (2003). State level assessment of physical education: The South Carolina experience. *Journal of Teaching in Physical Education*, *22*(5), 471–614.

Rovegno, I. (1998). The development of in-service teachers' knowledge of a constructivist approach to physical education: Teaching beyond activities. *Research Quarterly for Exercise and Sport*, *69*, 147–162.

Rovegno, I. (1993). The development of curricular knowledge: A case of problematic pedagogical content knowledge during advanced knowledge acquisition. *Research Quarterly for Exercise and Sport*, *64*, 56–68.

Savery, J. R. (2015). Overview of problem-based learning: Definitions and distinctions. *Essential Readings in Problem-Based Learning: Exploring and Extending the Legacy of Howard S. Barrows*, 5.

Schein, E. H. (1996). Kurt Lewin's change theory in the field and in the classroom: Notes toward a model of managed learning. *Systems Practice*, *9*(1), 27–47.

SHAPE America & Human Kinetics. (2014). *National Standards & Grade-Level Outcomes for K-12 Physical Education*. Retrieved from www.shapeamerica.org/pe

Shead, N. W., Walsh, K., Taylor, A., Derevensky, J. L., & Gupta, R. (2011). Youth gambling prevention: Can public service announcements featuring celebrity spokespersons be effective? *International Journal of Mental Health and Addiction*, *9*, 165–179.

Shen, L., Monahan, J. L., Rhodes, N., & Roskos-Ewoldsen, D. R. (2009). The impact of attitude accessibility and decision style on adolescents' biased processing of health-related public service announcements. *Communication Research*, *36*, 104–128.

Siedentop, D., Hastie, P. A., & van de Mars, H. (2011). *Complete Guide to Sport Education* (2nd ed.). Champaign, IL: Human Kinetics.

Sloane, B. C. & Zimmer, C. G. (1993). The power of peer health education. *Journal of American College Health, 41,* 241–245.

Welk, G. J. (1999). The youth physical activity promotion model: A conceptual bridge between theory and practice. *Quest, 51,* 5–23.

Welk, G. J., Eisenmann, J. C., & Dollman, J. (2006). Health-related physical activity in children and adolescents: A bio-behavioral perspective. In D. Kirk, D. Macdonald, & M. O'Sullivan (Eds.), *The Handbook of Physical Education.* Thousand Oaks, CA: Sage.

Witte, K. (1994). Fear control and danger control: A test of the extended parallel process model (EPPM). *Communications Monographs, 61,* 113–134.

Witte, K. & Allen, M. (2000). A meta-analysis of fear appeals: Implications for effective public health campaigns. *Health Education & Behavior, 27,* 591–615.

Wood, E. J. (1994). The problems of problem-based learning. *Biochemical Education, 22,* 78–82.

10

RICK: "ENERGIZE AND EDUCATE AT EVERY AGE"

Technology integration over a teaching career

Emily Jones, Rick Schupbach, Stephen Harvey, Sean Bulger and Dana Voelker

CHAPTER OVERVIEW

This case describes Rick's 32-year career teaching physical education and his strategic uses of digital technologies to improve his teaching, impact student learning, and enhance the quality of life for members of his community. Perspectives from experts in health oriented physical education, professional development and learning, and transformational leadership provide additional insights on the case. Using the Technological Pedagogical Content Knowledge (TPACK; Mishra & Koehler, 2006) as a framework, the authors identify two primary outcomes from Rick's technology integration in physical education: (a) inquiry and student-centered pedagogy, and (b) an elevated status for physical education.

Practitioner narrative (Rick Schupbach, as told by Emily Jones)

Rick is a recently retired 32-year veteran physical education teacher from a rural farming community in the Midwest region of the United States who claims that 'Technology has transformed the way I teach and do my job'. Rick teaches in a school district that serves 720 students who range in age from 5 to 18 years, many of whose families have farmed the land for generations. Rick began his career at the middle school level (ages 12–14 years) but found his calling at the elementary level (ages 5–11 years) where he established a state, national, and international reputation as an innovator in technology use in the gymnasium. Rick claims to be 'tech-phobic', and describes his technology skills to be 'laughable', yet his gymnasium was kitted out with a mounted projection system that syncs wirelessly to his laptop and iPad, and a surround sound system also controlled by iPad. His iPad has an extensive library of music, including classical segments with timed voice overlays tailored for instant activities and classroom management routines, and mobile applications used for instruction, assessment, and communication with administrators and parents. Rick had a class set of Polar® heart rate monitors (HRMs) and physical activity monitoring devices (i.e. pedometers and Polar Active® monitors) that were integrated into his classes. Table 10.1 provides an overview of technologies and functions used within Rick's classroom.

Despite the increase in technologies, Rick has been selective in which tools he uses and cites two primary factors in his decision to adopt any new technology: quality and efficiency. He selects tools that are robust and reliable with the ultimate goal of freeing him to devote increased time and creativity in designing engaging learning experiences. The alignment of teacher, learner, and technology has taken countless hours to develop and years to refine. This case describes Rick's professional journey and offers an analysis of the complex process of learning to teach with technology across a career.

TABLE 10.1 Sample digital technologies used in Rick's classroom

Technology/ application	General function of the technology/application	How the technology was used
Polar®Heart Rate Monitors	Displays real-time heart rate for individuals to see and respond to while participating in aerobic activities.	Students wore HRMS during class to monitor heart rate and modify exercise intensity to remain within target heart rate zone.
Sony™Sound Forge Pro software	Sound editing software that allows for layering of audio files (e.g., voice recording, music).	Edited sound clips were used to signal transition in activity, particularly during aerobic warm-up routine.
Mounted Projector System	Displays digital multimedia materials.	Instructional materials were displayed during class to supplement instruction, provide visual aids, and assist with classroom management (e.g., transitions).
Polar® Activity Monitors	Wrist activity trackers that calculate steps, calories burned, and time spent in moderate-to-vigorous physical activity.	Students wore activity monitors during class to track steps taken and time spent engaged in health-enhancing levels of physical activity.
Pocket PC and iPad	Portable, handheld computing devices.	Mobile devices were used by the instructor to track attendance, assess skill performance with electronic rubrics.

Early career (1983–1997)

Rick started his career in 1983 as a middle school physical education teacher and head coach for boys' basketball. During his fourth year of teaching, Rick realized he was spending more time and energy on coaching than teaching, so he began seeking new ideas to infuse into his teaching. In February 1987 he came across a LIFE Magazine article about a teacher whose physical education program was using innovative health-oriented technologies, namely HRMs, computerized running shoes, and electromyograms. He was delighted to find that the teacher, named Beth Kirkpatrick, taught only 20 miles from his school. He scheduled a day to meet Beth and observe her teach. What he saw made him begin to think differently about teaching, and, upon his return, Rick started making small pedagogical changes. He changed his warm-up routine, modified his lessons to increase the aerobic time for students (e.g. reducing transition time, integrating aerobic segments into each class), and infused more self-directed learning approaches. These low budget, technology-free pedagogical improvements spurred a desire in Rick for continuous improvement.

In his sixth year of teaching, Rick took a teaching position in Grundy Center, a neighboring community. He was not aware at the time that Beth lived in this community, and, moreover, her children were enrolled in his school district. When the time came, he felt tremendous pressure sitting across from Beth in parent-teacher conferences. He had limited data to support his program effectiveness. Rick embraced the opportunity to collaborate with Beth and began meeting with her regularly. Three years later, inspired by Beth, he wrote and received a $5,000 grant to purchase HRMs for his elementary physical education program. Rick was determined to take his program to a new level. With the HRMs able to provide instant feedback to learners about their exercise intensity, Rick (and Beth) foresaw an opportunity to teach concepts related to cardiovascular and health-related fitness and to empower students to assume ownership of their personal health and well-being.

Mid career (1997–2012)

As a mid-career professional, Rick maintained momentum in his quest for improvement and sought new collaborations. Taking advice from an administrator, Rick began working closely with his colleagues to refine their K–12 physical education curriculum, looking for strategic ways technology could enhance the teaching and learning environment. Rick created voice recordings over music to the lesson warm-up to reduce transition and increase activity time. These classroom routines freed him to interact with students and reinforced self-monitoring and student accountability. In the 2000s, Rick used hand-held computing devices (e.g., Dell Pocket PCs) to take attendance, assess student learning (e.g., electronic skill and fitness rubrics), and share documents with his colleagues. Data collected on the hand-held device synced to his desktop computer and were used to generate individual standards-based report cards delivered to parents, administrators, and school-level stakeholders. A mounted projector in the gymnasium enhanced Rick's ability to communicate and reinforce concepts with his learners, for example, he displayed text-based instructions, color-coded transitional prompts, videos of activities or tasks, and connected classroom content such as phonics and mathematics to physical education.

These technology-enhanced instructional practices caught the attention of parents, community members, and administrators. A collaborative effort between community stakeholders and Rick secured a grant for fitness equipment/technology and spurred a partnership with a regional YMCA to develop a school-based, community-accessible wellness center. This afforded community members access to the school-based fitness center before and after-school hours. Heart rate monitoring and fitness technologies were integrated within the YMCA and the motto for Grundy Center physical education became 'Energize and Educate at Every Age'.

PE4Life, a U.S. non-profit organization whose mission was promoting best practices and program advocacy, heard of Rick's passion, community outreach, and innovative teaching approaches. In 2003, Grundy Center was recognized as the first elementary PE4Life Academy in the country. Rick began hosting 1–2 day professional development workshops. The workshops allowed Rick to showcase his technology-rich environment, teaching practices, and curriculum, and the effects of community partnership. Rick encouraged visitors to take steps to enhance their programs through advocacy and technology-enhanced pedagogy. Across a 9-year period, over 200 visitors, including senators, congressmen, and even the U.S. Secretary of Education, attended the PE4Life Academy and observed the Grundy Center physical education program.

During this time, Rick was committed to collaborating with physical education teacher education faculty from regional universities. In 2004, Grundy Center Community Schools established a partnership with a University to host a 1-year Master's program. The Polar Scholar Master's program was a residency-based program that provided a venue for teacher education students to experience 'pedagogy of technology' and educational theory in practice. Across 7 years, 46 Master's students relocated to central Iowa to learn and teach within this rural, innovative wellness-focused community. The Polar Scholar program served to launch innovative physical educators into K–12 and collegiate levels and the health and fitness industry.

In May 2010, Grundy Center was host to 70 professionals from over 35 countries at the Global Forum for Physical Education Pedagogy. The focus of the 2-day forum was to revitalize health and physical education through technology. The culmination of the Forum was the development of a global consensus statement entitled Health and Physical Education Pedagogy in the 21st Century that included recommendations and calls to action for health and physical education professionals (see www.globalpeforumgc.org/consensus-statement).

Late career (2012–2015)

With changes in school/university administration and concerns regarding program sustainability, the final cohort of Polar Scholars completed their program of study in 2012. As Rick reflected upon 7 years of mentoring graduate students and the collaborative exploration of technology, he commented 'The Polar Scholars took me to a whole different level that I didn't know was possible'. However, in a much quieter gymnasium and with his students as the only audience, Rick continued to integrate and innovate using technology. Changes included transitioning to iPads for greater versatility and introducing the HRMs in sixth grade rather than fourth – both of which required Rick to re-conceptualize aspects of his teaching, understanding of learners, and learning environment.

Challenges and opportunities of integrating technology across a career

The integration of technology in physical education across a career required commitment and persistence, and, according to Rick, did not come without its challenges. Notable challenges included assessing the appropriateness of technologies, allocating time to plan and develop technology-rich lessons, pursuing new technologies, and financing innovation. Amidst the challenges, however, numerous opportunities were afforded to Rick, his students, and community, including enhanced experiences for learners, dynamic and strategic partnerships, continuous professional learning, and the capacity to promote health and wellness throughout the community. To offer additional insights into the development of Rick's personal technology pedagogies, his case is considered from three disciplinary perspectives: Health Optimizing Physical Education, Professional Development and Teacher Learning, and Transformational Leadership.

A health-optimizing physical education perspective (Sean Bulger)

Over the past two decades, the PE teaching profession has become increasingly engaged in a physical activity related public health agenda (Webster *et al.*, 2015). Although this health-related focus is not entirely new for physical education (Leonard, 1915), it has re-emerged as a societal priority. As proposed by Sallis and McKenzie (1991), health-oriented (or health-optimizing) physical education focuses on two primary public health goals: (a) providing school-age children and adolescents with the knowledge, skills, and attitudes needed to remain physically active across the lifespan, and (b) affording access to regular opportunities to engage in developmentally appropriate forms of physical activity as a predisposing factor to habitual behavior change. In response, physical educators, teacher educators, and researchers have been challenged to reconsider the role of school physical activity from a public health standpoint including the resultant implications for their pedagogies and curriculum design (McKenzie & Lounsberry, 2013).

Individual and interpersonal levels of influence: knowledge, skills, and attitudes

It is probable that emerging public health concerns related to childhood inactivity and obesity influenced Rick's use of technology to focus on the development of autonomous learners who assume responsibility for their physical activity and health-related fitness. When physical activity interventionists target behavior change at this individual level of influence, key factors include self-efficacy, behavioral skills, and behavioral capabilities (Ward, Saunders, & Pate, 2007). *Self-efficacy* is defined as "a person's belief in his or her ability to perform a particular behavior, including confidence to overcome barriers to engaging in that behavior" (Ward *et al.*, 2007: 25). Behavioral skill (self-control) represents the person's readiness to manage their physical activity through goal setting, planning, self-monitoring, modification, and self-reinforcement. Behavioral capability incorporates the motor/sports skills and performance concepts needed to engage in a specific form of activity. Within the interpersonal level of influence, the relationships and social interactions shared by teachers and students serve as important reinforcing variables regarding physical activity (Ward *et al.*, 2007). The related factors include the establishment of encouraging social environments for learners and the facilitation of supportive social networks among peers and families.

As evidenced in the practitioner narrative, PE teachers can employ instructional technology to address these individual and interpersonal influences on physical activity behavior. For example, pedometers and heart monitors have a long history of use in PE for measuring physical activity, motivating increased participation, providing individualized feedback to learners, and teaching health-related fitness concepts (Clapham, Sullivan, & Ciccomascolo, 2015). Other technologies are also applicable for these instructional purposes, including fitness testing and reporting software, mobile devices and applications, accelerometers and activity monitors, movement analysis software, computer and video games for health and physical activity, distance learning, and social media platforms (Jones, Bulger, & Wyant, 2012).

It is important to note that despite their possible benefits, these technologies do have inherent limitations and PE teachers are advised to prepare adequately before integrating them into their instruction (e.g. cost, validity, reliability, ease of use, maintenance, replacement) (Partridge, King, & Bian, 2011). Adequate teacher training and instructional planning represent another concern about the use of technology in that inappropriate practice can represent a barrier to participation and source of frustration for teachers (Wyant, Jones, & Bulger, 2015). Finally, teachers need to consider learner perceptions regarding technology use in PE settings and make certain that they understand its relationship to the intended learning outcomes (Partridge *et al.*, 2011). In a study investigating heart rate monitor use in high school physical education, Partridge *et al.* offered the following recommendations for PE teachers based on student perceptions:

1. Exercise caution when using tools like heart rate monitors, activity monitors, and/or pedometers as a basis for assigning letter grades, because the association of technology and grade as an extrinsic motivator might lower the intrinsic motivation to become more active.
2. Collaborate with learners to identify individualized uses of technology, increase student active engagement, and account for their unique interests and abilities.
3. Maintain a consistent focus on self-improvement to improve learner motivation and enjoyment as an alternative to absolute measures of achievement.

Organizational and community levels of influence: increasing opportunities

Effective physical activity interventions for children and adolescents often extend beyond the individual and interpersonal levels of influence with a goal of increasing access to physical activity opportunities through environmental modification (Ward *et al.*, 2007). Within schools, for example, changes at the organizational level of influence could include alteration of the daily schedule to provide access to more frequent opportunities for structured and unstructured play and/or the development of supportive policies mandating a sufficient amount of physical education for all learners across the developmental continuum. At the broadest level of influence – community/environmental – physical activity interventionists build collaborative partnerships in the community with the intent of enhancing program capacity, sharing facility spaces and equipment, eliminating barriers to existing resources, and creating new opportunities. Advocacy approaches can also be used at this level to raise public awareness about the benefits of physical activity and various resources available to the community.

These changes to the school environment are consistent with recommendations for the use of multi-component physical activity programming in schools. Leading professional and educational organizations have highlighted the importance of comprehensive school physical activity programs (CSPAP) that contribute to the accumulation of 60 minutes or more of moderate-to-vigorous physical activity each day in and around the school day (Centers for Disease Control and Prevention, 2013). Additionally, a range of coordinated opportunities should be provided for learners "to maximize understanding, application, and practice of the knowledge and skills learned in physical education so that all students will be fully educated and well-equipped for a lifetime of activity" (Centers for Disease Control and Prevention, 2013, p. 12). The CSPAP components are recommended to include physical education, physical activity during school, physical activity before and after school, family and community engagement, and staff involvement. There are multiple CSPAP resources available for teachers at www.shapeamerica.org/cspap/what.cfm.

A professional development and teacher learning perspective (Stephen Harvey)

Focusing on the key aspects that help improve the quality of teaching in an ongoing and systematic manner are key aspects of continual teacher success and retention (Armour & Yelling, 2007). In this section, some of the primary factors that research has shown are key aspects to effective Professional Development and Learning (PDL) are outlined and point to key aspects of 'Rick's story' that demonstrate links to effective PDL.

Curriculum and pedagogy to enhance student learning

Researchers have argued that curriculum and pedagogy to enhance student learning must be the primary focus and starting point of any PDL initiative (Armour & Yelling, 2007, 2004). Rick outlined intentional attempts to use technology tools to solve instructional dilemmas and problems. Technology tools were also selected to help him communicate difficult concepts. Paradoxically, Parker and Patton (in press) reported that only two research studies have examined the specific effects of a PDL initiative on student learning in physical education. Hunuk, Ince, and Tannehill (2012) concluded that a PDL initiative based on teachers' specific needs significantly improved students' learning on a health-related fitness knowledge pre-test to post-test. Previously, McKenzie, Alcaraz, Sallis, and Faucette (1998) reported improvements in children's manipulative skills after physical educators and classroom teachers received substantial training. Documenting resultant gains in student learning from PDL is imperative because it can validate teacher efforts and stimulate changes to beliefs and practice (Guskey, 2002).

Collaborative opportunities

Contrary to the traditional forms of PDL where external experts or school administrators establish the agenda, it has been suggested that effective PDL occurs when learning occurs among a collaborative network of professionals (Deglau *et al.*, 2006; Armour & Yelling, 2007; Parker & Patton, in press). PDL programs that promote the development of communities of practice by encouraging discussion and debate among peers and enabling the sharing of concerns, ideas, knowledge, and experiences have been shown to be effective (Armour, 2006). Rick's personal initiative to begin using digital technologies within his teaching practices spurred higher-order pedagogical discussions and dialogue amongst him and his colleagues – thus a community of practice that focused on innovating in physical education was formed (Patton *et al.*, 2005). Moreover, programs such as East Valley outlined by Prusak *et al.* (2010) have shown that the requirement for teachers to attend monthly, collaborative in-service sessions that included interactive exchange of ideas and accountability were key aspects to systemic success in the district. Further, teachers helping other teachers via mentoring has been shown to be an effective strategy for PDL (Patton *et al.*, 2005). Conscious efforts were made by Rick early in his career to identify and seek out a mentor to expand his community of practice.

School-based initiatives that occur in school settings

Armour and Yelling (2004) suggested that more PDL initiatives should be school based and occur in school settings. Furthermore, PDL initiatives are more efficacious if they include members of the same school and/or district, because this is where the direct impact on student learning can be greatest (Goodyear *et al.*, 2014) and opportunities for interactions and follow-up can be facilitated within the school setting (Armour & Yelling, 2004). Rick's involvement with PE4Life and the Polar Scholar program were key influencers in his ongoing motivation for technology integration. Hunuk *et al.* (2012) found that a teacher-centered PDL initiative increased student engagement in physical education, and triggered motivation to continue in the program of learning.

Contextual factors

Additional research has also shown that contextual factors such as workplace conditions, micro-politics, school culture, and support are important for PDL initiatives to be successful (Bechtel & O'Sullivan, 2006). Research shows that the collaboration identified above should involve a range of stakeholders, including administrators, parents, teachers, and others. (Deglau *et al.*, 2006; Armour & Yelling, 2007). Rick realized the significance of developing relationships when building a new program. Therefore, Rick invested heavily in building relationships with his learners, parents, administrators, fellow teachers, and the community. Deglau *et al.* (2006) found that teachers' dialogue in a community of practice was centered on a teacher's consideration for administrators and, in particular, parents. Rick was able to make effective links to parents and the community through the integration of school- and community-fitness-based programming.

Initiatives that are not fully supported by school administrators or are inadequately resourced are not only perceived to be of low value, but can also be resisted by teachers (McCaughtry, Martin, Kulinna, & Cothran, 2006). McCaughtry *et al.* (2006) found that an appropriately resourced physical education department in terms of equipment and visual aids such as educational posters assisted in the delivery of the formal curriculum by teachers in urban and underprivileged school districts. They also noted that the provision of resources changed the emotions, feelings and attitudes of teachers and pupils to the physical education program. Without the support from the administration regarding resources, time and support, the development of Rick's program would have been confined to that of an 'individual maverick' (Bowman & Farrelly, 1992) and could have been marginalized at the school.

Psychological dispositions and teacher beliefs

Finally, psychological dispositions and teacher beliefs can affect teacher responses to PDL initiatives. Kullina, Silverman, and Keating (2000) examined the extent to which beliefs towards physical activity and fitness affected how teachers promoted this in their classes and found a misalignment between teachers' beliefs and actions. Thus, helping teachers to reflect upon their beliefs should be a key aspect of PDL initiatives (Guskey, 2002). An additional aspect of changing beliefs is reflection on practice. It was clear that Rick engaged in such 'cognitive housekeeping' on a regular basis, albeit in a less formal manner, such as in the bike ride to and from work. This form of learning has previously been reported to be commonplace for practitioners (Knowles, Tyler, Gilbourne, & Eubank, 2006). It is my contention that a lifelong learner such as Rick could not have progressed along his learning journey without daily reflection. Indeed, one critical factor in Rick's story is that he viewed himself as a continuous learner (Makopoulou & Armour, 2011).

In closing, consider the recent words of Armour *et al.* (2015), who recommend a refocus of teacher PDL using Dewey's concept of 'education as growth', which goes beyond policy and instead focuses on the nature of contemporary physical education and the needs of teachers as learners.

A transformational leadership perspective (Dana Voelker)

Over his career, Rick demonstrated qualities that many might consider characteristic of a good leader. His successful engagement with the community and completion of several innovative ventures suggests that he is an effective communicator, a critical thinker, and a doer. However, beyond effective leadership qualities, Rick demonstrated leadership behaviors that were transformational in nature. Specifically, his efforts to integrate technology into physical education with intention were an impetus for positive change that transformed him, his students, his community, communities beyond his own, and informed physical education as a profession. Transformational leaders supersede their own self-interests for the betterment of the group and motivate followers to do the same (Bass, 1985). They are characterized by four primary components:

- Idealized influence – being an exemplary role model;
- Inspirational motivation – developing and communicating a compelling vision that followers are eager to pursue;
- Intellectual stimulation – encouraging followers to be creative and innovative by challenging norms and inciting ideas for change; and
- Individual consideration – attending to the individual needs of followers (Bass & Riggio, 2006).

Rick's approach to technology integration aligns strongly with the tenets of transformational leadership theory, which has been shown to promote the enjoyment and engagement of students in physical education settings (e.g. Beauchamp *et al.*, 2014). The following examples from Rick's narrative show how he exemplified the four components of transformational leadership.

Rick exuded *idealized influence* by serving as an exemplary model of positive teaching practices for the profession. For example, building a self-determined physical education environment that supports autonomy (i.e. self-regulation), relatedness (i.e. connectedness with others), and competence (i.e. mastery over the environment), promotes sustained and internally driven motivation (Deci & Ryan, 2000) and optimally engages students and teachers in class (Cheon, Reeve, Yu, & Jang, 2014). Rick integrated technology in ways that not only preserved but also enhanced this self-determined environment. Through the use of heart rate monitors, for example, students still had the opportunity to interact with one another (i.e. relatedness) while also monitoring their intensity (i.e. autonomy) to achieve self-directed goals (i.e. competence). Embodying the notion of idealized influence, Rick's decisions to dramatically change his pedagogical strategies were rooted in personal values to positively impact his students.

Rick also demonstrated *inspirational motivation* in that he developed and communicated a vision that others became eager to follow. Importantly, this journey began with critical self-reflection on current practices, thereby identifying a need for the infusion of technology in the gymnasium. Initiating these changes required time, considerable funding and tremendous effort, especially when the idealized changes were 'ahead of the curve' and new to not only his community but also the profession. Based on the literature examining the link between transformational leadership and the engagement of followers (Mhatre & Riggio, 2014), it is likely that Rick garnered enthusiasm around his vision by first establishing trust. This trust allowed him to forge the key partnerships that made his technology-based vision for the classroom a reality.

Rick's compelling vision challenged extant teaching norms and encouraged others to also 'think outside the box' and begin 'doing' physical education differently. This type of *intellectual stimulation* resulted in a school-based and technology-integrated community wellness center, a technology-focused Master's physical education program, and international recognition for a mid-west rural farming town. Additionally, by showing students how technology often used for academic or social purposes can be used in physical education, Rick also showed them how to be creative in their learning. Although there is no direct evidence on how Rick's students began to innovate as a result of his leadership at this time, transformational teaching in physical education is indeed associated with positive psychological and behavioral changes in students, such as increased physical activity in and outside the classroom (e.g. Beauchamp *et al.*, 2014).

Finally, Rick exemplified *individual consideration* by adapting his practices to meet the needs of his students. By using technology, Rick met the learning preferences of a technologically savvy generation, and tailored their physical education experience through devices that helped them to regulate their progress. This technology usage also allowed Rick to reduce time spent on logistics and transitions and increase time spent on individualized attention and supportive feedback during class. Such consideration for individual strengths and needs has been identified as an essential component to fostering the personal growth of young people (Vella, Oades, & Crowe, 2013).

Although we do not have the perspective of Rick's 'followers' to know truly how they reached higher levels of motivation and were positively transformed because of his leadership, the transformational leadership components observed have been shown to predict positive developmental experiences for youth in similar contexts (Vella *et al.*, 2013). The development of such transformational leadership is a popular topic of inquiry in the scholarly literature. Effective leadership, in general, is explained by a blend of stable personal attributes (e.g. personality, values), attributes that are malleable and developed over time (e.g. problem-solving skills, expertise), and an environment that demands this leadership (Zaccaro, 2007). Congruent with the literature (Stavros & Seiling, 2015), the transformational leadership development observed in Rick's case involved critical self-reflection and awareness, an assessment of values, the creation of a vision, the development of key competencies, and some risk taking as his practices departed from the status quo. Rick's transformational leadership development was also shaped by his mentorship experiences in that he not only sought the expertise of those more experienced than him but also willingly engaged in 'reverse mentoring' in which the older learns from the younger (Bailey, 2009). As demonstrated by Rick's story, transformational leadership is invaluable to the continued advancement of pedagogies and practices in physical education.

A pedagogical perspective (Emily Jones)

Although digital technologies have been used by teachers to enhance instruction, communication, and student engagement (Tamim *et al.*, 2011), understanding how teachers navigate the affordances and constraints technology places on content and pedagogy is a relatively young concept. In 2006, Mishra and Koehler proposed a conceptual framework called Technological Pedagogical Content Knowledge (TPACK) as a way to represent teacher knowledge required for technology integration. TPACK, which is built upon and extends Shulman's (1986) conceptualization of pedagogical content knowledge, offers insights into the complex 'relationship between content, pedagogy, and technology' (Mishra & Koehler, 2006, p. 1026). TPACK emphasizes the development and application of each knowledge construct as well as the interplay and interactions among the constructs. The constructs of TPACK are represented in the case through Rick's understanding of the features and function of the different technologies (technological knowledge – TK); how technology enhances the efficiency of his instructional practices and pedagogy (technological pedagogical knowledge – TPK); how technology influences the way students interact with content (technological content knowledge – TCK); and, finally, how to create a technology-enhanced learning environment for students to achieve instructional goals and learning outcomes (technological pedagogical content knowledge – TPACK).

Critics of TPACK suggest it is far too broad and does not offer clear distinctions between constructs. For example, Brantley-Dias and Ertmer (2013) speculate that the original framework for teacher knowledge proposed by Shulman (1986) depicts knowledge that teachers must possess to select appropriate teaching methods *and* instructional tools. On a larger scale, others suggest that 'new paradigms for achieving learning outcomes with technology do not need new theories' (Mayes & de Freitas, 2013, p. 18). This perspective repositions pedagogy at the center of teaching and perhaps reduces the emphasis on technology. Further, this idea pulls away from 'technocentric' planning and assigns greater value to the process of establishing meaningful teaching, learning, and assessment strategies before identifying what role (if any) technology tools play and the value they have on the achievement of outcomes (Mayes & de Freitas, 2004).

Across his career, Rick developed TPACK and used this knowledge to make decisions about how he would implement change within his program and practices. Scholars emphasize that possessing TPACK is very different from actually using it (Brantley-Dias & Ertmer, 2013). That is, TPACK is not achieved within a single lesson but rather refined over time through deliberate and reflective practice, and with careful consideration of contextual variables such as student readiness, technology management, and the like. Based on an analysis of the case, two major outcomes of Rick's application of TPACK in physical education were observed: (a) inquiry and student-centered pedagogy, and (b) an elevated status for physical education.

Inquiry and student-centered pedagogy

As Rick evaluated and experimented with the digital technologies in his gymnasium with his students, he refined his strategies in a way that Mishra and Koehler (2006, p. 1033) describe as 'authentic program solving with technology'. These practices align with findings that exemplary teachers plan, coordinate, and blend technology tools into their instruction, whereas adequate or less exemplary teachers viewed technology integration as a specific activity (Pierson, 2001). Further, Pierson described exemplary technology-using teachers as having extensive teaching experience, technology training, and commitment to spending personal time learning and engaging with the technology.

Rick spent considerable time learning how to use digital technologies (TK), and even more time planning how to use and manage them (TCK and TPK). With this in mind, the PDL Rick engaged in across his career were largely school based and focused on curriculum, pedagogy, and student learning – with technology as a secondary agent. As he and his students became more comfortable using the HRMs, Rick noticed students appropriately responding to the audible 'beep' of the monitor and checking their HRMs during aerobic activities without teacher prompting, and he heard students encouraging one another to 'stay in your zone'.

He began using more student-centered approaches such as questioning, and guided and divergent discovery (Mosston & Ashworth, 2002). Eventually, Rick observed students self-regulating, using the data to make decisions, and challenging the established labels of 'biggest, fastest, or strongest'. The ownership of learning, acquisition of power, and elevation of students to a higher *status* within the learning environment are reflective features of post-modern pedagogy (Kilgove, 2004).

As Rick recognized the impact that data were having on student learning he began to consider how he might use those data to influence his instructional effectiveness (TPK). Outlined in the literature, inquiry and problem-based learning centers on the curiosity of the learner and engages learners in systematic processes of questioning, critical thinking, reflection, and problem-solving (Ermeling, 2012; Savery, 2015). Within the current case, Rick used inquiry-based approaches across his career by identifying problems within his classroom, exploring realistic solutions, reflecting on implementation, and engaging in collaborative dialogue about the impact of his efforts. For example, to reduce the percentage of time students spent in low-intensity activities (e.g. below the target heart rate zone), Rick used (a) sound-editing software to overlay voice commands to music for warm-up activities, (b) modified and small-sided game play to increase activity time and emphasize strategy and concepts (Harvey, Song, Baek, & van der Mars, 2015), and (c) the mounted projection system to supplement his instruction (TPACK).

Although research indicates that individuals who engage in inquiry and problem-based learning have been found to become more self-regulated lifelong learners (Vernon & Blake, 1993), Ermeling (2012) suggests that widespread adoption of this approach would require a significant shift in cultural routines and mind sets for many educators.

Elevated status for physical education

Once Rick recognized the impact digital technologies were having in his classroom and on the health and wellbeing of his learners, he explored ways to extend his sphere of influence into the community. He began to share data with parents, administrators, and community stakeholders to illustrate his vision for physical education and its potential to impact the health of children, families, and community members. From a social ecological perspective (McLeroy, Bibeau, Steckler, & Glanz, 1988), by broadening his influence across interpersonal, institutional, and community levels, Rick was able to enhance his capacity for reach and impact. Whole-school approaches to physical activity such as CSPAPs (Erwin et al., 2013) indicate that quality physical education is at the heart of school physical activity, yet should be supplemented by opportunities for physical activity before, during, and after school and within school and community settings. In Rick's case, he implemented a quality, innovative, health-oriented physical education program at the center of a school and community's physical activity programming.

An identified barrier to CSPAP planning, development, and sustainability is the availability of qualified individuals to lead programs (Jones et al., 2014). Proponents suggest that physical education teachers are well positioned to assume the role of physical activity director; however, many physical educators do not view directing a CSPAP as their responsibility, nor have they been formally trained to fulfill this role (Illg & Bulger, 2015). Illg and Bulger (2015) conducted an exploratory study to identify the knowledge, skills, and behavioral competencies needed for a school leader to develop, implement, and sustain a CSPAP. Findings indicate five primary areas: (a) team building and facilitating, (b) capacity building, (c) knowledge of instructional practices, (d) content knowledge, and (e) program development and management. Reflecting on this case, it appears Rick developed and exhibited these (and other) skills throughout his career, allowing him to successfully navigate social and organizational structures to immerse health and physical activity in the broader community, thus elevating the awareness and status of physical education.

Finally, collaborative partnerships developed over a 30-year period facilitated state, national, and international recognition of the physical education program in Grundy Center. PE4Life provided Rick with a platform upon which to share his and Beth's vision of technology-enhanced, health oriented physical education and encourage others to enact change within their programs. The partnership with the university was a significant undertaking and required a commitment from the community (Brusseau *et al.*, 2015). Rick's sphere of influence reached across ecological levels (McLeroy *et al.*, 1988) and community support for the Polar Scholars program was unwavering (Crisp, Swerissen, & Duckett, 2000). As previously noted, Rick demonstrated attributes of a transformational leader (Bass & Riggio, 2006) and was effective at motivating others to follow his lead of using digital technologies to improve teaching and learning in physical education and beyond.

Practitioner reflection (Rick Schupbach)

When I reflect on my professional journey, I think two things are paramount to delivering change within our schools and communities: building relationships and seeking mentors. First, an important aspect of being an agent for change is developing meaningful relationships with students. To build those relationships we must be present each day, each class, and every moment in the gymnasium and out in our communities. We need to create classroom environments that accept students as they are and challenge them to grow and explore. Therefore, I focused on finding ways that would allow me to interact in more meaningful ways with the students while they were in my gym. Technology assisted me in accomplishing this. When we believe that what we are teaching is important, and we care about whom we are teaching, I feel it naturally fuels a desire to pursue "best practice". Teaching has provided me with incredible memories. Paramount in all of these memories are the purposeful and meaningful relationships I have developed with so many of my students. These relationships have enriched my life in a way that cannot be adequately expressed in words.

Second, agents of change know they do not have all the answers but they seek out and surround themselves with individuals who can help them grow. I have had mentors that have taught me lessons that are pivotal to success within the classroom. My father was a divorced, self-employed painting contractor who raised three children on his own. He worked full time until age 83. My father taught me the value of hard work, dedication, perseverance and pride in a job well done. I needed all of these attributes to forge a path of pursuing cutting-edge technology practices in physical education. What an example he set for me!

Finally, a true technology pioneer and innovator in the field of physical education mentored me. Beth Kirkpatrick modelled the use of heart rate monitors and other technologies to me when I first visited her classroom. She gave me a vision for what was possible and challenged me to challenge the status quo. Beth taught me that we often accept less than we deserve; more importantly perhaps, we many times accept less than what our students deserve. Without her model and vision, I would not have travelled the path I did. I hope all professionals look to glean knowledge from others, because none of us has all the answers.

Lessons from the case: How can the use of digital technologies accelerate pupil learning in physical education?

- The value of engaging in career-long, inquiry-based learning is underpinned by strong mentorship.
- Transformational leadership is invaluable to being a progressive pedagogue.
- Have pupils (needs) driving the introduction of technology – rather than technology driving the pedagogy.
- Possess a passion for pedagogy and lifelong learning.

References

Armour, K. (2006). 'Physical education teachers as career-long learners: A compelling research agenda'. *Physical Education and Sport Pedagogy*, *11*(3), 203–207.

Armour, K. M. and Yelling, M. (2007). 'Effective professional development for physical education Teachers: The role of informal, collaborative learning'. *Journal of Teaching in Physical Education*, *26*(2), 177–200.

Armour, K. and Yelling, M. (2004). 'Continuing professional development for experienced physical education teachers: Towards effective provision'. *Sport, Education and Society*, *9*(1): 95–114.

Armour, K., Quennerstedt, M., Chambers, F., and Makopoulou, K. (2015) 'What is "effective" CPD for contemporary physical education teachers? A Deweyan framework', *Sport, Education and Society*, 1–13.

Bailey, C. (2009). 'Reverse intergenerational learning: A missed opportunity?' *AI and Society*, *3*, 111–115.

Bass, B. M. (1985). *Leadership and performance beyond expectations*. New York: Free Press.

Bass, B. M. and Riggio, R. E. (2006). *Transformational leadership* (2nd ed.). Mahwah, New Jersey: Lawrence Erlbaum Associates.

Beauchamp, M. R., Liu, Y., Morton, K. L., Martin, L. J., Wilson, A. H., Wilson, A. J., Sylvester, B.D., and Barling, J. (2014). 'Transformational teaching and adolescent physical activity: Multilevel and mediational effects'. *International Journal of Behavioral Medicine, 21,* 537–546.

Bechtel, P. A. and O'Sullivan, M. (2006). 'Effective professional development: What we now know'. *Journal of Teaching in Physical Education, 25*(4), 363–378.

Bowman, J. and Farrelly, J. (1992). 'Model physical education programs in South Carolina'. *Journal of Physical Education, Recreation and Dance, 63*(4), 77–79.

Brantley-Dias, L. and Ertmer, P. A. (2013). 'Goldilocks and TPACK: Is the construct "just right?"'. *Journal of Research on Technology in Education, 46*(2), 103–128.

Brusseau, T., Bulger, S., Elliott, E., Hannon, J., and Jones. E. (2015). 'University and community partnerships to implement comprehensive school physical activity programs: Insights and impacts for Kinesiology Departments'. *Kinesiology Review, 4,* 370–377.

Centers for Disease Control and Prevention. (2013). *Comprehensive school physical activity programs: A guide for schools.* Atlanta, GA: U.S. Department of Health and Human Services.

Cheon, S. H., Reeve, J., Yu, T. H., and Jang, H. R. (2014). 'The teacher benefits from giving autonomy support during physical education instruction'. *Journal of Sport and Exercise Psychology,* 36, 331–346.

Clapham, E. D., Sullivan, E. C., and Ciccomascolo, L. E. (2015). 'Effects of a physical education supportive curriculum and technological devices on physical activity'. *The Physical Educator, 72*(1), 102–116.

Crisp, B., Swerissen, H., and Duckett, S. (2000). 'Four approaches to capacity building in health: Consequences for measurement and accountability'. *Health Promotion International, 15*(2), 99–107.

Deci, E. L. and Ryan, R. M. (2000). 'The "what" and "why" of goal pursuits: Human needs and the self-determination of behavior'. *Psychological Inquiry, 11*(4), 227–268.

Deglau, D., Ward, P., O'Sullivan, M., and Bush, K. (2006). 'Professional dialogue as professional development'. *Journal of Teaching in Physical Education, 25*(4), 413–427.

Ermeling, B. A. (2012). 'Improving teaching through continuous learning: The inquiry process John Wooden used to become coach of the century'. *Quest, 64*(3),197–208.

Erwin, H., Beighle, A., Carson, R. L., and Castelli, D. M. (2013). 'Comprehensive school-based physical activity promotion: A review', *Quest, 65*(4), 412–428.

Goodyear, V. A., Casey, A., and Kirk, D. (2014). 'Tweet me, message me, like me: Using social media to facilitate pedagogical change within an emerging community of practice'. *Sport, Education and Society, 19*(7), 927–943.

Guskey, T. R. (2002). 'Professional development and teacher change'. *Teachers and Teaching, 8*(3), 381–391.

Harvey, S., Song, Y., Baek, J-H., and van der Mars, H. (2015). 'Two sides of the same coin: Student physical activity levels during a game-centered soccer unit'. *European Physical Education Review.* doi:10.1177/1356336X15614783

Hunuk, D., Ince, M. L., and Tannehill, D. (2012). 'Developing teachers' health-related fitness knowledge through a community of practice: Impact on student learning'. *European Physical Education Review, 19*(1), 3–20.

Illg, K. and Bulger, S. (March, 2015). 'Identification of school physical activity leader competencies using concept mapping.' Paper presented at the National SHAPE Conference, Seattle, WA.

Jones, E. M., Bulger, S. M., and Wyant, J. (2012). 'Moving beyond the stopwatch and whistle: Examining technology use in teacher training'. *The Global Journal of Health and Physical Education Pedagogy, 1,* 210–222.

Jones, E. M., Taliaferro, A. R., Elliott, E., Bulger, S., Kristjansson, A. L., Neal, W., and Allar, I. (2014). 'Feasibility study of comprehensive school physical activity programs in Appalachian communities: The McDowell CHOICES project'. *Journal of Teaching in Physical Education*, 33(4), 467–491.

Kilgove, D. (2004). 'Promoting critical practice in adult education'. *New Directions for Adult and Continuing Education*, *102*, 45–53.

Knowles, Z., Tyler, G., Gilbourne, D., and Eubank, M. (2006). 'Reflecting on reflection: Exploring the practice of sports coaching graduates'. *Reflective Practice*, 7(2), 163–179.

Kullina, P. H., Silverman, S., and Keating, X. D. (2000). 'Relationship between teachers' belief systems and actions toward teaching physical activity and fitness'. *Journal of Teaching in Physical Education*, *19*(2), 206–221.

Leonard, F. E. (1915). *Pioneers of modern physical training*. New York: Association Press.

McCaughtry, N., Martin, J., Kulinna, P. H., and Cothran, D. (2006). 'What makes teacher professional development work? The influence of instructional resources on change in physical education'. *Journal of In-Service Education*, *32*(2), 221–235.

McKenzie, T., Alcaraz, J., Sallis, J., and Faucette, N. (1998). 'Effects of a physical education program on children's manipulative skills'. *Journal of Teaching in Physical Education*, *17*(3), 327–341.

McKenzie, T.L. and Lounsberry, M. A. F. (2013). 'Physical education teacher effectiveness in a public health context'. *Research Quarterly for Exercise and Sport*, *84*, 419–430.

McLeroy, K. R., Bibeau, D., Steckler, A., and Glanz, K. (1988). 'An ecological perspective on health promotion programs'. *Health Education Quarterly*, *15*, 351–377.

Makopoulou, K. and Armour, K. M. (2011) 'Physical education teachers' career-long professional learning: Getting personal'. *Sport, Education and Society*, *16*(5), 571–591.

Mayes, T. and de Freitas, S. (2004). 'Review of e-learning theories, frameworks and models'. London: Joint Information Systems Committee. Retrieved from www.webarchive. org.uk/wayback/archive/20081225004835/http://www.jisc.ac.uk/whatwedo/programm es/elearningpedagogy/outcomes.aspx

Mayes, T. and de Freitas, S. (2013) 'Technology-enhanced learning: The role of theory'. In H. Beetham and R. Sharpe (Eds.), *Rethinking pedagogy for a digital age: Designing for 21st century learning* (2nd ed.). New York: Routledge.

Mhatre, K. H. and Riggio, R. E. (2014). 'Charismatic and transformational leadership: Past, present, and future'. In D. V. Day (Ed.), *The Oxford handbook of leadership and organizations*. New York: Oxford University Press. pp. 221–240.

Mishra, P. and Koehler, M. J. (2006). 'Technological pedagogical content knowledge: A framework for teacher knowledge'. *Teachers College Record*, *108*(6), 1017–1054.

Mosston, M. and Ashworth, S. (2002). *Teaching physical education* (5th ed.). New York: Benjamin Cummings.

Parker, M. and Patton, K. (in press). 'What international research evidence tells us about effective and ineffective forms of teacher continuing professional development'. In C. D. Ennis (Ed.), *Handbook of physical education*. London: Routledge.

Partridge, J. A., King, K. M., and Bian, W. (2011). 'Perceptions of heart rate monitor use in high school physical education classes'. *The Physical Educator*, *68*(1), 30–43.

Patton, K., Pagnano, K., Griffin, L. L., Dodds, P., Sheehy, D., Arnold, R., Henninger, M. L., Gallo, A. M., and James, A. (2005). 'Chapter 2: Navigating the mentoring process in a research-based teacher development project: A situated learning perspective'. *Journal of Teaching in Physical Education*, *24*, 302–325.

Pierson, M. (2001). 'Technology integrtion practices as a function of pedagogical expertise'. *Journal of Research on Computing in Education*, *33*(4), 413–430.

Prusak, K. A., Pennington, T., Graser, S. V., Beighle, A., and Morgan, C. F. (2010). 'Systemic success in physical education: The East Valley phenomenon'. *Journal of Teaching in Physical Education, 29,* 85–106.

Sallis, J. F. and McKenzie, T. L. (1991) 'Physical education's role in public health'. *Research Quarterly for Exercise and Sport, 62,* 124–137.

Savery, J. R. (2015). 'Overview of problem-based learning: Definitions and distinctions'. In A. Walker, H. Leary, C. E. Hmelo-Silver, and P. A. Ertmer (Eds.), *Essential readings in problem-based learning.* West Lafayette, IN: Purdue University Press.

Shulman, L. S. (1986). 'Those who understand: Knowledge growth in teaching'. *Educational Researcher, 15*(2), 4–14.

Stavros, J. M. and Seiling, J. (2015). 'Transformational leadership development'. In W. J. Rothwell, J. M. Stavros, and R. L. Sullivan (Eds.), *Practicing organization development: Leading transformation and change* (4th ed.). Hoboken, NJ: Wiley. pp. 78–95.

Tamim, R. M., Bernard, R. M., Borokhovski, E., Abrami, P. C., and Schmid, R. F. (2011). 'What Forty Years of Research Says About the Impact of Technology on Learning: A Second-Order Meta-Analysis and Validation Study'. *Review of Educational Research, 81*(1), 4–28.

Vella, S. A., Oades, L. G., and Crowe, T. P. (2013). 'The relationship between coach leadership, the coach—Athlete relationship, team success, and the positive developmental experiences of adolescent soccer players'. *Physical Education and Sport Pedagogy, 18*(5), 549–561.

Vernon, D. T. A. and Blake, R. L. (1993). 'Does problem-based learning work: A meta-analysis of evaluative research'. *Academic Medicine, 68*(7), 550–563.

Ward, D. S., Saunders, R. P., and Pate, R. P. (2007). *Physical activity interventions in children and adolescents.* Champaign, IL: Human Kinetics.

Webster, C.A., Webster, L., Russ, L., Molina, S., Lee, H., and Cribbs, J. (2015). 'A systematic review of public health-aligned recommendation for preparing physical education teacher candidates'. *Research Quarterly for Exercise and Sport, 86*(1), 1–10.

Wyant, J. D., Jones, E. M., and Bulger, S. M. (2015). 'A mixed methods analysis of a single-course strategy to integrate technology into PETE'. *Journal of Teaching in Physical Education, 34,* 131–151.

Zaccaro, S. J. (2007). 'Trait-based perspectives of leadership'. *American Psychologist, 62*(1), 6–16.

11

JARROD: THE PROMISE AND MESSY REALITIES OF DIGITAL TECHNOLOGY IN PHYSICAL EDUCATION

Eimear Enright, Jarrod Robinson, Anna Hogan, Michalis Stylianou, Joe Hay*, Finn Smith* and Alice Ball*

CHAPTER OVERVIEW

Although there is currently a great deal of interest in the use of digital technology in physical education, there is the clear and as yet unaddressed risk that the transformative potential of digital technology will be squandered. Drawing on a practitioner narrative of an Australian physical educator, which presents a retelling of how he uses digital technologies to support learning, we consider the promise and messy realities associated with digital technologies in physical education. After analysing the narrative through multiple lenses (students' eyes, educational policy, effective instruction and critical pedagogy), we argue for a democratic and critical re-imagineering of physical education along digital lines.

Practitioner narrative (Jarrod Robinson)

I am a practicing physical education teacher and e-learning coordinator in a small, rural school in country Victoria, Australia. I am passionate and enthusiastic about the role emerging technologies play within teaching and learning, and have been integrating technology into my teaching practice for a long time. I am known in the online community as "The PE Geek", and I author a blog of the same name. Drawing on my interest and experience in digital learning, I have constructed the following case which highlights the possibilities associated with using technology to support learning.

* Pseudonyms of student researchers and co-authors

The case

I have chosen one lesson in my seventh grade (12–13-year-olds) volleyball unit to provide some insight into the integration of video assets like Sworkit Lite, QR Code Skill posters, Video Tagger Pro, and BaM Video Delay into physical education (see Table 11.1). These resources allow me to differentiate, and thereby strengthen, learning for individual students. Together with GoPro Hero 4 devices (see Table 11.1), these technologies help me teach my students tactical insight and provide a framework for them to analyse their own performance on individual and group levels. The specific outcomes/objectives are to:

1. develop students' skills and game strategies, which can then be employed throughout the game of volleyball; and
2. facilitate tactical and skill transfer from previous lessons in the unit (the lesson was part of a wider net and wall games unit).

All seventh grade students in my school have iPads and laptops. The flexibility afforded to students in choosing the appropriate device for activities gives them a sense of ownership over their learning.

Warm-up

After students have changed clothes, they grab their iPads, find a spot for a work out, and begin the lesson independently. The first application they engage with is Sworkit Lite. My students choose cardio and aerobic-based activities, and set a time limit for their warm-ups.

Students' ability to choose allows them to attempt tasks that are relevant to them. As well as this warm-up application, the second warm-up resource used is Joey Feith's QR Code Skill poster set (see www.thephysicaleducator.com). When a student scans the code with a QR reader application on their device, a video of a skill, broken down into basic elements, is displayed. The posters for this lesson contain skills for volleyball – for example, the forehand, forearm pass, overhead pass, and underarm serve. Students visit each poster station with their devices and scan codes for the skills they wish to exercise or improve. There are three levels per skill set, marked by different levels of difficulty. While differentiation is possible without technology, in this case the technology functions as a proxy in the learning process by carrying out some of the tasks of the teacher.

Digital technology supports students in taking responsibility for doing their own warm-ups and identifying skills which they perceive as their weaknesses or their strengths, and choosing exactly what they wish to improve. This prepares them to participate in a game while simultaneously helping them to become knowledgeable about the types of skills needed for successful play. In essence, this means that both teachers and technology position students as authorities in their own learning, by helping them seek mastery in whatever aspects of the sport they choose to master.

TABLE 11.1 Overview of technology use in this case

Technology/ application	Function	Used in this case to . . .
BaM Video Delay	A video delay and feedback application	record play with an 8-second delay; streamed onto the gym's big screen, allowing students to reflect on play after it had occurred
CoachNote	Application that works like a coach's whiteboard and allows you to draw plan and create sport plays and tactics	aid discussion of tactics with the class during and at the conclusion of the lesson
GoPro Hero 4	A small, light, durable, wearable and mountable camera	record video footage and enable Jarrod to see what the students are seeing, and provide further insight into their decision making
iPad	A tablet computer	support all the various applications the students engage with
Large screen display	Medium used for transmitting sound and moving images	display highlights from VideoTagger and BaM Video Delay recordings
QR code reader	An application that converts Quick Response code (a type of matrix bar code) to some useable form	scan the QR Code skill posters and to convert the embedded code to video
QR Code Skill poster set	Skill posters with QR codes embedded	facilitate warm-ups; a resource students use to scan codes to display video of the skill on their device
Sworkit Lite	An application that allows you to customise and play personalised video workouts	aid in the warm-up part of the lesson; presents students with different aerobic warm-ups (including stretching and yoga)
VideoTagger Pro	A video analysis and assessment tool	record and provide feedback on/tag student performance; in this case, for creating highlight reels according to the tags attributed to recorded actions; these highlights were shared with students as feedback

Development

In my experience working in this way has meant that their skill level and tactical awareness is more advanced than previous years. I believe this is partly due to the freedom digital technology affords them, but also due to the quality of feedback various applications help me to deliver as the lesson develops. For example, I use an application I created – VideoTagger – to record students' movement and tag it as either "good" or "in need of improvement". Those that were tagged as "good" had the appropriate formations and outcomes. VideoTagger creates highlight reels according to the tags attributed to recorded actions. After stopping the game play, I display the highlights to the students on the large screen in the gymnasium. Not only do the students watch videos via the big screen, they then also try to replicate what they have seen via the posters and accompanying video. This means their own actions at these stations became viable forms of data for me and for them. This enables me to measure the progress of the class, and aids students in analysing, questioning, and justifying their skill learning. As a result, VideoTagger Pro supports students by reinforcing the important points of the skill and by helping them to engage in peer teaching. I feel this is the essential teamwork a physical education class needs.

The highlight reel that follows the actual game is also accompanied by in-game highlights (via BaM Video Delay). It is immediately streamed onto the gym's big screen, giving the students an opportunity to view a particular play immediately after it occurred. I believe the use of BaM Video Delay actually increases my students' motivation. Not only do they like to see themselves play, but BaM also helps create teachable moments that helps the students and I focus on the reason behind individual and team success. BaM Video Delay also serves as an unbiased umpire and provides evidence to students on why and how particular decisions were made. As students are wearing the GoPro cameras, I am able to see what the students are seeing. In turn I am also able to gain insight into particular student reactions as they happen live. This aids discussions with the class during and at the conclusion of each lesson regarding the accuracy of the play, any stressors, distractions, or judgments. With the integration of the CoachNote app, a tactical approach to game play begins to take shape. Like a coach's whiteboard, different courts and field diagrams can be used to illustrate tactics and strategies. By moving players digitally around using the app, I can demonstrate to them where to stand and how to execute a proper skill. Conceptualising these through mere discussion and drawing on a board is difficult at times, and using CoachNote with GoPros makes tactics easier to illustrate and discuss. For example, visually showcasing a strategy for positioning the ball in readiness for a spike compliments the spoken instructions.

The information gathered through applications enriches the learning environment while providing various types of learning pathways for each student. The students do not just have to rely on the teacher in demonstrating or articulating a skill; they now have a variety of avenues to actualise the information. In turn, these applications help me record the progress of my class by providing raw evidence of student performance. This evidence is then translated into new material for learning. During one of the lessons, for example, the video evidence captured using VideoTagger enabled a student "Jack" to observe the fundamental flaws that occurred during his volleyball sets. This video evidence, used in conjunction with teacher advice, resulted in a measurable improvement in his ability to set the ball. Supported by digital tools, Jack was able to demonstrate that he was working towards curriculum objectives that require students to develop strategic thinking and tactical knowledge that improve individual and team performances.

The efficiency, creativity, and freedom these applications offer have not only revolutionised a lesson in volleyball but they have also impacted the expectations my students have around their learning and ability in the physical education environment.

Three student perspectives (Joe, Finn and Alice)

We are year-seven (12–13-year-old) students from Queensland, Australia. Eimear (the first author) has given us new names here so that nobody knows who we are. She has called us Joe, Finn and Alice. All three of us are doing a research project with Eimear that's about learning in our sports.

Joe

I'm a 13-year-old downhill longboarder. I like everything about this lesson, except that it's volleyball. I'm not that into volleyball, but there's so much cool technology I'd probably forget that it's about volleyball, so all good. The warm-up is the best – just you and your iPad, and a teacher who isn't afraid you'll trash the technology. I don't learn well from people telling me what to do. It helps with them telling me how to do it, but not what to do. I never thought about using QR codes like that but it makes sense. You're getting help from the iPad and from the teacher. You're getting a lot of help about how to do stuff. The only thing is, like, I'd do it, but would every kid in my class do what they're supposed to be doing? I don't know. I think they might want to be surfing the web on the iPad, checking out stoke-worthy videos on YouTube. Stuff like that. It's risky giving some kids that much control and an iPad in PE. You'd have to be the kind of teacher who we know not to mess with.

Finn

This lesson would definitely be fun. The teacher must be totally rad to come up with a lesson like that. I would be stoked about being a student in it. It could only be better if it was skating and not volleyball. I reckon using videos is great. I'm 13 and I'm a skater. When I started skating, videos really helped me – just like seeing those videos and knowing where your feet are – seeing where your feet are and how you can change. VideoTagger seems awesome but I wouldn't like seeing myself out there on the big screen in the gymnasium. The 'selfie sect' (students in Finn's class who enjoy taking and sharing photographs of themselves) and some of my mates would be pretty happy about that part though – seeing themselves blown up out there. I've got a GoPro for my skating, and yeah, I use that sometimes to get some footage with some mates. The footage from a GoPro is good, like to see where you've messed up and haven't and see how you could have got a better corner or you could have overtaken someone in the straight where you didn't. It really helps perfecting that kind of stuff, especially things you couldn't see or feel at first. It's cool to see a teacher using a GoPro in school. It's cool that they even know what it is!

Alice

My name is Alice and I'm 12. I think that lesson is nothing like the PE I have in my school. I didn't know about or understand all of it. I like social media, Instagram the most, but I don't really know anything about other apps or programmes. I'm not very good at doing anything with the iPad other than watching YouTube, 'how-to' surfing videos and Instragramming. I love surfing and I love volleyball. My Dad played volleyball and he taught me when I was like six. When we do volleyball for PE, we just play and I love it. If I was a student in this class I think I'd love the playing volleyball part the most and I'd worry that PE mightn't be as fun because there's so much technology that I don't know how to use. I showed my Dad the lesson and he thought that there was too much technology and not enough volleyball. I think I agree, but I think it's hard to fully imagine what it would be like. It's very cool that every student has their own laptop and iPad in Mr. Robinson's school. Is that what happens in Victoria? That doesn't happen in my school.

An education policy perspective (Anna Hogan)

I am an education policy scholar, interested in the emerging role of edu-business in education, and the ways in which corporations seek to influence education policy and affect education practice as opportunities for profit. Jarrod's narrative, and the augmented desire for the use of technology to support teaching and learning in schools more broadly, is interesting to analyse. Digital, online, technologically advanced teaching and learning materials make up the largest and most profitable sector of the education market (Burch, 2009). The US education industry is estimated to now be worth over \$1 trillion and is growing rapidly each year (Fallon, 2015). Within this market, digital technologies are often sold by edu-businesses as a 'solution' to improving learner outcomes (see Ball, 2012; Hogan *et al.*, 2015). Digital products are marketed by edu-businesses as 'transformative' in that they provide opportunities for students to 'take charge of their own learning' (DiCerbo & Behrens 2014). Jarrod speaks of these benefits in his class. For example, students use the app Sworkit Lite to select their own warm-up activities, which according to Jarrod, presents them with a more personalised and autonomous learning experience. This integration of a more student-centred approach to learning is a positive development that can be associated with the increasing use of technology in physical education, and education more generally (Casey, 2013). However, we need to be cautious when attributing these effects to 'technology' rather than a teacher's expertise in their use of digitally constructed pedagogies.

The reason that this distinction is important can be aptly summarised by Pearson plc (2015, p. 7) when it observes: 'The real problem in education is not finding a great teacher or a really good school, but being able to replicate that excellence at scale. All our new digital products are focused on meeting that need'. This statement suggests that digital technologies can 'stand alone' to improve student learning and outcomes, irrespective of the teacher employing them, or the context of a school environment. Yet, it is clear from Jarrod's lesson, and his integration of five different apps to support the learning experiences of his students, that a teacher must have advanced technological and pedagogical competence to integrate digital resources in classrooms in meaningful ways. Moreover, the fact that each of Jarrod's students have access to an iPad and a laptop, and that his school has the resources to provide GoPro video cameras and a large screen in the gymnasium, is something that cannot necessarily be replicated in all schools across Australia. Clearly, Jarrod's lesson aligns with research that suggests the teacher's expertise and school context are significant in how technology is effectively implemented (see Pountney & Schimmel, 2015).

Despite the complexity that surrounds the effective implementation of tech- nology, edu-businesses continue to make the assertion that *technology is the answer*. Edu-businesses are thus working to promote a professional deficit where teachers are constructed as simply the implementers or enactors of digital products with no legitimate curriculum or pedagogical development interests (Hogan *et al.*, 2015). Indeed, Gard (2014) argues that rather than technology working to support the educative aspects of Health and Physical Education (HPE), it is a reform agenda being capitalised on by edu-businesses as a way to establish a presence within schools and drive up profits. This increasing commercialisation of digital technologies means that we need to be cautious in our implementation, and, as Gard (2014) suggests, ask ourselves, 'What responsibility do we as educators have when we involve students in the use of digital technology which, without most students' knowledge, exists to make money for someone else' (p. 838)?

In answering this question we need to consider what digital resources we are using, who developed these, their expertise and with what underpinning motivation? In the case of VideoTagger Pro, developed by Jarrod, and the QR Code Skill poster set developed by Joey Feith, another physical education teacher, it could be argued that both of these are worthwhile and educative because they have been developed by physical education teachers, with physical education curriculum expertise, specifically for physical education learning experiences. These apps are free to download and use, and represent technology designed from the standpoint of social good, otherwise interpreted as a desire to enhance student learning, without seeking to make a profit. However, if we take another app, such as Bust a Move (BaM) Video Delay, these questions become more complicated to answer. BaM is developed by Orange Qube, an independent design studio founded in 2011, by Marcin Jachmann, in Warsaw, Poland. Orange Qube's tagline is that it is dedicated to creating high quality applications and casual games. In Orange Qube's current portfolio of products, it has three apps, including:

- Tangled FX Photo Effect, available for $1.99, which is an app that works to turn iPhone photos and images into more abstract forms of art;
- Right Note Ear Trainer, available for $6.99 (also available in a free 'lite' version), is an app for interval, pitch and melody recognition that helps users develop their aural skills through both voice and instrument recording and playback; and
- BaM Video Delay, available for $6.49 (see Table 11.1).

This portfolio represents a company whose expertise lies in app development, not physical education, and arguably, not video analysis software. The question here, as Gard (2014) highlights, is are we paying for a technology which has little connection to educative value in our classrooms? I am not suggesting that BaM should not be utilised to support physical education learning experiences. As Jarrod has argued, BaM works to increase students' motivation and provides 'teaching moments' for reflection. However, I do wonder if we are supporting these for-profit, non-educative apps for the right reasons. Jarrod's lesson presents an evolution of technology in PE, not a revolution.

To explicate this thinking through a particularly critical lens, I question whether this technologised volleyball lesson is still a lot like a traditional volleyball lesson. Students wearing GoPro cameras in which the footage is instantaneously broadcast to the big screen in the gymnasium through the assistance of the BaM app represents an exciting evolution of technology, but it is not fundamentally different from the 1980s when a bulky camera set up on a tripod recorded student performance which they later analysed on VHS. Similarly, by allowing students to use an app (rather than a text book, peer discussion, or individual autonomy) to select warm-up activities, can we really claim that we are fundamentally changing how we are teaching and how students are learning? The reason this is problematic is because of what technology *promises*. Teachers are told that they must effectively integrate ICT into their lessons to improve student learning outcomes. Yet while technology is getting sexier, learning is still fundamentally the same. We seem to be investing (with our limited school resource budgets) in new technologies, but we are still interpreting these from the perspective of the preceding pedagogical paradigm. If we are not using technology to revolutionise teaching and learning, are we not just inviting edu-business and their for-profit agendas into our classrooms and paying them to produce services that we are more than capable of providing ourselves? To use the Trojan Horse analogy, are we blindly inviting corporations into our classrooms without understanding the long-term consequences of these developments?

An instructional effectiveness perspective (Michalis Stylianou)

I am a researcher with a particular interest in instructional effectiveness and curriculum links. In this section, I reflect on Jarrod's narrative with regard to instructional effectiveness and the curricular and policy directives that seek to guide the use of technology in the context in which Jarrod is teaching.

As a secondary teacher in Victoria, Jarrod and his school are subject to state and national curricular and policy mandates that have been formulated to inform and shape the uses of technology. The Victorian Curriculum represents a hybrid of the recently endorsed Australian Curriculum (AC) and the previous Victorian Essential Learning Standards. In the AC (Australian Curriculum, Assessment, and Reporting Authority [ACARA] 2015a), the general capabilities encompass the knowledge, skills, behaviours and dispositions that will assist students to live and work successfully in the twenty-first century. These general capabilities span all curricular areas. One of the seven general capabilities is the information and communication technology (ICT) capability. The following description provides an overview of how the ICT capability is addressed in the AC: HPE (F–10):

> Enhances ICT learning by helping students to effectively and safely access online health and physical activity information and services to manage their own health and wellbeing. Students further develop their understanding of the role ICT plays in the lives and relationships of children and young people. They explore the nature of ICT and the implications for establishing and managing relationships in the twenty-first century. Students develop an understanding of ethical online behaviour, including protocols and practices for using ICT for respectful communication. Students use ICT as key tools for communicating, collaborating, creating content, seeking help, accessing information and analysing performance in the Health and Physical Education field. They use a range of ICT to analyse, measure and enhance movement performances and to access and critically evaluate health information, products and services. They also use ICT to develop personalised plans for nutrition and physical activity participation. (ACARA, 2015b)

Consistent with this description, Jarrod is helping students use a range of digital technologies to, amongst other things, access online physical activity information and services to manage their own health and well-being, as well as analyse, measure and enhance movement performances. For instance, Jarrod incorporates Sworkit Lite in the warm-up section of his lesson and uses QR Code skill posters that connect students to videos of the different volleyball skills broken down into basic elements to support skill development. Beyond alignment with the ICT capability in the AC, the use of digital technologies by Jarrod might also be read as a direct response to the position adopted by the Victorian Curriculum regarding the importance of embedding ICT in the curriculum (Victorian Curriculum and Assessment Authority, 2015).

In Victoria, like in many other Australian states, there is a digital learning strategy that seeks to inform the day-to-day activities within Jarrod's classroom. The current (2014–2017) strategy 'Unlocking the potential' outlines the Victorian Government's plan to 'strengthen digital learning in order to improve learner outcomes' (Department of Education and Training, 2014, p. 3). Five actions are identified as key to supporting teachers in unlocking the potential of digital technology for learning, including fostering learner-centred, personalised and flexible learning and teaching; and providing access to real-time, learner-centred formative assessment tools. These actions can be easily mapped onto Jarrod's narrative. The Sworkit Lite application, as well as the QR Code skills posters with varying difficulty levels, have the potential of supporting a learner-centred and flexible learning environment that caters to individual student needs (e.g. volleyball skills that need improvement) and interests (e.g. types of warm-up routines). The use of VideoTagger Pro and BaM Video Delay applications are actually explicitly referred to in the strategy document as exemplars of providing real-time learning-centred formative assessment tools. As Jarrod points out, applications like these can also be used to facilitate peer teaching. According to Casey and Jones (2011), the use of record and playback technologies resulted in deeper understanding of the targeted skills, facilitated peer teaching/assessment, and also helped students feel less marginalised. The findings of this study as well as others (e.g. Harris, 2009; Harvey & Gittins, 2014) legitimise Jarrod's practices and lend support to the use of similar technologies in physical education to help improve student outcomes, not only in the psychomotor domain but also the cognitive and affective domains, which is the focus of the current Victorian digital strategy.

As well as identifying the potential of digital technologies to enhance learning, the Victorian digital strategy (Department of Education and Training, 2014) outlines potential challenges associated with the use of digital technologies. One of these challenges is being learning centred rather than technology driven. Of course, this is more an issue of whether digital technologies are organically integrated in the lesson in a way that supports student learning (Department of Education and Training, 2014), and less an issue of quantity. But a cogent question is whether all the applications Jarrod is using are necessary or whether the use of all the different technologies actually interferes with student learning? In other words, would 'less be more'?

A second challenge identified in the Victorian digital strategy (Department of Education and Training, 2014) relates to promoting safe, responsible and discerning use of digital technologies, which includes accessing appropriate and reliable information. The accuracy of content accessed through digital technologies as well as its developmental appropriateness are often proposed as key criteria in evaluating digital technologies for use in teaching and learning (e.g. Eady & Lockyer, 2013). The Sworkit Lite application does individualise the warm-up but some of its content is questionable. For example, a user will find shoulder push-ups in a cardio routine and pilates under the yoga category. Additionally, the developmental appropriateness and inclusivity of some of its exercises are somewhat concerning; for instance, there is no push-up modification for students who may not be able to perform regular push-ups. Third, while there is video demonstration of exercises, there is a lack of teaching cues to help students perform the exercises correctly and safely (e.g. what body part should you use in bridging to avoid over-extending the lower back?). These are issues that may arise when applications that are not developed by teachers are used in school settings.

In summary, the use of digital technologies presents many opportunities in terms of enhancing learning experiences and learner outcomes. However, integrating digital technology appropriately also poses several challenges including managing the risk of prioritising technology over learning and maintaining vigilance to ensure the safe, responsible and discerning use of digital technologies in the physical education context.

A pedagogical perspective (Eimear Enright)

> Schools are becoming new kinds of spaces and places as they are rebuilt and re-designed, figuratively and literally. They stand for, are icons of, new policy, new modalities of learning – the products of a re-imagineering. They have new kinds of social and architectural ecologies, which promise new kinds of learning experience, in technologically rich, flexible learning environments (Ball, 2007, p. 189).

There is no doubt that the narrative presented by Jarrod will challenge many people's ideas about what physical education is and might be. The 'technologically rich, flexible learning environment' Jarrod constructed is a re-imagineering of physical education, and presents a challenge to the notion that physical education remains a monolithic subject resistant to change. My intent in the following paragraphs is to extend critically enhanced conversations about how the educative potential of technologies (such as those Jarrod identifies) might be best realised in our subject. To do this, I engage with Jarrod's narrative together with the various responses, which all highlight the promise and the messy realities of engaging with digital technology in schools (Selwyn, 2010) and in physical education specifically. Some of the key pedagogical issues raised relate to: the privatisation of physical education, physical education policy and curriculum making, and the lived experiences of physical education teachers and students.

Digital technology and the privatisation of physical education

Digital technology undoubtedly represents a significant recent privatisation of PE. While the outsourcing or external provision of physical education has been subject to sustained critique in the literature (e.g. Evans & Davies, 2015; Williams, Hay,

& Macdonald, 2011), digitally based or digitally enhanced products and services have not yet received the same scrutiny. Jarrod's smorgasboard of technology might easily be justified as a wholly worthwhile and largely beneficial collection of educational resources, however, the Trojan Horse analogy reminds us to consider the networks of private sector interests and agendas that might underlie the applications and digital devices that finds their way into our classrooms. Any profit-driven intervention in schools, digital or not, results in a blurring of the line that might separate benign concern for student learning and self-interested entrepreneurship (Menchik, 2004, p. 197).

Other significant boundaries that become blurred are those concerning expertise. The educational policy and instructional effectiveness perspectives draw attention to the blurring of boundaries between the field of expertise and the site of intervention. When hybrid collectives (e.g. physical education teachers, technologists, Big Business etc.) create new networks and reconfigure boundaries, the educative translation of knowledge in the school context arguably becomes more important. The content knowledge, pedagogical knowledge, pedagogical content knowledge (Shulman, 1987), and technological pedagogical content knowledge (Mishra & Koehler, 2006) of the physical education teacher, and their ability to recognise and respond appropriately to the assemblages of material devices (technological devices and apps in this case), and other interests and agendas (e.g. commercial, global economic and political policies, etc.) become paramount to the realisation of the educative potential of our subject. In Jarrod's case, his expertise as both a physical education teacher and technologist means that he is fully involved in shaping many of the technologies he uses, and arguably better positioned then most to resist non-educational ideologies that might be 'hardwired' into commercial products by either modifying them, turning to open-source software or hardware or creating alternatives (Selwyn, 2010).

PE policy and curriculum making

As the instructional effectiveness perspective highlights, Jarrod and his school are subject to numerous curricular and policy mandates, formulated to direct their use of technology. These policies and curricula are expressions of particular perspectives on the nature and form of digital technology use. While policy rhetoric often, and understandably, supports ambitious aims, the gulf between the rhetoric of educational technology policy and the reality of its translation has been an enduring disappointment for educational technologists and academic commentators (Selwyn, 2010). Numerous theories have been proposed for why this gulf exists and why teachers have not enthusiastically embraced technological innovation; one such theory is that educational technology policies seem to prioritise narrow economic and political motivations rather than educational agendas. Zhao *et al.* (2005, p. 674), for example, suggest that these policies tend to be directed by an 'economic driven mind-set towards learning' and show scant regard for pedagogical implications. Nivala (2009, p. 445) criticises this economically driven policy making as not paying due regard to 'the agency of teachers or pupils, on whom the information society narrative is imposed, but "forces" them to use ICT whether they find it useful or not'. It should go without saying that the addition of technology is not always the answer to the complex pedagogical questions and problems teachers face in their classrooms, however, considering the prevalence of hyperbolic claims about digital technology in schools, one might be forgiven for thinking otherwise. What this means is that teachers often feel pressure to make sense of and enact policies and curricula that are sometimes messy, internally inconsistent, unrealistic, and not always underpinned by sound educational rationales: often without much support or expertise. Jarrod and the policies and curriculum supporting his use of technology may be aberrations in this regard. Jarrod highlights that he uses technology to create a context in which students make meaningful decisions about their own learning. Given technology is Jarrod's passion, it is probably safe to say, therefore, that he is not being coerced into using it. Questions remain, however, as to the relationship between educational technology policy making and in-school curriculum making.

Re-reading the curricular and policy documents that inform Jarrod's work, together with the students' perspectives above, raises some significant questions regarding digital equity. By digital equity I mean ensuring that all students have equitable access to digital technology and to teachers with the pedagogical skills to integrate technology in meaningful ways. While Jarrod has been instrumental in the creation of a context where all students have access to iPads and laptops, and has the pedagogical and digital expertise to develop effective e-pedagogies that are specific to his learning context (Mehenna, 2004), Alice and Finn highlight that this does not align with their respective experiences of physical education. Alice asked if all students in Victoria have access to technology, as this is not what happens in her school in Queensland, and Finn shared surprise that Jarrod is using a GoPro in physical education and that a physical education teacher actually knew what a GoPro was. What these student narratives suggest is that Jarrod's narrative may be the exception rather than the norm, and there is a need to seriously reflect on digital technology use in physical education from an equity perspective. These students also support my claim that digital equity is about more than access (although that can be a significant issue); digital equity is also a pedagogical issue that is intimately connected to the digital and pedagogical expertise of the teacher.

The democratic re-imagineering of physical education

I now move my focus to the micro-level of the gymnasia and classrooms in which students like Alice, Joe, and Finn move and learn. Firstly, let's consider the role of the teacher and how digital technology articulates with that role. Jarrod is a technophile who is enthusiastic about the role emerging technologies can play in teaching and learning. Jarrod is not a passive recipient of the various education technology polices now emerging. He is doing what he loves doing – designing and using technology in creative ways to support student learning – and has in some ways been active in the construction of the educational technology policies that seek to shape his and other teachers' work. The Australian Professional Standards for Teachers now stipulate, however, that all teachers, including those who may not share Jarrod's enthusiasm, demonstrate they are able to 'use effective teaching strategies to integrate ICT into learning and teaching programs to make selected content relevant and meaningful' (Australian Institute for Teaching and School Leadership, 2015). This, taken together with previously shared curricular and policy stipulations, means that teachers' choices to resist using technology are being curtailed. In Australia at least, it seems reasonable to suggest that physical education might begin to be re-imagineered along digital lines. I fundamentally believe that for this re-imagineering to be transformative, we need teachers to be working in partnership with students like Alice, Joe, and Finn. We need digital physical education curricula to be negotiated with rather than prescribed for students. This negotiated approach to curricula will be especially important for those teachers who, unlike Jarrod, are neither comfortable with nor excited about using technology to support and enhance some of their learning experiences.

Recent research I have undertaken with young alternative sport enthusiasts (including Joe, Finn, and Alice) is suggesting that digital media seems to have made new ways of participating and learning in and about sports possible (Enright & Gard, 2015). Participants see digital media having a strong and multifaceted impact on learning. It is, for some, the means through which they learn that the sport (in their case) actually exists; it seems to make it easier to engage in self-education, and can accelerate the learning process; it supports the creation and maintenance of community; it is a source of inspiration; and a new medium through which people can create and express themselves. Joe and Finn point to some of these impacts in their commentaries, and share their excitement that Jarrod's lesson reflects some of the ways they learn to move outside of school. Preliminary analysis of the most recent data generated with and by Joe, Finn, Alice, and their peers also suggests that many of these young people are excited about any prospect of negotiating physical education curricula with their teachers along digital lines.

In summary, the development of effective, equitable, and democratic pedagogies of technology to support young people's learning in physical education is an issue that deserves our immediate attention. My thanks to Jarrod for opening up his practice in ways that helped us to reflect in generative ways upon physical education in 'the digital age'.

Practitioner reflection

One of my earliest memories of technology in physical education occurred during my school years in the early 1990s. While the pedagogical case I constructed for this chapter may not be hugely different to some of the movement lessons I participated in as a student, the fact remains that technology has made some new pedagogical pathways available. Another indisputable fact is that technological advances mean that the integration of technology in the teaching space can now be done almost seamlessly. This is the opposite of the environment in which

I experienced technology in education for the first time. I remember the inclusion of the bulky camcorder as being marred by multiple issues, including the lack of technological knowledge of the teacher who was attempting to use said tool. Compare this to my own teaching where technology has always played a major role and continues to allow me to enhance the teaching and learning experience for all students. Through this written piece, and thinking with the comments of others, I have been able to reflect on my use of technology in my classroom. This reflection has been rewarding, and has prompted me to restate one of my fundamental beliefs about education. I remain convinced that the single most important thing in a classroom is the teacher. There really is no substitute for good teaching. There is no magic app that will transform your lesson.

Therefore, I view any emerging technology as a mere tool in an array of pedagogical options. These tools are drawn on whenever situations arise that they are most appropriate in. In the same vein, if a situation would be best served by the use of zero technology, then that's the pedagogical path taken. As a result, the successful inclusion of technologies in my classroom comes from my ability to appropriately utilise advanced digital and technological pedagogies intertwined with my curriculum objectives. These skills have been learnt through many hours of personally led professional development, and I acknowledge that these skills and knowledge may not exist to the same degree for every physical education teacher. Therefore, lessons I complete with relative ease and a sustained focus on the learning objectives, might for another teacher, result in a messy lesson that takes away from the learning objectives. Eimear highlights the privileged position my technological knowledge places me in, and I am aware that some of what I do might be difficult for a teacher who is not as technologically savvy. Teacher skill, training, and expertise are paramount to the success of any digital technology utilised. In my opinion, issues tend to appear when educational institutions hand over technology to teachers and students without the necessary training, support, and guidance. This, for me, is the key issue.

I found the student commentaries on my case to be particularly interesting, and they highlighted some common themes I have experienced working with thousands of teachers all over the world. There still appears to exist large variations between what constitutes quality physical education both here in Australia and overseas, and even within states, cities, and towns in the same country. While many teachers fight to raise the quality of physical education through the use of varying and appropriate pedagogical styles and high quality teaching, there remain too many teachers still happy simply "rolling out the ball". This is perhaps echoed in the comment made by Alice, who states that the lesson in question "is nothing like the physical education we have". My immediate thought surrounding this was "good", as it is my belief that far too many physical education teachers are forgetting that they have a responsibility to teach. For me this means ensuring that the students in the classroom have opportunities to question their learning, reflect on their actions, and meet curriculum milestones. It seems that far too many physical education classrooms are measured solely by how much "fun" the students are having.

Finally, in terms of the comments on the privatisation of physical education, I wish to offer an alternative perspective. I am mostly thankful for the opportunities and resources that the edu-business sector has provided me with. While governments and educational institutions have mostly failed to innovate to a level needed by our classrooms, individuals and private companies all over the globe have done so. The net result has been the availability of tools that I can employ in my classroom to help me seek improved learning outcomes for my students. Again, however, it is not the tools, but how these tools are used that I believe matters more.

Lessons from the case: How can the use of digital technologies accelerate pupil learning in physical education?

- The addition of digital technology is not always the answer to the complex pedagogical questions and problems teachers and students face in sports halls and classrooms. Digital technology alone does not necessarily accelerate student learning. Various technologies must be sensibly and meaningfully integrated into physical education experiences if they are to support learning. Teacher expertise and school context play a significant role in whether and how this integration occurs.
- The rapidly changing technological landscape means that teachers and students will need to work together and constantly examine how they learn and how they might help others to learn using digital technology. One powerful way of harnessing the potential of digital technology to enhance student learning is by recognising learners' expertise and engaging them in the negotiation of physical education curricula.
- Digital equity is about more than access (although that can be a significant issue); digital equity is also a pedagogical issue that is intimately connected to the digital and pedagogical expertise of the teacher. To accelerate student learning, physical education teachers will need to be better supported in the development of their own digital and pedagogical expertise.
- Any profit-driven intervention in schools, digital or not, results in a blurring of the line that might separate concern for student learning and self-interested entrepreneurship. Teachers need to critically engage with the many digital technologies that are targeted at them and their students and work to ensure that the digital technologies they choose to draw on have an educative value, and are not simply obscuring commercial interests.

References

Australian Curriculum, Assessment, and Reporting Authority (ACARA). (2015a). 'Health and Physical Education F-10 Curriculum: General capabilities'. Retrieved from www. australiancurriculum.edu.au/generalcapabilities/overview/introduction
Australian Curriculum, Assessment, and Reporting Authority (ACARA). (2015b). 'Health and Physical Education F-10 Curriculum: Information and Communication Technology (ICT) Capability'. Retrieved from www.australiancurriculum.edu.au/generalcapabilities/

information-and-communication-technology-capability/introduction/in-the-learning-areas

Australian Institute for Teaching and School Leadership (AITSL). (2012). 'Australian professional standards for teachers'. Retrieved from www.teacherstandards.aitsl.edu.au/

Ball, S. (2012). *Global Education Inc: New Policy Networks and the Neo-liberal Imaginary*. London: Routledge.

Ball, S. (2007). *Education PLC: Understanding Private Sector Participation in Public Sector Education*. London: Routledge.

Burch, P. (2009). *Hidden Markets: The New Education Privatization*. New York: Routledge.

Casey, A. (2013). '"Seeing the trees not just the wood": Steps and not just journeys in teacher action research'. *Educational Action Research*, vol. 21, no. 2, pp. 147–163. doi:10.1080/09650792.2013.789704

Casey, A. & Jones, B. (2011). 'Using digital technology to enhance student engagement in physical education'. *Asia-Pacific Journal of Health, Sport and Physical Education*, vol. 2, no. 2, pp. 51–66.

Department of Education and Training. (2014). 'Unlocking the potential: A digital learning strategy for Victorian learning and development settings (2014–2017) '. Department of Education and Early Childhood Development, Victoria.

DiCerbo, K. E. & J. T. Behrens. (2014). *Impacts of the Digital Ocean*. London: Pearson.

DiCerbo, K. E., Behrens, J. T. & Barber, M. (2014). 'Impacts of the digital ocean on education'. Retrieved from www.alexandriava.gov/uploadedFiles/dchs/childrenfamily/DigitalOcean.pdf

Eady, M. J. & Lockyer, L. (2013). 'Tools for learning: technology and teaching strategies'. In M. J. Eady & L. Lockyer (Eds.), *Learning to Teach in the Primary School*. Queensland, AUS: Queensland University of Technology. p. 71.

Enright, E. & Gard, M. (2015). 'Media, digital technology and learning in sport: A critical response to Hodkinson, Biesta & James'. *Physical Education and Sport Pedagogy*, vol. 21, no. 1, pp. 40–54.

Evans, J. & Davies, B. (2015). 'Physical education, privatisation and social justice'. *Sport, Education and Society*, vol. 20, no. 1, pp. 1–9.

Fallon, J. (2015). 'A year of helping to make progress'. Retrieved from http://blog.pearson.com/a-year-of-helping-to-make-progress/

Gard, M. (2014). 'eHPE: A history of the future'. *Sport, Education and Society*, vol. 19, pp. 827–845. doi:10.1080/13573322.2014.938036

Harris, F. (2009). 'Visual technology in physical education using Dartfish video analysis to enhance learning: An overview of the Dartfish project in New Brunswick'. *Physical & Health Education Journal*, vol, 7, no. 4, pp. 24–25.

Harvey, S. & Gittins, C. (2014). 'Effects of integrating video-based feedback into a Teaching Games for Understanding soccer unit'. *AGORA for Physical Education and Sport*, vol. 16, no. 3, pp. 270–290.

Hogan, A., Sellar, S. & Lingard, B. (2015). 'Network restructuring of global edu-business'. In W. Au & J. Ferrare (Eds.), *Mapping Corporate Education Reform: Power and Policy Networks in the Neoliberal State*. New York: Routledge.

Mehenna, W. N. (2004). 'E-pedagogy: the pedagogies of e-learning'. *ALT-J, Research in Learning Technology*, vol. 12, no. 3, pp. 79–293.

Menchik, D. A. (2004). 'Placing cybereducation in the UK classroom'. *British Journal of Sociology of Education*, vol. 25, no. 2, pp. 193–213.

Mishra, P. & Koehler, M. (2006). 'Technological pedagogical content knowledge: A framework for teacher knowledge'. *The Teachers College Record*, vol. 108, no.6, pp. 1017–1054.

Nivala, M. (2009). 'Simple answers for common problems: Education and ICT in Finnish Information Society strategies'. *Media, Culture and Society*, vol. 31, no. 3, pp. 433–448.

Pearson (2014). Chief executive's strategic overview. Retrieved from www.pearson.com/content/dam/corporate/global/pearson-dot-com/files/annual-reports/ar2014/0220 ChiefExecutivesOverview.pdf.

Pountney, R. & Schimmel, H. (2015). 'Developing professional knowledge and expertise in educational technology: Legacy, change and investment'. *The Journal of Technology Enhanced Learning, Innovation & Change*, vol. 1, no. 1, pp. 1–17.

Selwyn, N. (2010). *Schools and Schooling in the Digital Age: A Critical Analysis*. London: Routledge.

Shulman, L. (1987). 'Knowledge and teaching: Foundations of the new reform'. *Harvard Educational Review*, vol. 57, no.1, pp. 1–23.

Victorian Curriculum and Assessment Authority. (2015). 'Victorian Curriculum F-10: Learning Areas and Capabilities'. Retrieved from http://victoriancurriculum.vcaa.vic.edu.au/overview/curriculum-design/learning-areas-and-capabilities

Williams, B. J., Hay, P. J. & Macdonald, D. (2011). 'The outsourcing of health, sport and physical educational work: A state of play'. *Physical Education & Sport Pedagogy*, vol. 16, no. 4, pp. 399–415.

Zhao, Y., Lei, J. & Conway, P. (2005). 'A global perspective on political definitions of e-learning'. In J. Weiss, J. Nolan & J. Hunsinger (Eds.), *International Handbook of Virtual Learning Environments*. Netherlands: Kluwer.

12

TOM: USING DIGITAL TECHNOLOGY IN PHYSICAL EDUCATION TO TRANSFORM PEDAGOGY

Helena Baert, Tom Winiecki, Matthew Madden, Rebecca Bryan and Catherine MacDonald

CHAPTER OVERVIEW

In this chapter, Tom provides a narrative describing his experiences related to how he introduced and integrated digital technology in his classroom. Three perspectives: educational change, humanistic theory, and self-determination theory are used to examine the impact of technology integration within Tom's physical education classes. A pedagogical review synthesizes and summarizes the different perspectives in relation to the narrative. Insights into Tom's process of technology integration reveal that by focusing on student learning, technology can be a powerful vehicle to help motivate and empower learners and ultimately transform pedagogy.

Practitioner narrative (Tom Winiecki)

I am a K–4 (age 5–10) physical education teacher, as well as the K–12 (ages 5–18) curriculum coordinator for physical education in a suburban district in the north-eastern region of the United States. My coordinator role includes making sure all physical education teachers within the schools at each level (elementary: K–4, ages 5–10; middle school: grade 5–8, ages 10–14; and high school: grade 9–12, ages 14–18) within the district provide instruction according to the pre-designed curriculum that was framed using state and national learning standards and grade-level outcomes (see Society for Health and Physical Educators, 2014). Consequently, I must ensure the coordination and scaffolding of the district's curriculum between the different levels.

In my teacher role, I began integrating technology by using heart rate technology, then pedometers, and more recently video recording within my K–4 physical education classes. The instructor of a graduate course at a nearby university asked me if her graduate students could try out some technologies in my classes, and I welcomed that opportunity. During their first visit we were playing small-sided games, and the graduate students used heart rate batons to measure heart-rate and video analysis to evaluate running gait (see Table 12.1). Not only were students engaged, the digital technologies used prompted my students to ask questions about their bodies. This experience sparked an interest in learning more about how digital technologies could be used within my program. I began to question my approach to teaching physical education, and felt I needed a reason for physical education beyond simply helping students become proficient at many physical skills. My goal was not to create "gym class heroes", or students who always dominate in physical education due to their level of skill, but to provide a learning environment where students understood why those skills were good for them. In other words, I felt that students should learn the physical, affective, and cognitive benefits of physical education so they can apply them outside of the gymnasium.

Initially, the change started with kindergarten (age 5–6) and when students came into my gymnasium, sat down, and put their hand on their heart. They were amazed at simply feeling their heartbeat. Next, they were challenged to move around and check their pulse after increasing their pace. When they started to run, you would have thought they all just won $1,000,000! The wonder and excitement on their faces after checking their heart rate told me that this could be what ties everything together. The children's excitement for learning more about their bodies sparked me to include heart rate into my instruction.

Prior to implementing digital technology to measure heart rate, my elementary (ages 5–10) students checked their pulse manually and shared their number. It was somewhat successful. However, I did not want them to feel that they had to compare their heart rate to a peer. They needed to learn how to monitor their individual

TABLE 12.1 Digital technologies used by elementary PE students

Digital technologies used	Function	How to use the technology	Learning tasks
Strapless heart rate monitor	To accurately see student heart rate and to allow students to see if individual heart rates hit the target heart rate zone or not.	Students would wear a watch that would provide a reading of heart rate.	(i) station work to collect heart rate data used by students to create individual graphs tracking heart rate; and (ii) during general class activities to monitor heart rate to see if student is participating in activity correctly, by reaching their target heart rate zone.
Baton heart rate monitor	To accurately see student heart rate and to allow students to see the number and learn about their own heart rate.	Students would grab a baton and hold on to the brass parts to receive a heart rate reading.	

effort by measuring their heart rate. Consequently, I utilized pre-printed charts that used a 10-second heartbeat and converted it to beats per minute to make it easier for my students. They counted for 6 seconds, then added a zero to get their beats per minute. I placed a poster in the gymnasium with the numbers 140, 150, 160, 170 and 180 on it (see Figure 12.1).

The utilization of heart rate posters evolved into seeking digital technologies that could provide a more individual and accurate reading of heart rate. I ordered a few baton style heart rate monitors (see Table 12.1) with my yearly supply budget. These are similar in size and shape to a track relay baton. The students hold them on the brass rings with both hands to get their heart rate. I depleted the budget but viewed the purchase as a good long-term investment for my teaching. The heart rate batons were a big hit with the students! They wanted to know their number (heart rate). As a result, my instruction shifted to focus on what the actual numbers meant. I made sure the students understood that anything in the range of 140–180 beats per minute was in essence an A+, or a 4 on our 4-point grading/assessment scale. It didn't take very long for the students to grasp this concept, especially for those kids who weren't the "gym class heroes". They now saw that they were working just as hard as someone else who was in the zone.

At one point I tried the heart rate monitor watches with chest straps. While the baton style monitors read the student's heart rate through the brass rings on the baton, these monitors had two devices: a watch that received a signal from a strap worn around the student's chest. I found, especially with younger students, even after trying the smallest sizes of chest straps available, that they weren't practical for an elementary setting. They were too big to snugly fit on each student and we could not receive an accurate reading. In addition, putting on the straps took far too much time away from active instruction and deliberate practice. The monitors with a chest strap just weren't the most practical way to go about it initially. After researching digital heart rate monitors online, district leaders agreed on strapless watches. These watches proved to be much easier to use than those with chest straps, and if smaller students had a difficult time with the strapless watches due to the small size of their wrists, they always had access to the baton style monitors.

Using the heart rate monitor watch along with the baton style monitors had enhanced my instruction at the elementary level to the point where students analyzed

FIGURE 12.1 Heart rate poster.

FIGURE 12.2 Grade 2 student (age 7) using a heart rate baton.

FIGURE 12.3 Grade 2 student (age 7) interpreting results from heart rate baton with me.

their own heart rates (see Figure 12.2, 12.3 and Table 12.1). After collecting the heart rate data, I entered them into an Excel spreadsheet for the first and second graders. This spreadsheet created a visual (graph) for students to interpret. Students then identified the activities that produced the highest and lowest heart rate levels. Further, they explained what they would do differently next class to make a slow heart rate speed up. The student's verbal response was an effective way for me to assess their fitness knowledge. The third and fourth graders entered their own data which also produced graphs showing their heart rates and whether they hit the target heart range at each particular learning station (see Figure 12.4). I purposely included learning stations that may not increase their heart rates. The students were able to identify "less active" stations, as well as share how their heart rate was affected or not. My objective was for students to recognize that exercises such as arm curls, climbing a cargo net or hula-hoop activities are still effective physical activities to strengthen muscles, but may not increase their heart rate. This introduced the notion that multiple exercises affect the body differently.

In conclusion, I believe that digital technology integration in physical education can be very beneficial. In the simplest sense, it gave each student immediate and accurate feedback on their own efforts. Students learned how their heart reacts to physical activity and why that is important to them. By exposing students to a few forms of digital technology in a developmentally appropriate way, my goal was to use these technologies as a tool to help them learn about the importance of fitness.

In the following sections, this narrative is discussed from educational change, humanistic theory and self-determination theory perspectives. The narrative and perspectives are then analyzed together to consider the pedagogical implications of digital technologies in physical education.

An educational change perspective (Matthew Madden)

Researchers are interested in the factors that influence educational change, or, more specifically, the extent to which teachers change their practices and beliefs (Fullan, 2015). Although educational reform efforts have focused largely on the areas of literacy, math, science, and technology education, all curricular areas have been impacted. Physical education teachers and researchers want to be involved in the process, but its recognition is still limited (Bechtel & O'Sullivan, 2007). However, reform and physical education teacher and curricular change efforts have been studied (e.g. Bechtel & O'Sullivan, 2007; Casey, 2012; Goodyear & Casey, 2015; Kirk, 2012; Parker et al., 2010). Despite recent efforts focused on educational reform, findings from each respective work indicated very little significant change around teaching and learning in physical education (Goodyear & Casey, 2015). Further, continued investigation of change is needed in physical education, and existing theoretical frameworks must guide the inquiry.

Fullan (2015) identified three broad phases of the change process: initiation, implementation, and continuation. *Initiation* refers to the adoption of a new innovation and the process that leads up to and includes the decision to proceed

a)

b)

c)

d)

FIGURE 12.4 Photographs a–d show a grade 4 student (age 9) measuring heart rate with a strapless monitor, inputting the results into Excel and interpreting the results using graphs.

with a change. *Implementation* (first 2 or 3 years of use) involves the first experiences of attempting to put the innovation into practice. *Continuation* refers to whether the innovation becomes an ongoing part of the program.

Each of the three phases includes multiple characteristics throughout the change process. But two prominent characteristics influenced Tom's beliefs and eventually informed his pedagogy: his belief that change was needed, and his ability to change the materials and practice to facilitate the change.

Tom's belief that change was needed

Previous experience often influences the change in one's belief and approach to teaching. When teachers implement change, they are not blank slates. Their attitudes and beliefs stem from what they have previously learned and experienced, and thus inform the decisions they make and strategies they employ (Ferry & McCaughtry, 2013). The combination of what is learned through these experiences is the process of developing a teacher's knowledge. In fact, teachers are not born with knowledge to teach effectively, but construct their knowledge over time and through their experiences (Rovegno, 2003). Therefore, understanding a teacher's past experiences may provide insight into why and how certain decisions are made by teachers (Ferry & McCaughtry, 2013; Kirk, 2009). Tom's belief of "what was important for students" changed during the process of implementing technology into his school's curriculum and his own pedagogy.

Previously, his curriculum focused on skill acquisition of skill themes or the development of "gym class heroes". He took pride in his ability to teach movement skills as they related to sport and games. However, he questioned whether his students were applying the skills learned outside of his classroom, and he viewed a new importance on fitness knowledge. Tom used his previous experiences and beliefs to not only recognize a need but also to pursue change.

The need for change refers to a teacher's initial belief that the innovation is compatible with the teacher's personal teaching philosophy and culture, beneficial for their program, and more importantly for their students (Casey, 2012; Fullan, 2015; Parker *et al.*, 2010). Tom is very clear about his intentions or need for change. He wanted his curriculum to incorporate more than what had been offered in the previous years for the benefit of his students. These notions parallel with the idea that teachers must value the process of change and understand that change can positively impact their programs where change is seen as beneficial for their students' learning and engagement (Cothran, 2001; Parker *et al.*, 2010).

Unfortunately, teachers implementing curricular change may view any attempt as beneficial to their program and the students initially, but sustaining that belief may be short lived. In fact, there is very little evidence that teachers move beyond the initial point of implementation or what Goodyear and Casey (2015) described as the "honeymoon period" (p. 188) which would describe where Tom was within his narrative. Tom not only recognized the need for change but he also put his plan into action. The actions included purchasing new equipment and modifying a few of his pedagogies.

Change in materials and practices

In most attempts at change, materials are the first and "relatively easy" items to be changed by the teacher (Fullan, 1982, p. 30). Furthermore, changing or acquiring different materials and equipment are referred to as *surface level*, or superficial change (Sparkes, 1990). Ideally, the easiest way for Tom to change the curriculum would have been to purchase the new tools (heart rate monitors) first and equate the new equipment as new curriculum (Fullan, 2015).

Tom indicated that throughout the implementation he changed the materials and equipment in order to continue effective change into the program. But the heart rate monitors were implemented after his beliefs were challenged, Tom did not purchase the equipment until he was positive that the technology was necessary. This shift in thinking was beyond considering the equipment as the change, but more importantly how it benefitted his students. Therefore, this case is not supported by the idea that material or superficial change is the easiest or first process of change (Fullan, 1982; Sparkes, 1990).

Tom's first step was to modify his instruction, and changing one's teaching approach is more difficult (Fullan, 2015). Prior to implementing the digital technology (materials) he had the students check their pulse manually (practice). Then, he searched and created heart rate posters for students to utilize. Tom's adoption of different teaching practices continued to change with the use of the new technology and eventually he viewed the technology as a form of student accountability and assessment.

Summary

Tom's narrative illustrated that the effective integration of digital technology within his pedagogy ultimately led to successful change initially. What was yet to be known was whether or not the change continued or was sustainable. For teachers to continue the process of curricular change, their values and beliefs must change (Fullan, 2013). Two concepts affected change in this case study. First, Tom believed, sought, and recognized a need for change. Next, he changed the equipment and practice. Overall, Tom perceived the implementation of new technology as benefitting his current curriculum and pedagogy.

A humanistic theory perspective (Rebecca Bryan)

Humanistic theory focuses on personal growth and the affective elements of self-concept, values and emotions (Johnson, 2014). The theory is often applied to fitness education because of its focus on individual goals and the affective elements that can affect one's learning and participation in fitness and physical activity content

(Virgilio, 2012). Fitness education, viewed through a humanistic lens, enhances learning by making connections to individuals' lives, emotions and experiences while emphasizing the reciprocal relationship between learning and the learner (Zhou, 2007). This is achieved by developing students' cognitive capabilities in conjunction with their emotional development (Lei, 2007). Connecting on a personal level provides the potential for students to learn the elements of fitness more deeply and relate them to their own health and well-being (Prewitt *et al.*, 2015). Furthermore, the theory provides the context for personal growth and development of the knowledge, skills and values necessary to live a physically active lifestyle. The humanistic approach to teaching and learning is, therefore, centered around the student and is concerned with students' (1) self-direction, (2) intrinsic motivation, (3) reflection of self and (4) personal growth that is realized through the process of learning (Leonard, 2002).

Supporting self-direction

Tom demonstrated how he made his students' learning more personal and self-directed through the use of digital technology. It was Tom's student-centered approach rather than the digital technology itself that determined the effectiveness of the learning experience. For example, Tom used the heart rate monitors to provide immediate and accurate feedback to students and directed them to reflect on what that meant regarding their own health. It was not the use of the digital technology alone but rather how it was applied to facilitate student learning in a very personalized and meaningful way. In Tom's classroom, students were provided with more opportunities to be self-directed, self-motivated and self-evaluated which empowered the learners through both experiential and reflective learning. It is how the students were taught (methodology) rather than the tool (digital technology) that determined the meaningfulness of the students' learning, as also shown by Zhou (2007).

Tom paid particular attention to his students and their excitement around feeling their heart and how it beats differently during a variety of activities. It is in his attention to his students emotions that Tom taught from a humanistic frame and created a student-centered environment that focused on both the cognitive and affective learning of his students. Tom's teaching addressed the needs and wants of the learner, which is the key to humanistic learning according to Rogers and Freiberg (1994). Thus, Tom provided a platform for students to accurately control and direct their own learning through the use of heart rate monitors.

Intrinsic motivation

Intrinsic motivation, a motivation that comes from within or can be described as doing an activity for its own sake, is effective in promoting long-term behavioral change. Intrinsic motivation is the most desirable form of motivation in an achievement domain (Ferrer-Caja & Weiss, 2000). Therefore, it is essential to establish a learning environment that promotes intrinsic motivation to encourage students to develop a long-term commitment to a physically active lifestyle (Virgilio, 2012). The integration of the heart rate monitors supported the elementary students' development of intrinsic motivation by providing a safe and supportive environment where students explored their heart rate through self-directed and success-oriented activities. According to Deci and Ryan (1985), when students are intrinsically motivated they experience enjoyment, are interested and more likely exert effort and continue participation in the activity.

Physical education class climates that emphasize effort, learning and self-improvement help maximize intrinsic motivation in students (Deci & Ryan, 1985; Ferrer-Caja & Weiss, 2000). In Tom's physical education environment, students managed their own heart rate through self-checks and graphs, which quantified their results and challenged each student to examine their effort and focus on self-improvement. Focusing on self-improvement can lead to goal setting and self-monitoring which have been shown to significantly improve physical activity in school-age students (McDonald & Trost, 2015). The implementation of the heart rate monitors allowed Tom to emphasize effort, learning and self-improvement to support intrinsic motivation.

Self-reflection and personal growth

Reflection is the process of thinking about an experience while pursuing a deeper understanding (Bard, 2014). Strategies to foster reflective practice include, but are not limited to, student writing and constructive feedback from the teacher. Constructive feedback from teacher, self or peers allows students to evaluate their actions and level of understanding and plan for future learning (Dennick, 2012). Consequently, students are encouraged to take responsibility for their own learning, and personal growth is supported through feedback and reflection. In the narrative, the digital technologies empowered learners by providing physical and cognitive artifacts to use for reflection (Zhou, 2007). The elementary students were provided with multiple opportunities to reflect on their learning and construct their personal understanding of heart rate and physical activity behavior from the graphs provided by the digital technologies.

Summary

Tom's narrative demonstrates how he adopted a humanistic approach to teaching by supporting and personalizing the content which empowered students strengthening self-efficacy and encouraged students to reflect and take responsibility for their learning. Digital technologies allowed for the students to be self-directed in learning about heart rate. The pedagogy and digital technology supported a greater understanding of heart rate and provided the students multiple ways to demonstrate their learning, personal growth and development of the knowledge and skills necessary to maintain a healthy heart.

Tom utilized a humanistic approach that was enhanced with his integration of heart rate monitors to focus instruction on fitness content. He explored a variety of heart rate monitoring technologies that helped him design developmentally appropriate learning experiences that address grade level outcomes in a student-centered and intrinsically motivating way. When students are intrinsically motivated they are more likely to exert effort and persistence in activity (Deci & Ryan, 1985), which is essential to developing the knowledge, skills and values for lifelong health-related fitness and physical activity behaviors in students.

A self-determination theory perspective (Catherine MacDonald)

The value of self-determination is clear: It has been described as the ultimate goal of education (Halloran, 1993) and is associated with positive educational and post-school outcomes (Wehmeyer & Schwartz, 1997). *Self-determination* is defined as "acting as the primary causal agent in one's life and making choices and decisions regarding one's quality of life free from undue external influence or interference" (Wehmeyer, 1997, p. 305). Self-determination has become increasingly important in the field of special education over the last several years due to several factors including evolving views of disability (Polloway, Patton, & Smith, 1996), changes in legislation, and advances in teaching. Recently, researchers have attempted to apply self-determination to physical education (MacDonald & Reid, 2013; Robinson & Lieberman, 2004), as a way of supporting the learning of all students, including those with a disability. Despite evidence that claims self-determination should be taught starting at a young age (Wehmeyer, Sands, Doll, & Palmer, 1997) its promotion among educators, including physical educators, remains limited. Yet, some dedicated practitioners, like Tom, make strong efforts to help students develop the skills and behaviors essential to the development of self-determination (Wehmeyer, 2015). While his implementation of self-determination instruction may not be explicit, his use of instructional strategies and digital technology helps promote associated skills and behaviors.

Teaching self-determination

While several theories of self-determination exist, Wehmeyer's (1996) functional model emphasized that self-determination can be developed and taught using a variety of instructional methods and strategies. Physical education teachers, like Tom, play an important role in helping students develop a sense of self-determination and may help all students take responsibility over their own physical activity needs (Calzonetti, 2003).

Specifically, four essential and interrelated characteristics must be present to be self-determined. *Autonomy* involves acting according to personal preferences, desires, and abilities, and in an independent manner (Wehmeyer, 1996). *Psychological empowerment* involves students believing that (a) they have the capacity to perform behaviors needed to influence outcomes in their environment, and (b) if they perform such behaviors, anticipated outcomes will result (Wehmeyer, 1997). *Self-regulation* refers to making decisions about what skills to use in a situation, examining the task at hand and using an available repertoire of skills to formulate, enact, and evaluate a plan of action, and revise the plan when necessary. *Self-realization* involves using a comprehensive and reasonably accurate knowledge of strengths and limitations in a meaningful way (Wehmeyer, 1997). Self-determination can be enhanced by promoting skills associated with the four essential characteristics described above. These skills include choice making, problem solving, and an having internal locus of control (Wehmeyer, 1997). Tom implemented many of these strategies and created an environment to support self-determined learning.

Self-determination and digital technology

Technology-mediated instruction has the potential to promote self-determination by helping students participate in activities at school, facilitating social opportunities with peers, and increasing opportunities for independence (Wehmeyer, 2007). Tom placed students in situations that were student centered (rather than teacher driven) and relied on active learner participation. Through this approach, Tom promoted self-determination by having students take control and responsibility for their learning (Wehmeyer, 2007) and used digital technology to facilitate teaching some of the components of self-determination. Below are examples as to how Tom supported the development of self-determination by incorporating effective instructional strategies, such as providing choice, and creating a mastery climate and encouraging self-directed learning.

Provide choice

Expressing preferences and making choices is an important way that students can demonstrate self-determined behavior (Wehmeyer *et al.*, 1997). Some of the research examining individuals with a disability has addressed the use of alternative communication to express preferences (Singh *et al.*, 2003; Wacker *et al.*, 1988). Physical education teachers can support self-determination, implementing choice making in their teaching (Reid & Hermo, 1998), by providing even simple choices, such as having students decide on which type of equipment they would like to use to complete a task. Tom allowed his to students to express their preferences by allowing them to choose the activities they completed throughout the lessons.

Create a climate of mastery

A mastery climate emphasizes personal improvement and progress. While it is difficult to teach students explicitly that they are capable of achieving their desired goals, Tom allowed students to explore their capabilities and develop positive perceptions of control by focusing on personal improvement and progress. He stated, "They now saw, in very concrete terms that they were working just as hard as someone else who was in the zone," and he recognized the importance of his students "comparing themselves to their past efforts, not against anyone else". Tom used the heart rate monitors for students to gather specific information about their performance and helped them to recognize that their actions can lead to success.

Encourage self-directed learning

Self-directed learning can lead to more positive student outcomes and a greater ability to generalize skills (Agran, 1997). Tom presented several opportunities for exploration by allowing students to be in charge of their own learning. He structured the environment using activities where students learned how to measure their heart rate and recognize that their heartbeat changed with different physical activities. By allowing students to identify a particular activity and talk about why it didn't allow them to reach the target zone, they practiced using the heart rate monitor and evaluated how their bodies responded to different exercises. In addition, students were to graph and chart their own progression based on individual goals.

Summary

Self-determination is a critical educational outcome (Wehmeyer, 1997, 1996). Educators like Tom play an important role in enabling students to become self-determined by teaching skills like choice making, goal setting, and problem solving. Tom successfully used digital technology as a way to assist students in acquiring the skills and attitudes they need to be in control of their own learning. By teaching his students to take an active role in their participation, they may be more likely to engage in lifelong physical activity.

A pedagogical perspective (Helena Baert)

What sparked Tom's decision to implement technology? Did he effectively implement technology? How do we know if it was done effectively? These questions formed the basis for the analysis of the narrative by the three perspectives as well as the understanding of the relationship between technology and pedagogy as the central theme of this book. This section of the chapter takes a closer look at this powerful relationship by drawing on the revelations the three perspectives shared.

A pedagogy of technology: The new pedagogy?

Tom's decision to integrate technology came from watching the engagement of his students as they manipulated new tools such as heart rate batons and video analysis tools, which in turn pulled the students into learning. When teachers watch how new tools can spark engagement and learning, they naturally gravitate towards these new pedagogies (Fullan & Langsworthy, 2014). Fullan and Langsworthy (2014) explain how a new pedagogy is necessary when we focus our attention on learning rather than teaching, when teachers become partners in learning and when technology can be used to explore deeper learning opportunities. Tom watched and listened to his students as they explored new tools. His decision to use digital technology was not because of the tools, it was about the engagement and the deeper learning that happened when students interacted with those tools. This event sparked a change in Tom's pedagogy. Tom began to question the deeper meaning of teaching physical education and explored the relationship between technology and pedagogy.

Technology integration vs. pedagogy of technology

The term *integrating technology*, often used in a simplistic way to explain the process of how to infuse technology within pedagogy, was explored further by Prensky (2012) and Fullan and Langsworthy (2014). They questioned the relationship between pedagogy and technology. Richardson (2013) once said that "simply adding a layer of expensive tools on top of the traditional curriculum does nothing to address the learning needs of modern learners" (p. 10). Richardson, too, was referring to a much more complex relationship between pedagogy and technology, one that should aim at meeting the needs of students as well as create more opportunities for learning. Casey (2014) once questioned whether or not we should adopt a pedagogy of technology, or a new way of thinking about how technology can be a catalyst for deeper learning, rather then using technology to teach. In 1998, Neil Postman stated that "technological change is not additive; it is ecological" (p. 4). He cautioned us about the nature of technological innovation and that a new technology may not simply "add" to what is there but may in fact change it (i.e. the pedagogy). Tom may have known about technology tools in physical education after his 20+ years of service, but it was the change technology caused in his students that made him take a closer look at the transformation technology can create.

Transformative technology is not about enhancing education but more about changing education. A question researchers in educational technology often ask is whether or not technology in itself can transform teaching and learning. In this narrative, the transformation Tom saw was that technology allowed students to gain a deeper understanding of why they should be active and why they are attending physical education in the first place. Tom shifted the focus within his physical education class from becoming proficient in motor skills to enhancing the quality of life. He believed that digital technology could help him make his lessons more relevant to the students and shift their focus to themselves and how students can use the information gained through his lessons to enhance their own knowledge and outlook on life. But it was not the technology alone that transformed his teaching and his students' learning.

Tom questioned his own beliefs on what to teach, what tools to use, how the content should be taught and how to effectively use technology to help his students learn. He questioned the purpose of his approach to teaching elementary physical education and whether or not the acquisition of fundamental motor skills should be the prominent goal. His need to reflect and refocus his pedagogy was inspired by the elementary students who questioned what they were learning and why they needed to learn the skills he taught. Prensky (2012) stated that good pedagogy should be a bottom-up curricular approach, where the teacher finds out "what the students need and how the teacher can provide that" (p. 1).

As teachers implement new technology it is important to examine how the technology should be used and how it can match the needs of the students. In essence, teachers must make crucial decisions about how content, technology and pedagogy work together to meet the learning needs of the students. Mishra and Koehler (2006) theorized that appropriate teaching with technology can occur when those three components are integrated effectively to create a triad called the Technological, Pedagogical and Content Knowledge (TPACK) framework. Other researchers (Cox & Graham, 2009; Porras-Hernandez & Salinas-Amescua, 2013) found TPACK to be an effective framework to examine teacher's knowledge based on their own reflection of their practice. Once Tom understood the digital technology, how to use it and how to teach with it, the connections between technology, content and pedagogy and how technology can transform learning became clear. The new connections made by Tom not only justified his change but also strengthened his ongoing belief that digital technology can have a positive effect on learning. The TPACK framework was developed once he acquired an understanding of the relationship between the three constructs (see Figure 12.5).

Focusing on the student: Learning comes first

Surrounding the TPACK constructs (see Figure 12.5) is a circle that represents the context in which learning takes place. Central to any context are the students. All three perspectives analyzing this narrative examined the impact of technology integration within Tom's physical education classes and commonly agreed upon the force students had on Tom's questions and decisions about pedagogy and technology. Using the educational change perspective, in order to create the change he did, Tom questioned his own delivery, curriculum and the skills students were learning. Consequently, Tom responded to his students' needs by implementing change in pedagogy that involved changing the equipment used to support student learning and changing his beliefs around technology. Bai and Ertmer (2008) suggested that teachers' beliefs must focus on meaningful learning rather than the digital technology in order to enhance learning. Ultimately, his decisions in changing the tools and how to implement the tools were based on the needs of Tom's students.

The students were always central to Tom's decision to use technology and change his pedagogy. The humanistic and self-determination perspectives identified that promoting self-determination and self-direction is about providing students with opportunities to create meaningful connections to their own personal life outside the classroom so they could make effective decisions about their own future. When

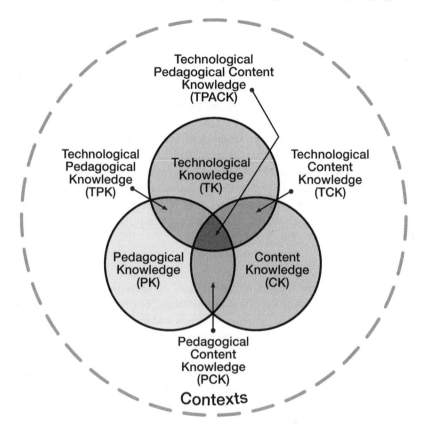

FIGURE 12.5 The TPACK framework.

Reproduced by permission of the publisher, © 2012 by tpack.org

students become more self-directed, intrinsically motivated and self-reflective, they can take accountability of their own personal growth in learning. The humanistic perspective argued that Tom maximized the positive effects of digital technology on learning by focusing on creating developmentally appropriate instruction, routines and teaching strategies. Technology alone will not drive the change but how a teacher uses the technology within teaching can. Tom discovered that by listening to his students, questioning his own beliefs on teaching and learning in physical education and experimenting and ultimately implementing a variety of technologies, his students were able to acquire skills for life.

Can technology transform learning and/or learners?

The narrative showed how technology could create change in learners by changing how they learn. Simply adding a tool will not create the transformation in learning and pedagogy, but rather the way the teacher uses the tool is a key factor in that transformation. Teachers must learn the affordances each technology has to offer that will allow them to make appropriate decisions about the specific technology and how to implement it within teaching.

In order for technology to transform learning, and adopt a pedagogy of technology, the TPACK framework can be used to effectively implement technology. The following questions can guide the decision making process:

1. Will the technology enhance learning of the specific content that must be learned?
2. Does the teacher have the knowledge and experience to effectively implement a technology without impeding the engagement level in the lesson?
3. Can the teacher integrate the technology in a developmentally appropriate way while addressing student past experiences and current needs?

Summary

The narrative illustrated effective integration of technology within physical education, which ultimately led to successful change. The narrative and discussions showed how the relationship between pedagogy and technology can be powerful and, if questioned and understood, one that can transform learners, teachers and ultimately education. A personal reflection from Tom on the analysis of his narrative will allow for a deeper understanding into the process of thinking related to teaching and learning with technology.

Practitioner reflection

Learning to be fit just to avoid a heart attack in 50 years isn't meaningful for my students now. Fitness for their favorite game or increasing brain power in school is what is important to them. If technology is used, it should be to better meet these needs. Any form of technology should be used to make students better learners, not better technology users. Heart rate monitors offer that to me.

My students show higher engagement levels and deeper learning when interacting with the digital technologies. They gravitate toward seeing their results personally displayed. I also agree that technology should be a catalyst for deeper learning, rather than using it simply to teach. The technology allows me to create a student-centered environment where I can apply specific fitness knowledge learned using heart rate monitors to other content throughout the year. The technology did not determine this way of teaching. Rather it made me more effective in relating my curriculum to each student. While students work on skills in my class, we check our pulse. They now clearly understand whether their bodies will get stronger or not, based just on their heart rate. They also learn that if their heart is going too fast, that won't help either. We learn that more is not always better; an effective lesson for this age student. This is also helpful with my lesser skilled students, who discover that they no longer have to feel like they need the most points to be successful. They now know that their heart doesn't care if they made every shot or not (though we will keep working on that). It just cares if it went fast enough to get stronger. Knowing this, they are more willing to participate, knowing that they will benefit from my class. They will be able to focus better and be able to play longer at recess. These two outcomes make my class relevant to them, so I am better able to meet their needs. Simply put, with the use of the heart rate monitors, my students become owners of their own fitness knowledge, becoming more intrinsically motivated and self-directed as learners.

Learning motor skills is still important! But teaching skills just to be skillful isn't enough. Knowing how and why to use those skills is more important. We must remember that learning to simply have an active lifestyle is not an end to itself. Rather it is a means to an end. It enables them function better as people, not just as better athletes. Teaching students to enjoy personalizing an active lifestyle is why we are teaching physical education in the first place. Heart rate technology allows students to learn how to fit fitness into their daily lives, which can then help them avoid that heart attack in 50 years.

Lessons from the narrative: How can the use of digital technologies accelerate student learning in physical education?

An in-depth look at how and why a teacher decided to implement technology, alongside a multi-disciplinary and pedagogical analysis of the narrative, has revealed many connections between theory and practice, and has allowed us to present three common valuable lessons:

1. Listen to the students: Students are central to the learning and teaching process. When teachers make decisions related to integrating digital technologies based on student needs and experiences, technology can help make learning authentic and meaningful to the student.
2. Pedagogy drives the change, not digital technology: When the focus lies with digital technology without regards to the needs of the students, good pedagogy goes missing. It is crucial to make change for learning. Ultimately, the purpose of educational change has to benefit the students.
3. Digital technology can be transformative and can motivate and empower students to be critical thinkers, problem solvers and owners of their own knowledge and learning.

These three key points exemplify that transforming education or creating a "new pedagogy of technology" does not come easy. When teachers put students and pedagogy first and learn to understand the relationship between pedagogy, content and technology, however, technology has the potential to do much more than support learning.

References

Agran, M. (1997). *Students-directed learning: Teaching Self-Determination Skills*. Pacific Grove, CA: Brooks/Cole.

Bai, H. & Ertmer, P. A. (2008). Teacher educators' beliefs and technology uses as predictors of pre-service teachers' beliefs and technology attitudes. *Journal of Technology and Teacher Education,16*(1), 93–112.

Bard, R. (2014). Focus on reflective learners & feedback. *The Electronic Journal for English as a Second Language, 18(3)*.

Bechtel, P. A. & O'Sullivan, M. (2007). Enhancers and inhibitors of teacher change among secondary physical educators. *Journal of Teaching in Physical Education, 26*, 221–235.

Calzonetti, K. (2003). Facilitating Independence. In R. D. Steadward, G. D. Wheeler, E. J. Watkinson (Eds.), *Adapted physical activity*. Edmonton, AB: University of Alberta Press. pp. 213–228.

Casey, A. (2012). A self-study using action research: Changing site expectations and practice stereotypes. *Educational Action Research, 20*(2), 219–232.

Casey, A. (2014). *Developing a pedagogy of technology in physical education*. Keynote presentation at afPE London, February 14, 2014.

Cothran, D. J. (2001). Curricular change in physical education: Success stories from the front line. *Sport, Education, and Society, 6*, 67–80.

Cox, S. & Graham, C. R. (2009). Diagramming TPACK in practice: Using an elaborated model of the TPACK framework to analyze and depict teacher knowledge. *Techtrends: Linking Research & Practice To Improve Learning, 53*(5), 60–69.

Deci, E. L. & Ryan, R. M. (1985). *Intrinsic motivation and self-determination in human behavior*. New York, NY: Plenum.

Dennick, R. (2012). Twelve tips for incorporating educational theory into teaching practices. *Medical Teacher, 34*, 618–624. doi:10.3109/0142159X.2012.668244

Ferrer-Caja, E. & Weiss, M. R. (2000). Predictors of intrinsic motivation among adolescent students in physical education. *Research Quarterly for Exercise and Sport, 71, 3*.

Ferry, M. & McCaughtny, N. (2013). Secondary physical educators and sport content: A love affair. *Journal of Teaching in Physical Education, 32*, 375–393.

Fullan, M. (1982). *The new meaning of educational change*. New York, NY: Teachers College Press.

Fullan, M. (2013). *Stratosphere: Integrating technology, pedagogy, and change knowledge*. Toronto, ONT: Pearson Canada, Inc.

Fullan, M. (2015). *The new meaning of educational change* (5th ed.). New York, NY: Teachers College Press.

Fullan, M. & Langworthy, M. (2014). *A rich seam: How new pedagogies find deep learning*. London, UK: Pearson. Retrieved from www.michaelfullan.ca/wp-content/uploads/2014/01/3897.Rich_Seam_web.pdf

Goodyear, V. & Casey, A. (2015). Innovation with change: Developing a community of practice to help teachers move beyond the 'honeymoon' of pedagogical renovation. *Physical Education and Sport Pedagogy, 20*(2), 186–204.

Halloran, W. D. (1993). Transition services requirement: Issues, implications, challenge. In R. C. Eaves & P. J. McLaughlin (Eds.), *Recent advances in special education and rehabilitation*. Boston, MA: Andover. pp. 210–224.

Johnson, A. P. (2014). *Theories of learning and human development*. National Science Press. Retrieved from www.nsspress.com

Kirk, D. (2009). A physical education for the future or a future for physical education? In L. D. Housner, M. W. Metzler, P. G. Schempp, & T. J. Templin (Eds.), *Historic traditions and future directions of research on teaching and teacher education in physical education.* Morgantown, WV: Fitness Information Technology. pp. 137–148.

Kirk, D. (2012). What is the future for physical education in the 21st century? In S. Capel & M. Whitehead (Eds.), *Debates in physical education.* London: Routledge. pp. 220–231.

Lei, Q. (2007). EFL teachers' factors and students' affect. *US-China Education Review, 4*(3), 60–67.

Leonard, D. C. (2002). *Learning theories A to Z.* Westport, CN: Oryx Press.

MacDonald, C. & Reid, G. (2013). Instructional strategies of inclusive physical education teachers: Developmental and validation of self-determination survey. *European Journal of Adapted Physical Activity, 6,* 43–56.

McDonald, S. M. & Trost, S. G. (2015). The effect of a goal setting intervention on aerobic fitness in middle school students. *Journal of Teaching in Physical Education, 34,* 576–587.

Mishra, P. & Koehler, M. J. (2006). Technological Pedagogical Content Knowledge: A framework for teacher knowledge. *Teachers College Record, 108*(6), 1017–1054.

Parker, M., Patton, K., Madden, M., & Sinclair, C. (2010). From committee to community: The development and maintenance of a community of practice. *Journal of Teaching Physical Education, 29,* 337–357.

Polloway, E. A, Patton, J. R, & Smith, T. E. C. (1996). Historical changes in mental retardation and developmental disabilities. *Education and Training in Mental Retardation and Developmental Disabilities, 31,* 3–12.

Porras-Hernandez, L. H. & Salinas-Amescua, B. (2013). Strengthening TPACK: A broader notion of context and the use of teacher's narratives to reveal knowledge construction. *Journal of Educational Computing Research, 48*(2), 223–244.

Postman, N. (1998). *Five things we need to know about technological change: A talk delivered in Denver Colorado.* Retrieved from www.technodystopia.org/

Prensky, M. (2012). *From digital natives to digital wisdom: Hopeful essays for 21st century learning.* Thousand Oaks, CA: Corwin.

Prewitt, S. L, Hannon, J. C., Colquitt, G., Brusseau, T. A., Newton, M., & Shaw, J. (2015). Effect of personalized system of instruction on health-related fitness knowledge and class time physical activity. *The Physical Educator, 72,* 23–29.

Reid, G. & Hermo, J. (1998). Beyond skill development. *International Journal of Practical Approaches to Disability, 22,* 17–22.

Richardson, W. (2013). Technology-rich learning: Students first, not stuff. *Educational Leadership, 70*(6), 10–14.

Robinson, B. L. & Lieberman, L. J. (2004). Effects of visual impairment, gender, and age on self-determination. *Journal of Visual Impairment & Blindness, 98,* 351–366.

Rogers, C. R. & Freiberg, H. J. (1994). *Freedom to learn* (3rd ed.). Columbus, OH: Merrill/Macmillan.

Rovegno, I. (2003). Teachers' knowledge construction. In S. Silverman & C. Ennis (Eds.), *Student learning in physical education: Applying research to enhance instruction* (2nd ed.). Champaign, IL: Human Kinetics. pp. 295–310.

Society of Health and Physical Educators, (2014). *National standards & grade-level outcomes for K–12 physical education.* Champaign, IL: Human Kinetics.

Singh, N. N., Lancioni, G. E., O'Reilly, M. F., Molina, E. J., Adkins, A. D., & Oliva, D. (2003). Self-determination during mealtimes though microswitch choice-making by an individual with complex multiple disabilities and profound mental retardation. *Journal of Positive Behavior Interventions, 5,* 209–216.

Sparkes, A. (1990). *Curriculum change and physical education: Towards a micropolitical understanding.* Geelong, AUS: Deakin University.

Virgilio, S. J. (2012). *Fitness education for children* (2nd ed.). Champaign, IL: Human Kinetics.

Wacker, D.P., Wiggins, B., Fowler, M., & Berg, W.K. (1988). Training students with profound or multiple handicaps to make requests via mircoswitches. *Journal of Applied Behavior Analysis, 21,* 331-343.

Wehmeyer, M. L. (1996). Self-determination as an educational outcome: Why is it important to children, youth and adults with disabilities? In D. J. Sands & M. L. Wehmeyer (Eds.), *Self-Determination across the lifespan: Independence and choice for people with disabilities.* Baltimore, MD: Paul H. Brookes. pp. 15–34.

Wehmeyer, M. (1997). Self-determination as an educational outcome: A definitional framework and implications for intervention. *Journal of Developmental and Physical Disabilities, 9*(3), 175–209.

Wehmeyer, M. L. (2007). *Promoting self-determination in students with developmental disabilities.* New York, NY: The Guilford Press.

Wehmeyer, M. L (2015). Framing the future self-determination. *Remedial and Special Education, 36*(1), 20–23.

Wehmeyer, M. L., Sands, D. J., Doll, B., & Palmer, S. (1997). The development of self-determination and implications for educational interventions. *International Journal of Disability, Development, and Education, 44,* 305–328.

Wehmeyer, M. L. & Schwartz, M. (1997). Self-determination and positive adult outcomes: A follow-up study of youth with mental retardation or learning disabilities. *Exceptional Children, 63,* 245–255.

Zhou, L. (2007). Supporting humanistic learning experiences through learning with technology. *International Journal of Learning, 13*(11), 131–136.

13

GARETH: THE BEAUTY OF THE IPAD FOR REVOLUTIONISING LEARNING IN PHYSICAL EDUCATION

Kathleen M. Armour, Gareth Evans, Matt Bridge, Mark Griffiths and Sam Lucas

CHAPTER OVERVIEW

Gareth is more interested in student learning than traditional ways of teaching, and claims that the iPad and the apps to which it gives access are effective for engaging a range of students. For Gareth, e-pedagogy is about using digital technologies to make learning interesting, relevant and personalised. Gareth's narrative is considered from three perspectives: neurophysiology, motor learning and situated learning. In the pedagogical and practitioner analyses, Dewey's concept of learning continuity illustrates the challenges of developing effective and dynamic pedagogies of technology and the need for researchers and practitioners to work together to address practice challenges.

Practitioner narrative (Gareth Evans)

I qualified as a teacher in 2008, and have since achieved the status of an 'Advanced Skills Teacher' (AST). In the English education system, this means that I have been recognised as an outstanding practitioner, and part of my role is to support the professional development of my colleagues.

When I qualified as a PE teacher, I was told by my mentor that one of the great things about a career in teaching is that it constantly evolves. My mentor explained that I'd never find myself stuck in a rut because education doesn't stand still and my professional development will keep driving me forward. At the time, I didn't really appreciate or understand the importance of this. Teaching has been a profession for such a long time; surely we've tried everything and got it right by now?

I think back to those words from my mentor and reflect on how accurate they were. Luckily, I work in a school that encourages career progression and supports me every step of the way. Now, as an AST and Head of PE, I support my colleagues. In fact, I'm not a teacher anymore. Sure, 'teacher' is my job title and it's what I tell people I do, but, in reality, all I am is a facilitator – a tool to support learners.

Children love technology. Their worlds are dominated by texting friends, watching videos on YouTube, social media, reading the news online, playing games, capturing and replaying their favourite moments through camera or video . . . the list goes on. Handheld digital technology is a huge part of everyday life and I want to jump on that in my role as a facilitator. Using an iPad has allowed me to do just that, although, in reality, the iPad is simply an example of one of many devices that could have facilitated access to exciting and relevant apps.

My iPad journey in education began a few years ago when my school issued one to each member of staff with the aim of improving teaching and learning. Some teachers found success, others didn't. Many members of staff felt discouraged from using iPads because they simply didn't know how they could support learning and they were scared they might lose control of lessons. Reflecting on it, I believe that I found success because I focused on the learning rather than the teaching.

Examples of iPad being used in my PE lessons

The beauty of the iPad is its adaptability and the diverse ways in which it can be used, for example, as a tool to challenge students to reach their potential and to engage students and provide excitement in lessons. The way iPads are being used in PE is evolving. There are new apps being designed with the specific aim of supporting PE teachers, and the iPad is just one example of a device that enables me to use them. Below are two examples that demonstrate ways in which I have used iPads and apps to support two very different students in PE.

Supporting more able learners

'Fred' is a very talented cricketer. He plays at a high level out of school and has started to lose focus in school-based cricket lessons because the standard is not high enough. His enthusiasm levels have dropped and his behaviour has become disruptive – mainly as a result of boredom – and this is having a negative impact on others in the class.

Analysis of the problem

When it comes to gifted and talented students, PE teachers can be lazy. On many occasions I've seen teachers simply using these students to support the less able, justifying this as allowing them to make progress as a leader and developing social interaction. I believe, however, that we should be looking to further improve the skills and knowledge of these talented students.

Solution

In this situation, an iPad was used to improve Fred's batting technique through qualitative analysis. Using the knowledge gained from his club out of school, Fred created a checklist of key points to remember when hitting various shots (e.g. straight drive, pull shot, etc.). While the rest of the class was concentrating on very basic techniques and making contact with a stationary ball, Fred was using slow-motion video to compare his technique against professional players on the same screen, using his checklist to identify strengths and areas to develop.

Supporting less able learners

'Jimmy' hates PE. He has always hated it, even at primary school (up to age 11). Now that he is in secondary school (age 11–16), there is more emphasis on physical sports and competence, so he hates it even more. He struggles to see the importance of PE when he knows he isn't very good at it. In reports on his achievements, he sees that his lack of ability is preventing him from making progress and this serves to de-motivate him even more.

Analysis of the problem

For some children, PE just isn't for them and it seems as if no matter what we do as teachers, they will dislike anything physical and fail to see its benefits. A common question asked of PE teachers in a job interview is "How will you engage students who aren't interested in PE?" Standard answers to this question include praise and motivation, while better answers include the use of roles other than a performer, for example becoming a manager, coach or referee. In his book *An Ethic of Excellence*, Berger (2003, p. 65) discusses his belief that excitement plays a key role in excellence, and states, "The first step in encouraging high quality student work is to have assignments that inspire and challenge students". For less physically able learners, iPads can add that pedagogical excitement, supporting teachers to address the misconception that talent is a requirement for enjoyment. Basic apps that utilise movie creators, cameras, numbers and stopwatches can be used, and a whole range of scorekeeping and tournament tracking apps can be accessed easily, offering students the opportunity to run competitions independently.

Solution

Jimmy was taken out of the physical element of PE lessons – temporarily – and reintroduced slowly in a variety of roles. As he became increasingly confident in these roles, Jimmy responded by showing more enthusiasm, and other students began to recognise him as an important part of the lesson. By taking pictures and videos, he was able to review the learning that was taking place and demonstrate progress in his knowledge and understanding in new ways. Eventually, Jimmy gained enough confidence to take part in some activities.

The beauty of the iPad

By using the iPad, lessons can be planned with student independence in mind. I like to create worksheets and resources available on the iPad that students can follow throughout the lesson. Rather than stop the class to introduce a new skill, students can attempt it when they are ready, and so they can progress at their own pace. Resources can be made so much more exciting in their presentation using a variety of apps, with Comic Life being a perfect example (see Table 13.1). QR codes, with links to websites or YouTube clips, and augmented reality apps, are great ways to make resources interesting (Table 13.1)

To conclude, the iPad as a device, and the apps it gives access to, have not revolutionised the way I teach my lessons, but they have revolutionised the way students learn. iPads can be used across the ability range to engage students and accelerate their learning by providing opportunities to work independently, research key information and even compare themselves against a perfect model. These observations are based on trial and error in my practice, so it will be interesting to see whether my beliefs about enhanced learning are borne out in the research that follows.

TABLE 13.1 Technologies used by Gareth and his students

Technology/app	Function	How it was used
iPad (device)	A portable tablet computer that can be used to access a range of apps and that includes a camera and video function	By students to support engagement with multiple apps to support learning
Comic Life app	Allows the user to make unique resources that look like comic books	To create user-friendly resources
QR codes app	QR codes act as a hyperlink to a web page, a video, a photo – whatever the creator wants; the function is similar to a barcode	QR codes were created and displayed on walls or on resources to support students' learning by providing easily accessible key information (i.e. website showing rules and regulations of a sport)
iBeacons	Similar to a QR code; offers key information but without scanning a barcode; instead, it detects iPads in close proximity	Offers an alternative way to provide resources (iPad to iPad); could be very useful in fitness classes and orienteering

A neurophysiology perspective (Sam Lucas)

One of the most significant advances in neuroscience is the move away from the traditional view of the brain being unable to adapt beyond its initial development during early life (i.e. ontogenesis). It is now well established that the human brain preserves its capacity for functional and structural changes throughout life (Boyke et al., 2008; Draganski et al., 2004; Scholz et al., 2009), and this concept is known as *brain plasticity*. Importantly, structural and functional changes occurring within the adolescent brain have been identified as a key period for brain development (Fuhrmann, Knoll, & Blakemore, 2015), illustrating the opportunities in and importance of the environment to which the brain is exposed during this stage of development (e.g. through school pedagogical practices).

Development of technologies such as magnetic resonance imaging (MRI) have given us greater access to non-invasive observations of structural changes that can occur within the human brain during development (inclusive of learning and memory) and how those structures are connected and communicate with each other. Consequently, rather than solely relying on post-mortem assessment of human brain tissue or animal-based studies to illustrate how the human brain may change, we can now examine real-time changes occurring in the human brain during both skill execution or following a specific intervention (e.g. treatment or training/ learning). However, while such advances in neuroimaging technology and the associated approaches used with them (e.g. blood oxygen level-dependent imaging, diffusion-weighted imaging, voxel-based morphometry) have opened the door to observing structural and functional changes within the brain, understanding what these changes signify and in particular the behaviours associated with them is not well understood. For example, while we now know that learning-related structural alterations in humans can be observed after just 2 weeks of complex motor skill learning (Driemeyer et al., 2008; Filippi et al., 2010), we don't know how these alterations correlate with individual learning success, and, if so, which are the most relevant (Taubert, Villringer, & Ragert, 2012).

In humans, changes in activation patterns from regions of the brain associated with higher order, cognitively demanding tasks (i.e. prefrontal cortex) to regions more associated with habitual and less attention-demanding tasks (e.g. basal ganglia) have been shown to occur across the learning cycle with practice and development of expertise in a skill (Pennartz et al., 2009; Ericsson, 2006). Collectively, such observations indicate that the early stages of learning are associated with a larger and higher order neuronal 'footprint', which reduces in size and changes its activation location within the brain as the skill becomes more autonomous. This reflects greater efficiency of neuronal activation and/or communication within the brain as learning advances.

How to optimise this brain plasticity response (i.e. structural and functional change) in humans through effective pedagogical practice in the classroom is a challenging question (e.g. Blakemore & Frith, 2005; Dubinsky, Roehrig, & Varma, 2013). Despite the relatively little we know about how the brain adapts and what this may mean for function and performance, the ability of the brain to respond and adapt to new learning experiences seems unequivocal, so we should maximise learning environments to take advantage of the brain's plasticity.

One of the most exciting prospects for researchers, educators and health professionals interested in brain health and development is the link between physical activity and brain function (e.g. Voss, Nagamatsu, *et al.*, 2011). Regular physical activity has repeatedly been shown to be a key mediator for improved brain function across the lifespan, and to induce brain plasticity (Voss, Vivar, *et al.*, 2013). Further, physical activity and an enriched environment (i.e. offering greater opportunity for social interaction, physical activity and learning) improve the rate of cell growth in the brain (i.e. neurogenesis) and maintenance of these new cells (Kempermann & Gage, 1998; Gage, 2002). Physical education in schools, its associated experiences and the consequences for lifelong engagement in physical activity, have, therefore, important implications for brain health and disease prevention throughout life, including academic performance while at school (Hillman, Erickson, & Kramer, 2008).

A neurophysiological perspective on the iPad cases

Example 1

'Fred' has been tasked with observing expert batting technique and mapping it against his own technique. From a neuroscience perspective, there is certainly support for this pedagogical approach. Studies in both animals and humans have shown that observation of a specific action stimulates similar activation patterns in the regions of the brain associated with movement (e.g. motor cortex) to actually performing the action (e.g. di Pellegrino *et al.*, 1992; Hari *et al.*, 1998). Thus, as pedagogical strategies, mental rehearsal and observation of best practice have a neurobiological foundation; essentially they can enhance performance of a skill via improved coordination of brain activation in the various regions of the brain required for execution of that skill. This visualisation approach may also stimulate deeper learning of the combination of actions required to execute a movement in order to replicate an expert (Howard-Jones, 2009).

Example 2

As explained above, the role that physical activity plays in developing and maintaining healthy brain function throughout life is well established. Thus, it could be argued that 'Jimmy's' experience of physical education classes is not optimal. As presented, however, the narrative illustrates strategies to engage the student in the class in ways that seek to reduce and prevent a negative association with physical activity.

Of more significance, perhaps, is the brain activation associated with the creative thinking and planning required for Jimmy to organise league tables and media production. All these types of activities can strengthen connections within the brain regions associated with these types of functions. Bridging both examples is the involvement and progression of the student's social interaction in this class. Social interaction is a key component of the enriched environment that stimulates brain plasticity, with the effects of environmental enrichment on short-term brain plasticity shown to be independent of the physical activity itself (Birch, McGarry, & Kelly, 2013). Therefore, Jimmy's increased involvement in the class (including participating in the physical activity) and the social interaction associated with it has the potential to create an enhanced environment for the brain to change its structure and function as skills are developed.

Summary

The development of a positive outlook towards PE through a combination of teacher/facilitator, technology and pedagogy and the resultant increased participation in practical components of the lessons are likely to lead to positive physical activity-related effects on the brain. Future questions include: How does digital learning compare to traditional learning and how, exactly, does the iPad facilitate an enriched environment? Answering these questions will require a combined approach from neuroscience, psychology and education.

A motor learning perspective (Matt Bridge)

Over the past 5–10 years, there has been an explosion in mobile devices, such as iPads, that capture high quality video, including more recent advances in increased frame rates for slow motion capture and replay. At the same time, a plethora of coaching-related video apps for mobile devices have been developed. Coaches typically use these apps to provide augmented feedback that is not otherwise available to the performer (Trout, 2013). Equally, the apps may be used to carry out notational analysis and record timings and scores within games (Legg *et al.*, 2012). Gareth's narrative raises a number of issues that are widely discussed in the motor learning literature.

In the example of 'Fred', Gareth uses video captured on the iPad to provide Fred with feedback and the opportunity to compare personal technique to that of a professional player. The use of feedback in an appropriate manner is well known to increase motor learning, but the most effective method to provide this feedback is still a matter of debate (Sigrist, Rauter, Riener, & Wolf, 2013). Feedback can be provided in a number of different forms, for example, visual, auditory, haptic/touch or multimodal, and be given at differing points in time. Typically coaches use verbal feedback but there is a growing use of technology to monitor players in different ways through real-time monitoring of heart rate or movement using GPS, or the provision of augmented feedback in the form of video replays and analysis (Wilson, 2008).

For Fred, the use of observational learning is linked with both direct perception (Scully & Newell, 1985) and cognitive motor control perspectives (Bandura, 1986), and, as such, is a valuable form of feedback (Ste-Marie *et al.*, 2012). Yet, understanding the mechanisms by which observational learning 'works' is unclear. For example, we see Fred comparing himself to a professional on the same screen and highlighting strengths and areas to develop. The practitioner argues that this offers a template of movement within which certain features must be present, such that faults can be identified and corrected. This desire for consistency and the creation of a specific movement pattern and its automaticity is often used to define expertise (Seifert, Button, & Davids, 2013). Glazier and Davids (2009), however, have suggested that the notion of a common optimal movement solution in a sporting skill that is generalisable to all performers is inappropriate because of the complex and degenerate nature of neurobiological systems. The temptation to seek a more consistent movement pattern, thereby reducing its variability, may lead to a lack of exploration and reduce the ability of learners to create unique solutions to the movement problems encountered in competition (Glazier & Davids, 2009). Indeed, it has been suggested that the drive to find a common movement pattern tyrannises practice in sport pedagogy and distorts learning (Phillips *et al.*, 2010).

Another consideration when technical correction is provided as feedback is how this information is presented and conveyed. There is a risk that through the provision of technical points (strengths and weaknesses) a learner may develop explicit rules for carrying out movements rather than learning in an implicit manner. This can have the effect of increasing the potential for performance reduction under pressure (Masters & Poolton, 2012). It has also been argued that directing a young learner's attention to internal features, such as body movements (internal focus), is less effective in preparing for performance than directing the attention to the movement effect (external focus) (Wulf, 2013).

One potential solution to these problems is to simplify the information provided. It has been shown in laboratory tasks that the simplification of augmented feedback that, for example, conveys the angle between two limbs rather than the position of the limbs themselves (Wilson, Snapp-Childs, Coats, & Bingham, 2010) may promote an external focus of attention (Magill & Anderson, 2012). Furthermore, it is important to consider model–observer familiarity. For novice performers, there is little or no model–observer familiarity when viewing an expert model, which may lead to feeling the skill is unobtainable or an inability to pay close attention to the critical movement elements (Jennings, Reaburn, & Rynne, 2013).

A different approach is to have the learner as the model. There are two potential alternatives here – self-modelling and self-observation (Clark & Ste-Marie, 2007). Self-modelling is where through editing and the use of multiple videos, a coach creates an edited version which removes the 'errors' in performance so that learners can see themselves executing a skill as it is meant to be performed. The more commonly used self-observation approach is where the video contains errors and is unedited (Dowrick, 2000). The aim is to address the errors by having the performer as the model in order to increase ownership and attention to the modelled skill. This, it is argued, can lead to learners becoming actively engaged in exploration and the problem solving process within the movement rather than simply trying to copy the model (Hodges & Franks, 2002).

What is commendable in the approach taken in both practitioner examples is the focus on developing learner autonomy. The needs of individual pupils are analysed and met so that none are over- or under-challenged. For Jimmy, we see a different approach to the use of technology in learning by focusing on promoting learner engagement in the overall lesson rather than specific technical skills. Time keeping and scoring, and areas such as statistics, kinematics and kinetics are introduced alongside the more conventional areas, such as feedback and instruction. It is also clear from Gareth's narrative that he offers students opportunities to work in small groups and to shape the use of the iPad device, which further creates an optimal learning environment in terms of autonomy support, peer feedback and social learning.

In summary, the use of technology such as the iPad allows practitioners to enhance motor skill learning and engage students in a broader curriculum. Caution must be exercised, however, in the temptation to over-use the 'perfect model' and the ways in which augmented feedback is provided for pupils of different skill ranges. One further – and pivotal – consideration for the whole of this case (and indeed book) is pupil data security, particularly on easily portable devices. This issue is picked up in the final chapter in this book.

A situated learning perspective (Mark Griffiths)

In Gareth's rich and detailed practitioner account, words such as *engage*, *progress*, and *needs* are used to illustrate the ways in which he views the role of technology in facilitating pupil learning. Implicit in his narrative is an understanding of the learning process mediated by pupil engagement, and a belief that digital technology is particularly effective in 'satisfying needs'. Taken as a whole, Gareth's account appears to resonate with contemporary research that continues to question the relevance of PE, particularly in terms of transfer value to activities outside school (Gard *et al.*, 2012). It is interesting, therefore, to consider Gareth's narrative in this context, and to pose questions about whether and how the initial novelty of digital technologies can be developed into more substantive and creative pedagogies to support deeper pupil engagement and learning.

A situated learning perspective is helpful in framing learning as a dynamic process of decision making and perception (Lave & Wenger, 1991). Learning is perceived as active and dynamic as individuals actively seek to construct meaning resulting in learning being more than simply 'learning by doing' or experiential learning. Hence, knowledge is personal, learning involves making sense of the world, and effective learning requires meaningful problem solving (Fox, 2001). From a practical perspective, encouraging teachers to find authentic ways to engage young people offers possibilities to engage them in ways that have value and relevance.

Questions about curriculum 'relevance' are not new and are discussed in a large body of research arguing for the development of culturally relevant PE curricula (e.g. Ennis, 2011; Kirk, 2006). The National Curriculum for Physical Education in England, for example, states that all pupils should become physically confident in pursuing healthy and active lives outside school through community links (Department of Education, 2013), Similarly, in SHAPE America (2014) and the Australian Curriculum (2015) among others, there are ambitions to develop physically literate young people who are equipped to exploit physical activity opportunities in their communities. If, therefore, one purpose of PE is to socialise young people into activity in their communities, it is important to reflect on Gareth's account of technology from a situated learning perspective. Can iPads be helpful in connecting learning across the educational spaces of school and community?

In one of the few studies that examined the role of iPads in PE, Sinelnikov (2012) described the experiences of 12- and 13-year-old pupils in a 20-lesson volleyball unit. A variety of free and purchased apps was used to create and edit videos, search the Internet, analyse performance statistically, clarify refereeing signals, and give team presentations to the whole class. Although the focus was on iPads as tools in the learning process, Sinelnikov (2012) concluded that "the iPad seems to offer numerous innovative outlets for advancing and using technology in physical education classes – an opportunity that can be fostered by teachers' and students' creativity and imagination" (p. 45). Gareth's experience seems to be similar. He reported an interesting example of the creative use of iPads for Fred who was able to use video footage from his community club performance in a PE lesson. In this example, the iPad was used as a two-way knowledge conduit between school and community learning contexts, providing Fred with "scaffolding" that gave meaning and understanding to PE content knowledge.

There is some research available on the optimal ways of using iPads in educational contexts. Higgins *et al.* (2012) suggested that: (a) collaborative use (in pairs or small groups) is usually more effective than individual use; (b) short and focused deployment has a more powerful impact than sustained use over a longer period (e.g. 3 x per week, over 5–10 weeks); (c) there is clear added value when iPads are used to support students to catch up with their peers; and (d) teachers need to consider pedagogical application rather than focusing on teaching technological skills. In a PE context, however, while there is a growing body of research that focuses on the impact of digital technologies on the learning process (e.g. heart rate monitors, web-based portfolios, exergaming; Palao *et al.*, 2015), there is very little evidence on the impact of such technologies to support learning across contexts and into the life-course.

Even though digital technologies transcend specific contexts and also generations, the sustained and critical pedagogical value of these technologies remains unclear (Beetham & Sharpe, 2013). There is some evidence that mobile devices give young people learning freedom by offering immediate guidance and feedback (Higgins *et al.*, 2012) and this aligns with Gareth's experience. Yet, we need to know more about the educational role of technologies such as iPads in engendering and sustaining behaviour change beyond school in sport or physical activity community settings and though the life-course. The application of a situated learning perspective broadens the view of learning and in so doing, promotes educational activities that make available authentic and real-world scenarios in pursuit of more meaningful learning.

If, as Biesta (2015) argued, the last two decades have seen a proliferation of learning research, with a decline in the concept of education, then it is clear that, as Evans (2014) observes, "the new problematic for education and PE will, indeed, be how it can help children to see what they have in common with other people/s, the environments they inhabit and the communities they serve" (p. 555). In this new digital landscape, it is interesting and timely to consider whether and how technologies such as iPads might be used even more effectively to bridge learning across different situated contexts and move beyond novelty to inform more relevant and sustainable pedagogies.

A pedagogical perspective (Kathy Armour)

In concluding the practitioner narrative that opened this chapter, Gareth makes a bold claim: 'iPads haven't revolutionised the way I teach my lessons, but they *have revolutionised the way students learn*'.

Threading through his narrative is a strong belief that it is a teacher's professional responsibility to find new ways to support learning. Indeed, Gareth argues:

> I'm not a teacher anymore. Sure, 'teacher' is my job title and it's what I tell people I do but, in reality, all I am is a facilitator – a tool to support learners.

Moreover, underpinning all Gareth's views is an understanding that effective practitioners are those who learn continuously across their careers. In this sense, Gareth's beliefs resonate powerfully with the professional development research literature. For example, Dadds (2014, p. 9) states that continuing professional development (CPD) should 'meet the continuing needs of teachers as learners in a changing society'. In physical education, similarly, there is a large body of literature highlighting the importance of sustained CPD (e.g. Armour & Makopoulou, 2012; Patton, Parker, & Pratt, 2013) and also the shortcomings of much existing provision (i.e. Armour, Quennerstedt, Chambers, & Makopoulou, 2015). Gareth might, however, be disappointed – although not wholly surprised – to find that there is little robust evidence on what constitutes 'effective' CPD (Hill, Beisiegel, & Jacob, 2013).

There is no question that Gareth views himself as a pedagogue who is able to recognize numerous professional learning opportunities in his daily practice. It is also notable that his philosophy on professional learning can be traced back to a mentor whom he met early in his career. It can be argued that to qualify as a 'pedagogue' is to be an expert in all the different components of pedagogy and to understand the complexity of their interaction (see Armour, 2011). Gareth's description of his practice, the diagnostic processes in which he engages to tailor curriculum and learning support for individual students, and his determination to be a continuous and active learner, mark him out as a pedagogue.

One key point about Gareth's narrative is the clarity of his position on the pedagogical role of the iPad: it is a *tool* to support his bigger pedagogical goals, rather than an attractive educational gimmick. His mission is to use digital and mobile technologies to achieve his aim of making learning interesting, relevant and personalised so that it meets the needs of each individual pupil. Yet, there is limited research available to support Gareth. Lupton (2012, 2013), for example, suggests that we have little robust knowledge about how practitioners are using digital technologies for educational purposes. Indeed, Fullan (2013) has argued that used uncritically, these technologies can be more negative than positive, especially if they are simply used to replace teaching or reinforce a transmission model of learning. Certainly when we look at the three disciplinary perspectives on Gareth's narrative in this chapter, some interesting questions emerge in the quest to develop complex and nuanced 'pedagogies of technology'.

In the neurophysiological perspective, Sam Lucas points out that whereas we now know that the brain can change its functional capacity throughout life, and changes can be observed after even short bursts of motor skill learning, we still don't know whether and how these changes are linked to specific learning success. We do know that optimising the brain's plasticity is essential, and that pedagogical practices that support this are to be encouraged, but we don't yet know whether use of the iPad in PE is more – or less – optimising in this regard. It could be argued, therefore, that these are the kinds of research questions that must be answered before we can develop advanced pedagogies of technology. There may be much more that we could do to enhance students' learning if we had a more detailed understanding of what works and how.

In the motor learning perspective, Matt Bridge is able to link the approach taken by Gareth to a range of literature on the pros and cons of providing different types of feedback. Here again, the research highlights a series of questions that need to be answered. On the one hand, Gareth was able to use the iPad to support Fred to capitalise on his existing cricket expertise. On the other hand, there are important questions to be addressed about whether the 'perfect digital model' approach to feedback is appropriate and whether, in practice, it can act to reduce learner creativity in a game situation. This is the kind of question that needs to be addressed by motor learning researchers working closely with practitioners and youth. At the same time, we might wish to explore how these different forms of feedback are reflected in the development of brain plasticity, so we could usefully bring in our neurophysiologist too.

From a situated learning perspective, Mark Griffiths examines the issue of sustaining and enhancing learning across contexts. As he points out, there have long been claims that learning in school should be linked to learning outside of school in order to bridge the gap between school and community. The aim is to engender a disposition towards lifelong learning post school which, in the case of physical education, has implications for increasing physical activity engagement for lifelong health and well-being. This is captured by Akkerman and Van Eijck (2013, p. 60) who argue that 'the learner should be approached . . . as a whole person who participates in school as well as in many other practices'. We might speculate that in the example of Jimmy, the positive learning experiences facilitated by Gareth are likely to encourage activity outside school and through life, but we don't have any strong evidence to support that assertion. Indeed, at this stage, it is little more than a hope.

It is interesting to consider the tone of the practitioner narrative alongside that of the three disciplinary perspectives. Gareth is positive, upbeat and enabling. He faces pedagogical challenges on a daily basis and he seeks solutions that can meet his pupils' immediate learning needs. From a practitioner's perspective, there is simply no time to waste. The three researchers, on the other hand, see much of value in Gareth's narrative, yet they also make links to big research questions in their fields. We could guess that Gareth and other dynamic practitioners like him would love to work alongside researchers to address such questions. By taking Gareth's pedagogies and practices as the starting point, it is possible to see exactly where research efforts need to be directed – and with whom we need to collaborate – to understand the bigger pedagogical questions about PE and technology.

In the end, as Gareth points out, his practice is all about supporting pupil learning, and his pedagogical approach is endorsed in the learning theories literature. Armour *et al.* (2015) revisited John Dewey's influential theories of education to look afresh at questions about effective CPD for PE teachers. Dewey's (1916/1951) under-pinning concept of education as 'growth' and continuity is particularly important for this discussion. Dewey (1938/1997) explains it as follows:

> The principle of continuity of experience means that every experience both takes up something from those which have gone before and modifies in some way the quality of those which come after. (p. 27)

The take-home message is that each learning experience should be evaluated for the further learning it stimulates. This applies equally to pupils' and teachers' learning so the pressing research question is: Can digital technologies be used to promote the kind of dynamic learning that Dewey describes? The concept of continuity, however, could have another meaning in the context of digital technologies: the continuity of the presence of images and digital footprints. This essentially ethical concern is raised in several chapters in this book.

Finally, a word about the use of a practitioner narrative as the focal point for this pedagogical case. In their seminal work, Clandinin and Connelly (1995) highlight the importance of teachers' stories in the 'professional knowledge landscape'. Moreover, Keats Whelan *et al.* (2001) argue that practitioners need opportunities to retell and relive stories of practice in order to imagine new storylines; engaging in 'storytelling with diverse responses that leads to restorying with growth and change' (p. 154). The final questions, therefore, are for Gareth to answer in his practitioner reflection: How does he react to reading his narrative in the context of the three disciplinary perspectives and the pedagogical comment, and does his reading prompt any new storylines for the future?

Practitioner reflection

It is fascinating to see how my work looks from other perspectives. Firstly, it would be interesting to see research on technology's neurophysiological impact so teaching could be adapted to support learning even further and facilitate brain development. I also agree with the motor learning perspective of Matt Bridge that skills do not have an exact or consistent technique which must be followed to be successful. However, to counter this, I believe the use of quantitative analysis is an invaluable tool to use in the first instance. If the technique is successful, then there is no need to change it, unless it is an illegal technique or the cause of injury. From a teacher's perspective, while I do see merit in the suggestion that perfect models can reduce creativity, I see such models as a good starting point for skill development. As learners develop I then look to focus on abstract thinking, including creativity – although I can appreciate there is a challenge to this view.

As well as developing skills and a knowledge and understanding of healthy, active lifestyles, it is my belief that a high quality PE curriculum should develop teamwork, social skills and resilience which help students develop into well-rounded learners who are ready for the real world. This aligns with situated learning perspective on the importance of promoting lifelong learning through PE. Technology is a key part of our world and it should help students to be better prepared for life after school. As noted, however, short and clearly focused deployment is essential and we shouldn't become reliant on this technology as it is the pedagogy that really counts.

I have concluded that the value and impact of iPads on learning is too difficult to assess from my perspective alone. Robust and multi-disciplinary research is needed to see whether they generate deep and sustained learning. Undertaking such research will begin to inform the development of a more complex pedagogy of technology.

Lessons from the case: How can the use of digital technologies accelerate student learning in physical education?

- The use of devices and apps can help teachers to cater for a wide range of learner abilities and paces, thereby accelerating learning.
- Learner facilitation and pedagogy are the keys to using digital technologies effectively.
- Practitioners and researchers can learn much that is essential from each other.

References

Akkerman, S. F. & Van Eijck, M. (2013). Re-theorising the student dialogically across and between boundaries of multiple communities. *British Educational Research Journal, 39*, 1, 60–72.

Armour, K. M. (Ed.). (2011). *Sport Pedagogy: An Introduction for Teaching and Coaching*. London: Pearson.

Armour, K. M. & Makopoulou, K. (2012). Great expectations: Teacher learning in a national professional development programme. *Teaching and Teacher Education, 28*, 3, 336–346.

Armour, K. M., Quennerstedt, M., Chambers, F. C., & Makopoulou, K. (2015). What is effective CPD for contemporary physical education teachers: A Deweyan Framework. *Sport, Education and Society*, i-first. doi:10.1080/13573322.2015.1083000

Australian Curriculum. (2015). *Health and Physical Education*. Retrieved from www.australian curriculum.edu.au/health-and-physical-education/rationale

Bandura, A. (1986). *Social Foundations of Thought and Action: A Social Cognitive Theory*. Upper Saddle River, NJ: Prentice Hall.

Beetham, H. & Sharpe, R. (2013). *Rethinking Pedagogy for a Digital Age: Designing for 21st Century Learning* (2nd ed.). New York and London: Routledge Taylor and Francis Group.

Berger, R. (2003). *An Ethic of Excellence*. Portsmouth, NH: Heinemann.

Biesta, G. J. (2009). Good education in an age of measurement: On the need to reconnect with the question of purpose in education. *Educational Assessment, Evaluation and Accountability* (formerly: *Journal of Personnel Evaluation in Education*), *21*, 1, 33–46.

Biesta, G. J. (2015). *Beautiful Risk of Education*. Abingdon, UK: Routledge.

Birch A. M., McGarry N. B., & Kelly Á. M. (2013). Short-term environmental enrichment, in the absence of exercise, improves memory, and increases NGF concentration, early neuronal survival, and synaptogenesis in the dentate gyrus in a time-dependent manner. *Hippocampus, 23*, 437–450.

Blakemore, S.-J. & Frith U. (2005). The learning brain: Lessons for education: A précis. *Developmental Science, 8*, 459–465.

Boyke, J., Driemeyer, J., Gaser, C., Büchel, C., & May, A. (2008). Training-induced brain structure changes in the elderly. *The Journal of Neuroscience, 28*, 7031–7035.

Clandinin, D. J. & Connelly, F. M. (1995). *Teachers' Professional Knowledge Landscapes*. New York: Teachers' College Press.

Clark, S. E. & Ste-Marie, D. M. (2007). The impact of self-as-a-model interventions on children's self-regulation of learning and swimming performance. *Journal of Sports Sciences, 25*, 5, 577–586.

Dadds, M. (2014). Continuing professional development: Nurturing the expert within. *Professional Development in Education, 40*, 9–16.

Department of Education. (2013). *National Curriculum in England: Physical Education Programmes of Study*. Accessed at www.gov.uk/government/publications/national-curriculum-in-england-physical-education-programmes-of-study

Dewey, J. (1916/1951). *Democracy and Education*. New York: The Macmillan Company.

Dewey, J. (1938/1997). *Experience and Education*. New York: Touchstone.

di Pellegrino, G., Fadiga, L., Fogassi, L., Gallese, V., & Rizzolatti, G. (1992). Understanding motor events: A neurophysiological study. *Exp Brain Res, 91*, 176–180.

Dowrick, P. W. (2000). A review of self modeling and related interventions. *Applied and Preventive Psychology, 8*, 1, 23–39.

Draganski, B., Gaser, C., Busch, V., Schuierer, G., Bogdahn, U., & May, A. (2004). Neuroplasticity: Changes in grey matter induced by training. *Nature, 427*, 311–312.

Driemeyer, J., Boyke, J., Gaser, C., Büchel, C., & May, A. (2008). Changes in gray matter induced by learning – revisited. *PLoS ONE, 3*, e2669.

Dubinsky, J. M., Roehrig, G., & Varma, S. (2013). Infusing neuroscience into teacher professional development. *Educational Researcher, 42*, 317–329.

Ennis, C. D. (2011). Physical education curriculum priorities: Evidence for education and skillfulness. *Quest, 63*, 1, 5–18.

Ericsson, K. A. (2006). The influence of experience and deliberate practice on the development of superior expert performance. In K. A. Ericsson, P. Charness, P. Feltovich, R. & Hoffman (Eds.), *The Cambridge Handbook of Expertise and Expert Performance.* Cambridge, UK: Cambridge University Press. pp. 685–706.

Evans, J. (2014*)*. Neoliberalism and the future for a socio-educative physical education. *Physical Education and Sport Pedagogy, 19*, 5, 545–558.

Filippi, M., Ceccarelli, A., Pagani, E., Gatti, R., Rossi, A., Stefanelli, L., Falini, A., Comi, G., & Rocca, M. A. (2010). Motor learning in healthy humans is associated to gray matter changes: A tensor-based morphometry study. *PLoS ONE*, e10198.

Fox, R. (2001). Constructivism examined. *Oxford Review of Education, 27*, 1.

Fuhrmann, D., Knoll, L. J., & Blakemore, S.-J. (2015). Adolescence as a sensitive period of brain development. *Trends in Cognitive Sciences, 19*, 558–566.

Fullan, M. (2013). *Stratosphere: Integrating Technology, Pedagogy, and Change Knowledge.* Toronto, ONT: Pearson.

Gage, F. H. (2002). Neurogenesis in the adult brain. *The Journal of Neuroscience, 22*, 612–613.

Gard, M., Hickey-Moody, A., & Enright, E. (2012). Youth culture, physical education and the question of relevance: After 20 years, a reply to Tinning and Fitzclarence. *Sport, Education and Society, 18*, 1, 97–114.

Glazier, P. S. & Davids, K. (2009) Constraints on the complete optimization of human motion. *Sports Medicine, 39*, 1, 15–28.

Hari, R., Forss, N., Avikainen, S., Kirveskari, E., Salenius, S., & Rizzolatti, G. (1998). Activation of human primary motor cortex during action observation: A neuromagnetic study. *Proceedings of the National Academy of Sciences of the United States of America, 95*, 5061–15065.

Higgins, S., Xiao, Z., & Katsipataki, M. (2012). *The Impact of Digital Technology on Learning: A Summary for the Education Endowment Foundation.* Retrieved from https://education endowmentfoundation.org.uk/uploads/pdf/The_Impact_of_Digital_Technologies_on_Learning_(2012).pdf

Hill, H. C., Beisiegel, M., & Jacob, R. (2013) Professional development research: Consensus, crossroads, and challenges. *Educational Researcher, 42*, 9, 476–487.

Hillman, C. H., Erickson, K. I., & Kramer, A. F. (2008) Be smart, exercise your heart: Exercise effects on brain and cognition. *Nature Reviews Neuroscience, 9*, 58–65.

Hodges, N. J. & Franks, I. M. (2002). Modelling coaching practice: The role of instruction and demonstration. *Journal of Sport Science, 20*, 10, 793–811. Retrieved from www.ncbi. nlm.nih.gov/entrez/query.fcgi?cmd=Retrieve&db=PubMed&dopt=Citation&list_uids=12363296

Howard-Jones, P. A. (2009). Neuroscience, learning and technology (14-19). *E-learning, 16*, 17–18.

Jennings, C., Reaburn, P., & Rynne, S. (2013). The effect of a self-modelling video intervention on motor skill acquisition and retention of a novice track cyclist's standing start performance. *International Journal of Sports Science and Coaching, 8*, 3, 467–480.

Keats Whelan, K., Huber, J., Rose, C., Davies, A., & Clandinin, D. J. (2001). Telling and retelling our stories on the professional knowledge landscape. *Teachers and Teaching: Theory & Practice, 7*, 2, 143–156.

Kempermann, G. & Gage, F. H. (1998). Closer to neurogenesis in adult humans. *Natural Medicine, 4*, 555–557.

Kirk, D. (2006). The 'obesity crisis' and school physical education. *Sport, Education and Society, 11*, 2, 121–133.

Lave, J. & Wenger, E. (1991). *Situated Learning: Legitimate Peripheral Participation.* Cambridge, UK: Cambridge University Press.

Legg, P. A., Chung, D. H. S., Parry, M. L., Jones, M. W., Long, R., Griffiths, I. W., & Chen, M. (2012). MatchPad: Interactive glyph-based visualization for real-time sports performance analysis. *Computer Graphics Forum, 31*, 1255–1264. doi:10.1111/j.1467-8659.2012.03118.x

Lupton, D. (2012). M-health and health promotion: The digital cyborg and surveillance society. *Social Theory & Health, 10*, 3, 229–244.

Lupton, D. (2013). Understanding the human machine. *IEE Technology and Society Magazine,* Winter, 25–30.

Magill, R. A. & Anderson, D. I. (2012). *The Roles and Uses of Augmented Feedback in Motor Skill Acquisition.* London: Routledge.

Masters, R. S. & Poolton, J. M. (2012). Advances in implicit motor learning: Skill acquisition in sport. *Research, Theory and Practice, 59*.

Palao, J. M., Hastie, P. A., Cruz, P. G., & Ortega, E. (2015). The impact of video technology on student performance in physical education. *Technology, Pedagogy and Education, 24*, 1, 51–63.

Patton, K., Parker, M., & Pratt, E. (2013). Meaningful learning in professional development: Teaching without telling. *Journal of Teaching in Physical Education, 32*, 441–459.

Pennartz, C. M. A., Berke, J. D., Graybiel, A. M., Ito, R., Lansink, C. S., van der Meer, M., Redish, A. D., Smith, K. S., & Voorn, P. (2009). Corticostriatal interactions during learning, memory processing, and decision making. *The Journal of Neuroscience, 29*, 12831–12838

Phillips, E., Davids, K., Renshaw, I., & Portus, M. (2010). Expert performance in sport and the dynamics of talent development. *Sports Medicine, 40*, 4, 271–283.

Scholz J., Klein, M. C., Behrens, T. E. J., & Johansen-Berg, H. (2009). Training induces changes in white-matter architecture. *Nature Neuroscience, 12*, 1370–1371.

Scully, D. & Newell, K. (1985). Observational learning and the acquisition of motor skills: Toward a visual perception perspective. *Journal of Human Movement Studies, 11*, 169–186.

Seifert, L., Button, C., & Davids, K. (2013). Key properties of expert movement systems in sport. *Sports Medicine, 43*, 3, 167–178.

SHAPE America. (2014). *National standards: Physical education.* Retrieved from www.shapeamerica.org/standards/

Sigrist, R., Rauter, G., Riener, R., & Wolf, P. (2013). Augmented visual, auditory, haptic, and multimodal feedback in motor learning: A review. *Psychonomic Bulletin & Review, 20*, 1, 21–53.

Sinelnikov, O. A. (2012). Using the iPad in a Sport Education Season. *Journal of Physical Education, Recreation & Dance, 83*, 1, 39–45.

Ste-Marie, D. M., Law, B., Rymal, A. M., Jenny, O., Hall, C., & McCullagh, P. (2012). Observation interventions for motor skill learning and performance: an applied model for the use of observation. *International Review of Sport and Exercise Psychology, 5*, 2, 145–176.

Taubert, M., Villringer, A., & Ragert, P. (2012). Learning-related gray and white matter changes in humans: An update. *The Neuroscientist, 18*, 320–325.

Trout, J. (2013). Digital movement analysis in physical education. *Journal of Physical Education, Recreation & Dance, 84*, 7.

Voss, M. W., Nagamatsu, L. S., Liu-Ambrose, T., & Kramer, A. F. (2011). Exercise, brain, and cognition across the lifespan. *Journal of Applied Physiology, 111*, 1505–1513.

Voss, M. W., Vivar, C., Kramer, A. F., & van Praag, H. (2013). Bridging animal and human models of exercise-induced brain plasticity. *Trends in Cognitive Sciences, 17*, 525–544.

Wilson, A. D., Snapp-Childs, W., Coats, R., & Bingham, G. P. (2010). Learning a coordinated rhythmic movement with task-appropriate coordination feedback. *Experimental Brain Research, 205*, 513–520.

Wilson, B. D. (2008). Development in video technology for coaching. *Sports Technology, 1*, 34–40. doi:10.1002/jst.9

Wulf, G. (2013). Attentional focus and motor learning: A review of 15 years. *International Review of Sport and Exercise Psychology, 6*, 1, 77–104.

14

JACOB AND MARTIN: DEVELOPING DIGITAL TECHNOLOGY COMPETENCE IN PHYSICAL EDUCATION TEACHER EDUCATION

Dean Barker, Jacob Nielsen, Martin Wahlström, Natalie Barker-Ruchti, Urban Carlén and Ninitha Maivorsdotter

CHAPTER OVERVIEW

This chapter provides an illustration of how digital technologies (DTs) are experienced by Physical Education Teacher Education (PETE) students. The illustration is based on the reflections of two students at the University of Gothenburg, Sweden. The students received an assignment that involved demonstrating how a specific DT could be implemented. Three perspectives of the practitioners' experiences are provided. A Deweyan perspective shows how the students and their situations are transformed by DTs. A Foucauldian perspective focuses on the regulating aspects of technology. An applied Information Technology perspective demonstrates how DTs become part of the social practices of physical education.

Practitioner narrative (Jacob Nielsen and Martin Wahlström)

We are two teacher education students in our second-to-last semester. Both of us are specialising in physical education and English. We are slightly more interested in teaching physical education, but course programming has meant that we have more English in our teacher education program. In terms of technology, we are both 'tech savvy'. Jacob is a competitive cyclist and uses tools such as heart rate monitors, power meters, and global positioning system devices (GPS). Martin used to spend a great deal of time playing computer games when he was aged 13–15 and uses various forms of technology in his life now. Apart from using PowerPoint and a short written assignment on technology in the English part to our program, the assignment we are going to discuss is our first real encounter with digital technologies as educational tools.

Essentially, we had a short introduction of two lectures to the topic. We discussed some general themes and read some literature that covered technological strategies like wikis, podcasts, and Excel documents (for example, Gibbs, Almqvist, Meckbach, Quennerstedt, & Öhman, 2012; Papastergiou, 2009). These texts gave us some ideas about the kinds of things that could be done in physical education. We then tried out a swimming application, Mr Smooth, which provides computer-generated animations of swimming strokes as well as technique tips. Our lecturer asked us to download the free version of the app and bring it along to the pool for our lesson. There, we worked in groups to analyse and try to improve our freestyle strokes.

Alongside lectures, we had an assignment where we needed to work in groups to investigate a digital technology and develop a 'how to' guide for teachers. After completing the guide, we needed to prepare a walk-through lesson where we showed and discussed our chosen strategy to our peers. We had to structure this like a 'real lesson' but also provide 'freeze frame' moments where we stopped the lesson and discussed practical or technical points related to the technology. It is this assignment and the process that we went through while completing it that we want to describe here.

We should start by mentioning that there were actually three of us working together. Our colleague was out of the country while this chapter was being prepared and was not able to contribute. When the three of us started brainstorming, we were interested in heart rate monitors. We were not sure that the faculty had enough heart rate monitors nor were we convinced that we could produce a fun lesson if we based it on measuring heart rates, so we decided against it. We also briefly considered using something like Kinect (a line of motion-sensing input devices designed by Microsoft which enables users to interact with their computer via gestures and spoken commands), but again, we were not sure if we had access to equipment. In the end, it made sense to use smart phones and tablets because we all have them.

We decided that we would focus on the complex movement objective in the Swedish National Curriculum[1] and create a mini-lesson dealing with shot putt, hurdles, and high jump. We chose three different disciplines so that we could split the class into groups and each of us could work with smaller groups. In a school setting, we would do something like this over three lessons rather than just in one. Each of us started by showing a video clip from YouTube (a video-sharing website that allows users to upload, view, and share videos – see Table 14.1 for detail) where good technique was demonstrated. It was actually harder than we expected to find clips – we wanted to have someone that our peers could relate to, but we were not sure if the amateurs were doing the movements correctly. We are not track-and-field experts and we did not want our students to learn the wrong technique. Actually, our first freeze frame was about this point. We talked about the benefits of using video clips, such as being able to slow down and pause the

TABLE 14.1 Technology used by the practitioners

Technology	Function	How they were used in this case
Coach's Eye	An app that enables users to record and view captured video footage at different speeds; along with other features, users can diagram the video material with tools such as a screen pen.	The practitioners modelled how the app could be used to teach track and field motor competencies, drawing attention to several of its features. Practitioners also discussed specific practical considerations and concerns when using the app.
YouTube	A video-sharing website that allows users to upload, view, and share videos.	The practitioners showed videos of experts doing three track and field activities (shot putt, hurdles, and high jump) as a way of introducing the activities to their peers. Peers were then provided with opportunities to practice their technique and compare their performances with the YouTube experts.

demonstration and talk over it, but we also talked about issues finding appropriate video clips.

After practising, we asked our peers to film themselves with their smart phones. They could then watch themselves and attempt to correct their technique. In the second freeze frame, we talked about how students can benefit from seeing themselves, especially if they do not have the body awareness to actually know what they are doing. We pointed out that students might be more likely to accept feedback if they see areas that they can improve and explained that the camera angle is important if you want to be able to compare your own performance with the YouTube performance. We also covered organisational issues. For example, we discussed how teachers need to be careful when using smart phones since things can get out of hand quickly with other technologies such as Snapchat and Instagram.[2] We suggested that students should be filmed with their own phones so that they maintain possession of footage of themselves. We also noted that we would not use this strategy unless we knew the class well and could trust the students to use the technology sensibly. But there were other questions that we could not answer. We did not know, for example, if schools have policies on smart phone use or on film storage. Film material could be useful for demonstrating student learning (and therefore assessment) for example, but we are not sure if we need consent or if there are any legal obligations.

In the third part of the lesson, we introduced the Coach's Eye app (see Table 14.1 for detail). We only had this on one laptop and one phone. This meant that when we demonstrated, we all had to look at the laptop. We had used the camera function on the laptop to record student performance and we could run our film clip beside the YouTube material without having to transfer clips from phone to laptop. Unfortunately, watching parallel performances was not possible with Coach's Eye which cannot be viewed at half screen. At this point, we conducted our third freeze frame where we talked about some of the features of the app like the screen pen. We mentioned possible barriers such as the cost and having wifi in the gym. Finally, we pointed out that being able to view students' movements multiple times could be really valuable in situations where we need to assess their complex movements.

In terms of facilitating learning around digital technologies in physical education for our peers, we think we did a reasonable job. They were all familiar with the technologies that we used so we did not need to tell them the basics – for example, they all knew how to use the film function on their phones. The focus was more about going through what you need to do before the lesson and then how to manage the technologies during the lesson. We thought that by doing this task ourselves, we were able to identify and communicate quite a number of points to our peers. Our peers were really keen to discuss these technologies once we had finished, and we had a long discussion about the possible benefits of smart phones, YouTube, and Coach's Eye following the session. We talked, for instance, about filming for assessment. This could be done as formative peer assessment. Self-assessment is also possible and might be useful if learners do not want to be filmed by someone else. Alternatively, students could submit clips of their performance to the teacher. This would mean that the teacher would not necessarily need to watch each student during the lesson. Assessment aside, having access to ideal performances on smart phones during lessons would also enable students to view ideal performances in their own time. This could shift the lesson in a more student-centered direction where students could make more decisions about their learning.

After doing this task, our take-home message would be that there are a lot of advantages to using digital technologies in physical education lessons, but you need to be careful and sensitive because there are risks. On a more practical note, it also pays to know your content well. Technology does not reduce the need for the teacher to be familiar with what he or she is teaching and explain, demonstrate, encourage, and so forth as he or she would do in a lesson without technology.

In the following sections, our co-authors provide analyses of our case from a Deweyan perspective, a Foucauldian perspective, and an applied Information Technology perspective. This is followed by a more general discussion of pedagogical implications. The chapter is concluded with some of our own reflections.

A Deweyan perspective (Ninitha Maivorsdotter)

My research has mainly been directed towards the significance of aesthetic experiences for learning. The frequent use of aesthetic judgments such as, 'beautiful', 'boring' or 'fine' in sport and physical education have drawn my attention to how feelings expressed in aesthetic judgments are involved in learning. Recently, my research has focused on how young people learn about sport through the use of exergames (a form of video games that relies on technology that tracks movements and reactions). Therefore, it was with great interest that I took note of the lesson described by Jacob and Martin.

As illustrated throughout this book, learning can be understood in many different ways. Drawing from the work of John Dewey (Dewey, 1938, 1934), I use a transactional perspective on learning in order to interpret the narrative and the two practitioners' lesson. A transactional perspective puts process first and treats distinctions such as those between people and environment as functional distinctions emerging from process, rather than starting points or metaphysical givens (Biesta & Burbules, 2003). From a transactional perspective, students' physicality is understood as biological and cultural, and digital tools are seen both as technical and cultural in nature, bringing values and norms into the learning.

Dewey (1938) also uses transaction to describe how people are connected to and part of reality: students face the consequences of their own actions and this close connection between doing and suffering is what Dewey calls *experience*. Experience is continually transformed in transaction; that is to say, students and their situation are in continual transformation. However, in order to understand learning, one must also understand the location of meaning and the process of students' meaning making. Dewey (1925) proposes that meaning is not to be found in the world itself but is located in the practices in which students are involved. In other words, meaning is not an invisible mental structure that the students capture in their heads, but something that works in action through consequences, and meaning making is the process in which students respond to a social practice through action. If different kinds of meaning making are desirable in physical education, then different kinds of actions must be possible for the students. This assertion is particularly interesting when it comes to employing digital technologies in physical education. Specifically, how can digital tools provide various actions that support student learning? Jacob and Martin's lesson provides a useful example with which to consider this question.

Based on his transactional perspective, Dewey understands learning as a reflected experience that supports action. Learning is therefore connected to observing, understanding and controlling the relation between actions and their consequences (Biesta & Burbules, 2003). Jacob and Martin's use of digital tools enables the students to observe, understand and control their actions. However, Dewey (1938) understands learning not only as overt reflection, but as something that happens through slow, often unreflective, contingent transformations of habits and customs. Learning in this way can more generally be understood as transformations of habits and ways of acting. Experiences are thus continually transformed in transaction with what occurs, especially as no two situations are identical. This transformation makes it possible for us to continually learn new things. Dewey (1938) captures this idea through his principle of continuity. This principle of learning suggests that students' prior experiences are made use of in current experiences. In this way, every experience influences possible future experiences and potential learning.

In his work, Dewey (1934) makes little distinction between aesthetic experience and any other kind of experience. Instead, he suggests that every experience – such as watching yourself doing a high jump on your smart phone – has aesthetic qualities that are perceived as moving towards or away from consummation and fulfilment – that is, whether divergent parts tend to become one whole.

Although we are connected to the world through experience, Dewey (1934) does not call every event an experience. An experience has a clear start, middle and ending, which separates an experience from the flow of events in people's lives. An experience is one that runs its course to fulfilment and is savored as a whole. Many experiences cannot be savored in this immediate way, but are paths where aesthetic judgments are used to communicate whether and in what ways different courses of action lead to fulfilment (or not). In this process we learn whether and how we belong in the activity that makes up the experience. These processes of relation and differentiating are emotional and hence aesthetic experiences (Maivorsdotter, Lundvall, & Quennerstedt, 2014). Teachers should be aware that smart phones are not 'neutral' technology but bearers of social norms and values. Using smart phones or other technologies clearly affects student learning. Educational decisions should therefore not only be directed by biomechanical knowledge of complex movements, but also by sociocultural knowledge of how smart phones are used in young peoples' lives. We might well wonder if it is even possible for a student to observe the position of his or her legs in a movement if the aesthetical fulfilment of being filmed is, for example, to look good with perfect hair.

To summarise the key points that can be drawn from a Deweyan perspective: by adding YouTube clips or filming movements with a smart phone for educational purposes, the teachers provide possibilities for reflection on the same experience. Both the teacher and student(s) can observe together and support each other's understanding in order to facilitate the students' control of action. In this way, the experience can turn into an experience with a clear start, middle and ending that distinguishes the experience from the flow of experiences during a lesson in physical education. It can become an aesthetic experience supporting student learning of the complex movement objectives set by the Swedish National Curriculum.

A Foucauldian perspective (Natalie Barker-Ruchti)

I will discuss technology as part of physical education and will do this employing Michel Foucault's (1978) theory of discipline and normalisation. This section builds on other Foucauldian work to argue that physical education is a disciplinary, regulating practice (Webb & Macdonald, 2007; Webb, McCaughtry, & MacDonald, 2004; Wright, 2000). Specifically, I discuss: (a) the two students' understanding and utilisation of digital technology in physical education, and (b) consequences that technologised forms of knowing may have for physical education classes. In so doing, my analyses take up and build on Gard's (2014) claim that the use of digital technologies in physical education should be considered carefully.

Foucault suggests that dominant discourses shape knowledge and that accepted ways of understanding phenomena regulate individuals' thinking and conduct. From this perspective, ways of knowing about something are not intellectual acts of freedom, but products of subjectification and normalisation (Foucault, 1978). With regard to this chapter's practitioner narrative, knowledge relating to modernisation and commercialisation currently tells us that technological advancements are indicators of constructive and valuable progress (Gard, 2014). Indeed, numerous technologies save lives (e.g. pacemakers, cell phones, GPS) which adds to the perceived importance of technological development in general. It is thus perhaps of little surprise that the two PETE students approach technology positively and are familiar with and employ a number of digital technologies in their lives. Of course, not all digital technologies are life saving. Recently, I read of an application that enables you to identify the destination of planes flying overhead, a facility that seems to have rather limited use for most people. Regardless of utility though, digital technologies have and will continue to shape our lives, sometimes profoundly (Säljö, 2010). With specific reference to the above case narrative, I want to discuss three ways the technologies that the two PETE students employed can be seen to have influenced teaching practice and student learning. Foucault's ideas of subjectification and normalisation are used to consider the focus and purpose of the lesson and the objectification of the performing bodies within the lesson. The Foucauldian analysis is then concluded with a summary of how the two PETE students' understanding of technology shapes student-centered learning.

An important rationale for the use of digital technologies in competitive sport is the improvement of movement technique. This is related to the focus and purpose of lessons. Certainly, technical proficiency enhances performance and can reduce adverse health consequences such as overuse injuries (Elphinston & Hardman, 2006). With relevance to the practitioner narrative, the complex movement skills and their official learning outcomes which relate to the importance of technical proficiency relate to quality of movement, improvement of physical ability, and ergonomic adaptation of movement (SNAE, 2011). To achieve the learning outcomes, the two students claimed that gaining knowledge of 'good' and 'bad' technique is necessary. YouTube clips were used as a way to move closer to technically correct performances. The slowing down and pausing of video footage to point to detailed technical information was considered particularly useful in providing learners with visual evidence of 'good technique'. Once the students had filmed their own performances using smart phones, video footage helped the students to detect performance deficiencies and provided an impetus for further optimisation of performance. While the benefits of movement analysis and learning through video feedback have been documented (see for example, Poppe, 2007), my point is that video-based technology may focus lesson content and purpose on particular aspects of performance, as well as learning opportunities. In Foucauldian terms, however, this focus can be seen to have been influenced by contemporary dominant discourses of (movement) efficiency and control, as well as currently accepted knowledge of particular movement techniques. Videoing enhanced this influence through presenting the students with particular performances. The lesson was consequently limited in stimulating other contents and learning outcomes, such as, for instance, the exploration of different kinds of techniques for the performance of the shot putt, high jump, and hurdle movements that the lesson focused on.

Physical education has been interpreted as a space and practice of surveillance where bodies are objectified (Webb *et al.*, 2004). Indeed, literature argues that surveillance is a characteristic of physical education through which students are normalised according to pre-set standards (Kirk, 1998). Surveillance is considered to not only have a concrete source in a physical education teacher, but by drawing on Foucault (1978), this can also occur through students evaluating their bodies and performances in comparison to norms presented to them. Foucault uses the concept of the panopticon to theorise how this process of knowing about and judging oneself against ideals involves individuals being reduced to objects that can be gazed upon (for an example from physical education, see Cockburn & Clarke, 2002). In our case narrative, ideal forms of the complex movement skills were presented to the students through the YouTube clips. Once the students had filmed their own movements, comparison between the 'good technique' and their own became possible. This watching and filming and being watched again contained both subjectification and objectification (see Webb *et al.*, 2004), which in Foucauldian terms are understood as top–down and bottom–up disciplinary pressures that regulate individual conduct. Indeed, Shogan (1999) suggests that the more complex and difficult sporting skills are, the more thorough these disciplinary effects are on the body. This self-regulation, according to Foucault (1978) is productive, however, it also creates docile individuals who cannot make decisions, create routines, or reflect on their lives beyond idealised standards.

In summary, the Foucauldian perspective demonstrates how the use of technology may have led to docility. This conclusion runs counter to the two PETE students' impression that video-based feedback can create student-centered learning experiences. Although possibilities for independent learning through video feedback have been outlined in scientific literature (e.g. O'Loughlin, Chróinín, & O'Grady, 2013), the Foucauldian perspective would challenge these assumptions. I have discussed above how normalisation occurs both through top–down and bottom–up regulation, and through these processes, creates individuals that adapt to expectations. Hence, although individuals may consider themselves independent and self-driven citizens, this agency can be seen as limited by their subjectivity. In the narrative, such subjectivity may explain the PETE students' lack of critical appraisal of digital technologies beyond organisational and ethical aspects.

An applied information technology perspective (Urban Carlén)

As a discipline, applied Information Technology (IT) is made up of various research fields. Some researchers focus on IT and learning to try to understand the conditions that lead people to adopt and use various digital tools at work, in everyday life, and in education (e.g. Haythornthwaite, 2008; Rainie & Wellman, 2012). Since most tools and applications are designed with commercial interests in mind, and are only later introduced into educational settings, questions about conditions for learning and how digital tools change the nature of students' learning are often only asked once tools have been in use for some time (Cuban, 1986; Lupton, 2015). Importantly, IT tools can be seen as both physical and intellectual (Säljö, 2010). A laptop can be considered a physical tool whereas the installed software applications are considered intellectual tools. Gibson (2013) introduces the term *affordance* to denote that former experiences of tools, activities and environments influence how people use tools in ways that exceed their technical properties.

Within applied IT, I have investigated how people participate online as they share knowledge and experiences around common interests (see for example, Carlén & Lindström, 2011). The adoption of digital technologies in physical education is interesting since it challenges common sense conceptions of what physical education is about and what it should be about (i.e. movement in its broadest sense). Research focusing on participation, generally, concentrates on the characteristics of activities that make up social practices (Wenger, 1998). In social practices, learning becomes situated and knowledge is distributed among participants who engage with one another (Lave & Wenger, 1991). This means that learning is a constant process that takes place in all situations, whether the activity is explicitly educational or not. As people engage online, they create situations of learning that challenge our traditional conceptions of how we socialise and share knowledge in social practices. Using ideas from this perspective, I will comment on several of the conditions for participation when digital technologies are introduced in a physical education lesson. By doing this, I hope to provide insights into the organisation of learning activities described by Jacob and Martin.

Some schools in Sweden provide students with laptops in a 'one-to-one' scheme (Tallvid, 2015). Research also suggests that about one third of Swedish students have their own computers at school (Findahl, 2014). Smart phones are also widespread and these devices provide a 'thick' infrastructure for learning that fosters digital competences within the collectives of young citizens. These digital tools and wireless networks connect activities that are performed at school with those that are performed at home. In the case narrative, teachers are challenged by students' authorised, as well as unauthorised, use of digital technologies, as they negotiate the meaning of how teaching and learning can be organised (Tallvid, 2015; Wenger, 1998). According to Swedish curricula, the introduction of digital technologies must include a didactic dimension and not simply focus on the content of digital technologies. Rather than working out how to use the technologies, the challenge for teachers seems to be to develop a rationale for how and why filming body movements with smart phones can complement learning in a didactic sense. Students need to learn how to direct the scenes and then analyse the situations in order to increase their understanding of how to participate as high jumpers. Students are required to watch and imitate athletic physical movements. In addition, the video clips become complementary material for analysing student performances in relation to the athletes. Knowledge about how to watch and understand physical movements becomes highly relevant if one is to learn about one's own capabilities and this applies to both the students and teachers in the narrative. Digital technologies bring to the scene an array of challenges that extend the meaning of participation in physical education. Using digital tools should not reduce or deemphasise the role of the teacher, but rather change the role to one of facilitator of physical movements. The teacher should, as a consequence, learn new things and expand their field of knowledge when introducing digital technologies as they need to reorganise their teaching.

Before digitalisation, using video was expensive and often only teachers were allowed to use camcorders (Cuban, 2001). In the narrative, the teachers assume that all students can use their own smart phones and become owners of their recorded video clips. In such an arrangement, they can look instantly at their results in order to adjust their performances, as students continue with another attempt, recording once again their actions. Thus, the video material has the potential to challenge their understanding of high jump, since they might fail the height even if they are using the correct body movements. This makes the facilitation role of the teacher crucial.

Unsurprisingly, those teachers who view themselves as technology enthusiasts are more willing to introduce technology in education (Cuban, 2001). Tallvid (2015) explains that teachers may be simultaneously accepting and resistant to using tools, but should discuss digital technologies on social and material accounts. Hence, there is little point blaming teachers for being conservative or resistant to change as they struggle to translate their use of technologies for organisational purposes into teaching (Tallvid, 2015). With teacher education and continuing professional development, it is worth fostering both the courage to use digital tools as well as critical points of view. In the narrative, we imagine that the scenario in physical education could become integrated with other school subjects such as biology, physics, and media education that could extend the lesson in high jump. From an applied IT perspective, learning about teaching with digital technologies becomes a project of pedagogical digital competence situated in a social practice of education. In such a scenario, teachers can adopt digital tools together, inviting both tech savvy educators and novices to master the challenges of educational technologies, and to develop didactics that support learning and teaching in PE.

A pedagogical perspective (Dean Barker)

There are a number of issues that emerge from the narrative and the three perspectives that relate to both the work of teachers in schools and the work of teacher educators with student teachers. I will focus on four key issues and limit the discussion to pedagogical work that takes place in schools. These issues concern: (1) meaning making, (2) student agency and possibilities for student decision making, (3) the effects of technology on lesson content, and (4) students' digital competence.

Much has been written about the meaningfulness of physical education and how, for some students, physical education is either not particularly meaningful or takes on negative connotations (Sykes & McPhail, 2008; Tannehill, MacPhail, Walsh, & Woods, 2015). Both a Deweyan perspective and an applied IT perspective draw attention to meaning-making processes and discuss how meaning is created in and through action. From these perspectives, introducing digital technologies as a new set of practices has the potential to change the way that students do, and therefore make sense of, physical education. Indeed, this is consistent with expectations that technologies will increase interest and help young people to connect their experiences in physical education with their technologically saturated lives (Papastergiou, 2009). This is obviously an exciting prospect for physical education practitioners and scholars. We may ask, however, about the scope of this potential. Granted, in Martin and Jacob's lesson students were: connected to the internet, using an application that they had never used before, individually filming motoric performances in an attempt to facilitate biomechanical analysis, and basing discussion on observations occurring almost in real time. In a sense, these actions are genuinely new and do constitute quite a radical shift from physical education practices occurring in many schools.

At the same time, the narrative calls to mind Kirk's (2010) work on the idea of the idea (idea^2) of physical education. Kirk suggests that despite superficial changes, physical educators have continued to teach sports techniques for almost a century. According to Kirk, sports techniques are different from sports skills since techniques are de-contextualised and can be done with little understanding of the sport's rules, tactics, or culture. If we accept Kirk's thesis, we may ask whether the introduction of technological advances will shift physical educators' focus away from techniques. Martin and Jacob's lesson suggests that it probably will not. In fact, their narrative suggests that digital technologies such as Coach's Eye actually provide effective ways of isolating particular movements and techniques and present opportunities for learning movements without any knowledge of the context-specific rules or cultural norms that go with them. Other technological advances may lead to alternative ways of making sense of physical education, but this expectation should be made with caution. Students that have covered the same track and field techniques in grades six, seven, eight, nine and ten may continue to struggle to make meaning in physical education, even if they are able to integrate their mobile phones and various applications in their learning tasks.

From a Foucauldian perspective, there was a concern that even while Martin and Jacob made claims to a student-centred pedagogy that encouraged independent work and decision making, the use of cameras and video clips increased discipline and cultivated student docility. From a pedagogical perspective, it is important to note that: (1) disciplinary techniques have always been a part of physical education and schooling in general (Kirk, 1998), and (2) these techniques are productive in that they create ways of being and acting. Digital technologies could be seen simply as *contemporary* forms of control. This is not to downplay the gravity of concerns inspired by Foucauldian thinking (see also Gard, 2014): Cameras, heightened monitoring, and idealised ways of moving have the potential to normalise, and therefore to alienate and exclude. Over time, increased use of digital technologies could lead young people to become even more comfortable with sharing aspects of their private lives with friends, strangers, and multinational corporations. All of this suggests that the practitioner has an extremely important role to play, and with the introduction of different technologies comes opportunities for discussion and reflection. Practitioners may well ask questions such as: What kinds of bodies are used in instructional clips? What kinds of language are used to describe movement? What aspects of movement are left out? These kinds of questions could be used in critical pedagogical approaches (Macdonald & Brooker, 2000; Tinning, 2002) and may be a more constructive way forward than avoiding digital technologies altogether.

In line with the above observation, a Foucauldian view also drew attention to the way the directive to implement digital technologies not only shaped the structure but also the content of the lesson. Martin and Jacob had the explicit task of using technology while basing their lesson on the Swedish curriculum. Their description of their planning process illustrates their thinking nicely. They ruled out various options on the grounds of fun or availability before settling on phones, Coach's Eye, and the complex movement curricular aim. Such considerations are not necessarily unique to technology. Making lessons engaging as well as utilising available equipment are basic elements of planning physical education lessons (Siedentop, 1991). Further, once equipment has been selected from the equipment room, it tends to 'talk to us'. As Quennerstedt and colleagues (2011) suggest, a basketball wants to be bounced. A Foucauldian view suggests that Coach's Eye encourages teachers and students to measure, compare, and calculate. This does not mean, however, that we must use it in these ways, for these purposes. Coach's Eye could be used as an artistic tool or a prompt for reflection. Cameras on phones could be used to capture expressions or emotions. In other words, new artefacts will make certain kinds of content and particular practices more obvious, just as 'old' artefacts currently do. Being aware of this is crucial and there is nothing to say that digital technologies could not be used in alternative or unorthodox ways. Creativity and imagination would seem to be just as important in the process of teaching in new times (Wright, Macdonald, & Burrows, 2004) as they were in 'old' times.

Finally, it is worth considering the 'digital competence' of school students. Martin and Jacob assume that students at upper secondary level are already digitally competent and expect these students to use phones and their features capably within the learning context. From an applied IT perspective, using phones for video-assisted movement analysis may be asking too much. Of course, digital competence found in any class is likely to vary a great deal. Still, this perspective raises several important issues for practitioners. First – in line with a Deweyan perspective – it is important to discern students' competencies. At a time when young people have unprecedented access to technology, it is possible to overestimate their capacity to use it. Second and related, practitioners should be clear on the prerequisite knowledge required for the task. It is not clear that Jacob and Martin knew which points regarding movement analysis would need to be taught, even if they were relatively clear on the biomechanical and technological cues on which they wanted to focus. Teachers would probably develop sensitivity over time and a reflexive approach would be useful when setting out. Third, practitioners would need to consider whether they are prepared to teach students digital competence. Here, I use 'prepared' in two senses. Teachers should ask themselves whether they have the *capacity* to foster digital competence. In other words, do they know enough about digital technologies to teach others about them? Additionally, teachers would have to ask themselves whether they are *willing* to foster digital competence. Rationales for physical education have been discussed at length with many arguing that claims made on behalf of the school subject have been too broad (Bailey *et al.*, 2009; Evans, 2004). Do physical education teachers really want to lay claim to developing digital competence as well?

Practitioner reflection

Deweyan thinking draws attention to how smart phones bear social norms and values. We think it might pose a problem for teachers that their students normally use smart phones for entertainment, rather than learning. When we planned our lesson, this problem crossed our minds and our conclusion was that the social environment in the class is of great importance in this aspect. If the class is mature and if they have a good relationship to each other, it might be effective in bringing about learning and not too problematic to use smart phones. On the other hand, if the group is immature smart phones would probably cause more 'damage' to the classroom environment than helping the learning process. No matter what the group looks like, we think that smart phones should just be seen as a complementary tool for the teacher, until they have been tested with success in the classroom. However, in order to change these social norms connected to smart phone use, we think that students need to be challenged. The change we want to achieve in this case is to show students that their smart phones can be used as an aid to their learning and not only as a technological device used for entertainment.

In the perspectives, there seems to be a general skepticism towards students' skills in using smart phones for educational purposes. The students might lack the prerequisites to be able to carry out exercises such as the ones described in the case above. That is a plausible claim and we think that a thorough introduction will be needed in order for the students to understand how to handle the application. However, what is needed from the students regarding technological skills is filming videos in different angles with their smart phones and the ability to draw lines in the Coach's Eye application. We are confident enough to say that we think students already possess sufficient skills for this with minimal guidance.

By using their smart phones, the students can be responsible for their own learning with the teacher monitoring the process and guiding them. When using the smart phone for analysing the video, students get the chance to identify their needs for improvement. This can lead to a more meta-cognitive learning than when the teacher provides all the answers, which is often the case in a classic physical education lesson. This could be seen as a step towards individualisation in teaching, which we see as positive. It should also be noted that the point is not to use technology "for the sake of using technology", but rather because we think that it will be a valuable aid in learning these complex movements.

The points made in each of the case analyses are all good points worthy of taking into consideration. However, we think that teachers must not be afraid of using technological aids in their teaching when it is justified. With some practice from both teachers and students, we retain our optimism that digital technologies in some situations can add new and valuable dimensions to teaching and learning in physical education.

Lessons from the case: How can the use of digital technologies accelerate pupil learning in physical education?

- Introducing movement analysis technologies has the potential to change the ways that young people make sense of their bodies, their movements and movement cultures. These changes may be in line with young people's experiences outside of physical education. Digital technologies could therefore be seen to increase the relevance and authenticity of learning that takes place in physical education.
- Observing, recording and comparing one's body/performance against social norms can extend forms of self-discipline and create particular ways of being and acting. This can be productive in the sense that students may become more effective in performing sports techniques that are valued in certain contexts. Additionally, and somewhat alternatively, the use of digital technologies can provide opportunities to critique norms that relate to bodies and movement.
- Using different forms of technology can increase students' digital competence as it relates to physical education and movement. Two points should be noted here: (i) the digital competence found in any class is likely to vary a great deal; and (ii) physical educators should consider how this kind of learning relates to the objectives of physical education in their given context.

Notes

1 The statement suggests that students will be provided with opportunities to develop movement capacities in a range of activities, and generally improve physical ability (SNAE, 2011).
2 Snapchat is a video messaging application that allows users to take photos, record videos, add text and drawings to recorded material, and send this material to controlled lists of recipients. Instagram is an online mobile photo-sharing, video-sharing, and social networking service that enables its users to take pictures and videos, and share them on a variety of social networking platforms.

References

Bailey, R., Armour, K. M., Kirk, D., Jess, M., Pickup, I., & Sandford, R. (2009). The educational benefits claimed for physical education and school sport: An academic review. *Research Papers in Education*, *24*(1), 1–27.

Biesta, G. & Burbules, N. C. (2003). *Pragmatism and educational research*. Lanham, MD: Rowman & Littlefield.

Carlén, U. & Lindström, B. (2011). Informed design of educational activities in online learning communities. In A. D. Olofsson & J. O. Lindberg (Eds.), *Informed Design of Educational Technologies in Higher Education*. Hershey, PA: IGI Global. pp. 118–134.

Cockburn, C. & G. Clarke. (2002). "Everybody's looking at you!": Girls negotiating the "femininity deficit" they incur in physical education. *Women's Studies International Forum*, *25*(6), 651–665.

Cuban, L. (2001). *Oversold & underused: Computers in the classroom*. Cambridge, MA: Harvard University Press.

Cuban, L. (1986). *Teachers and machines: The classroom use of technology since 1920*. New York: Teachers College Press.

Dewey, J. (1938). *Experience and education*. New York: Touchstone.

Dewey, J. (1934). *Art as experience*. New York: Perigee Books.

Dewey, J. (1925). *Experience and nature*. New York: Dover.

Elphinston, J. & Hardman, S. L. (2006). Effect of an integrated functional stability program on injury rates in an international netball squad. *Journal of Science and Medicine in Sport*, *9*(1), 169–176.

Evans, J. (2004). Making a difference? Education and ability in PE. *European Physical Education Review*, *10*(1), 95–108.

Findahl, O. (2014). Swedes and the Internet 2014 – An annual study of the Swedish people's internet habits. Retrieved from http://en.soi2014.se/

Foucault, M. (1978). *Discipline and punish: The birth of the prison*. New York: Random House.

Gard, M. (2014). eHPE: A history of the future. *Sport, Education and Society*, *19*(6), 827–845.

Gibbs, B., Almqvist, J., Meckbach, J., Quennerstedt, M., & Öhman, M. (2012). TV-spel som läromedel i idrott och hälsa. *Idrott och hälsa*, *8*, 11–14.

Gibson, J. J. (2013). *The ecological approach to visual perception*. Hillsdale, N.J: Psychology Press.

Haythornthwaite, C. (2008). Learning relations and networks in web-based communities. *International Journal of Web Based Communities*, *4*(2), 140–158.

Kirk, D. (2010). *Physical education futures*. London: Routledge.

Kirk, D. (1998). *Schooling bodies: School practice and public discourse, 1880–1950*. London: Leicester University Press.

Lave, J. & Wenger, E. (1991). *Situated learning: Legitimate peripheral participation in communitities of practice*. New York: Cambridge University Press.

Lupton, D. (2015). Data assemblages, sentient schools and digitized health and physical education (response to Gard). *Sport, Education and Society*, *20*(1), 122–132.

Macdonald, D. & Brooker, R. (2000). Articulating a critical pedagogy in physical education teacher education. *Journal of Sport Pedagogy*, *51*(1), 51–63.

Maivorsdotter, N., Lundvall, S., & Quennerstedt, M. (2014). Being a competent athlete or a competent teacher? Aesthetic experiences in physical education teacher education. *European Physical Education Review*, 1356336X14535058.

O'Loughlin, J., Chróinín, D. N., & O'Grady, D. (2013). Digital video: The impact on children's learning experiences in primary physical education. *European Physical Education Review*, *19*, 165–182. doi:10.1177/1356336X13486050

Papastergiou, M. (2009). Exploring the potential of computer and video games for health and physical education: A literature review. *Computers & Education, 53*(3), 603–622.

Poppe, R. (2007). Vision-based human motion analysis: An overview. *Computer Vision and Image Understanding, 108*(1), 4–18.

Quennerstedt, M., Almqvist, J., & Öhman, M. (2011). Keep your eye on the ball: Investigating artifacts-in-use in physical education. *Interchange, 42*(3), 287–305.

Rainie, H. & Wellman, B. (2012). *Networked: The new social operating system.* Cambridge, MA: Mit Press.

Säljö, R. (2010). Digital tools and challenges to institutional traditions of learning: technologies, social memory and the performative nature of learning. *Journal of Computer Assisted Learning, 26*(1), 53–64.

Shogan, D. (1999). *The making of high-performance athletes: Discipline, diversity and ethics.* Toronto: University of Toronto Press.

Siedentop, D. (1991). *Developing teaching skills in physical education* (3rd ed.). Mountain View, CA: Mayfield.

Swedish National Agency for Education (SNAE). (2011). *Läroplan, examinsmål, och gymnasiegemensamma ämnen för gymnasieskola 2011.* Stockholm: Skolverket.

Sykes, H. & McPhail, D. (2008). Unbearable lessons: Contesting fat phobia in physical education. *Sociology of Sport Journal, 25*(1), 66–96.

Tallvid, M. (2015). *1:1 in the classroom – Analysis of an educational practice in change.* (PhD). University of Gothenburg, Gothenburg, Sweden. Retrieved from http://hdl.handle. net/2077/37829

Tannehill, D., MacPhail, A., Walsh, J., & Woods, C. (2015). What young people say about physical activity: The Children's Sport Participation and Physical Activity (CSPPA) study. *Sport, Education and Society, 20*(4), 442–462.

Tinning, R. (2002). Toward a "modest pedagogy": Reflections on the problematics of critical pedagogy. *Quest, 54,* 224–240.

Webb, L. & Macdonald, D. (2007). Dualing with gender: Teachers' work, careers and leadership in physical education. *Gender and Education, 19*(4), 491–512.

Webb, L., McCaughtry, N., & MacDonald, D. (2004). Surveillance as a technique of power in physical education. *Sport, Education and Society, 9*(2), 207–222.

Wenger, E. (1998). *Communities of practice: Learning, meaning, and identity.* Cambridge: Cambridge University Press.

Wright, J. (2000). Disciplining the body: Power, knowledge and subjectivity in a physical education lesson. In A. Lee & C. Poyton (Eds.), *Culture and Text: Discourse and Methodology in Social Research and Cultural Studies.* Sydney: Allen & Unwin. pp. 152–169.

Wright, J., Macdonald, D., & Burrows, L. (Eds.). (2004). *Critical inquiry and problem-solving in physical education.* London: Routledge.

15

ARTICULATING "PEDAGOGIES OF TECHNOLOGY" THROUGH THIRTEEN "PEDAGOGICAL CASES"

Ashley Casey, Victoria A. Goodyear and Kathleen M. Armour

CHAPTER OVERVIEW

The purpose of this chapter is to consider whether there are any lessons to be learnt from the preceding pedagogical cases. We comment on three areas: (i) new information that helps us to conceptualise 'pedagogies of technology' or 'e-pedagogies', (ii) a challenge to pedagogues to 'be brave' in the ways in which we think about and use technology in physical education, and (iii) suggestions for the future. In particular, we identify a pressing need for an inclusive 'big conversation' or 'grand debate' in the physical education profession about the potentially transformative role of technologies in physical education in a digital age.

Introduction

In writing this book we set out to explore the relationship between pedagogy and technology, and, subsequently, examine how digital technologies impact on young people's learning in physical education. Pedagogical cases offered us an innovative framework within which to explore these issues. In particular, the pedagogical cases model allowed us to construct case studies of technology, pedagogy and learning in action and to analyse them from multi-disciplinary perspectives. Building on the first edited volume (see Armour, 2014), we saw the potential for pedagogical cases to be a useful professional development mechanism in the topical area of digital technologies and learning in physical education. We aimed to achieve this by exploring the dynamic pedagogical concerns of teachers and teaching, learners and learning, context and content as illustrated through a practitioner's experiences. It is important to reiterate that the practitioner narrative was the starting point for the construction of each pedagogical case, thus ensuring that practice was driving theory.

The aim of this concluding chapter is to consider what we have learnt from the chapters in this second volume of pedagogical cases, and to suggest some possible ways forward for pedagogy, technology and learning, and the pedagogical cases model. The chapter is organised into three sections: (i) pedagogies of technology, (ii) a challenge to pedagogues to 'be brave', and (iii) what next?

Pedagogies of technology

The first point to be made is that, similar to the experience of putting together the first volume of pedagogical cases, there were numerous challenges to be overcome in seeking to work across disciplinary boundaries. Terminology, writing style, referencing and understandings of the key concepts of pedagogy, technology and learning are different across disciplines and, at times, these were significant barriers. That said, shared learning from the process was a valuable outcome and there are common messages that can be taken from the cases.

As was explained in Chapter 1, the Introduction, each chapter team was tasked with constructing a pedagogical case centred on a practitioner's narrative about the ways in which they use digital technologies in physical education. Specifically, we asked the lead authors and their multi-disciplinary teams to problematise the fledgling concept of pedagogies of technology from their different perspectives and to offer new insights into the meaning of the term and potential ways forward for the development of robust pedagogies of technology for the field. The lead chapter authors were free to select any disciplines that they felt could offer useful insights into the practitioner narrative.

Looking across the thirteen chapters, twenty-six (inclusive of physical education and sport pedagogy) different disciplines considered the notion of pedagogies of technology. Since there was some replication in the perspectives found in different chapters, notably in psychology, motor learning, literacy and teacher learning, we might conclude that these disciplines have close alliances with pedagogy, technology and learning in the context of physical education. On the other hand, diversity across the perspectives was also evident, and some practitioner narratives were analysed from disciplines such as anthropology, neurophysiology and digital humanities that we might not typically associate with physical education.

As was noted earlier, working across disciplines presented challenges for our chapter teams. Yet, the synthesis undertaken by the pedagogical experts in our field (the first author on each chapter) and the practitioner reflections at the end of each chapter demonstrate that in both research and practice we do broadly agree on three key things. In constructing pedagogies of technology for our field, the pedagogical cases in this book seem to suggest that: (i) technology is a tool for teaching and learning, (ii) technology promotes a student-centred approach, and (iii) practitioner learning is a significant and important aspect of pedagogies of technology. These are now discussed in turn.

Technology is a tool for teaching and learning

Although viewed in distinctively different ways to other forms of PE equipment – such as a bat, ball or net – technology was consistently positioned as a teaching and learning tool, resource or artefact to be used by students and teachers. The varying devices (e.g. tablet computers, exergames, algorithm monitors), their compatible features (e.g. apps, kinetic sensors, cameras) and functions (e.g. social networking, freeze-frame capabilities, video examples) were presented as tools capable of supporting students' engagement with learning tasks and helping them to manage and organise their learning individually, in pairs or small groups. In some chapters, however, it is also apparent that technology was conceptualised as a kind of 'super tool' – a tool that is contemporary, socially relevant, politically important and culturally accepted across international boundaries.

Technology promotes a student-centred approach

While technology was seen as, essentially, a tool to support learning, there is agreement across the case chapters that it was methods of teaching, processes of learning and the broader pedagogical context created by teachers that ensured developmentally appropriate learning outcomes were met. To support these assertions, chapters (implicitly or explicitly) drew on features of constructivist learning theories. Authors argued that technology enhanced a teacher's ability to create a student-centred (or self-directed) pedagogical context where learning was situated (or contextually relevant), active and transferable to other aspects of young people's lives outside of formal physical education lessons. In sum, it was argued that the student-centred pedagogy afforded by technology was capable of extending teachers' capabilities to promote a range of learning outcomes in the physical, cognitive, social and affective domains.

Practitioner learning is a significant and important aspect of a 'pedagogy of technology'

Practitioners' uses of technology as presented in their narratives were often informed by an intensely personal and often emotional learning journey that involved reflection, experimentation and mentoring from colleagues and other practitioners within their professional learning networks. Notably, the different uses of digital technologies were underpinned by the practitioners' invested interest in both student learning and – as important – their own learning. As such, and in order to develop pedagogies of technology, it is apparent that innovative and confident practitioners were those who were willing to position themselves as ongoing learners, learners who inquire into their practices, strive to keep up to date with the latest pedagogies and practices, and seek to learn how digital technologies can support their pedagogical ambitions.

In Chapter One, the Introduction, we offered a tentative definition of pedagogies of technology:

> Pedagogies of technology are critically aware and technically competent pedagogies that can be developed in practice to maximise the latent potential of technologies to accelerate learning in meaningful ways that meet the individual needs of diverse learners. The starting point for a pedagogy of technology is a desire to do things differently, rather than to the same things using 'flashy' tools and gizmos.

In returning to this definition, we are encouraged by the manner in which it reflects the experiences and practices of the thirteen pedagogues in the book. They all reflected on their attempts to 'maximise the latent potential of technologies to accelerate learning in meaningful ways that meet the individual needs of diverse learners'. Yet, as editors, when we reflected on this definition and these three key – and rather obvious – learning points from the case chapters (technology as a tool, student-centred pedagogy, and practitioner professional learning), we felt that there might be more to learn. Most articles in education, physical education and sport pedagogy journals have made similar points. So, is it possible that we can push the analysis further, taking advantage of the pedagogical-cases format?

A challenge to pedagogues to 'be brave'

In this second section, we challenge the field and us (as editors and chapter authors) to 'be brave' in the ways that we think about pedagogy and technology. As yet, we do not fully understand the basis for teachers' decisions to use technology in physical education, nor the impact of this choice on teaching and students' learning outcomes. Indeed, although we found much practitioner and researcher enthusiasm for the use of digital technologies in physical education, we found rather less robust knowledge of impact. Questions emerge, therefore, about the ways in which these technologies have been introduced into physical education and whether these were the most appropriate ways to support learning. It is worth noting, for example, that practitioners were often unaware of the wider literature on learning from other academic fields that would have informed alternative approaches. This is not a criticism, merely an observation. It could also be argued that there was a sense in which the excitement and 'buzz' around digital technologies in society were strong push factors in the decision to adopt them in education.

As we outlined in Chapter 1, there can be little doubt that digital technologies are a prominent aspect of young people's lives outside of school (see Lenhart, 2015), and that they can deliver forms of knowledge to young people in ways that are engaging, immediate and attractive (Greenhow & Lewin, 2016; Rich & Miah, 2014; Selwyn & Stirling, 2016). At the same time, there are dangers presented by digital technologies. Arguments urging caution appear in several chapters in this book focusing on areas such as power, social justice and the influence of edu-business.

For example, the public displays of personal data in lessons (see Jarrod's use of video delay feedback, Béatrice's use of exergames, and Tom's use of Baton heart rate monitors) or the sharing of students responses through social media (see Andy's desire to use student blogs and Antonio's use of social media in his undergraduate class) all prompt ethical questions about what should or should not be shared with others. Halford (2016) recently raised questions about what is considered public or private on social media sites. In challenging what might be considered private, Halford (2016) suggested that a person, a company or even the host site (e.g. Facebook) will be able to access the digital data, regardless of privacy protection plans, guidelines and regulations. Consequently, there is a need not only for researchers to consider how and what data are reported from research using digital technologies (Halford, 2016) but also for practitioners to consider the digital footprints they are encouraging young people to create. We should consider, for example, whether digital images, and personal data about the body and/or a child's health may be accessible by others outside of a physical education context. There is a pressing need for further critical debate around these ethical issues. Certainly we should be critically reflecting on the current uses of and research on digital technologies in physical education to ensure we are not glorifying the capacity of digital technologies to educate, while remaining only dimly aware of the ethical implications of public data.

Looking across the practitioner narratives, there is some evidence of teachers who have been early adopters of digital technologies and who, understandably, enjoy the position in which this has placed them within their practitioner communities. Yet, at the same time, these teachers have a professional responsibility to be cognisant of the ease with which young people could learn about physical activity and health from the widespread unsolicited public health information that is shared through social media (British Medical Association, 2011; Lupton, 2015) and/or the problems with 'benchmarked' data accessed from apps or wearable technologies (Williamson, 2015). This implies that teachers, as professional practitioners, can never be satisfied with being knowledgeable techno-enthusiasts. Instead, they need to be brave enough to enter the digital worlds of their students to fully grasp the sheer power and pervasiveness of the knowledge and processes that are freely available to young people; young people who have been described as 'digital natives' (Prensky, 2010) or the 'iGeneration' (Rosen, 2010), and while such terms are highly contested (Helsper & Eyon, 2010), there is strong agreement that technology is ubiquitous in young people's lives (Kretschmann, 2015). How, for example, can teachers respond to some of the undesirable learning outcomes emerging from young people's engagement with health-related digital technologies outside of physical education?

Most practitioner narratives provided detailed insights into how technology was used to support learning. The focus was not on how practitioners might respond to young people's awareness, knowledge of, or learning about health and physical from digital technologies outside of physical education contexts (Rich & Miah, 2014). There was little evidence of a desire to support young people to critically evaluate physical activity and health data accessed from digital technologies, nor to navigate through potentially negative messages learnt about the body. Taking the information from these pedagogical cases, therefore, and the arguments made by Gard (2014), Öhman et al. (2014), and Rich and Miah (2014), it seems clear that an important future direction for the physical education profession is a focus on practitioners' critical pedagogical responses to digital technologies. Similar arguments were made about the need for practitioners to consider the influence of the media and magazines on young people's learning about the body (Kerner, 2013; Oliver & Kirk, 2016). In the case of digital technologies, such concerns are likely to be exaggerated, placing an even larger responsibility on professional practitioners and pedagogy researchers.

Another question that arises as we look across the chapters is what came first: the pedagogy or the technology; or, more bluntly, what cause generated what effect? Do, for example, the arrival of new technologies (cause) trigger the need to teach differently (effect)? Alternatively, does the desire to teach differently (cause) trigger the desire to use new technologies (effect)? Or, perhaps of even more interest, does the arrival of new technologies (cause) trigger a desire – or even a requirement – to use them in one way or another to generate a certain type of learning experience in the gymnasium (effect)? If this book has shown us anything then all of these questions, or none of them, are potential reasons why practitioners have chosen to use digital technologies in physical education. Indeed, different practitioners have used digital technologies for different reasons and each has come from different starting points and is working towards different end points. It could be argued, therefore, that our physical education profession has been poorly prepared to deal with the digital technologies tsunami. At no stage have we as a physical education profession debated the role of digital technologies in our lessons. We have no professional consensus on what is or is not acceptable, what is more or less effective, or what position we should take on the proliferation of physical activity and physical activity/health-related knowledge that impinge on the ways in which we would like physical education to be taught and learnt. When we asked the pedagogy lead authors in each pedagogical case to 'be brave' in their analysis of the learning from their pedagogical case many struggled (ourselves included). We now know why. We were asking these authors to take the first steps in a profession-wide analysis that has yet to begin in earnest.

What next?

The cases in this book illustrate diverse viewpoints on the concepts of pedagogy, technology and the notion of 'pedagogies of technology'. Looking ahead, it seems clear that attempting to develop a complex, multi-disciplinary understanding of effective pedagogies of technology (critical or uncritical) is going to be a challenging task. This is made more challenging when there is little in the way of an agreed consensus about what the respective terms mean individually, let alone collectively.

For example, Dron (2012) argued that how pedagogy is defined and used is diverse; it can be used to identify an area of study, an aspect of teaching, subject matter or to describe a particular method of teaching. The terms *pedagogical* or *pedagogic* relate back to that broader definition of the subject matter. 'In some cases the word is just a qualifier to say that we are talking about something to do with teaching' (Dron, 2012, p. 24), engendering such poetic phrases as 'pedagogic love' (Vandenberg, 2002). Similarly, Arthur (2009) argued that there is no overall theory of technology, and, as such, every definition and conception is corralled under the same umbrella term – *technology*.

In considering the term *pedagogies of technology*, which is where we started the book, and seeking to identify the impact of teachers' practices and technologies on learning in the pedagogical cases, the challenges become clear. The chapters are replete with authentic and believable examples of teacher learning about technology, but are less certain in their explanations of how the inclusion of technology into the pedagogical context impacted on student learning. Indeed, Passey (2014) cautions against the claims made about the impact of technology on learning:

> Learning is a wide conceptual term encompassing very many specific and distinctive elements and processes. When it is stated that a digital technology enhances or supports learning, such a statement is likely to be over-generalising in terms of describing influence or impact. It would be extremely unlikely that any specific digital technology or application would enhance or support all aspects or elements of learning. (p. 9)

Looking ahead, therefore, it could be argued that one vital part of the pedagogies of technology jigsaw is a focus on understanding 'teacher intent', or, in other words, what 'causes' generate what 'effects'? Drawing on the concept of 'commander's intent' (Heath & Heath, 2007), it can be suggested that a focus on teacher intent is an essential pedagogical starting point if the concept of pedagogies of technology is to have wider purchase. Heath and Heath (2007, p. 26) argued that 'a crisp, plain-talk statement that appears at the top of every order, specifying the plan's goal, [and] the desired end-state of an operation' allows for an understanding of desired effect where key and central practices or ideas can then be easily used by others. This focus on intent also chimes with Hattie's (2012) views on 'visible learning'. Hattie (2012) argued that we should not be concerned with the software or hardware of schooling but the 'processing' attributes that make learning visible. To achieve this, Hattie (2012) suggested that teachers should identify their targeted learning aims, learning intentions and success criteria. Evidence of 'visible' learning can then be determined and used to evaluate the effect of specific teaching practices on student learning.

At one level, this understanding of teacher intent could be viewed as overly simplistic. Yet, Saldaña (2014) and Heath and Heath (2007) reminded us of the importance of keeping (or making) ideas simple (or, perhaps, intelligible) if they are to 'stick' and impact on the practices of others. On the other hand, it may be that in the case of 'technology' we need to complicate the arguments. The work of Arthur (2009), Golding (2000), and Selwyn (2014), for example, suggested that it is important to move beyond understanding technology as a singular (i.e. a tablet or a camera) or a plural (i.e. a school network or class set of iPads) and to see it in a more 'general sense'. In seeking to define technology in this broader sense Arthur (2009) coined the phrase *technology-general*.

While Arthur's work is useful in understanding different micro, meso and macro notions of technology, he did not focus his work on education or educational technology. In applying these ideas to education, Casey (2015) argued that the adoption of 'technology-general' perspective on education-specific technology would necessitate a fundamental shift in thinking: from viewing technology as a noun to thinking of it as a verb. Thus, technology ceases to be about a specific item or tool and becomes, instead, about the wider educational milieu. In broadening our thinking, we become concerned less with how a child experiences the use of technology by one teacher and more about how the wider pedagogies of the school impact on the young person as learner. In other words, education as a technology becomes gestalt – the sum of its collective parts. As such we begin to see that those parts need to operate coherently in order to work collectively to support learning. This is certainly a more complex view of technology and is not one that was found in the pedagogical cases in this book.

A question that remains, therefore, is: What might a technology-general view of technology mean for the approaches we could take to the use of digital technologies in physical education? If we take the iPad – which features in several chapters in this book – as an example of a technology that has infused itself into schools, we are quickly able to see how it has been positioned to support an individual's learning. Tay (2016) recently concluded that while iPads helped teachers transform their lessons through significant task redesign, it was not the device per se but how it was used that facilitated deep learning and helped teachers to transform their roles. Apple argue that the iPad is 'a device like no other' which 'changes the way you do things and what you think is possible'. Tay's study, which we use here anecdotally, supports Apple's argument but it still focuses on technology as a singular (i.e. a single class, a single teacher, a single subject area, a single type of technology). Even though Tay reports on the outcomes from four pilot classes where every student had an iPad, she is only able to talk about 'singles'. She does not explore the 'plural' of technology in the school – the other technologies required for the iPads to go online (servers, wifi) or available in the school (laptops, projectors) – nor does she position the school as a technology system itself.

As noted earlier, it is not technology that allows teachers to collaborate and structure new ways of thinking and doing education. If we are to achieve this, we will need to develop new frameworks to guide and challenge our thinking. Certainly, in the cases presented in this book, there is very little evidence of a revolution in learning. As Selwyn (2014, p. vii) put it 'a gulf . . . persists between the rhetoric of how digital technologies could be used in education and the realities of how digital technologies are actually used'. Fundamentally, education is recycling the same practices but using different technologies to achieve the same or very similar aims.

When we consider 'what next' for pedagogies of technology, we could do worse than acknowledge the lack of a revolution in education as our starting point. Despite all the enthusiasm expressed for digital technologies in our pedagogical cases, there is little that is radical or new in practice. As Selwyn (2014, p. 7) points out, education is beset by 'exaggerated expectations over the capacity of the latest "new" technology to change education for the better, regardless of context and circumstance'. Moreover, as Golding (2000) reminded us, technology rarely enables us to do things that were previously impracticable or inconceivable. Instead, it allows us to do 'things' a little better, more speedily, efficiently and with less effort. This is a good description of the pedagogical cases in this book. As inspiring and fascinating as the cases are, there is nothing unthinkable that even comes close to Golding's (2000) description of 'type two technology' that 'enables wholly new forms of activity previously impracticable or even conceivable' (p. 171). We have clearly seen examples of 'further, faster, stronger' teaching and learning but a critical eye suggests that we have seen little that could be regarded as wholly new.

So – what's next? In short, we need to think bigger and braver in physical education if we are to develop pedagogies of technology that are worthy of the name. In this book we attempted to create something new, using a new concept and working within an innovative pedagogical cases framework. Yet, although we see glimpses of innovation, they did not come where we expected them. The traditional concept of physical education remained largely intact, with technology acting to reinforce its practices. It seems clear to us that what we are lacking is an inclusive 'big conversation' or 'grand debate' reaching the widest possible corners of the physical education profession to consider how critically aware pedagogues, pedagogically aware researchers and technologically innovative educators can collaborate to rethink the possibilities of physical education in a digital age.

In many respects, while we might have added parts to our education assembly-line model, allowing it to gain in complexity and refinement, we have not yet found ways to supersede it with something entirely new. Like Robinson (2011), we believe that education remains enthralled with finding twenty-first century solutions to twentieth-century problems rather than understanding and seeking to solve the problems of the twenty-first century. To move forward, we will need to do more than add to what exists, and instead take a radical standpoint on how pedagogies of technology can redefine the nature of physical education in a relentlessly digital age.

Lessons learned from the book

- The pedagogical cases in this book seem to suggest that currently: (i) technology is a tool for teaching and learning, (ii) technology promotes a student-centred approach, and (iii) practitioner learning is a significant and important aspect of 'pedagogies of technology'.

- That said, we need to move beyond enthusiasm and passion for digital technologies and begin to develop a robust evidence base that details the impact of digital technologies on student learning in physical education contexts.
- The influence of digital technologies on learning about physical activity and health occurs within and beyond the physical education classroom. Practitioners and researchers, therefore, need to be prepared to critically respond to young people's contemporary learning needs in a digital age.
- The use of technology in schools raises ethical questions about what should or should not be shared and prompts us to consider 'what happens' to what we share.
- We need to engage in a profession-wide and multi-disciplinary analysis of pedagogies of technology. Fundamentally, we need to move our thoughts beyond the individual and the group and start to see education as a technology in and of itself. In so doing, we can start to post questions about how the infrastructure of education can be changed to do things that were previously thought impossible or impractical.

References

Armour, K. M. (Ed.). (2014). *Pedagogical cases in physical education and youth sport.* Oxon: Routledge.

Arthur, W. B. (2009). *The nature of technology: What it is and how it evolves.* New York: Free Press.

British Medical Association. (2011). *Using social media: Practical and ethical guidance for doctors and medical students.* Retrieved from www.bma.org.uk/support-at-work/ethics/ethics-a-to-z

Casey, A. (2015). *Developing a theory of technology for physical education pedagogy.* Paper presented at the British Educational Research Association's Annual Conference, Queens University, Belfast, 3–5 September 2015.

Dron, J. (2012). The pedagogical-technological divide and the elephant in the room. *International Journal on E-Learning, 11*(1), 23–38.

Gard, M. (2014). eHPE: A history of the future. *Sport, Education and Society, 19*(6), 827–845.

Golding, P. (2000). Future features: Information and communications technologies and the sociology of the future. *Sociology, 34*(1), 165–184.

Greenhow, C. & Lewin, C. (2016). Social media and education: Reconceptualizing the boundaries of formal and informal learning. *Learning, Media and Technology, 41*(4), 6–30.

Halford, S. (2016, March). *The ethical disruptions of social media research: Tales from the field.* Paper presented at the Social Media & Social Science Research Ethics conference, London, UK.

Hattie, J. (2012). *Visible learning for teachers: Maximizing impact on learning.* London: Routledge.

Heath, C. & Heath, D. (2007). *Made to stick.* London: Random House Books.

Helsper, E. J. & Eyon, R. (2010). Digital natives: Where is the evidence? *British Educational Research Journal, 36*(3), 503–520.

Kerner, C. (2013). *Relationships between body image, motivation and physical education (PE) experiences in 13–14 year old boys and girls* (Unpublished PhD thesis). University of Bedfordshire.

Kretschmann, R. (2015). Physical education teachers' subjective theories about integrating information and communication technology (ICT) into physical education. *The Turkish Online Journal of Educational Technology, 14*(1), pp. 68–96.

Lenhart, A. (2015). *Teens, social media and technology.* Pew Research Centre. Retrieved from www.pewinternet.org/files/2015/04/PI_TeensandTech_Update2015_0409151.pdf

Lupton, D. (2015). Data assemblages, sentient schools and digitized health and physical education (response to Gard). *Sport, Education and Society, 20*(1), 122–132.

Öhman, M., Almqvist, J., Meckbach, J., & Quennerstedt, M. (2014). Competing for ideal bodies: A study of exergames used as teaching aids in schools. *Critical Public Health, 24*(2), 196–209.

Oliver, K. & Kirk, D. (2016). Towards an activist approach to research and advocacy for girls and physical education. *Physical Education and Sport Pedagogy, 21*(3), 313–327.

Passey, D. (2014). *Inclusive technology enhanced learning: Overcoming cognitive, physical, emotional and geographic challenges.* London, UK: Routledge.

Prensky, M. (2010). *Teaching digital natives: Partnering for real learning.* Thousand Oaks, CA: Corwin Press.

Rich, E. & Miah, A. (2014). Understanding digital health as public pedagogy: A critical framework. *Societies, 4*(2), 296–315.

Robinson, K. (2011). *Out of our minds: Learning to be creative.* Chichester, UK: Capstone.

Rosen, L. (2010). *Rewired: Understanding the iGeneration and the way they learn.* New York: Palgrave MacMillan.

Saldaña, J. (2014). Blue-collar qualitative research: A rant. *Qualitative Inquiry, 20*(8), 976–980.

Selwyn, N. (2014). *Distrusting educational technology: Critical questions for changing times.* London: Routledge.

Selwyn, N. & Stirling, E. (2016). Social media and education . . . now the dust has settled. *Learning, Media and Technology, 41*(1), 1–5.

Tay, H. Y. (2016). Longitudinal study on impact of iPad use on teaching and learning. *Cogent Education.* doi:10.1080/2331186X.2015.1127308

Vandenberg, D. (2002). The transcendental phases of learning. *Educational Philosophy and Theory, 34*(3), 321–344.

Williamson, B. (2015). Algorithmic skin: Health-tracking technologies, personal analytics and the biopedagogies of digitized health and physical education. *Sport, Education and Society, 20*(1), 133–151. doi:10.1080/13573322.2014.962494

INDEX

Page numbers in italics refer to figures. Page numbers in bold refer to tables.